German Division as Shared Experience

German Division as Shared Experience

Interdisciplinary Perspectives on the Postwar Everyday

Edited by Erica Carter, Jan Palmowski and Katrin Schreiter

berghahn
NEW YORK · OXFORD
www.berghahnbooks.com

First published in 2019 by
Berghahn Books
www.berghahnbooks.com

Library of Congress Cataloging-in-Publication Data
Names: Carter, Erica, editor. | Palmowski, Jan, editor. | Schreiter, Katrin,
  editor.
Title: German division as shared experience : interdisciplinary perspectives
  on the postwar everyday / edited by Erica Carter, Jan Palmowski and Katrin
  Schreiter.
Description: New York : Berghahn Books, 2019. | Includes bibliographical
  references and index.
Identifiers: LCCN 2019007584 (print) | LCCN 2019011545 (ebook) | ISBN
  9781789202434 (ebook) | ISBN 9781789202427 (hardback : alk. paper)
Subjects: LCSH: Germany (East)--Social life and customs. | Germany
  (West)--Social life and customs. | Germany (East)--Intellectual life. |
  Germany (West)--Intellectual life. | Intercultural communication--Germany
  (East)--History. | Intercultural communication--Germany (West)--History. |
  Germany (East)--Relations--Germany (West) | Germany
  (West)--Relations--Germany (East) | Germany--History--1945-1990.
Classification: LCC DD282 (ebook) | LCC DD282 .G46 2019 (print) | DDC 943.
  087--dc23
LC record available at https://lccn.loc.gov/2019007584

British Library Cataloguing in Publication Data
A catalogue record for this book is available from the British Library

ISBN 978-1-78920-242-7 hardback
ISBN 978-1-78920-243-4 ebook

Contents

Figures

Acknowledgements

Interdisciplinary scholarship demands patience and a willingness to engage across the divides of distinct disciplinary cultures, scholarly vocabularies and historical epistemologies. Colleagues who accompanied the editors and volume contributors during those discussions include Leora Auslander, Silke Arnold-de Simine, Jeremy Aynsley, Paul Betts, Beate Binder, Martin Brady, Kathleen Canning, Alex Clarkson, Robin Curtis, Greg Eghigian, Anne Fuchs, Neil Gregor, Anna Hájková, Donna Harsch, Jeff Hayton, Maria Hetzer, Helen Hughes, Jason Johnson, Valentina Rozas Krause, Kate Lacey, Richard Langston, Eric Limbach, Thomas Lindenberger, Iga Nowicz, Petra Rethmann, Annemarie Sammartino, Ben Schofield, Catherine Smale, Katie Stone, Camillo de Vianco, Elizabeth Ward and Daniel Wolpert. Thanks are due to all the above for giving generously of their time, energy and expertise.

Funding from King's College London and the University of Warwick for developing our ideas through a number of seminars and workshops is gratefully acknowledged. We also thank Iga Nowicz for summarizing the discussions of the 2014 symposium at King's College London in a report and to Frank Sterkenburgh for his help with editing the final manuscript. The Artists Rights Society (ARS), New York / VG Bild-Kunst, Bonn gave kind permission for the reproduction of Heidrun Hegewald, 'Child and Parents (Kind und Eltern), 1977'; Klaus Weber, 'The Youngest Fliers (Die jüngsten Flieger)'; and Doris Ziegler, 'The Rosa Luxemburg Brigade - Eva (one panel from a pentaptych), 1974/75'. Permission to use screenshots from Jürgen Böttcher's *Verwandlungen* (*Transformations*, 1981) was generously granted by the DEFA-Stiftung/Filmmuseum Munich.

We are grateful to three anonymous readers whose comments helped us to hone our arguments in the final editorial stages. At Berghahn Books, Chris Chappell, Soyolmaa Lkhagvadorj, Amanda Horn and Marion Berghahn have been unstinting in their backing for this volume, and we thank them most warmly for their practical and scholarly support.

Abbreviations

ARD	German Public Television Broadcasting Station (FRG)
BArch	Bundesarchiv
CDU/CSU	Christian Democratic Party/Christian Social Party
DFF	German Television Broadcasting Service (GDR)
DRA	Deutsches Rundfunkarchiv Babelsberg
FDJ	Free German Youth
FRG	Federal Republic of Germany
GDR	German Democratic Republic
HO	National retail organization (GDR)
KGV	Small Garden Allotment Association
LHA	Landeshauptarchiv Schwerin
MJ2	Movement June Second
RAF	Red Army Faction
SAPMO	Stiftung der Parteien und Massenorganisationen der Ehemaligen DDR
SED	Socialist Unity Party
SMAD	Soviet Military Administration in Germany
VBKD	East German Association of Visual Artists
ZDF	Second German Television Broadcasting Station (FRG)
ZIJ	East German Central Institute for Youth Research

Introduction
German Division as Shared Experience

Erica Carter, Jan Palmowski and Katrin Schreiter

In 1988, the Stasi clandestinely recorded a conversation between two loyal socialists, Fred Müller, Director of East Berlin's International Press Centre, and Heinz Felfe, arguably the KGB's most famous spy in 1950s Bonn.

Felfe: I was in Lusitania and couldn't get hold of sauerkraut. They say that deliveries go to Berlin first, then to the district capitals. We get the leftovers. But try shopping in West Berlin: all the shops are full! oranges, bananas, peaches … .

Müller: Just what I've always said! I've been crossing the border for twenty years now. If you go to the market in any small or medium-sized town, they have everything.

Felfe: My wife has seen fruit that she had never even heard of: nectarines, avocatoes [sic] … And the traffic on the *Kurfürstendamm*, heavy traffic: it runs, it hums, no noise, no two-stroke engines, no broken exhaust pipes, … . Then back to the lousy border: … nothing but greyness, drabness.[1]

This brief exchange from the late 1980s speaks volumes about the dissatisfaction of many East Germans with the conditions of everyday life. It also reproduces narrative tropes that became pervasive after 1989 in accounts of life across the German-German divide. The conversation contrasts the turgid grey of the GDR with the bright colours of the Kurfürstendamm. It juxtaposes the tastes and smells of the West with the 'leftover' sensations of Germany's eastern half; and it makes of West Berlin a throbbing soundscape that drowns the stuttering put-put of the GDR two-stroke.

The West, then, is plenitude, abundance, fullness, the East a place of scarcity and sensory lack. This divided image of the sensory pleasures and unpleasures of life across the German-German border fuelled, as is well known, a post-1989 'Ostalgia' wave in German popular culture.[2] In post-*Wende* German heritage culture, consumer objects and practices became sites for an idealized memorialization of divided sociopolitical identities. East German consumer goods and cultural artifacts – food brands, TV shows, cars, traffic light insignia (the GDR *Ampelmann*) clothing, films – became the retrostyle avatars for a GDR way of life that was both repudiated, and somehow also nostalgically missed.[3] Controversies over the meaning of GDR heritage came to one kind of head in 2006. That year saw the publication of the Sabrow report, a public commission headed by the historian Martin Sabrow, whose recommendation that the public memory of the GDR focus, amongst others, on the everyday triggered public controversy amidst claims that it would constitute a memory of the GDR 'lite'.[4] Beneath the noise caused by this debate, 2006 also saw the opening of the private Berlin GDR Museum, criticized in its early years for preserving the GDR in its status as the 'other' Germany: an irredeemably foreign rump state whose idiosyncrasies might be charming, but whose history was at best a museum attraction, and one radically divorced from the political realities of the postwar FRG.[5]

Historical scholarship also emphasized for many years the 'peculiarities' of GDR 'life', seeing it as set apart from the processes of democratization and consumerization, or the social and political tensions of the 1960s and 1970s that so affected the FRG. This view of the GDR as *sui generis* in the context of German history gained plausibility from the GDR specificity of state machinations via the Stasi, of mass organizations like the Free German Youth, or of consumer goods shortages, none of which had parallels in West Germany. Attempts to understand each German state in its distinctiveness seemed of particular significance for the GDR, which in 1990 presented itself as a *terra incognita* to historians (notwithstanding the quality of GDR scholarship in the political sciences up until that point).[6] Social historians used such notions as the 'bounded dictatorship' (Jessen and Bessel) or the 'welfare dictatorship' (Jarausch) to capture the specificity of GDR society, and the conjoining of an authoritarian political system with varying levels of social and civic participation.

Yet more recently, historians have also posed questions about the many interconnections between the histories of the two Germanies.[7] Even scholars working within the relatively distinctive historiographies of East and West Germany have recognized an East-West commonality in the key postwar challenges confronting all Germans. Both states struggled to reintegrate displaced populations, to mend the ruptures of exile, to rebuild flattened cities, to mend family and kinship relations while meeting new demands for gender equality, or to come to terms with a substantial Cold War foreign military presence.[8] Cross-border relationships amongst families, friends, political allies, or later, subcultural communities and cross-border social movements – environmentalism, feminism, third world politics, the peace movement – also cut across the German-German border, building on older links, or forging new connections across Cold War divides.

Though the scholarship on this entangled binational history remains in its infancy, historians have certainly made headway with new approaches to what Christoph Kleßmann has called the 'asymmetrical parallel history' of the two postwar Germanies.[9] The proposal that historians explore the 'divided' but 'not disconnected' history (Lindenberger) of the two postwar German states finds resonance across a broad field of current historical research, including, as Frank Bösch has noted, 'energy and environmental history ... the history of consumption, sports history, the history of medicine ... media history [or] global history'.[10] Fruitful studies by Eli Rubin, Katherine Pence, Judd Stitziel and others have shown how consumption functioned as a site where both asymmetry and connectivity between the two Germanies played out. Without denying that GDR consumers, within the socialist planned economy, shared many experiences with citizens in other socialist states,[11] this work has shown how GDR consumer desires were shaped in close reference to West Germany.[12] Other historians have suggested that the failure to fulfill these desires chipped away at the foundations of the legitimacy of socialism in the GDR state.[13] The Federal Republic, from this perspective, functioned as a society of reference for GDR citizens, who at the same time developed their own strategies to achieve happiness within their means.

West Germany, of course, mattered for consumer behaviours in the GDR in ways that was simply not the case in reverse. It is no accident that the West German historiography of consumption has been less concerned with German-German relations, focussing instead on the transatlantic and transnational forces that shaped the FRG's postwar consumer economy. As early as the early 1990s, studies were emerging that explored the embedding of the Federal Republic, through consumption, in western liberalism. West Germany's economic success inspired histories of the 'German Model' of ordoliberalism, with its distinctive social market approach to state, industry and consumer relations, as well as its attention to gendered consumption as a structuring force for economic development.[14] This emphasis on 'westernized' or 'Americanized' economic and consumer models deflected attention from the GDR as West Germany's significant other, and highlighted instead West Germany's relations with its western European neighbours and transatlantic partners, especially, though not exclusively, the USA.[15]

The picture in social, cultural or political history is arguably less clearly divided. Social historians have highlighted the need to 'break out of the strait-jacket of parallel stories', and to emphasize instead the similar problems faced by both Germanies, even while each found different solutions in line with their ideological bent and geopolitical dependencies.[16] Studies of history and memory have also explored similarities in Germans' dealings with the Nazi past, even if the two populations addressed that shared history in very different environments.[17] Political historians have shown increasing interest in cross-border relations within a politics of national division. There is for instance a growing body of work on Willy Brandt's *Ostpolitik*, the NATO double-track decision in the 1980s, and Stasi infiltration into the political and economic institutions of the FRG.[18] Further important scholarship explores the interconnectedness of the two Germanies in the realm of culture. Uta Poiger's early research on jazz culture in East and West set an important standard, showing how both parts of Germany were influenced, albeit differently, by American jazz.[19] Even here, however, the 'West' remained the society of reference for the East, in contrast to sport, which was a rare field of genuine exchange, competition and mutual reference. As Uta Balbier has shown, the GDR's athletic prowess made of competitive sports one arena where West Germans were as eager to learn from the GDR as vice versa.[20]

Yet such perspectives still remain the exception. The necessary distinction between a GDR society shaped by authoritarian state structures, and an FRG counterpart deeply entangled with western capitalism and a liberal international order, continues to present problems for historians seeking to identify commonalities across the German-German border. It is to these problems that the present volume is addressed. *German Division as Shared Experience* draws on, and seeks to supplement with a German-German perspective, a body of historical work that suggests lived experience as a route to understanding the relation between politics and power. That relation, this volume proposes, was one that was in part negotiated in the postwar period, both internally within each German state, and across the boundaries between them, at the level of everyday social relations and aesthetic practice. The volume takes its cue in the first instance from GDR history, which has been pioneering in a field that explores from an everyday perspective the broad range of human emotions, behaviours and sensibilities that colour the relation of individuals and communities to structures of power.[21] As the East German author Kerstin Hensel puts it: 'Every individual had a life-story, not a preliminary one, but one lived over decades ... history can neither be reconstructed nor come to terms with. It can only be grasped through the everyday'.[22] Hensel's insight is confirmed by histories whose exploration of the everyday offers a rich understanding of how socialism shaped individual assumptions of the private;[23] how state planning affected individual experience and identity;[24] how the tenacity of the GDR state system might be explained by studying its citizens' 'subjectivities, values, beliefs and mentalities';[25] and how the Party's desire for control affected personal attitudes towards sexuality and the body.[26]

There have, admittedly, been concerns that an emphasis on individual everyday experience may deliver a rose-tinted view of GDR-history that glosses over the state's repressive instruments,[27] even while fulfilling popular desires to remember the past.[28] In an effort to counter the danger of history as nostalgia, GDR history has turned for one conceptual anchor to the historian Alf Lüdtke, as well as to other histories that Lüdtke's writing has inspired. There are important affinities between Lütdke's approach and the work of fellow oral historians including Dorothee Wierling, Alexander von Platho and Lutz Niethammer, whose 1980s studies focused on working-class histories of East and West.[29] Nonetheless, it is Lüdtke's work that has been especially influential in GDR historiography, and indeed for historians exploring other authoritarian regimes, including the Soviet Union and Nazi Germany.[30] Central to Lüdtke's approach is his notion of *Eigensinn*, which explores the relationship between political domination and social action through a close-up look at individual action, signals and meanings. For Lüdtke, there is a 'disjunction' between formal politics, and acts of negotiating and appropriating socio-political structures and relations. In the social gestures of *Eigensinn* – which translates literally as obduracy or obstinacy – that disjunction is articulated through acts of recalcitrance, 'spontaneous self-will', or 'prankish, stylized, misanthropic distancing from ... constraints'.[31] Lüdtke's historical-anthropological approach shares with early subcultural studies in the Anglophone tradition, as well as with Chicago School urban sociology, the anthropological 'thick description' of Clifford Geertz, or the phenomenology of Georg Simmel or Michel de Certeau, a focus on the everyday as a locus of human agency. But his work also privileges, and has inspired a number of further studies that trace, both the deep contours of power within everyday life, and the 'obstinate' behaviours that signal a 'reappropriation' by individuals and groups of a 'world' or a 'society' which otherwise presents itself in the form of external interest or constraint.[32]

By examining closely the meanderings of the individual away from the lofty summits of political history, everyday history has made it possible to understand how power is transmitted, transformed and evaded, and thus – crucially for the present volume – to reveal the gap between structural

histories of state socialism or liberal democracy, and the ambiguous realities of politics as they are lived on the ground.[33] To be sure, for the GDR
context, marked by stark power imbalances that could not be articulated
and negotiated openly, Lüdtke's work has offered particularly powerful
ways of reading between the lines of official GDR documents, examining
carefully the social practices beneath citizens' public acts, and uncovering the contrast between lived experience and memory. This approach
poses important questions, however, regarding heuristic value, the
specific question being how *Eigensinn* and everyday history can be fruit-
fully applied to West Germany, or to cross-border flows between East
and West. A key issue here is how to conceptualize the ground of the
everyday as a field of social action. For Lüdtke, the practice of *Eigensinn*
relates to an individual experience (*Erfahrung*) of social agency. Andrew
Bergerson, Leonard Schmieding and others have used that insight to
offer perspectives on German history that approach the shifting relations between centre and periphery through stories of everyday lives
from the ground up. The lives of Germans, they have argued, have
been determined by rupture, and by a concomitant process of making
sense and meaning within life worlds determined by extrinsic structure
and agency.[34] These authors' emphasis on power that becomes effective through individuals' self-authorization, dissociates power's exercise
from a particular ideological or political context and shows how everyday history might in principle provide an important lens for the study of
German history across East and West.

Lüdtke himself, while his work has focused on unsettling easy binaries between domination and the apparently powerless, has also noted
that everyday history can be applied in any context to alert historians to
the physicality of their human subjects' existence, their subjective experiences, their sociabilities, their anxieties and aspirations, and their 'shifting
involvements' (Hirschman).[35] Studies of the 'situational', the (literally)
concrete settings of individuals, are already producing fruitful new perspectives, as shown by Eli Rubin's examination of the impact of the built
environment of the Berlin suburb of Marzahn on the memories and sensibilities (through sight, sound and smell) of their residents.[36] A focus
on the situatedness of human subjects within the time and space of the
everyday requires, however, a careful awareness of the social and political
structures within which their actions unfold, and the cultural meanings of
contexts and actions. A key challenge, then, is to develop an analysis of
'historically formed and historically shaping actions, insights and perceptions in their culturally specific entanglements, differences, ruptures and
commonalities'.[37] Such a perspective cannot focus solely on human action
in systems characterized by great imbalances of power, but it has to ask

precisely how actions, symbols and ideas are transmitted across different social, political and cultural divides.

This question, which has become of growing interest to historians of postwar Europe, also fuels this volume's search for a rearticulated focus on the everyday that might offer a better understanding of German history across the East-West divide. Some cultural histories have already offered potential frameworks for comparative or transnational studies. Rana Mitter and Patrick Major's 2004 comparative sociocultural history of the Cold War allots to popular cultural industries and forms 'across the blocs' an important role in shaping both shared and divided modes of 'mass experience'. Mitter and Major coin the oxymoronic, but heuristically rich term 'mirror opposite' for the relations of simultaneous affinity and difference that shaped Cold War sociocultural relations.[38] They also argue persuasively for the value of cultural history in mapping East-West interrelations. But if culture is an important starting point, there is a need also for careful scrutiny of questions of method. Mitter and Major identify social histories, alongside anthropologies of everyday culture, as the dual methodological pillars on which their 'home front' Cold War history rests. Clifford Geertz is cited as one of many possible sources for an understanding of culture as 'interworked systems of construable signs'.[39] Culture, then, is located here in the field of symbolic representations and practices, which are seen in turn to be productive of individual and social subjectivities, as well as structures of feeling and experience across and between nations or supranational blocs.

Our book aims to take further this exploration of culture and the everyday within and across the inner German border. The volume seeks to energize cross-disciplinary debate, further probing Major and Mitter's history of 'mirror opposites' by bringing together scholars working not only in history and anthropology, but also in art history, cultural, literary, media and visual culture studies. The shared aim of the volume's contributors is to examine how approaches from the perspective of the everyday might further illuminate the history of shared but divided belonging that shaped the two postwar German states. The common perception of chapters in the collection is that individuals and communities are actively involved, through their own idiosyncratic (or 'obstinate' – *eigensinnig*) modes of linguistic, narrative, poetic or performative cultural production, in shaping their relation to larger political and social formations – in this case, the two postwar Germanies. This will come as no surprise either to historians of *Alltagsgeschichte*, or to practitioners of cultural studies. But the focus of all the volume's contributors on questions of cross-border belonging will, we hope, contribute a new perspective on the place of cultural practice – which we understand in the broadest sense, as the production of oral and written language, image, sound, or performance, as well as practices of reading, viewing, tasting, touching, smelling – in shaping shared experiences of socio-political community in a divided Germany.

Volume Overview: Methods and Approaches

This methodological concern with capturing in a new way the idea of *Eigensinn* and moving beyond it for a cross-disciplinary exploration of experience in postwar Germany was the subject of intense discussions that began with a departmental seminar series at King's College London in 2012, and continued with a conference at King's College London in 2014, as well as the US German Studies Association Conference in Washington DC in 2015. Those events were the starting point for the interdisciplinary dialogue that threads its way through the book. Emerging from these cross-disciplinary conversations is no single methodology or theory. To generate such a unified approach was neither heuristically desirable nor feasible in our view. Instead, our discussions on research and method (including the consideration of key framing texts) yielded multiperspectival approaches articulated from multiple disciplinary standpoints. This perspective has guided our approach to this volume and its contributions, and we believe – and set out to show in the overview of those approaches presented below – that our approach to postwar German experience in the everyday is all the richer for that heterogeneity. It allows historical methods that develop in specific relation to objects, artifacts, events, collective and individual cultural practices, and thus reflect the ontological complexity of the historical ensembles that shape everyday experience.

At the same time, the volume's eleven chapters, generated as they are in part in response to shared readings and collective debate, converge in their methods and approaches around a series of distinct concerns. The first relates to questions of narrative. In numerous contributions to this volume, narrative form figures as a site of intersection between macro-histories of political division, and the experiences of social actors negotiating those histories within quotidian life. Historians across a range of fields have regularly explored the role of narrative – whether as oral narration, prose fiction, life-writing, or indeed historical scholarship[40] – in shaping both social experience and its recorded, remembered, fictional or fantasized histories. Narrative 'grammar', as well as the 'larger conventions of discourse'[41] to which storytelling adheres, make of narrative a communicative mode that is at once ineffably individual (no two stories are ever quite the same), and necessarily collective. Even avant-garde literary narration, or in everyday speech, the fantastical or nonsensical stories of children and eccentrics, either adhere to the conventions of what the Russian formalists termed *fabula* (the basic story material) and *syuzhet* (the story's organization in space and time), or retain those conventions as a common point of reference against which to pitch more playful or experimental forms.[42] That narrative form has a normative status not only in cultural production, but in broader social relations, is confirmed by the long-standing equation of narrative disorder with social marginality or outsider status. Thus in mental illness for instance, 'narrative disruption' – the inability to tell coherent stories – is one diagnostic marker for a mental state seen to place patients beyond the bounds of ordinary social life. In psychosis particularly, a loss of narrative frameworks produces a collapse of that sense of progressive time, bounded space, or coherent self-other relations, which is the stuff both of cohesive life stories and of effective communication amongst individuals or larger social groups.[43]

Conversely, as Jan Palmowski shows in his chapter below on GDR television, fictional narrative enters the daily life of so-called ordinary people – here, GDR TV viewers – as a means both of individual and collective meaning-making, and of a spatio-temporal and affective ordering of social reality. In the GDR, Palmowski contends, television was a 'central reference point of social and cultural communication', and played a key role therefore in forging 'socialist ways of living and ... feeling'. In his account, narrative form features as a means of regulating everyday contingencies, giving form and meaning to experienced events, but also managing everyday life's unforeseen or uncanny elements by locating them in the time and space of familiar stories. Palmowski's focus in particular is on the temporality of television narratives, and on the subjunctive mood ('what might have been, or what might yet transpire if ...') as a means of containing both the melancholy of lost utopias (which might include the utopia of a grass-roots democratic socialism), and the subjective as well as social instability induced by imagined alternative futures.

While Palmowski's chapter, then, explores institutionally generated narrative as a means of organizing and containing an unruly popular imaginary (an ultimately failed project in GDR television, as Palmowski also shows), Heidi Armbruster considers autobiographical narration in oral testimony as a means of self-positioning within social and historical discourses of belonging. The assumption by the everyday historians of the 1970s and 1980s that history was made in 'microhistorical moments of interaction' produced what Sarah Maza has termed a return 'with a vengeance' of storytelling, both as source and method, to the historical disciplines.[44] Armbruster shows the value of the pluralist method for evaluating storytelling in everyday history. The first of several chapters focusing on migrant groups – here, white German post-1945 immigrants to the former German settler colony of Namibia – Armbruster's contribution draws on socio-lingustic accounts of 'positioning' as a form of 'relational work' performed by storytelling to show how stories of being 'German' amongst this white minority expatriate group function as 'ambiguous narrative act[s] of racial and historical self-positioning' in the postcolonial context of post-independence Namibia.

While Armbruster's anthropological and sociolinguistic approach reveals storytelling as a mode through which social actors (including herself as researcher) locate themselves in historical relations of space, time and micropolitical power, Katharina Karcher's reading of autobiographical writings produced by Red Army Faction (RAF) member Inge Viett during a five-year prison sojourn from 1992 to 1997 shows Viett using similar narrative acts of self-positioning to locate herself within German history as the story of 'an ongoing revolutionary struggle against fascism and for a socialist society'. Without defending Viett's commitment to revolutionary violence, Karcher explores her life-writing as an interventionist communicative act that 'stubbornly' (*eigensinnig*) resists absorption into established postwar historical narratives. Particularly significant for Karcher is Viett's dual life as a revolutionary activist on both sides of the German-German border, as Karcher shows how Viett created spaces of *Eigensinn* that defied conformity or resistance, through practices better described as footdragging to maximize her own desires. Charting Viett's account of a life lived underground between the two Germanies, Karcher shows how, despite its political 'peculiarities', her case illustrates the part played by self-narration in generating or refiguring Cold War subjectivities.

Karcher's argument that autobiographical narratives from Cold War Germany involve the narrator in a necessary positioning 'towards the other [Germany] and the relationship between both' has purchase, moreover, not only on such radically politicized subjects as Viett. In subsequent chapters on, respectively, oral histories from villagers living at some distance from the border, in Saxony and Baden-Württemberg, and German-language short prose by migrant writers, Marcel Thomas and Áine McMurtry show how national belonging was shaped after 1949 by a cross-border or transnational imaginary, whether in the West German imagination of the GDR as a structural absence (Thomas), or in migrant imaginings of the inner German border as a symbolic cipher for other forms of spatial fracture between *Heimat* and *Fremde* (McMurtry).

That the inner German border shaped German imaginations and everyday experiences is hardly surprising, nor is a recognition that Germany's division was created through social practices on both sides of the border, beyond the physical separation that it most tangibly produced. There is now a rich literature on inner German border communities that demonstrates how social practices on both sides of the border gave it meaning and effect.[45] Yet, curiously, historians still have only a partial understanding of how the division affected cultural meanings and sensitivities beyond these communities, in the contexts of the everyday. Here again, this volume's cross-disciplinary investigations yield helpful insights. Thomas follows Michael de Certeau in searching within his interviews for evidence of the 'spatial practices' that defined his subjects' relation to German division. Unlike Inge Viett, who uses written narrative to insert herself temporally as the active agent of a (failed) history of revolutionary progression, Thomas's interviewees use spatial markers in oral narration to locate their personal stories within the political history of the German Cold War. While his West German respondents thus obliterate the GDR as a quotidian presence by locating it narratively in a distant elsewhere, his GDR villagers tell stories that are haunted by the Federal Republic as an ever-present site of longing. Here too, however, narrative constructions of the FRG as a distant and unattainable space help Thomas's GDR subjects to manage the melancholy of spatial division, either through the stress they place on their geographical distance from the East-West border (rural Saxon Neukirch is described by one interviewee with a degree of approbation as 'far away from it all [*weit ab vom Schuss*]'), or by repudiation: 'a rather forced narrative of lacking knowledge about the West'.

Thomas's oral history of Germans living at some distance from the border shows, then, how the absence of the frontier's physical presence intensifies the capacity of narrative form to shape an imagined affective geography of divided Germany. His chapter also highlights a second common thread uniting contributions to this volume, namely their shared understanding of form (in Thomas's case, forms of narrative) as a material force within both everyday and macro-political history. In recent media, cultural and literary theory, cultural form figures not simply as a vector of symbolic meaning and value, but as a vehicle for what the literary historian and theorist Caroline Levine terms 'the ordering of bodies and spaces, hierarchies and narratives, containments and exclusions'.[46] Developing insights from Foucault on the 'organisations and arrangements' through which power works at the micro-level of lived culture, Levine extends Foucault's linguistically-influenced understanding of form as discourse, presenting form instead as a larger category of 'shapes and configurations ... ordering principles, patterns of repetition and difference' that are simultaneously aesthetic and social, and that thus shape social perceptions of the material world.

Levine's political aesthetics of social form is distinguished both from Foucauldian accounts of discourse, and from classical narratology in

its emphasis on what are termed the 'affordances' of form. Deriving
from design and material culture theory, Levine's notion of affordance
describes the 'potential uses or actions latent in materials or designs':
thus glass 'affords' transparency and brittleness, steel 'affords' strength,
smoothness and durability, straw by contrast 'affords' a dessicated
warmth coupled with bristle and fragility, and so on.[47] This account of
form begins to move cultural analysis towards an understanding of form
as productive of specific modes of embodied historical experience.[48] The
affordances of narrative, for instance, include, as Palmowski, Armbruster
and Thomas show, its capacity for spatio-temporal positioning. Narrative
locates not only its stories' protagonists, but also speakers, writers, readers and audiences within specific historical temporalities and spaces: in
Palmowski's case, the subjunctive temporality of West German television, in Armbruster's and Thomas's, the stretched space of cross-border
belonging experienced by German expatriates in Namibia, and, albeit
differently, by Thomas's hinterland citizens of a divided postwar state.
But narrative also has affordances that are significant in other ways for
storytelling across borders. Narrative form is structured by the tension
between what narratology calls 'disruption' – the experience of conflict
between opposing forces that triggers new storylines; sequentiality – the
ordering of events through time; and equilibrium – the opening state of
expectant inertia that precedes the story's unfolding, or the closure that
remains part of narrative convention, however much it may have been
challenged by modernist or postmodern modes of narrative fragmentation and textual bricolage.

The tension between narrative disruption and closure, or stasis, reveals
within narrative – as indeed in any form – affordances that are potentially
in a state of mutual conflict. That these conflicting affordances can generate contestation of social and political arrangements is evident below
in three chapters on dissident forms that contest the border narratives
of a divided Germany. In Levine's understanding of form, narrative, by
virtue of its drive towards closure, becomes a subset of what she terms
'bounded wholes': aesthetic but also social totalities whose contradictory
'affordances' include, first, the containment or, at worst, imprisonment
within their borders of imagined and actual social actors; second, the
drive to exclude those who do not belong; and third, more alluringly, the
appeal of inclusion, alongside the certainty of a world whose contours
are familiar, secure, and invested with senses of belonging.

Levine's work offers interesting perspectives on the FRG-GDR border,
a frontier that might figure in a version of her socially embedded formalism not solely as ideological or physical boundary, but as a line of
demarcation between 'contending wholes'.[49] In Levine's account then,

the border comes under pressure as a site of collision between the competing affordances of bounded wholes. That it is in what Ernest Renan famously termed the 'plebiscite of the everyday' that the felt implications of those formal collisions are registered is demonstrated below in Áine McMurtry's account of short written prose by two postwar migrant writers, Herta Müller and Emine Sevgi Özdamar.

McMurtry's chapter focuses on two key works that span the transition from divided to reunified Germany: Müller's 1989 *Reisende auf einem Bein* (Traveling on One Leg), and Özdamar's *Mein Berlin* (My Berlin), a text written during the years following unification, and first published in the short story collection *Der Hof im Spiegel* (The Courtyard in the Mirror, 2001). As exiles finding refuge in divided Berlin from authoritarian regimes (Müller fled to West Berlin following political persecution in Ceauşescu's Romania, Özdamar escaped Turkish military repression to pursue an acting career in 1970s East Berlin), Müller and Özdamar share common experiences of migrant flight. The two writers also have recourse to prose strategies that are identified in McMurtry's analysis as significant for this volume's discussion of the interplay between aesthetic form and divided everyday experience. The first such is a use of staccato textual constructions that block fluid narration, favouring instead a montage or collage structure that reinvents through poetic narration the fractured experience of a divided Cold War Berlin. For both Müller and Özdamar, Berlin, as McMurtry shows, is at once a place of 'resettlement and new beginnings' and a site of division that captures the migrant, refugee or exile's 'sensed experience of everyday strangeness'. To recast this in Caroline Levine's terms: the 'temporal, spatial and perspectival play' identified by McMurtry as a shared feature of Müller and Özdamar's experimental prose foregrounds precisely those ambivalent 'affordances' – the simultaneous presence of disruption or fracture, and a containment that fosters senses of space, place and belonging – which Levine might identify in the Berlin urban milieu as 'bounded whole'.

McMurtry's analysis secondly casts light on a spatial practice that differs markedly from the cross-border imaginings of Thomas's East-West villagers. As McMurtry stresses, *Reisende* and *Mein Berlin* derive from a historical moment of 'structural transformation' in which both the 'former East-West coordinates of Cold War division' and the 'binaries of Orient and Occident' are in a state of transition to a new post-Cold War order of globally dispersed community and multipolar power. That experience of precarious spatio-political transition is captured by Müller and Özdamar through an emphasis in their prose on modes of transnational and local mobility, from the migrant journey into exile, to walking as a practice that 'establish[es] connections and contrasts without providing explicit commentary'. McMurtry's account of the journey recalls Lüdtke's observations on 'meandering', a practice for which he uses a nautical parallel, of boats tacking in the wind. Tacking is a manoeuvre that appears random at first sight, but that in fact establishes a trajectory through space and time through multidirectional movements that avoid confronting head-winds straight on.[50] The strategy is identified by Lüdtke as a means by which social actors negotiate the 'commando heights' of history, developing their own meanings, and frustrating, evading or amending identifications or behaviours constructed from 'above'. An analogous mode of what Lüdtke might identify as 'obstinate' subjective reinvention can be observed in McMurtry's prose narratives in a dislocated and imagistic writing style that 'reduplicate[s]' their protagonists' 'state of disconnectedness', while also forging new understandings of mobile belonging in the similarly fractured city of pre- and post-unification Berlin.

A third insight from McMurtry connects her discussion with the numerous contributions to this volume that explore multiple belongings in geopolitical spaces beyond the nation state. In McMurtry's reading, both Müller and Özdamar are seen to associate everyday repressive acts encountered in daily life in Berlin with 'forms of coercion and exclusion' experienced back home. For Müller's protagonist Irene, familiar types of 'wardrobe, demeanour and speech patterns' encountered in interviews with the *Bundesnachrichtendienst* (Federal Intelligence Service) recall the 'formulaic turns of phrase and contrived gestures' of her former Romanian interrogators. The links Irene makes between these cognate modes of 'coercion and exclusion' (McMurtry) are replicated in Özdamar's account of memories of the Turkish military regime conjured by small signals of everyday constraint on East Berlin streets (the conspicuous absence of graffiti for instance). Özdamar's simultaneous delight in passing reminders of socialist utopias – streets and squares named after Marx, Engels, and Rosa Luxemburg, or dreams of social equality rekindled by fixed prices for cucumbers (40 Pfennig 'no matter where you bought them') – demonstrates meanwhile, as McMurtry also shows, the potential of migrant movement both to facilitate insight into the transnational character of political repression, and to point up 'possibilities for solidarity' that may generate 'as yet unthought and unimagined … forms of perceptible community'.

McMurtry's ultimately optimistic account of transnational belonging as an experience facilitated (or in Levine's terms, 'afforded') by open aesthetic form and fluid movement is echoed by the volume's two subsequent chapters on, respectively, East German experimental film, and East-West subcultural style. Franziska Nössig's contribution on the DEFA filmmaker Jürgen Böttcher examines the relation between experimental form and spatial imaginings in the 'only experimental film ever produced' by the GDR studio, Böttcher's short film trilogy *Verwandlungen* (Transformations, 1981). In McMurtry's chapter, experimental literary technique in Özdamar is compared to cinematic montage as a means of drawing together distinct spaces (Turkey/Germany, Istanbul/Berlin) within a single narrative frame. Nössig's chapter shows Böttcher using film montage proper, but also more painterly collage forms deriving from his own practice as a visual artist, to produce similar forms of simultaneous collision and linkage across disparate spaces of quotidian experience and artistic practice. Perhaps the most significant 'transformation' of Böttcher's film is thus the metamorphosis of his own private apartment – where the entire film is shot – into an experimental playground for avant-garde film art. Contextualizing Böttcher's oeuvre within a GDR film industry constrained by censorship as well as socialist realist artistic norms, Nössig presents his 'sensuous [cinematic] experiments', performed as they are within the confines of domestic space, as signaling something more than homage to the underground filmmaking of artists such as Andy Warhol, Stan Brakhage or Kenneth Anger. Nössig instead reads Böttcher's practice spatially, exploring how it 'imaginatively extends his everyday boundaries' (the four walls of his flat) into the 'cultural space of the international film avant-garde'.

Nössig thus follows historian Paul Betts in understanding private space in the GDR as a site of 'alternative identity formation' as well as a 'semipermeable refuge from public life'.[51] But her chapter also emphasizes the capacity of artistic practice to remodel quotidian experience by calling forth a transnational presence within private space. Böttcher does this, admittedly, from a relatively privileged position as 'the most significant GDR documentarist, and one of its most influential visual artists' (Nössig). Alissa Bellotti's contribution, by contrast, pursues visual evidence of similar transnational borrowings in the street-level modernism of West and East German 1980s youth subcultures. Drawing on contemporary interviews as well as oral history, memoirs, fanzines, photographs and other popular ephemera, Bellotti highlights how subcultural practices of self-fashioning (dress, hairstyle, music, dance and other elements of subcultural style) situated 1980s punks within a cross-border community of dissident youth. Bellotti is not unusual in reading punk's nihilistic aesthetic as the signal of a breakdown in social consensus: a resistant response then, as Birmingham cultural studies scholar Dick Hebdige famously suggested, to the 'continued subordination' of groups that find no place in the prevailing social order – in Bellotti's case, disaffected German youth.[52]

But Bellotti's work also yields novel insight into punk's role in what her co-contributor McMurtry terms 'new kinds of subject formation at historical moments of structural transformation'. The subject emerging here is the post-socialist individual formed in the wake of the collapse of GDR state socialism in 1989; and Bellotti's chapter charts the emergence of punk as an early signal of that subjective transformation. She discovers in the archive as well as oral history interviews a set of shared stylistic elements amongst East and West German punks, including 'irreverent, aggressive postures; clothing transformed through ripping/tearing, the addition of handwritten slogans or by mismatching pieces of an outfit; and short, spikey hair, especially on young men'. As Bellotti notes, shared modes of self-construction through such 'signifiers of chaos' did not however locate punk as a new universal language of East-West dissent. 1980s social scientists concurred in their identification of punk style as a resistant stylistic mode that funnelled youthful protest towards locally specific objects of discontent. In the West, rising youth unemployment, environmental destruction and the nuclear threat fed punk's anarchic 'no-future' attitude. GDR punk, by contrast, directed its inchoate ire at the deadening conformity of a sclerotic authoritarian regime.

Bellotti is especially interesting on vibrant colour as an aesthetic element in GDR punk that disrupted the ambient drabness to which we point in our opening quote. But she also identifies a tendency in East German punk that locates it as more than an empty signifier of youthful discontent. Naming the spread of youth subcultural style as part of a 'broader turn towards lifestyles as a mode of identity construction', Bellotti pinpoints a historical development that is of signal interest for this volume. Historians of the last years of Cold War have shown how the GDR's turn to a consumer economy from the late 1960s set in motion struggles over the individualism seen to derive from the country's adoption of economic models from the capitalist West.[53] Bellotti's chapter shows a different cross-border dynamic at work in the demand for individualized lifestyles. For her, it is not only mainstream consumerism, but also underground transnational traffic in dissident cultural forms that fuels a longing for the expressive possibilities contained in dress, music, visual culture, literature, and everyday performance. The sonic, visual and performative styling of the self appears in this context as a practice fuelled not by consumer desires for commodity acquisition, but by demands for an individual stake in the process of production of social forms and institutional arrangements.

Bellotti's analysis resonates once again with Lüdtke's account of *Eigensinn* in terms of acts of stubborn awkwardness that highlight the 'frictions, malfunctions, disturbances and attritions' inherent in social orders.[54] Punk style, or indeed any dissident cultural expression, appears in this light no longer in the mode of 1980s cultural studies analysts, who read subcultural styles as semiotic ensembles expressing 'resistance through rituals', but as an 'obstinate' embodied intervention into the ordered social arrangements that Levine associates with closed form.[55]

At the same time, an understanding of stylistic self-fashioning as an embodied challenge to established arrangements of power reveals some potential limits to Levine's avowedly formalist approach. That cultural practice not only engages 'form', but also bodies, spaces, temporalities, sensibilities and subjectivities, is demonstrated by four final contributions to this volume from Katrin Schreiter, April Eisman, Michael Schmidt and Alice Weinreb. Schreiter enters the fray first with a contribution on the urban allotment garden (*Schrebergarten*). Considering the allotment as a physical space whose specifically German history she traces to origins in nineteenth-century health and urban reform movements, Schreiter also addresses this volume's interdisciplinary concerns by placing the 'experienced history' of gardens in dialogue with the allotment as a postwar literary *topos*. She draws on Pierre Nora's notion of *lieu de mémoire*, as well as Henri Lefèbvre's account of what he terms 'social spatial production', to explore the role of literature in producing the garden as a phenomeno-logical entity (a concrete space possessing material substance) and thus a place of embodied experience and either affective belonging, or aliena-tion from social norms.

In Lefèbvre's resonant formulation, space 'takes on body' through representational practices (in this case, literary narration) as well as spa-tial practices ('behaviours triggered and defined by space': Schreiter) that produce within larger social spaces determinate places of embodied experience and feeling.[56] Schreiter's approach to Lefèbvre distinguishes his work from more formalist accounts of spatial production by empha-sizing the capacity he identifies in space to produce feeling, affective attachment, and concrete spatio-temporal location in history. Analysing two Berlin novels by Paul Gurk and the East German Ulrich Plenzdorf, which she counterposes to post-unification texts set by authors Jost Baum and Michael Kleeberg respectively in the Ruhr region, and on the former German-German border, Schreiter presents the garden as more than an imagined space of seclusion or privatized belonging. The allot-ment garden is instead produced within literary representation as both the material repository (or 'palimpsest') of traces of collectively shared troubled pasts (and it is in this sense that the garden is a social, not an individual 'place of memory'), and a space of imaginative production in which both literary and actual social subjects negotiate new relationships to sociopolitical orders in present time.

Even the most reclusive everyday space, the allotment garden, is not able, then, to defy questions of politics and power. Schreiter also echoes other contributors when she stresses the political importance of belonging in everyday social practice: an importance clearly recognized by postwar political regimes, as is evident for instance in Palmowski's exploration of how the Socialist Unity Party, through GDR television, encouraged both distinctive quotidian viewing practices, and socialist communities and behaviours. In the volume's penultimate chapter, April Eisman follows both Palmowski and Schreiter when, in a study of painting in East Germany, she presents fine art practice as a form of socialist 'work' that strives to 'connect individuals to larger narratives'.

Eisman's approach is distinguished from Palmowksi's however by her critique of historiographical maps that locate the GDR uniquely in a topo-graphical and ideological relationship to the German West. The asym-metry of a relationship that places the GDR at several steps behind more 'advanced' forms of Western modernism is countered by Eisman when she draws on writers including Dipesh Chakrabarty and Piotr Piotrowski to argue for an East German art history located more centrally in relation to the global East and South.[57] What links East German art to non-West-ern cultural domains is, for Eisman, its eschewing of high modernism, and its embedding of art production and consumption within the realm of the socialist everyday. Ranging historically across forty years of GDR policy and practice, Eisman shows how East German artists, museums, galleries, curators, critics and policy makers strove to make of painting a 'public medium' enjoyed not solely by specialist, elite or connoisseur audiences, but by the socialist collective, or simply, the 'people'.

Especially notable in Eisman's contribution is an attentive use of quantitative method to explore the reach of GDR painting into popular culture and daily life. As she shows, GDR policies designed to extend public encounters with contemporary art practice were shaped by audi-ence surveys and representative polls that probed reasons for exhibi-tion and museum attendance. Data from those quantitative surveys are set in Eisman's account alongside visual analyses of paintings by art-ists Heidrun Hegewald and Doris Ziegler, as well as considerations of the extensive paratextual framework of popular magazine articles, exhibition reviews and other critical responses that contextualized art-ists' work for popular audiences. Her pluralist method affords multi-perspectival insight into the actualization in art and museum practice of a socialist critique of Western models of fine art as elite intellectual and economic capital. It shows too how the consumption of painting did indeed become a key component of everyday leisure culture in the GDR. But Eisman's work also points towards a final field of enquiry

shaping contributions to this volume. Her chapter ends with a sugges-
tive reference to the 'alternative structures of feeling' revealed by GDR
art history as framing East German quotidian life. Her reference here
is to Raymond Williams 1961 *The Long Revolution*, the *locus classicus* of
accounts of 'structures of feeling' as the constitutive framework for historical relationships between subjectivity, collective experience, and the
formal or institutional structures of nation, economy and state.[58] Of the
various shared readings on method discussed in the workshops which
inspired this volume's approach, Williams' text was amongst the most
productive in generating shared approaches to the postwar German
everyday; and it is most comprehensively examined in the chapter that
follows Eisman's, Michael Schmidt's analysis of the place of jazz and
pop within the 'perceptual fabric and everyday practices' of East and
West Germany after 1945.

As Schmidt explains, structures of feeling are 'forms of present-oriented thinking and sensing that do not fit into established institutions
or received cultural tendencies and movements'. Schmidt's summary
shows Williams sharing with Alf Lüdtke a commitment to exploring the
frictions between lived cultures and the structures of domination within
which they are constrained. But Williams reorients everyday history as
practised by Lüdtke when he further defines structures of feeling as
'meanings and values as they are actively … felt'.[59] His approach, then,
is one that decisively foregrounds questions of social affect: an emphasis
mirrored in Schmidt's study of West and East German post-1945 jazz and
pop culture, which similarly accentuates the affective entanglements of
bodies and subjectivities in everyday cultural practice. His chapter charts
a postwar history first of hot jazz and its differential embedding in the
musical cultures of East and West Germany, and second, of pop songs
or *Schlager*, seen specifically in their intermedial relation to film, television and celebrity culture. Importantly, Schmidt also adds to Williams'
account a spatial dimension that refigures 'structures of feeling' as 'perceptual-medial *zones*' traversing the inner German border as well as the
external frontiers of German nation. Against regime efforts on both sides
of the border to contain popular experience within Cold War bounds,
Schmidt thus identifies in popular music a historical attachment to transnational black music cultures, as well as to North American and trans-
European popular music modes.

Such affective attachment depends for Schmidt on engagements of
the body, primarily through dance: engagements that in turn demand
conceptual frameworks which move beyond Williams' ideas of structure
to capture the mobility and fluidity of the embodied self (Schmidt's suggested starting point is Roland Barthes' notion of *musica practica*). What

Schmidt further identifies as a lacuna in William's approach is a sensitivity to processes of transnational circulation and distribution which, in
his musical case studies, 'reorient ... daily practices and experiences ...
away from racial insularity and towards a sense of community and subjectivity beyond the nation'. Schmidt turns here therefore, albeit briefly,
to a second key text in our workshop discussions, Jacques Rancière's
The Politics of Aesthetic.[60] Rancière explores in that study what he terms a
'distribution of the sensible' that disperses sensed experience across hier-
archically organized sociopolitical domains, forging popular affiliations
as well as opposition to institutional structures, and becoming therefore
profoundly implicated in practices of domination as well as of contestation and dissent.

Schmidt makes use of this circulatory model to trace within postwar music history the transnational distribution of popular music practices and sensitivities. His focus is on patterns of perceptual and sensory
organization that drew communities together around common reference
points (a shared musical past, the cultural pull of the US, similar generational conflicts), but that also divided musical culture between industries
and publics that subsisted under the different material conditions and
contrasting political agendas of the two postwar German states.

The final chapter in this volume, Alice Weinreb's study of 'gustatory
tastes' in West and East Germany, replicates Schmidt's focus on sensory
experience and the body, but amplifies it with a detailed history of the
two countries' postwar food cultures. Indebted less centrally to Rancière
or Williams, Weinreb turns instead initially to Bourdieu's account of
social taste as a factor in 'social ordering and hierarchy', as well as to
Foucault's understanding of biopolitics as a 'politics that operates on the
body to determine the organisation, distribution and limitation of powers
in a society'.[61] Those writers are used by Weinreb to determine how GDR
and FRG food policy and practice forged links between 'bodies, taste
and economic development'. Central here is her account of 1970s nutritional education in both Germanies, which she sees as creating a common
pathologization of fatness across the inner German divide. Although
pathologies of obesity intersect differently in the two Germanies with the
hierarchical ordering of bodies around divisions of class, 'race', gender
and other social identities, there remains nonetheless a shared 'pathologization of popular tastes' that Weinreb shows to have persisted well
beyond unification in 1990. At the same time, divisions in culinary, food-
industrial and agricultural practice, as well as divergent 'moral economies' of gustatory taste in the GDR and FRG, generated frameworks for
everyday eating that shifted through time and diverged across social
groups and national boundaries.

Weinreb's exhaustive history of fluctuating German food economies charts the transition for instance from a celebration of overeating in the *Fresswelle* (eating frenzy) of an increasingly prosperous 1950s West Germany, to differently contoured moral panics over class and obesity in both Germanies from the 1970s on. Weinreb's conclusion that obesity became in both Germanies 'a useful expression of the troubled relationship between state economies and individual bodies' returns this introduction finally to questions of the everyday. As Weinreb also indicates, neither Foucault nor Bourdieu offer ways of fully accounting for the part played by everyday practices – which in her chapter take the most mundane possible form, as cooking and eating – in determining the specific relation of social subjects to larger relations of domination. Her solution is to interweave a discursive history of German-German obesity with an examination of taste as embodied experience within everyday food cultures. Other contributors to this volume explore from other perspectives the relation of everyday to larger political histories, drawing on historical anthropology, sociolingustic, narratological and politico-aesthetic accounts of form, as well as social theories of space, place, affect and the body, to explore the commonalities and distinctions that patterned German experience across Cold War divides. In thus rearticulating the complex relationship between the cultural, the social and the political, we hope to have begun to meet suggestions by Thomas Mergel at the beginning of the millennium for an intersecting history of the cultural and the political. In considering how culture might enrich our understanding of political history, Mergel suggested that the cultural perspective enabled historians to look at the political with a new sense of distance, as an 'Amazonian' terra incognita that was there to be discovered afresh.[62] Our volume proposes that the same is true for the social praxis of Germans, informed as it was by the political, the cultural, the social – but also by emotions and sensibilities, memories and affect. This has required us to take the commitment of everyday history, and the wider field of historical anthropology, into the realm of transdisciplinary scholarship and dialogue: a dialogue that we hope will continue as readers now engage with the eleven chapters below.[63]

Erica Carter is Professor of German and Film Studies at King's College London, and Chair of the UK German Screen Studies Network. She has published extensively on German cinema and cultural history; her publications include *How German Is She? Postwar West German Reconstruction and the Consuming Woman* (University of Michigan Press, 1997), *Dietrich's Ghosts: The Sublime and the Beautiful in Third Reich Film* (2004), *The German Cinema Book*, 2nd edition (Bergfelder, Carter & Göktürk, 2019) and *Béla*

Balázs: Early Film Theory (Berghahn, 2010). She is currently writing a monograph on cinema and late colonial sensibilities in the European 'white Atlantic' after the Second World War.

Jan Palmowski joined King's College London in 1999, and became a professor in 2009. In 2013, he was appointed Professor of Modern History at the University of Warwick. He is a specialist on the history of the GDR and of contemporary Germany, and his books include *At the Crossroads of Past and Present: Contemporary History and the Historical Discipline* (ed. with Kristina Spohr-Readman, special issue of the *Journal of Contemporary History* 3/2011), *Inventing a Socialist Nation: Heimat and the Politics of Everyday Life in the GDR* (Cambridge University Press, 2009, translated into German in 2016), and *Citizenship and National Identity in Twentieth-Century Germany* (ed. with Geoff Eley, Stanford University Press, 2008).

Katrin Schreiter is Lecturer in German and European Studies at King's College London. Her research focuses on the interplay of economics and culture of the Cold War era, and how these areas are connected to the politics of German diplomacy and ideas about nationhood. Her monograph *Designing One Nation: The Politics of Economic Culture and Trade in Divided Germany, 1949–1990* is forthcoming with Oxford University Press. She has published on related topics in *Business History Review* and *Europeanisation in the 20th Century: The Historical Lens* (Peter Lang, 2012). Her work on the gendered experience of Second World War trauma was published in *Central European History.*

Notes

1. Knabe, *Der Diskrete Charme der DDR*, 85–86.
2. For one of the best discussions of Ostalgie, see Leeder, *From Stasiland to Ostalgie.*
3. Berdahl, '(N)Ostalgie for the Present'.
4. Sabrow et al., *Wohin treibt die Erinnerung?.*
5. Paver, 'Colour and Time in Museums of East German Everyday Life'; Penny, 'The Museum für Deutsche Geschichte and German National Identity'; Arnold-de Simine, '*Ostalgie* – Nostalgia for GDR Everyday Culture?'.
6. For an overview of the breadth of GDR scholarship in the political sciences up to 1989, see Glaeßner, *Die DDR in der Ära Honecker.*
7. See, for instance, the enlightening reflections of a number of some of Germany's most prominent contemporary historians in Möller and Mählert, *Abgrenzung und Verflechtung.*

8. With a focus on West Germany, see for instance Biess, *Homecomings*; Demshuk, *The Lost German East*. For the GDR, see Jacobson, 'Integration of East German Resettlers into the Cultures and Societies of the GDR'. For insights into shared challenges around gender and sexual equality, see Brühöfener,Hagemann and Harsch, *Gendering Post-1945 German History*.

9. Kleßmann, 'Verflechtung und Abgrenzung'; Kleßmann, 'Spaltung und Verflechtung'.

10. Lindenberger, 'Divided, but not Disconnected'; Bösch, A History Shared and Divided, 5. This introduction addresses in particular entangled histories of culture, politics and consumption. For further scholarship on media history, see also Fengler, 'Westdeutsche Korrespondenten in der DDR'; Beutelschmidt and Oehmig, 'Connected Enemies?'; Badenoch, Fickers and Heinrich-Franke, *Airy Curtains in the European Ether*; Carter, 'Contact Zones and Boundary Objects'; Allen and Heiduschke, *Re-Imagining DEFA*. On environmental histories, see (on the German-German nuclear industry), Radkau and Hahn, *Aufstieg und Fall der deutschen Atomwirtschaft*; Eckert, 'Geteilt, aber nicht unverbunden'.

11. Bren and Neuburger, *Communism Unwrapped*.

12. Crew, *Consuming Germany in the Cold War*; Stitziel, *Fashioning Socialism*; Rubin, *Synthetic Socialism*.

13. See also Hertle, *Der Fall der Mauer*.

14. Moeller, *Protecting Motherhood*; Carter, *How German Is She?*; Heineman, *What Difference Does a Husband Make?*

15. Lüdtke, Marßolek and von Saldern, *Amerikanisierung*. For an approach that looks more closely at German-German connections, see Swett, Wiesen and Zatlin, *Selling Modernity*.

16. Kleßmann, *The Divided Past*; Jarausch, 'Divided, Yet Reunited'. See also Lindenberger, 'Ist die DDR ausgeforscht?'.

17. Jarausch, *After Hitler*.

18. See, for instance, Rödder and Elz, *Deutschland in der Welt*; Sarotte, *Dealing with the Devil*; Gray, *Germany's Cold War*.

19. Poiger, *Jazz, Rock and Rebels*.

20. Balbier, *Kalter Krieg auf der Aschenbahn*.

21. This is the starting point of Fulbrook, *The People's State*, 1–2.

22. Billardt and Hensel, *Alles war so. Alles war anders*, 6–7.

23. Betts, *Within Walls*.

24. Rubin, *Amnesiopolis*.

25. Fulbrook and Port, *Becoming East German*, 24.

26. McLellan, *Love in the Time of Communism*.

27. 'DDR-Alltag – das war nicht nur die private Idylle', interview with Culture Minister Bernd Neumann, *Berliner Zeitung*, 25 May 2006.

28. Hodgkin and Pearce, *The GDR Remembered*, especially part 2 on museums and the everyday.

29. Niethammer and von Platho, 'Die Jahre weiss man nicht, wo man die heute hinsetzen soll'.

30. Two of the most important examples include Fitzpatrick, *Everyday Stalinism* and Wildt, *Generation des Unbedingten*.

31. Eley, 'Glossary'.

32. Lindenberger, *Volkspolizei*; Palmowski, *Inventing a Socialist Nation*; Lüdtke, 'Introduction', 16. R. Hürtgen, *Der lange Weg nach drüben: Eine Studie über Herrschaft und Alltag in der DDR-Provinz* (Göttingen: Vandenhoek and Ruprecht, 2014).

33. Lüdtke, 'Alltagsgeschichte'.

34. Bergerson and Schmieding, *Ruptures in the Everyday*.

35. Lüdtke, 'Introductory Notes', 4–7.

36. See Rubin, *Amnesiopolis*, esp. chapter 3 on 'Material, Sensory, and Mnemonic Ruptures'.
37. Medick, '"Quo Vadis historische Anthropologie?"', 92.
38. Mitter and Major, *Across the Blocs*, 11.
39. Ibid., 3; Geertz, *The Interpretation of Cultures*, 3.
40. See Koselleck, *Futures Past*, esp. Part II, 'Theory and Method of the Historical Determination of Time', 75–154.
41. Tonkin, *Narrating our Pasts*, 2, c.f. Chamberlain and Thompson, *Narrative and Genre*, 10.
42. On *fabula* and *syuzhet* in Russian formalism, see for instance Cobley, *Narrative*, 15–16 and 243.
43. See France and Uhlin, 'Narrative as an Outcome Domain in Psychosis', 53. France and Uhlin in fact challenge notions of the psychotic's lack of narrative capacity, and explore developments in talking therapy that allow psychotics to renarrate their lives in ways that 'deconstruct oppressive narratives and generate alternative stories' (54).
44. Maza, 'Stories in History'.
45. Sheffer, *Burned Bridge*; Shaefer, *States of Division*; Johnson, *Divided Village*.
46. Levine, *Forms*, xii.
47. Ibid., 6. 'Affordances' is also a key term in the study of multimodal communication (communication in multiple and simultaneous semiotic form, as for instance in film, which may include speech, writing, music, image, etc.). In multimodal analysis, each semiotic mode is examined for its specific affordances, and meaning and aesthetic pleasure or unpleasure are seen as derived from the experience of these multiple modes in space and time: see Kress, *Multimodality*.
48. Examples of these disciplinary shifts include the recent rise of the history of emotions and the body, whose prominent exponents include the Berlin-based Centre for the History of the Emotions, https://www.mpib-berlin.mpg.de/en/research/history-of-emotions. See also Kalof and Bynon, *A Cultural History of the Body*; Porter, 'History of the Body Reconsidered'.
49. Levine, *Forms*, 37.
50. Lüdtke, '"Fehlgreifen in der Wahl der Mittel"'.
51. Betts, 'Building Socialism at Home', 114.
52. Hebdige, *Subculture*, 14.
53. Merkel, *Utopie und Bedürfnis*.
54. C.f. T. Lindenberger, 'Eigen-Sinn, Herrschaft und kein Widerstand', Version: 1.0, *Docupedia-Zeitgeschichte*, 2 September 2014. http://docupedia.de/zg/lindenberger_eigensinn_v1_de_2014. Retrieved 20 September 2018.
55. The reference is to one of the classical texts of 1970s and 1980s subculture studies, Hall and Jefferson, *Resistance through Rituals*.
56. Lefèbvre, *The Production of Space*, 220.
57. See Chakrabarty, *Provincializing Europe*; Piotrowski and Mickiewicz, 'Towards Horizontal Art History'.
58. Williams, *The Long Revolution*.
59. Williams, *Marxism and Literature*, 132.
60. Rancière, *The Politics of Aesthetics*.
61. Bourdieu, *Distinction*; Foucault, *The Birth of Biopolitics*, 13.
62. Mergel, 'Überlegungen zu einer Kulturgeschichte der Politik', 588–89.
63. Medick, '"Quo Vadis"', 84–87.

Bibliography

Allen, S. and S. Heiduschke (eds). *Re-Imagining DEFA: East German Cinema in its National and Transnational Contexts*. Oxford and New York: Berghahn, 2016.

Arnold-de Simine, S. '*Ostalgie* – Nostalgia for GDR Everyday Culture? The GDR in the Museum', in S. Arnold-de Simine, *Mediating Memory in the Museum: Trauma, Empathy, Nostalgia* (Basingstoke: Palgrave Macmillan, 2013), 160–86.

Badenoch, A., A. Fickers and Chr. Heinrich-Franke (eds). *Airy Curtains in the European Ether: Broadcasting and the Cold War*. Baden-Baden: Nomos, 2013.

Balbier, U. *Kalter Krieg auf der Aschenbahn: Deutsch-deutscher Sport 1950–72, eine politische Geschichte*. Paderborn: Schöningh, 2007.

Bauerkämper, A., M. Sabrow and B. Stöver (eds). *Doppelte Zeitgeschichte: Deutsch-deutsche Beziehungen 1945–1990*. Bonn: J.H.W. Dietz Nachfolger, 1998.

Berdahl, D. '(N)Ostalgie for the Present: Memory, Belonging, and East German Things'. *Ethnos* 64(2) (1999), 192–211.

Bergerson, A.S., and L. Schmieding (eds). *Ruptures in the Everyday: Views of Modern Germany from the Ground*. New York and Oxford: Berghahn, 2017.

Betts, P. 'Building Socialism at Home: The Case of East German Interiors', in K. Pence and P. Betts (eds), *Socialist Modern: East German Everyday Culture and Politics, Social History, Popular Culture, and Politics in Germany* (Ann Arbor: University of Michigan Press, 2008), 96–132.

_____. *Within Walls: Private Life in the German Democratic Republic*. Oxford: Oxford University Press, 2010.

Beutelschmidt, T. and R. Oehmig. 'Connected Enemies? Programming Transfer between East and West during the Cold War and the Example of East German Television'. *VIEW Journal of European Television History and Culture* 3(5) (2015), 60–67.

Biess, F. *Homecomings: Returning POWs and the Legacies of Defeat in Postwar Germany*. Princeton and Oxford: Princeton University Press, 2006.

Billardt, T. and K. Hensel. *Alles war so. Alles war anders: Bilder aus der DDR*. Leipzig: Kiepenheuer, 1999.

Bösch, F. (ed.). *A History Shared and Divided: East and West Germany since the 1970s*. Translated by J. Walcoff Neuheiser. Oxford and New York: Berghahn, 2018.

Bourdieu, P. *Distinction: A Social Critique of the Judgement of Taste*. Cambridge, MA: Harvard University Press, 1984.

Bren, P. and M. Neuburger. *Communism Unwrapped: Consumption in Cold War Eastern Europe*. Oxford: Oxford University Press, 2012.

Broszat, M. and E. Fröhlich. *Alltag und Widerstand: Bayern im Nationalsozialismus*. Munich: Piper, 1987.

Brühöfener, F., K. Hagemann and D. Harsch (eds). *Gendering Post-1945 German History: Entanglements*. Oxford and New York: Berghahn, forthcoming 2019.

Brunner, D., U. Grashoff and A. Kötzing (eds). *Asymmetrisch verflochten? Neue Forschungen zur gesamtdeutschen Nachkriegsgeschichte*. Berlin: Ch. Links, 2013.

Carter, E. 'Contact Zones and Boundary Objects: The Media and Entangled Representations of Gender', in F. Brühöfener, K. Hagemann and D. Harsch (eds), *Gendering Post-1945 German History: Entanglements*. Oxford and New York: Berghahn, forthcoming 2019.

_____. *How German Is She? Postwar West German Reconstruction and the Consuming Woman*. Ann Arbor: University of Michigan Press, 1997.

Chakrabarty, D. *Provincializing Europe: Postcolonial Thought and Historical Difference*. Princeton: Princeton University Press, 2000.

Chamberlain, M. and P. Thompson (eds). *Narrative and Genre: Contexts and Types of Communication*. London and New York: Routledge, 1998.

Cobley, J. *Narrative*. Hove: Psychology Press, 2001.

Crew, D.F. (ed.). *Consuming Germany in the Cold War*. Oxford and New York: Berg, 2003.

'DDR-Alltag – das war nicht nur die private Idylle'. *Berliner Zeitung*, 25 May 2006.

Demshuk, A. *The Lost German East: Forced Migration and the Politics of Memory, 1945–1970*. Cambridge: Cambridge University Press, 2012.

Dillon, M.C. *The Ontology of Becoming and the Ethics of Particularity*. Athens: Ohio University Press, 2012.

Eckert, A.M. 'Geteilt, aber nicht unverbunden: Grenzgewässer als deutsch-deutsches Umweltproblem'. *Vierteljahreshefte für Zeitgeschichte* 62 (2014), 69–100.

Eley, G. 'Glossary', in A. Lüdtke (ed.), *The History of Everyday Life: Reconstructing Historical Experiences and Ways of Life*, translated by W. Templar (Princeton, NJ: Princeton University Press, 1989), 313–14.

Enzensberger, H.M. *Hammerstein oder Der Eigensinn: Eine deutsche Geschichte*. Frankfurt am Main: Suhrkamp, 2008.

Felski, R. and S. Fraiman (eds). *In the Mood*, special issue of *New Literary History* 43(3) (2012).

Fengler, D. 'Westdeutsche Korrespondenten in der DDR', in J. Wilke (ed.), *Journalisten und Journalismus in der DDR* (Cologne, Weimar and Vienna: Böhlau, 2007), 79–216.

Fitzpatrick, S. *Everyday Stalinism: Ordinary Life in Extraordinary Times: Soviet Russia in the 1930s*. Oxford: Oxford University Press, 2000.

Foucault, M. *The Birth of Biopolitics: Lectures at the College de France, 1978–79*. New York: Palgrave Macmillan, 2008.

France, C.M. and B.D. Uhlin. 'Narrative as an Outcome Domain in Psychosis'. *Psychology and Psychotherapy: Theory, Research and Practice* 79(1) (2006), 53–67.

Fulbrook, M. *The People's State: East German Society from Hitler to Honecker*. New Haven: Yale University Press, 2005.

Fulbrook, M. and A.I. Port (eds). *Becoming East German: Socialist Structures and Sensibilities after Hitler*. New York and Oxford: Berghahn, 2013.

Geertz, C. *The Interpretation of Cultures*. New York: Basic Books, 1973.

Glaeßner, G.-J. (ed.). *Die DDR in der Ära Honecker: Politik – Kultur – Gesellschaft*. Opladen: Westdeutscher Verlag, 1988.

Gray, W.G. *Germany's Cold War: The Global Campaign to Isolate East Germany, 1949–1969*. Chapel Hill: University of North Carolina Press, 2003.

Hall, S. and T. Jefferson (eds). *Resistance through Rituals: Youth Subcultures in Postwar Britain*. London and New York: Routledge, 2006 [1976].

Hebdige, D. *Subculture: The Meaning of Style*. London and New York: Routledge, 1988 [1979].

Heineman, E.D. *What Difference Does a Husband Make? Women and Marital Status in Nazi and Postwar Germany*. Berkeley: University of California Press, 1999.

Hertle, H.-H. *Der Fall der Mauer: Die Unbeabsichtigte Selbstauflösung des SED-Staates.* Wiesbaden: Westdeutscher Verlag, 1999.

Highmore, B. and J.B. Taylor (eds). 'Introduction'. *Mood Work, New Formations* 82 (2014), 5–12.

Hodgkin, N. and C. Pearce (eds). *The GDR Remembered: Representations of the East German State since 1989.* Rochester, NY: Random House, 2011.

Hürtgen, R. *Der lange Weg nach drüben: Eine Studie über Herrschaft und Alltag in der DDR-Provinz.* Göttingen: Vandenhoek and Ruprecht, 2014.

Jacobson, A. 'Integration of East German Resettlers into the Cultures and Societies of the GDR'. PhD thesis, University College London, 2015.

Jarausch, K. *After Hitler: Recivilizing Germans, 1949–1995.* Oxford: Oxford University Press, 2006.

———. 'Divided, Yet Reunited – The Challenge of Integrating German Post-War Histories'. H-German Forum, 1 February 2011. Retrieved 13 October 2015 from http://h-net.msu.edu/cgi-bin/logbrowse.pl?trx=vx&list=H-German&month=11 02&week=a&msg=lNK7XIEc2qqANKFyP6tmew.

Johnson, J.B. *Divided Village: The Cold War in the German Borderlands.* Abingdon: Routledge, 2017.

Kalof, L. and W. Bynon (eds). *A Cultural History of the Body,* 6 vols. London: Berg, 2010.

Kleßmann, C. 'Spaltung und Verflechtung: Ein Konzept zur integrierten Nachkriegsgeschichte 1945-1990', in C. Kleßmann and P. Lautzas (eds), *Teilung und Integration: Die doppelte deutsche Nachkriegsgeschichte als wissenschaftliches und didaktisches Problem* (Bonn: Wochenschau, 2005), 20–37.

———. 'Verflechtung und Abgrenzung: Aspekte der geteilten und zusammengehörigen deutschen Nachkriegsgeschichte'. *Aus Politik und Zeitgeschichte* 29–30 (1993), 30–41.

——— (ed.). *The Divided Past: Rewriting Post-War German History.* Oxford and New York: Berg, 2001.

Knabe, H. *Der Diskrete Charme der DDR.* Berlin: Ullstein, 2001.

Koselleck, R. *Futures Past: On the Semantics of Historical Time.* New York: Columbia University Press, 2004.

Kress, G. *Multimodality: A Social Semiotic Approach to Contemporary Communication.* London: Routledge, 2010.

Leeder, K. (ed.). *From Stasiland to Ostalgie: the GDR 20 Years After, Oxford German Studies* 38(3) (2009), special issue, 234–344.

Lefèbvre, H. *The Production of Space.* Oxford: Blackwell, 1991.

Levine, C. *Forms: Whole, Rhythm, Hierarchy, Network.* Princeton, NJ: Princeton University Press, 2015.

Lindenberger, T. 'Divided, but not Disconnected: Germany as a Border Region of the Cold War', in T. Hochscherf, C. Laucht and A. Plowman (eds), *Divided, but not Disconnected: German Experiences of the Cold War* (London and New York: Berghahn, 2010), 11–33.

———. 'Ist die DDR ausgeforscht? Phasen, Trends und ein optimistischer Ausblick'. *Aus Politik und Zeitgeschichte* 24–26 (2014), 27–32.

———. *Volkspolizei: Herrschaftspraxis und öffentliche Ordnung im SED Staat 1952–68.* Cologne, Weimar and Vienna: Böhlau, 2003.

Lüdtke, A. 'Alltagsgeschichte – ein Bericht von Unterwegs'. *Historische Anthropologie* 11(2) (2003), 278–95.

――. '"Fehlgreifen in der Wahl der Mittel": Optionen im Alltag militärischen Handelns'. *Mittelweg* 36 (2003), 61–75.

――. 'Introductory Notes', in A. Lüdtke (ed.), *Everyday Life in Mass Dictatorship: Collusion and Evasion* (Basingstoke: Palgrave, 2016), 3–12.

Lüdtke, A. (ed.). 'Introduction: What Is the History of Everyday Life and Who Are its Practitioners?', in *The History of Everyday Life: Reconstructing Historical Experiences and Ways of Life* (Princeton: Princeton University Press, 1995), 3–40.

Lüdtke, A., I. Marßolek and A. von Saldern (eds). *Amerikanisierung: Traum und Alptraum im Deutschland des 20. Jahrhunderts.* Stuttgart: Steiner, 1996.

Maza, S. 'Stories in History: Cultural Narratives in Recent Works in European History'. *American Historical Review* 101(5) (1996), 1493–515.

McLellan, J. *Love in the Time of Communism: Intimacy and Sexuality in the GDR.* Oxford: Oxford University Press, 2011.

Medick, H. '"Quo Vadis historische Anthropologie?" Geschichtsforschung zwischen Historischer Kulturwissenschaft und Mikro-Historie'. *Historische Anthropologie* 9(1) (2001), 78–92.

Mergel, T. 'Überlegungen zu einer Kulturgeschichte der Politik'. *Geschichte und Gesellschaft* 28(4) (2002), 574–606.

Merkel, I. *Utopie und Bedürfnis: Die Geschichte der Konsumkultur in der DDR.* Cologne: Böhlau, 1999.

Mitchell, W.J.T. *Picture Theory: Essays on Verbal and Visual Representation.* Chicago: University of Chicago Press, 1994.

Mitter, R. and P. Major. *Across the Blocs: Cold War Cultural and Social History.* London and Portland: Frank Cass, 2004.

Moeller, R.G. *Protecting Motherhood: Women and the Family in the Politics of Postwar West Germany.* Berkeley: University of California Press, 1993.

Möller, F. and U. Mählert (eds). *Abgrenzung und Verflechtung: Das geteilte Deutschland in der zeithistorischen Debatte.* Berlin: Metropol, 2008.

Negt, O. and A. Kluge. *Geschichte und Eigensinn*, 2 vols. Frankfurt am Main: Suhrkamp, 1981.

Niethammer, L. and A. von Platho (eds). *'Die Jahre weiss man nicht, wo man die heute hinsetzen soll': Lebensgeschichte und Sozialkultur im Ruhrgebiet 1930 bis 1960*, 3 vols. Berlin: Dietz, 1983–1986.

Palmowski, J. *Inventing a Socialist Nation: Heimat and the Politics of Everyday Life in the GDR 1945-1990.* Cambridge: Cambridge University Press, 2009.

Paver, C. 'Colour and Time in Museums of East German Everyday Life', in A. Saunders and D. Pinfold (eds), *Remembering and Rethinking the GDR: Multiple Perspectives and Plural Authenticities* (Basingstoke: Palgrave, 2012), 132–48.

Penny, H.G. 'The Museum für Deutsche Geschichte and German National Identity'. *Central European History* 28(3) (1995), 343–72.

Piotrowski, P. and A. Mickiewicz. 'Towards Horizontal Art History', in J. Anderson (ed.), *Crossing Cultures: Conflict, Migration, Convergence* (Melbourne: Melbourne University Publishing, 2009), 82–85.

Poiger, U.C. *Jazz, Rock and Rebels: Cold War Politics and American Culture in a Divided Germany.* Berkeley: University of California Press, 2000.

Porter, R. 'History of the Body Reconsidered', in P. Burke (ed.), *New Perspectives on Historical Writing* (Cambridge and Malden: Polity Press, 2001), 233–60.

Radkau, J. and L. Hahn. *Aufstieg und Fall der deutschen Atomwirtschaft.* Munich: oekom, 2013.

Rancière, J. *The Politics of Aesthetics: The Distribution of the Sensible.* Translated and with an introduction by Gabriel Rockhill. London: Continuum, 2004.

Rödder, A. and W. Elz (eds). *Deutschland in der Welt: Weichenstellungen in der Geschichte der Bundesrepublik.* Göttingen: Vandenhoek und Ruprecht, 2010.

Rubin, E. *Amnesiopolis: Modernity, Space and Memory in East Germany.* New York: Oxford University Press, 2016.

———. *Synthetic Socialism: Plastics and Dictatorship in the German Democratic Republic.* Chapel Hill: University of North Carolina Press, 2008.

Sabrow, M. et al. (eds). *Wohin treibt die Erinnerung? Dokumentation einer Debatte.* Göttingen: Vandenhoek & Ruprecht, 2007.

Sarotte, M.E. *Dealing with the Devil: East Germany, Détente & Ostpolitik, 1969–1973.* Chapel Hill: University of North Carolina Press, 2001.

Shaefer, S. *States of Division: Border and Boundary Formation in Cold War Rural Germany.* Oxford: Oxford University Press, 2014.

Sheffer, E. *Burned Bridge: How East and West Germans made the Iron Curtain.* Oxford: Oxford University Press, 2012.

Steege, P., A.S. Bergerson, M. Healy and P.E. Swett. 'The History of Everyday Life: A Second Chapter'. *Journal of Modern History* 80 (June 2008), 358–78.

Stitziel, J. *Fashioning Socialism: Clothing, Politics and Consumer Culture in East Germany.* Oxford and New York: Berg, 2005.

Swett, P., J. Wiesen and J. Zatlin (eds). *Selling Modernity: Advertising in Twentieth-Century Germany.* Durham, NC: Duke University Press, 2007.

Tonkin, E. *Narrating our Pasts: The Social Construction of Oral History.* Cambridge: Cambridge University Press, 1995.

Wildt, M. *Generation des Unbedingten: Das Führungskorps des Reichssicherheitshauptamtes.* Hamburg: Hamburger Edition, 2002.

Williams, R. *The Long Revolution.* Peterborough and Ontario: Broadview Press, 2001 [1961].

———. *Marxism and Literature.* Oxford: Oxford University Press, 1977.

Chapter 1

Narrating the Everyday
Television, Memory and the Subjunctive in the GDR, 1969–1989

Jan Palmowski

This chapter asks how GDR television told stories creating boundaries and connections in the quotidian lives of East Germans, in the one arena where the GDR was perpetually challenged on equal terms. In his plea for future research agendas to focus on the entangled history of post-1945 Germany, Jürgen Kocka singled out television and radio as a particular instance in which 'West Germany and East Germany remained heavily interconnected and intertwined'.[1] And indeed, East German television offers a particularly rich and challenging prism for studying post-1945 German history. No other area of everyday life in the GDR was as marked by free and direct competition between East and West Germany. And yet, this competition only existed in the GDR; with fewer than one-sixth of West Germans able to receive GDR TV, West German channels were driven by competition amongst themselves, rather than looking toward the east. By contrast, for most East Germans, television defied the inner German border. Nowhere was it as easy for East Germans to emigrate mentally to the Federal Republic. Equally, nowhere were there greater opportunities (and greater needs) for the party to reach GDR citizens directly, in the privacy of their own homes.

In its endeavour to persuade viewers to accept its offerings rather than those of the West, GDR television had one distinct advantage over its West German rival: it could relate to the everyday experiences, localities and concerns of GDR viewers in ways that West German television was unable to. The party fully appreciated both the power and the vulnerability of GDR television in connecting to GDR citizens. No analysis of the SED's attempts to create a distinct sense of identity, realize a socialist society and popularize socialism is complete without a focus on television.

The specificity and the entanglement of GDR television requires particular attention, and yet it eludes many of the conventional tools of everyday historians. We can explore how power was transmitted though the programmes themselves, and we can also aim at a much better understanding of the limitations and possibilities faced by the makers of the programmes in the everyday. But it is virtually impossible to gauge the responses, gestures and communications of citizens about the programmes they watched, day in day out. The ephemeral nature of the experience of watching television defies specific memories of particular programmes that could be traced through oral history interviews, whilst letters to programme makers present an important, but partial perspective of viewers' responses. It is essential to access tools developed in other disciplines, notably literary and film studies, to gain a new understanding of the impact and meanings of television in the formation of East German identifications.

This chapter examines television not simply as something that linked the daily lives of most East Germans. Television, alongside other media, constitutes a structured framework enabling viewers to make meaning of the everyday.[2] Watching television acts as a central reference point of social and cultural communication.[3] In the GDR as elsewhere, television had the potential to relate the individual to wider cultural codes, allowing these to be shared.[4] Indeed, through the (fictional and nonfictional) stories it narrated, television offered symbolic interpretations of aspects of the world shaped by history and culture, thus establishing common ways of living and communicating.[5] Analysing television allows us to explore the symbolic worlds of viewers, and to uncover the narratives that were offered to citizens to order their social reality.[6]

Indeed, stories – whether presented through television or other media – allow us to make sense of our lives, ordering our own, fragmented memory into a wider narrative whole.[7] Stories are accepted if they accord to our experience, if they 'ring true', irrespective of whether they are formally fact or fiction. In that sense they are crucially linked to memory, because what we know is shaped by our memory. Television has the capacity to affect cognitive structures of individuals and societies, of how we see the world and understand it.[8] In these ways, television interacted with viewers, forming an integral part of the everyday and helping to constitute it in turn.[9]

It is important to note that narrative is more than just entertainment; stories invite us to 'reconsider the obvious. Great fiction is subversive in spirit, not pedagogical'.[10] Stories require something unexpected to happen. They invite us 'to see the world as embodied in the story', whilst 'the sharing of common stories creates an interpretive community', promoting cultural – and legal – cohesion.[11] Narrative is essential for the dynamism of society, and its ability to deal with the unforeseen. It subjunctivizes the familiar 'into what might have been and what might be', and this provides cultures with the tools to work out conflicts within the community and contain incompatible interests.[12] This chapter examines what stories were told on television, how they attempted to relate to the everyday, and the possibilities they provided for the subjunctive, to allow East Germans to imagine conflict – and its resolution.

Non-Fiction

Between 1960 and 1975, the proportion of households owning a television set increased from 16.7 per cent to nearly 100 per cent.[13] Between 1965 and 1975, the number of TV hours broadcast also doubled, from 58 to 116 hours per week.[14] Television became widely available, and constituted the most popular pastime of citizens, far ahead of gardening, entertaining friends and listening to music.[15] In 1967, watching TV represented the favourite weekend leisure activity for 68 per cent of the population,[16] and ten years later this figure had risen to almost 72 per cent.[17] Watching television constituted a central part of the East German everyday with East Germans spending on average 15 hours per week, a third of their spare time, in front of the box.[18]

At the same time, no other Western product could be consumed as freely as television. By 1965, between 70 and 80 per cent of East German viewers had access to the first channel of West German television (ARD). During the 1980s, reception of the two main West German television stations (ARD and ZDF) increased to between 80 and 90 per cent of households.[19] By contrast, at most one-sixth of West Germans could receive East German television, so that even if West German television actively engaged with its East German rival (and with the GDR), GDR television never presented the same challenges to West Germany's stations.

The German Television Broadcasting Service (DFF) was acutely conscious of West German television from its inception, its launch on 21 December 1952 hastily arranged to coincide with Stalin's birthday, to steal a march on West Germany's television launched four days later.[20] As early as the 1960s, it became abundantly clear just how much West German television had shaped GDR viewing habits. Where viewers could watch West German television, they often did so. The first comprehensive survey of viewing habits, conducted in 1965, noted with alarm that on one Saturday, only 11 per cent of those able to receive both Eastern and Western television watched the East German entertainment show *Melodie auf Abwegen* ('Melodic Meanderings'), lamenting that another 50 to 60 per cent of viewers would have seen its West German rival broadcast at the same time.[21] Moreover, those surveyed who could receive West German television tended to award the DFF's programmes significantly lower quality ratings, particularly when the ARD offered similar programmes.[22] And finally, West German television had a strong impact on viewers' expectations, as these began to expect the programming of GDR TV to mirror the structure of West German television.[23]

The availability of Western television reinforced the party's view of the DFF as constituting a propaganda tool of the utmost importance. According to Heinrich Adamek, the DFF's head between 1952 and 1990, television represented the most diverse and common instrument for agitation at the SED's disposal.[24] Better still, as one local functionary put it, television allowed the party to 'bring culture, the socialist culture, into every home',[25] and reach the individual in the privacy of her own living room.[26] In its programming decisions, the DFF thus directly sought to support the party's central endeavours, reinforcing every attempt to create a sense of identification with the GDR, and the party's ideals.[27] Because of its particular emotional access to viewers, DFF planners from the late 1960s argued that GDR television could help shape socialist aesthetic values characteristic of the socialist community of people.[28] Television programmes should represent the changed socialist individual, and make visible the nature of this transformation in individual thought and action, in the relationship with the state, and in the viewers' relations with each other.[29] Representing and reinforcing the love of the socialist homeland became a central task for GDR television, and the design of programmes in politics, entertainment and culture.[30]

The desire to represent the achievements of socialism could be realized most directly through journalistic programmes including the flagship news show, the *Aktuelle Kamera*, as well as programmes like the *Schwarzer Kanal*, which took a propagandistic look at West German news, or *Objektiv*, with its international reports. Because of their ideological significance, these occupied between 15 and 18 per cent of broadcast time during the 1970s and the 1980s. And yet, the DFF was under no illusion that these programmes suffered from low audience figures. The *Aktuelle Kamera* was watched by around 22 per cent of viewers in 1965–1966,[31] and appeared to reach well under 20 per cent of viewers by the early 1970s,[32] declining to 13.8 per cent in 1981, and to 9.5 per cent in 1988. As the proportion of functionaries watching the show continued to be overrepresented by a factor of two to three, this meant that by the 1980s, the show was barely watched by anyone who was not a party member.[33] By contrast, in the late 1960s, the DFF noted that within the FRG, the ARD's *Tagesschau* reached over 50 per cent of viewers, and the ZDF news programme *Heute* reached another 14 to 19 per cent. East German news shows were not popular,[34] with East German viewers lamenting the biased nature of news, its slowness to report breaking news, its drabness, and the monotony in its reports.[35] Even the *Aktuelle Kamera*'s makers were conscious that it was widely regarded as 'a sub-department of the Central Committee, de facto the party's trombone, its trumpet', with very strict codes through, for instance, the regular inclusion of workers' voices (who had to speak like their bosses). Indeed, over time the news show became more and more formulaic in its reporting,[36] even if programme makers tried to freshen the visual content to ensure more footage was included to underline the stories by the 1980s.[37] At best, then, makers of the programme could reach those parts of the population that were members of the mass organizations, and who were active volunteers in schools, or in the legal system.[38]

The low and declining ratings for news shows led to the development of socialist reporting packaged in entertainment formats. One example is *Rund*, a youth show originally created in 1973 to report on the World Youth Festival, and which was subsequently broadcast in 150 shows over almost fifteen years.[39] *Rund* featured the latest pop music available in the GDR, with the hottest homegrown bands including Karat and the Puhdys, and with international stars from other socialist countries, as well as the West. However, in the desire to fuse the Free German Youth (FDJ) and GDR youth culture,[40] *Rund* highlighted the FDJ's achievements, interviewed FDJ functionaries and reported on official FDJ festivals. For instance, in its eightieth show broadcast from Henningsdorf (Potsdam District) on 26 April 1980, one reportage featured the Wittstock Initiative in which over 1,200 youth brigades across then GDR were apparently inspired by the slogan 'A performance increase by ourselves is a performance increase for ourselves'. The reportage concentrated on Gerhard Piesler, a member of the youth brigade Heinrich Bartsch in the local steel works. Piesler was praised as a local FDJ secretary who translated the Wittstock motto into local practice by improving the manufacturing process, but who also never tired of improving himself through constant training. This feature was followed by an interview with Dieter Lining, sitting in the audience in a blue FDJ shirt, who was pleased to have been delegated to the fifth festival of friendship of GDR and Soviet Youth in Karl-Marx-Stadt that year, adding (to visibly bored faces in the audience around him) that the 1972 festival in Leningrad had been amongst the most memorable days of his life.[41] Even if *Rund* prided itself on two-thirds of the programme consisting of music, the remaining third of the programme left no doubt about the show's ideological provenance. In shows like *Rund*, the substance of ideology could not be compromised. Thus, the cultural codes transported through the show were never in doubt. While camera shots of dancing youths and the glitter of the rock stars' outfits were not unlike those of West German music shows,[42] the presence only of mainstream rock, with stars (and youths) all wearing aesthetically acceptable haircuts, transported unmistakeable ideological codes: individual fulfilment was to be sought within the boundaries of the collective.[43] And to leave absolutely no room for doubt, the two young presenters of the show, Bodo Freudl and Heidemarie Schröder, wore shirts that were a spitting image of the FDJ apparel, except that the FDJ insignia had been replaced by a badge sporting the letters of *Rund*.[44]

Despite low ratings, programmes like *Rund* and the *Aktuelle Kamera* were sustained as unmistakeably socialist frames for GDR TV. These shows were stymied by their high ideological visibility. The problem with these programmes was not simply the high ideological content in itself. The problem was that they did not contain any narrative features, as no surprise, no tension, no unforeseen events were allowed. The issue, thus, was not so much the ideology in itself, but the failure to connect to the narrative, the stories, of the everyday. The narratives transported through these shows became overspecialized, with ideology crowding out narrative that related to viewers.[45]

Stories of Joy

With its growing sense of urgency to appeal to viewers, the DFF had to develop other television programmes that were genuinely popular. From the late 1960s, the DFF became much more focused on the need to create popular light entertainment. In 1967 it created a central entertainment division (*Hauptabteilung Unterhaltung*) to stop the decline of viewing figures through a greater diversity of programmes, and the creation of more popular highlights. The DFF was keen to emphasize that socialism and entertainment did go together. The 1969 Annual Plan of the DFF's Entertainment Section demanded that the DFF go on the offensive against the shallow amusement offered by Western television, by communicating socialist optimism through Marxist aesthetic.[46] Indeed, entertainment could foster the individual's love of the socialist *Heimat*, their creative potential, and a respect for every individual, fulfilling her or his joy in leading a socialist life.[47] Television makers aimed at reflecting (and in turn demonstrating) the socialist citizens' new ways of living and their ways of feeling ('*Lebensweise und Lebensgefühl*').[48] This meant, for instance, truly capturing the creative talents of all, representing the culture and spirit that linked all socialist peoples in music and dance, and charting the transformation of the individual through socialism.[49] For entertainment, as for drama and other sections, GDR television sought to represent everyday life in the GDR in an optimistic way, but in a way that also connected to the experiences and desires of the population.

The late 1960s and early 1970s saw the emergence of a number of entertainment programmes which, in their heyday in the 1970s, regularly attracted 50 per cent of viewers or even more.[50] These shows represented entertainment linked to different parts or aspects of the socialist Heimat, including Heimat music (*Oberhofer Bauernmarkt*, from Thuringia), *Klock 8* (a variety show with a nautical theme, broadcast from Rostock), and – most popular of all – *Ein Kessel Buntes*, the variety show broadcast from Berlin from 1972. If GDR viewers wanted to watch the premier league of international stars in the German-speaking world like Abba, Boney M or Mireille Matthieu, they could do so by tuning in to the *Kessel*. Benefiting from the musical advice of Walter Kubiczek and others, and featuring some of the GDR's most popular cabaret performers, this show spared no expense to represent East Berlin as a 'cosmopolitan city' ('*Weltstadt*'), which offered entertainment at the very highest level, attracted global stars, and could afford to be relaxed about life – and attract viewers with its optimism.[51] These shows were popular because they connected with viewers' experiences, but also with their desires and dreams.

Together, the sounds and sights of the homeland, the glitter of the Friedrichstadtpalast in the 'Kessel', and the steel furnaces in Brandenburg in *Rund*, afforded viewers 'in novel and affective ways the spatial affordances of social life writ large'.[52] These sounds and sights were mediated by the particular conditions of music and image production in the GDR, their reception and reproduction, but also by the SED's relatively tight grip on who could and could not perform. The promotion of a German-language musical mainstream at the expense of innovative sounds such as glam or punk rock in the 1970s provided clear limitations to any sonic dissonances viewers might have been confronted with in GDR-produced shows. This was reinforced by a rigorous determination to keep within certain boundaries when it came to the appearances of individuals on TV – be they television presenters sporting everyday outfits, or musicians whose haircuts needed to conform to 'orderly' expectations. Indeed, a particular format for entertainment shows was never successfully imitated in the GDR: whilst quiz shows like *Der Grosse Preis*, *Wetten Dass* or *Am laufenden Band* were amongst the most popular programmes in West Germany (inviting viewers to imagine challenge, transformation and a life of plenty), these thrills were denied to viewers of East German television. A life of individual wealth was a subjunctive impossible for the party to entertain. In short, the range of sounds and sights of GDR shows was far narrower than it would have been in Western Germany. From this perspective, conversations in the *Bauernmarkt* around particular individual or collective achievements in realizing local folk traditions were not that far removed from the portraits of the Brandenburg foundry or the praises of the German-Soviet Youth Festival discussed in *Rund*. In sound and sight, as well as in narrative, the subjunctive had clear limits in the entertaining portraits of the GDR, the Heimat and its citizens.

Socialist Drama

An alternative way to connect to viewers' imagination was through drama, produced for GDR television either by DEFA or by the television studios themselves.[53] Here the 1960s proved to be formative in the evolution of a number of thematic tropes which formed the basis of a range of multi-part series. In particular, they contributed to a founding myth of the GDR by showing how it 'arose from ruins' following the moral perversion of Nazism and capitalism, against bitter and clandestine opposition from the West.[54] One example was the three-part series *Hannes Trostberg*, broadcast in 1966. It featured two protagonists, Hannes Trostberg and his superior, Edwin Spahn, returning to their village in Brandenburg in 1945. Whilst in Soviet imprisonment, Hannes had converted Spahn, heir to the local landowning dynasty, to communism. Back home, meanwhile, Spahn's mother had succumbed to the charms of the local Nazi leader, Grauling, falsely accusing Trostberg's wife who was consequently killed by the Nazis. Now returned from the war, Edwin Spahn developed an ambivalent relationship to socialism, with his brother finding success in the West as an advertising salesman. By contrast, Trostberg shone as a model of self-denial, wisdom and self-sacrifice, depicting the GDR's heroes of the first hour.[55] And indeed, the miniseries was praised in the GDR media as a paragon of new socialist art with the capacity to move hearts and minds.[56] A series that invoked in viewers, as far as the party was concerned, a natural pride in the GDR and its achievements, through the toil of individuals embracing the need for change – this won the author Seeger and the two lead actors the golden *Lorbeer*, the DFF's highest prize, in 1966.[57]

As the GDR matured, its founding myth retained a strong grip on the narratives of television dramas, even as these related more frequently to the present. In *Daniel Druskat* (1976), for instance, we witness, in the first episode, the ambivalent relationship between Daniel (Hilmar Thate) and his friend Max Stephan (Manfred Krug). Where Daniel sacrificed the love of his life for the party, Max was a pragmatic socialist who was trained not by the party, but by the 'school of life'. Living by the maxim of 'see much but appear little',[58] he was uninterested in the promise of tomorrow, preferring to focus on the here and now. The episode showed how Max used an impending state visit to his community to pressurize the party into building a new jetty at the lake and a swimming pool, diverting resources that were needed elsewhere. However, as the series unfolds, it becomes clear that the origin of the complex relationship between the two protagonists – and ultimately the reason for Daniel's downfall – were Daniel's actions in the dying days of the Second World War. In the final episode the viewers learned that as the NS regime collapsed, Daniel had been unable to prevent the murder of a Polish prisoner of war by the Nazi police inspector and – implicitly – the local Countess.

These tropes of the challenges of the socialist everyday with their origins in the heroic beginnings of 1945, which could only be mastered by individuals within the boundaries of the socialist community, which in turn grew with each of these challenges, were remarkably consistent in the flagship GDR drama productions. This is most evident in the dramatic series broadcast to celebrate the GDR's key anniversaries, *Dolles Familienalbum* ('Dolle's Family Album', October 1969), *Die lange Straße* ('The Long Road', October 1979), and the *Märkische Chronik* ('Chronicle of the Mark', broadcast to commemorate the fiftieth anniversary of the Nazi takeover, in early 1983). Designed for maximum popular effect, these programmes aimed at using folksiness (*Volkstümlichkeit*) and Heimat in order to show how socialist problems could be overcome in practice.[59] These each told the story of the GDR's founding years and its socialist transformation through the prism of relationships, but also – and increasingly – through a sense of place. Through the lens of a small local community, these series repeated, in different narratives, a number of tropes characteristic for the self-understanding of the GDR: the denial of immediate pleasures of consumption for a better tomorrow ('making do'), a collective responsibility for a just society versus the individualism of the West, a commitment to pacifism in the future through resolute anti-fascism and the social and cultural possibilities afforded to those who wanted to realize a socialist future.[60]

The depiction of the GDR in TV drama through the homeland climaxed in the *Chronik*, broadcast a year before Edgar Reitz's *Heimat* on West German television. Written by Bernhard Seeger, the *Chronik* was, in fact, a re-adaptation in twelve parts of *Hannes Trostberg*. But whereas the latter series had covered the period from 1945 to the late 1950s, the 'Chronicle' began in 1935, and ended in 1946. No longer set in a studio, it centred on the fictional community of Güterlohe in the Mark Brandenburg, showing 'in poetic images the straying and rise of our people'.[61] The rootedness in the land was unmistakeable – from the introduction of each episode through a voiceover: 'The summers are hot and dry. Frost presses the earth together so that it groans and tears in the night', to the imagery of the village and its church in the opening credits. It also featured consistent symbols of the Heimat, including the occasional depiction of a stork's nest between scenes throughout the series, symbolizing tradition, intimacy and new beginnings.

With this new series Seeger avoided many of the mistakes of the earlier miniseries which had become apparent, despite the media hype, at the time. In 1966 viewers found it hard to identify with any of the characters, with Trostberg just coming across one-dimensionally as secure, self-assured and flawless.[62] By contrast, in 1983 viewers could feel for Trostberg's all-too-human failures, for instance his inability to deal with the (renamed) Zahn family despite their responsibility for the Nazi's murder of his first wife, or his endearingly pathetic failure to communicate his affections to his new love, Paula.[63] And whereas the 1966 series featured only male protagonists, leaving the construction of socialism to 'homo-ingenuity', as one female reader of the *Neues Deutschland* complained,[64] in 1983 the female characters had critical and complex roles all the way through.

As the 1970s progressed and the GDR claimed its distinct heritage based on the traditions and cultures of its regions (*Erbe*), television started to produce historical drama series, about communist protagonists, and (increasingly) about classical German figures. With vast use of resources, DEFA produced the five-part drama *Martin Luther* to mark his five-hundredth birthday in 1983 whilst in 1987 the DFF broadcast the six-part series *Sachsens Glanz und Preußens Gloria*, a series on August the Strong of Saxony featuring the who's who of East German theatre. Other than the important implicit claim that August and Luther belonged to a specific canon of GDR history, there was nothing overtly socialist or ideological in these films. Even West German critics favourably commented on these programmes as evidence of the GDR's approach to its own history, in contrast to the shallow depiction and reflection of historical figures in comparable West German drama series.[65] And yet, while these programmes did make a point that the German classics were perfectly compatible with socialism, the GDR was particular amongst Eastern Bloc states in not being able to rely on high culture exclusively to claim a specific national identity because of the rivalry of West Germany. This was why the filmic representations of contemporary GDR novels, including Helmut Sakowski's *Druskat* and Seegers' *Menschenwege*, seen by the party as a culmination of the German traditions of the social novel,[66] were so critical for the popularization of the GDR and the myths of its creation.

Not every television drama was popular – indeed most failed to be watched by more than 40 per cent of viewers. And yet, shows like *Daniel Druskat* or the *Chronicle of the Mark* were widely watched, simply because they were good stories featuring popular actors. And whilst historical drama shows like *Martin Luther* or *Sachsens Glanz* tended to appeal more to educated, older viewers, *Druskat* and the *Chronicle* resonated amongst a cross section of the population. For instance, more and more young, urban viewers switched on to the *Chronicle* as the show progressed.[67] The GDR's narratives of hard beginnings, personal redemption through socialism, and material self-denial for the good of all and a better tomorrow were widely, and persistently, perceived.

At their best, drama series could articulate the real tensions of the everyday. It is not surprising that *Druskat* had such resonance, with its suggestion that the wily individuals who helped themselves were often more successful in getting results than ideological purists – and that they had more fun. But even in this programme, conflict could be articulated only because it remained firmly within the bounds of socialism, which in itself was never questioned. The subjunctive of narrative was only ever possible within clearly defined boundaries, which broadened or narrowed slightly depending on the SED's cultural policies. These programmes allowed viewers to relate to crises in the socialist everyday to a greater or lesser extent, but they never allowed a crossing of the imagination beyond the socialist prism.

Narratives of the Everyday

Dramatic narrative had a particular potential to kindle the imagination, and to allow possibilities of individual engagement with conflict and the unforeseen. But perhaps the most pervasive means by which television makers pointed to the breadth and the limits of social experience was by anchoring stories in manifest connection to everyday life. One of the GDR's most popular entertainment shows (from 1972) was *Außenseiter – Spitzenreiter* ('From Zero to Hero'), which presented curious facts about the GDR. In this show, viewers became coproducers by proposing ideas about the topics to be pursued, though the show also turned the tables, asking viewers questions over the everyday, inviting them to write in with the answers.[68] According to the GDR journalists' paper

Neue Deutsche Presse, the show demonstrated that most citizens had a close relationship with their television station, to which they contributed and which in turn served as their mouthpiece.[69] The twenty-first show broadcast on 22 October 1975, for instance, featured reports on whether the notion of the village beauty queen (*Dorfschönste*) still existed, whilst a viewer from Anklam wanted to know when a school lesson was officially over – at the sound of the school bell or when the teacher was finished. In one feature, the moderator, Joachim Wolfram, went to the Leipzig Interhotel to follow up on the question of what functionaries travelling on business did in the evenings. He asked them at check-in, when one after another protested that they worked. The reportage then showed Wolfram interviewing the same people in the bar at night, reminding them of their earlier statement – causing mild embarrassment amongst those interviewed. Another report explored the question of whether the GDR had any mountain peaks. The show revealed that since these were defined as any freestanding rocks above ten metres high, the GDR had, in fact, over one thousand, and so Wolfram was shown overcoming a twenty-metre high 'peak' in the Harz mountains. And a further report showed what cast and crew got up to when the *Kessel* stopped broadcasting. A number of stars were stopped on the corridor, and most noted that they were going home, but the bar was full also, as the sound engineer and a range of workers reflected on a job well done.

Aussenseiter was light-hearted, it entertained, and it told a story of the GDR, its citizens and the everyday in its rich diversity. And it defined community – through viewers writing in, glimpses of officials or stars in their private moments and through Wolfram travelling up and down the country, appearing to those he interviewed without introduction or script. It defined – and popularized – good behaviour and socialist law in the everyday, prompting one scholarly analysis to conclude that the show did, indeed, help to describe and define GDR identity and a sense of well-being.[70]

Shows with a clear connectedness to the everyday community were amongst the most important sites for mediating friction and examining the boundaries of socialist living. The popular crime drama *Polizeiruf 110* did this by concentrating on individual aberrations, showing how particular individual choices could lead to criminal behaviour, even in socialism.[71] Perhaps more interesting is the equally popular *Der Staatsanwalt hat das Wort* ('The State Attorney Takes the Word'), broadcast from 1965 in around six episodes per year. Watched regularly by over 50 per cent of viewers, each episode was framed by Peter Przybylski who introduced the case and made concluding remarks on it. Przybylski was a real-life member of the GDR attorney general's office, and appeared in a dark suit, with an SED badge on his lapel, wearing horn-rimmed glasses (just like the 'real-life' attorneys featured in *Aussenseiter*). The *Staatsanwalt* was striking because it was good drama, relating closely to viewers' experiences. The episode *Abseits* ('Off-Side', Episode 77 [1981]), for instance, tackled the problem of antisocial behaviour by young people amongst football supporter groups. It told the story of Thilo who felt rejected by his friends, and unable to communicate his feelings to his parents. Thilo found sympathy with Birke, and fell in love with her. Birke was part of a group of football supporters led by Okko, who went out with Birke. As Thilo tried to get closer to Birke, he became part of the supporter group, and was drawn into criminality by faredodging on the way to his first away match. The drama culminated with Thilo's participation in a fight between fans, leading to his arrest and criminal record. The *Staatsanwalt* episodes were loosely based on real criminal cases, and in his introduction, Przybylski underlined that antisocial behaviour was occurring all too often in the context of supporter groups. Significantly, whilst it was Thilo who made a number of poor choices that led him away from the 'moral' person that he evidently was, this case was presented as one where many other mechanisms of support had led to these decisions. This included his father confronting Thilo unnecessarily, the lack of opportunity for young people to hang out in safe spaces, and the lack of communication between generations. The message of the story was clear: there were plenty of diversions for young people in the GDR, and it was justified, and necessary, for them to socialize – in good measure. But molesting others invariably led to the path of criminal behaviour, and this was not tolerated under socialism.

Perhaps the most striking way in which GDR television attempted to mediate the socialist everyday was the journal *Prisma* ('Prism'). Much commented on by historians for how viewers brought their frustrations to the show by sending in petitions,[72] the programme was broadcast from 1963 to discuss everyday problems. While the letters sent to the show are indeed an important source on citizens' frustrations, it is worth examining the show as a television programme, to see how it changed over time. Episode 273, broadcast on 15 August 1974, featured three reports, beginning with youth in the Berlin suburb of Johannisthal. Shown on their motorbikes and partying to loud music – to the complaint of residents – the piece raised the question of where these young people could go given the absence of a youth club. The *Prisma* team was then featured speaking to functionaries to see if a room could be found, noting the desire of the young themselves to be off the street; and it ended with a discussion with the local mayor, who promised that this issue would be solved, though it would take time. The second report focused on an electrical company (VEB Straton), which was behind plan for the first time in living memory, yet was also faced with a charge in the 1975 Plan to increase productivity by 11 per cent. The feature concluded that this could only be done through open discussion of the challenges involved, involving all workers. And the third report asked how customer service could be improved. What all three reports had in common was that they tackled concrete problems that everyone could relate to; and these occurred anywhere in the GDR, in any walk of life. The show generated an understanding of the problem, showing that the members of the socialist community were well-meaning but had to overcome traditional ways of thinking. And they held out a clear (and credible) promise of resolution.

By the mid-1980s, the tone of *Prisma* had changed markedly. Episode 537, broadcast on 5 February 1985, began with a report on fashion as the SED had decided to improve the supply of innovative fashion in the GDR. In response, the FDJ had held a GDR-wide competition to create new designs, and the show asked why none of the winning designs generated by the contest had made it to the assembly line: large suppliers could not fit them into their plans, the supply of materials was insufficient, and the lead times from design to production were simply too long and inflexible. Indeed, one of the designs had almost made it, but the textile printing press required for the complicated design was broken, and very few others existed in the GDR. After the end of the report, the commentator concluded with breaking news: the Ministry of Light Industry had found an appropriate printing press, and this raised the hope that one of the designs could make it to the consumer. The second report was from Berlin's vast housing projects, noting the lack of communication between different construction teams, resulting in unacceptable and palpable waste; following the report the moderator was again able to bring good tidings, that the Building Ministry had found a way forward in creating a central point of coordination that would help all. And a final report came from Halle-South, where the local member of the People's Chamber was involved in improving the care for elderly people in their flats, organizing regular volunteers – and often finding it difficult (again the commentator noted after the report that one of the elderly featured in the programme had just been found a carer).

As with earlier programmes, in the 1980s the contributions looked at the problems of the everyday throughout the Republic, problems that could be solved. However, the tone had changed decisively. After more than 500 programmes the problems were presented with a greater sense of urgency, even desperation. The selfishness of Heads of Construction in Berlin never looking beyond their own concerns, or the inability of young designers to contribute, left programme makers clearly exasperated. Whilst examples were still local, the problems had become more systemic. Solutions appeared to be offered by the state higher up, rather than at the local level, but even then the vague resolutions provided offered much room for scepticism about whether they would ever come to pass.

To be sure, programmes embedded in the everyday were not unique to the GDR. But they did mark a particular feature through their breadth and depth in GDR programming, and they were shows that could – by definition – be 'original' to the GDR. They responded to a central focus of GDR TV, to address the experiences of viewers and their emotions, displaying with optimism the socialist individual and the socialist community in the full richness of life.[73] Complementing the optimism of Heimat shows or the dramatic narratives of *Druskat* or *Chronik*, the programmes of the everyday presented real-life conflict and provided the subjunctive for the imagination – but a subjunctive that was always resolved and closed down by the end of the show. As the economic, social and geopolitical challenges of the GDR increased during the 1980s, the ability of the socialist narrative to resolve conflict through clear and persuasive solutions, whilst also linking to the real-life experiences and imaginations of viewers, had increasingly come under strain.

The failure of socialist narrative was compounded by form. In the 1980s entertainment opportunities for West Germans increased dramatically through the advent of the CD player, video recorder and private television channels as mass consumer products.[74] Despite a far-reaching programme reform in 1983 that increased the amount of Western programming, viewing figures declined rapidly after 1983.[75] In the 1980s, the entertainment shows that had been so popular in the 1970s rapidly lost audience share as young viewers refused to switch on, and most drama programmes suffered the same fate.[76] The analysis produced for GDR television showed that these programmes increasingly failed to meet viewers' expectations of action, spectacle, tension and innovative yet plausible plots.[77] GDR television no longer had to compete just with ARD and ZDF, but with the glitz and glitter of private television, which in turn forced ARD and ZDF to transform their offerings. As social and cultural attitudes changed during the 1980s with accelerating pace, viewers' cultural expectations, the concerns they had and the stories they demanded were increasingly out of tune with the narratives, sounds and images produced by GDR television. Neither in content nor in form did television made in the GDR correspond to the social reality of the young, the middle-aged, as well as urban groups.

Conclusion

East German television had an important effect in describing the social reality for many, if not most, viewers in ways that no other GDR medium could. And it also created narratives that were unavailable on Western television, even if in form they were deeply influenced by it. GDR television told stories whose sheer popularity and repetitiveness ensured that its core narrative tropes became instantly recognizable, and part of an idealized or perceived reality that rang true, a way of organizing and interpreting a reality in which citizens 'had to cope'.[78]

Thus, GDR television programmes framed an image of the lived reality of the GDR everyday where citizens helped each other to selflessly overcome the concrete challenges of socialism. The success of making do and overcoming particular adversity was constructed as a founding myth: GDR citizens had overcome the particular deprivations of the postwar era against the adversity of capitalism, without the support (notably the provision of material goods through the Marshall Plan) enjoyed by the West. And this act of overcoming, improvising and 'making do', coupled with a desire to create a place that was more just, more equal, more caring, more cultured and more peaceful, infused GDR society with a spirit that enabled individuals to overcome the imperfections of the everyday. The stories constructed an image where, notwithstanding the limitations of alternative leisure pursuits, the classics could prosper and German heritage was truly respected. They suggested that every person's 'lived reality', in a society of scarce consumer goods and other frustrations of the everyday, could consist of fulfilment, joy and pleasure, in the intimacy of the community and the homeland, available to all.

Throughout the 1970s and much of the 1980s these stories were consumed, shared and enjoyed by millions: on television, in press reports about television and through word of mouth. These were stories that were accepted as consistent in themselves, connecting to the ordinary experience of viewers and thus becoming part of individual sense-making, symbolic systems that helped to shape human life and human mind in the GDR.[79] Television was so powerful precisely because it was not the sole storyteller, but instead its stories interacted with others; and yet its particular reach did provide a pervasive context for its stories to be shared. Crucial for the circulation of meanings,[80] television was able to produce codes that were widely consumed, understood and shared.

For Jerome S. Bruner, stories subjunctivize the familiar in to what might have been and what might be, with memory and imagination fusing.[81] They are an essential way for human culture to deal with foreseeable or unforeseeable imbalances in communal living. The narrative worlds created through television were important in allowing GDR citizens to create shared meanings and imaginations, and to deal – in limited forms – with imbalances. And indeed, a number of GDR TV's tropes were shared and recognized until the end. The surveys of the Central Institute for Youth Research, which became increasingly alarmed by the attitudes especially of sixteen to eighteen-year-olds during the 1980s, conducted repeated analyses of what led respondents to identify with the GDR. As late as (early) 1989, the GDR's anti-fascism was supported by 65 per cent of fourteen to sixteen-year-old pupils as a motive for identifying with the GDR, the fourth highest factor (out of twenty-five), with the two most popular identifying factors being non-political, the affinity with family and locality.[82] And indeed, narratives of locality, Heimat, war and anti-fascism corresponded with the most popular areas of historical interest amongst those questioned.[83]

And yet, the boundaries of narrative, image and sound, avoiding any subjunctives beyond socialism, whilst also insisting that within socialism only positive resolutions of tensions were imaginable, had clear limitations. They reduced society's ability to deal with the social, generational, ecological and geopolitical challenges which were not in themselves related to socialism (or indeed capitalism). From the mid-1980s, internal surveys of the Central Institute for Youth Research in Leipzig noted how those surveyed increasingly felt that the GDR was unable to respond to their anxieties about the future.[84] One theme persistently articulated in GDR television, the need for young people to find appropriate outlets for their energy and aspirations (within the boundaries of socialism), was persistently not met in practice, leading – according to the pollsters – to disillusionment and alienation with socialism and its ability to address personal concerns about the future. The evidence pointed repeatedly to the growing gap between the narratives of socialism told in school and in the media, and individual experience. This affected young people's anxieties about the environment, peace and their material well being. And this gap was experienced as most acute amongst those who consumed Western television, with the images transmitted on television, according to the pollsters, closely according to views about the GDR and West Germany.[85]

If narrative is a way for us to order – and give meaning to – our experience, then television – the GDR's most popular pastime – reinforced a failure of narrative. Because the stories of GDR television (as well as other media) did not allow society to probe, articulate and resolve its anxieties fully, it left the socialist everyday increasingly exposed as these challenges accumulated. Put differently, the limitations of narrative on generational conflict, pollution and nuclear disarmament, let alone social and political conflict, deprived GDR citizens of a critical mediation opportunity afforded by television in other societies.[86] They also increased the relevance of West German television despite its lack of direct references to the places, sounds and images of the GDR, precisely because its stories allowed much greater room for the contestation of tension and conflict. What became evident from the mid-1980s rested on foundations laid in the late 1960s: GDR television came to undermine itself, the clear boundaries it set for the imagination and dissonance undermining the credibility of its narrative, as distrust replaced interpretation.[87] The subjunctive could only be fully imagined through the West.

Jan Palmowski joined King's College London in 1999, and became a professor in 2009. In 2013, he was appointed Professor of Modern History at the University of Warwick. He is a specialist on the history of the GDR and of contemporary Germany, and his books include *At the Crossroads of Past and Present: Contemporary History and the Historical Discipline* (ed. with Kristina Spohr-Readman, special issue of the *Journal of Contemporary History* 3/2011), *Inventing a Socialist Nation: Heimat and the Politics of Everyday Life in the GDR* (Cambridge University Press, 2009, translated into German in 2016), and *Citizenship and National Identity in Twentieth-Century Germany* (ed. with Geoff Eley, Stanford University Press, 2008).

Notes

1. Kocka, *Civil Society and Dictatorship in Modern German History*, 61.
2. Pfaff-Rüdiger, 'Medien im Alltag'.
3. Lindenberger, 'Einleitung', 13.
4. Fiske and Hartley, *Reading Television*, 60 and 103.
5. Fisher, *Human Communication as Narration*, esp. xi, 48–66.
6. On these general points, see Shanahan and Morgan, *Television and its Viewers*, 192–94.
7. Fitzgerald, 'Intersecting Meanings of Reminiscences in Adult Development and Ageing'.
8. Kramp, *Gedächtnismaschine Fernsehen*.
9. Gorton, *Media Audiences*, 33.
10. Bruner, *Making Stories*, 10–11.
11. Ibid., 25.
12. Ibid., 93.
13. Staatliche Zentralverwaltung für Statistik, *Statistisches Jahrbuch 1978*, 274, table 10. The precise figures are unclear, as they differ between different yearbooks. The statistical yearbook for 1978 puts the proportion of households owning a TV set (as opposed to the households holding a license) in 1970 at 81.7 per cent, and at 82.7 per cent in 1976. In the

statistical yearbook for 1988, by contrast, the figures are 89.4 per cent and 102.3 per cent respectively. Staatliche Zentralverwaltung für Statistik, *Statistisches Jahrbuch 1988*, 291.

14. Staatliche Zentralverwaltung für Statistik, *Statistisches Jahrbuch 1978*, 311, table 41.

15. Stiftung Archiv der Parteien und Massenorganisationen der DDR im Bundesarchiv (BArch-SAPMO), Sozialistische Einheitspartei Deutschlands (DY30) IV/B2 9.06 – 85, Abteilung Kultur, 'Ergebnisse der Umfrage zu einigen Fragen von Geselligkeit und Unterhaltung', 3–4.

16. Weber, *Geschichte der DDR*, 245.

17. BArch-SAPMO, DY30 IV/B2 9.06 – 85, 'Ergebnisse', 3–4.

18. Bösenberg, *Die Aktuelle Kamera*, 229.

19. In the 1960s and the 1970s, only around 50 per cent of viewers were able to receive ZDF television. Lee, *Das Fernsehen im geteilten Deutschland*, 28–32.

20. Steinmetz and Viehoff, *Deutsches Fernsehen (Ost)*, 51. For an early history of GDR Television, see Gumbert, *Envisioning Socialism*.

21. DRA, H074-00-02/0015, 'Deutscher Fernsehfunk, Methodisches Kabinett. Berlin, im November 1965: Das Unterhaltungsprogramm des DFF im Urteil seiner Zuschauer im September 1965', 41–2.

22. Ibid., 72, 75.

23. Ibid.,10–16, 23–26.

24. On Adamek's role in trying to shape the DFF into a tool for the party, see Gumbert, *Envisioning Socialism*, passim. See also Riedel, *Hörfunk und Fernsehen in der DDR*, 58.

25. LHA, Kulturbund Kreisleitung Malchin 52, *Diskussion in der Arbeitsgruppe des Gen. Spitzkopf MTS-Bereich Dargun*, 23 March 1960.

26. Marßolek and von Saldern, 'Das Radio als historisches und historiographisches Medium', 32–33.

27. See, for instance, the extensive live reports to reinforce the GDR's anniversary celebrations, broadcast despite often dismal viewer ratings of well under 10 per cent. Fischer, 'Das DDR-Fernsehen in den Jubiläumsjahren'.

28. DRA, 'Vorbereitende Planmaterialien Unterhaltung. Stichworte für die Wahlversammlung der HA Unterhaltung', c.1968. See also DRA, 'Vorbereitende Planmaterialien Unterhaltung. Protokoll der Planverteidigung Bereich Unterhaltung vom 12. November 1970', as programme makers argued that entertainment programmes were to help realize the new socialist human image (*Menschenbild*).

29. DRA, 'Endgültiger Plan 1969. Vorgabe für die Programmtätigkeit des Deutschen Fernsehfunks 1969', 37–39.

30. DRA, 'Vorbereitende Planmaterialien Unterhaltung. Die Programmtätigkeit des Deutschen Fernsehfunks 1969 Teil 1, 25. Oktober 1968'.

31. DRA, 'DFF Methodisches Kabinett Sektor Zuschauerforschung. Berlin, im Juni 1966. Ergebnisse aus der repräsentativen DDR-Umfrage unter 2000 Zuschauern der DDR im September 1965. Ergänzt durch einen Anhang mit ersten Resultaten einer neuen repräsentativen DDR-Umfrage vom Mai 1966'.

32. Bösenberg, *Die Aktuelle Kamera*, 216–17.

33. Braumann, 'Fernsehforschung zwischen Parteilichkeit und Objektivität', 536–39.

34. DRA, 'Deutscher Fernsehfunk Programmdirektion/Zuschauerforschung. Berlin, im Juni 1969: Analyse der Bisherigen Forschungsergebnisse zur Wirkung der Journalistischen Sendungen im Programm des DFFs'.

35. Bösenberg, *Die Aktuelle Kamera*, 214–16, 219, 229–30.

36. Ibid., 224, 236. The quotation is from Michael Schmidt, editor at the news show in the 1980s and its local correspondent in the Mecklenburg Districts.

37. Hartmann-Laugs and Goss, *Deutschlandbilder im Fernsehen 2*, 33. On the attempts by the makers of the 'Aktuelle Kamera' to improve the show despite all the constraints

imposed by the SED's geriatric leadership, see the interview with H. Kipping in Ludes, *DDR-Fernsehen intern*, 164–90.

38. Herlt, *Sendeschluß*, 107–8.
39. For an excellent overview of 'Rund' in the context of the medialization of youth concerns between propaganda and popular reception, see Bauhaus, 'Jugendpresse', 174–76. Bauhaus assumes that 'Rund' had been popular because of its longevity, but he clearly did not have at his disposal the detailed viewers' surveys, which showed just how low audience figures had been throughout.
40. See, for instance, the note by Egon Krenz, FDJ first secretary, on *Rund's* fortieth broadcast: Krenz, 'Rund'.
41. 'Rund', broadcast Saturday, 26 April 1980, DDR1, 4 PM (90 min).
42. The structural similarity to West German shows of this kind is also noted in Hoff and Stiehler, 'Jugendfernsehen in der DDR', 79–80.
43. The counterpoint to these codes is discussed in Alissa Belotti's contribution to this volume (chapter 7).
44. On GDR TV's struggles to bring in stars with acceptable haircuts, see Herlt, *Sendeschluß*, 92–93.
45. Bruner, 'Entry into Meaning'.
46. DRA, 'Arbeits- und Programmplan 1969 der HA Unterhaltung', 1–4.
47. DRA, 'Vorbereitende Planmaterialien Unterhaltung 1966-71'. ('Referat zur ersten Bereichsparteiaktivtagung der APO Unterhaltung, 6. Dezember 1968'.)
48. DRA, 'Stichworte für die Wahlversammlung der HA Unterhaltung (1968)', 1.
49. DRA, 'Berlin, den 9. August 1967. Teil I: Planangebot der HA Unterhaltung zum Beschluss der Intendanz über die Vorgabe 1968, 7. Entwurf. Programmplan der HA Unterhaltung (zur Beratung in der Sitzung des Büros der Intendanz). Berlin, den 29. August 1966, 5–6. Protokoll, Programme- und Sendeleitung, 1.6.1967. Zu den Sendungen der HA Unterhaltung', 1.
50. Mühl-Benninghaus, *Unterhaltung als Eigensinn*, 290–98.
51. DRA, 'Vorbereitende Planmaterialien, HA Unterhaltung. Planangebot 1976', 7–8.
52. Born, *Music, Sound and Space*, 24.
53. Steinmetz and Viehoff, *Deutsches Fernsehen (Ost)*, 137–40. See also Herlt, *Sendeschluß*.
54. Schwab, 'Die fiktionale Geschichtssendung', 31–37.
55. Ibid., 46–55. For a good summary, see also 'Die Geschichte einer Freundschaft', *Leipziger Volkszeitung*, 24 July 1966.
56. 'Das Gerücht und die Wahrheit. Zur Wiederaufführung der Fernsehtrilogie "Hannes Trostberg" in der nächsten Woche', *BZ am Abend*, 11 September 1966.
57. 'Stolz auf unsere Republik. Leser schreiben zu "Hannes Trostberg"', *Neues Deutschland*, 16 August 1966. '"Hannes Trostberg" ausgezeichnet', *Neues Deutschland*, 18 August 1966.
58. Both quotations are from 'Daniel Druskat', Episode 1, broadcast 12 April 1976.
59. DRA, 'Vorbereitende Planmaterialien Unterhaltung: Planangebot 1971: Dolles Familienalbum'.
60. On the genesis of antifascism as part of the GDR's founding myth, see Eschenbach, 'Zur Umcodierung der eigenen Vergangenheit'.
61. DRA, *Märkische Chronik: Arbeitsprädikat: 'Märkische Chronik'*, 8 December 1982.
62. DRA, 'DDR3 – Heißer Fernsehsommer. Ergebnisse der repräsentativen DDR-Umfrage zum "heißen Fernsehsommer 1966". Berlin, im Juli 1967', 8–9.
63. 'Märkische Chronik', part 11, broadcast 12 February 1983.
64. Wiens, 'Die Geschichte eines Unruhvollen'.
65. For an example of the positive reception of the Luther series in the FRG, see Urban, '"Ein Genie sehr bedeutender Art"'.

66. 'Hier werden Fragen mit beantwortet, die Schriftsteller vor 50 oder 100 Jahren mit ihren Möglichkeiten gestellt haben'. Geerdts, 'Historische Erfahrungen und realistische Kunsttraditionen', 146. See also Nahke, 'Sozialistische Volksgestalten als Träger unserer Macht'.

67. DRA, '"Märkische Chronik". Vertraulich'.

68. Rosenstein, 'Ein "eigenes Gesicht"', 310.

69. 'Das Besondere einer Verbindung', *Neue Deutsche Presse*, 20 October 1974, 10.

70. Rosenstein, 'Ein "eigenes Gesicht"', 314.

71. Hoff, *Polizeiruf 110*.

72. Merkel, *Wir sind doch nicht die Meckerecke der Nation!*; Merkel, '"... in Hoyerswerda leben jedenfalls keine so kleinen viereckigen Menschen"'.

73. DRA, 'Deutscher Fernsehfunk, Bereich Unterhaltung und Musik, Planangebot 1971', 1–2.

74. Grunau and Stiehler, 'Medienalltage'.

75. Average viewing figures for both channels combined jumped from 32.9 per cent in 1982 to 40.1 per cent in 1983, before declining again to 37.6 per cent in 1987, and 32.1 per cent in the first half of 1989.

76. Average viewing figures for the 'Staatsanwalt' declined from 43.8 per cent (1983) to 37.3 per cent (1986).

77. DRA, 'Ergebnisse der Programmarbeit im Zeitraum 6.1. bis 30.6.1986' (Berlin, 30 July 1986), 11–12.

78. Fiske and Hartley, *Reading Television*, 30.

79. Bruner, 'Folk Psychology as an Instrument of Culture'.

80. Fiske, *Television Culture*, 64.

81. Bruner, *Making Stories*, 93.

82. BArch-SAPMO Zentralinstitut für Jugendforschung (ZfJ), Dr sc Harry Müller, 'Zur staatsbürgerlichen Identität und ihren Merkmalen im Bewußtsein Jugendlicher' (Ms. Leipzig, April 1989), esp. 5–6. The 'removal of the social roots leading to war' was also seen as a major point of difference between the GDR and West Germany, with 43 per cent of those polled attributing it to the GDR, and only 10 per cent to West Germany. BArch-SAPMO ZfJ, W. Friedrich, 'Aktuelle Ergebnisse zum ideologischen Entwicklungsstand unserer Jugend' (Ms. Leipzig, Ende Oktober 1987).

83. ZfJ, W. Friedrich, 'Das Geschichtsbewußtsein der DDR-Jugend zur 2. Hälfte der 80er Jahre' (Ms. Leipzig, 1989), 38–39.

84. Lange and Stiehler, 'Ausstieg aus der DDR'.

85. BArch-SAPMO, ZfJ, Sektor Jugend und Ideologie, 'Politisch-historische Einstellungen der Jugendlichen 1988 (Erstinformation) (Leipzig, Dezember 1988)', 6–9, 16–20. See also W. Friedrich, 'Aktuelle Ergebnisse zum ideologischen Entwicklungsstand unserer Jugend' (Ms. Leipzig, Ende Oktober 1987), 16.

86. Kramp, *Gedächtnismaschine*, 124.

87. Bruner, 'Entry into Meaning', 96.

Bibliography

Außenseiter – Spitzenreiter, presented by J. Wolfram, 21. Berlin: GDR Television, 22 October 1975.

Außenseiter – Spitzenreiter, J. Wolfram, 68. Berlin: GDR Television, 25 October 1984.

Bauhaus, A. 'Jugendpresse, -hörfunk und -fernsehen in der DDR: Ein Spagat zwischen FDJ-Interessen und Rezipientenbedürfnissen'. PhD thesis, University of Münster, 1994.

'Das Besondere einer Verbindung'. *Neue Deutsche Presse,* 20 October 1974.

Born, G. *Music, Sound and Space: Transformations of Public and Private Experience.* Cambridge: Cambridge University Press, 2013.

Bösenberg, J.-A. *Die Aktuelle Kamera: Nachrichten aus einem versunkenen Land.* Potsdam: Verlag für Berlin-Brandenburg, 2008.

Braumann, C. 'Fernsehforschung zwischen Parteilichkeit und Objektivität: Zur Zuschauerforschung in der ehemaligen DDR'. *Rundfunk und Fernsehen* 42 (1994), 524–41.

Bruner, J.S. *Acts of Meaning.* Harvard: Harvard University Press, 1993.

_____. 'Entry into Meaning', in J.S. Bruner, *Acts of Meaning* (Harvard: Harvard University Press, 1993), 67–98.

_____. 'Folk Psychology as an Instrument of Culture', in J.S. Bruner, *Acts of Meaning* (Harvard: Harvard University Press, 1993), 34–48.

_____. *Making Stories: Law, Literature, Life.* New York: Farrar, Straus and Giroux, 2002.

Daniel Druskat, written by H. Sakowski. 5 episodes. Babelsberg: DEFA, 1976.

Eschenbach, I. 'Zur Umcodierung der eigenen Vergangenheit: Antifaschismuskonstruktionen in Rehabilitationsgesuchen ehemaliger Mitglieder der NSDAP, Berlin 1945-46', in A. Lüdtke and P. Becker (eds), *Akten. Eingaben. Schaufenster. Die DDR und ihre Texte* (Berlin: Akademie Verlag, 1997), 79–90.

Fischer, J.-U. 'Das DDR-Fernsehen in den Jubiläumsjahren: Ideologische Leitlinien, Programme und Zuschauerreaktionen', in M. Gibas, R. Gries, B. Jakoby and D. Müller, *Wiedergeburten. Zur Geschichte der runden Jahrestage in der DDR* (Leipzig: Leipziger Universitätsverlag, 1999), 147–59.

Fisher, W. *Human Communication as Narration: Toward a Philosophy of Reason, Value and Action.* Columbia: University of South Carolina Press, 1987.

Fiske, J. *Television Culture.* London and New York: Routledge, 1989.

Fiske, J. and J. Hartley. *Reading Television.* London and New York: Routledge, 2003.

Fitzgerald, J.M. 'Intersecting Meanings of Reminiscences in Adult Development and Ageing', in D. Rubin (ed.), *Remembering our Past: Studies in Autobiographical Memory* (Cambridge: Cambridge University Press, 1996), 360–83.

Geerdts, H.-J. 'Historische Erfahrungen und realistische Kunsttraditionen', in *Fernsehdramatik im Gespräch: Theoretische Konferenz des Staatlichen Komitees für Fernsehen beim Ministerrat der Deutschen Demokratischen Republik 4. Februar 1969* (Berlin: Dietz Verlag, 1969), 142–47.

'Das Gerücht und die Wahrheit: Zur Wiederaufführung der Fernsehtrilogie "Hannes Trostberg" in der nächsten Woche'. *BZ am Abend,* 11 September 1966.

'Die Geschichte einer Freundschaft'. *Leipziger Volkszeitung,* 24 July 1966.

Gorton, K. *Media Audiences: Television, Meaning and Emotion*. Edinburgh: Edinburgh University Press, 2009.

Grunau, H. and H.-J. Stiehler. 'Medienalltage: Stabilität und Wandel im Mediengebrauch', in B. Schorb and H.-J. Stiehler (eds), *Neue Lebenswelt – neue Medienwelt? Jugendliche aus der Ex- und Post-DDR im Transfer zu einer vereinten Medienkultur* (Opladen: Leske und Buderich, 1991), 43–60.

Gumbert, H. *Envisioning Socialism: Television and the Cold War in the German Democratic Republic*. Ann Arbor: University of Michigan Press, 2014.

'"Hannes Trostberg" ausgezeichnet'. *Neues Deutschland*, 18 August 1966.

Hartmann-Laugs, P.S. and A.J. Goss. *Deutschlandbilder im Fernsehen 2. Politische Informationssendungen in der Bundesrepublik Deutschland und der DDR: Zeitvergleich und neue Aspekte*. Cologne: Verlag Wissenschaft und Politik, 1988.

Herlt, G. *Sendeschluß: Ein Insider des DDR-Fernsehens berichtet*. Berlin: Edition Ost, 1995.

Hoff, P. *Polizeiruf 110: Filme, Fälle, Fakten*. Berlin: Das Neue Berlin, 2001.

Hoff, P. and H.-J. Stiehler. 'Jugendfernsehen in der DDR: Die immerwährende Suche nach dem Zuschauer', in B. Schorb and H.-J. Stiehler (eds), *Neue Lebenswelt – neue Medienwelt? Jugendliche aus der Ex- und Post-DDR im Transfer zu einer vereinten Medienkultur* (Opladen: Leske und Buderich, 1991), 77–91.

Kipping, H. Interview in P. Ludes (eds), *DDR-Fernsehen intern: Von der Honecker–Ära bis 'Deutschland einig Vaterland'* (Berlin: Wissenschaftsverlag Volker Spiess, 1990), 164–90.

Kocka, J. *Civil Society and Dictatorship in Modern German History*. Hanover and London: University Press of New England, 2010.

Kramp, L. *Gedächtnismaschine Fernsehen. Band 1: Das Fernsehen als Faktor der gesellschaftlichen Erinnerung*. Berlin: Akademie Verlag, 2011.

Krenz, E. 'Rund – Ausdruck erfolgreicher Jugendpolitik'. *FF Dabei* 4 (1977), 32.

Kress, G. *Multimodality: A Social Semiotic Approach to Contemporary Communication*. London: Routledge, 2010.

Die lange Straße, written by G. Bengsch. 5 episodes. Babelsberg: DEFA, 1979.

Lange, G. and H.-J. Stiehler. 'Ausstieg aus der DDR: Politische Dimensionen von jugendlichen Lebenslagen und Befindlichkeiten im Wandel', in B. Schorb and H.-J. Stiehler (eds), *Neue Lebenswelt – neue Medienwelt?* (Opladen: Leske + Budrich, 1991), 29–42.

Lee, W.-S. *Das Fernsehen im geteilten Deutschland (1952–1989)*. Potsdam: Verlag für Berlin-Brandenburg, 2003.

Lindenberger, T. 'Einleitung', in T. Lindenberger (ed.), *Massenmedien im kalten Krieg: Akteure, Bilder, Resonanzen* (Cologne: Böhlau, 2006), 9–23.

Ludes, P. (ed.). *DDR-Fernsehen intern: Von der Honecker–Ära bis 'Deutschland einig Vaterland'*. Berlin: Wissenschaftsverlag Volker Spiess, 1990.

Marßolek, I. and A. von Saldern. 'Das Radio als historisches und historiographisches Medium: Eine Einführung', in I. Marßolek and A. von Saldern (eds), *Zuhören und Gehörtwerden. Vol. I: Radio im Nationalsozialismus* (Tübingen: ed. discord, 1998), 11–45.

Märkische Chronik, written by B. Seeger. 12 episodes. Babelsberg: DEFA, 1983.

Merkel, I. '"… in Hoyerswerda leben jedenfalls keine so kleinen viereckigen Menschen": Briefe an das Fernsehen der DDR', in A. Lüdtke and P. Becker (eds), *Die DDR und ihre Texte. Akten. Eingaben. Schaufenster* (Berlin: Akademie Verlag, 1997), 279–310.

———. *Wir sind doch nicht die Meckerecke der Nation! Briefe an das Fernsehen der DDR.* Berlin: Schwarzkopf&Schwarzkopf, 2000.

Mühl-Benninghaus, W. *Unterhaltung als Eigensinn: Eine ostdeutsche Mediengeschichte.* Frankfurt am Main: Campus, 2012.

Nahke, H. 'Sozialistische Volksgestalten als Träger unserer Macht', in *Fernsehdramatik im Gespräch: Theoretische Konferenz des Staatlichen Komitees für Fernsehen beim Ministerrat der Deutschen Demokratischen Republik 4. Februar 1969* (Berlin: Dietz Verlag, 1969), 9–45.

Palmowski, J. 'Citizenship, Identity and Community in the German Democratic Republic', in J. Palmowski and G. Eley (eds), *Citizenship and National Identity in Twentieth-Century Germany* (Stanford: Stanford University Press, 2008), 73–94.

Pfaff-Rüdiger, S. 'Medien im Alltag: Methodenprobleme qualitativer Nutzungsforschung', in S. Pfaff-Rüdiger and M. Meyen (eds), *Alltag, Lebenswelt und Medien: Qualitative Studien zum subjektiven Sinn von Medienangeboten* (Münster: Lit-Verlag, 2007), 9–46.

Prisma, presented by K.-H. Gerstner, 273. Berlin: Fernsehen der DDR, 15 August 1974.

Prisma, presented by R. Ebner, 537. Berlin: Fernsehen der DDR, 5 February 1985.

Riedel, H. *Hörfunk und Fernsehen in der DDR: Funktion, Struktur und Programm des Rundfunks in der DDR.* Cologne: Literarischer Verlag Braun, 1977.

Rosenstein, D. 'Ein "eigenes Gesicht" der Unterhaltung: Zur Geschichte unterhaltsamer Magazine im DDR-Fernsehen', in H. Heinze and A. Kreuz (eds), *Zwischen Service und Propaganda: Zur Geschichte und Ästhetik von Magazinsendungen im Fernsehen der DDR 1952–1991* (Berlin: Vistas, 1998), 279–329.

Rund, presented by B. Freundl and H. Schröder, 80. Berlin: Fernsehen der DDR, 26 April 1980.

'Rund um Stendahl; Auf Schusters Rappen'. *Fernsehdienst,* 7–13 August 1989.

Sachsens Glanz und Preußens Gloria, directed by H.-J. Kaspzik. Babelsberg: DEFA, 1985.

Schwab, U. 'Die fiktionale Geschichtssendung im DDR-Fernsehen der 60er Jahre: Forschungsprämissen und Charakteristik', in U. Schwab (ed.), *Fiktionale Geschichtssendungen im DDR-Fernsehen: Einblicke in ein Forschungsgebiet* (Leipzig: Leipziger Universitätsverlag, 2007), 9–66.

———. 'Der historische Mehrteiler *Die lange Straße – eine Familienchronik in fünf Teilen* (1979)', in U. Schwab (ed.), *Fiktionale Geschichtssendungen im DDR-Fernsehen (II): Analyse und Dokumentation* (Leipzig: Leipziger Universitätsverlag, 2008), 8–70.

Shanahan, J. and M. Morgan. *Television and its Viewers: Cultivation Theory and Research.* Cambridge: Cambridge University Press, 1999.

Staatliche Zentralverwaltung für Statistik (ed.). *Statistisches Jahrbuch der Deutschen Demokratischen Republik 1978.* East Berlin: Staatsverlag der Deutschen Demokratischen Republik, 1978.

Staatliche Zentralverwaltung für Statistik (ed.). *Statistisches Jahrbuch der Deutschen Demokratischen Republik 1988.* East Berlin: Staatsverlag der Deutschen Demokratischen Republik, 1988.

Steinmetz, R. and R. Viehoff (eds). *Deutsches Fernsehen (Ost): Eine Programmgeschichte des DDR-Fernsehens*. Berlin: Verlag für Berlin-Brandenburg, 2008.

'Stolz auf unsere Republik. Leser schreiben zu "Hannes Trostberg"'. *Neues Deutschland,* 16 August 1966.

Urban, D. '"Ein Genie sehr bedeutender Art": Bemerkungen zu einem Lutherfilm im DDR-Fernsehen'. *Deutschlandarchiv* 12 (1983), 1253.

Weber, H. *Geschichte der DDR*. Munich: DTV, 1999.

Wiens, E. 'Die Geschichte eines Unruhvollen: Leser schreiben zu Bernhard Seegers Fernsehspiel "Hannes Trostberg"'. *Neues Deutschland,* 20 August 1966.

Chapter 2

Tensions of Germanness in the Global South

German Immigrants in Namibia

Heidi Armbruster

Die namibische Historie war für mich eigentlich die Grundlage für den relativ leichten Start.
(Namibia's past gave me a chance to get off to a fairly easy start.)

The above quotation is from the life story of a German immigrant in Namibia whom I met in Namibia's capital Windhoek, in the mid-2000s. By then he had been living in Namibia for twelve years. A mid-level manager in a big German corporation before his departure, he created a tourism-related business after settling in Namibia and achieved considerable economic success. He told his story with the confidence of a man in his mid-50s who had gladly left his German life behind 'to start again' 5,000 miles from home, and never looked back.

This chapter extends the geographical relations which constitute 'postwar Germany'. As this volume shows these have been dominantly framed around 'East' and 'West' and the entanglements of the two German states in the competing powers of the Cold War. Following Germans to their émigré destinations in Namibia will bring to the discussion postcolonial history, and the way in which it shapes a migratory route for these Germans as well as questions of belonging and identity. In fact, the migrant stories presented below expose the obliviousness a term such as 'postwar history' can imply, given its insinuation of a history with fixed beginnings. While the Second World War and the spatio-temporal demarcations associated with it play a major role in European historical consciousness, the notion of the 'postwar' may bury other, pre-war pasts and the way in which they continue to shape us in the present. This includes colonialism. The period I have in mind is the colonialism of the late nineteenth and early twentieth century when Germany sought to realize its colonial ambitions alongside other European colonial powers. Scholars have identified European colonialism of the nineteenth and its dismantling in the twentieth century as particularly consequential for the postcolonial present, not least for the economic and political inequalities that continue to map onto historic geographies of colonial expansion, or the lingering hierarchies and ideologies of race inscribed in the politics of 'development' or immigration.[1]

Thus, acknowledging European postwar histories also as postcolonial histories inevitably situates any national history in a wider global framework.[2] German historiography in particular has been criticized for being oblivious to this fact. Largely writing from a Eurocentric perspective, historians have frequently suggested that German colonialism was too short-lived to have left significant effects on Germany.[3] While some historians have begun to challenge this view,[4] postcolonial scholars have shown that legacies of European colonialism are not solely attached to the formal rule over specific territories but also to wider cultures of knowledge and thought; this has sustained and legitimized the political and social power that colonialism had, and moulded colonial mindsets in a global and transhistorical sense.[5]

These comments notwithstanding, colonialism has had little impact on postwar German public consciousness. In both German states the Nazi dictatorship became a key concern of German history. As observers have shown, this popular amnesia has left the pre-1945 image of a benign German colonialism largely intact.[6] While there has been renewed interest in the subject, particularly since the 1990s, the debate has largely remained confined to scholars and intellectuals.[7] However, as Lora Wildenthal states, Germany's 'provincial postcolonial identity'[8] has been richly exposed in the writings of black Germans who have challenged the racial norms that associate Germanness with whiteness. These works also show that the postwar black experience in Germany has been marked by racialized exclusion and confrontations with constructions of 'Africa', which perpetuate racist and colonial discourses.[9]

In what follows I do not investigate the memories of colonialism among the heirs of the first colonial settlers in 'German South West Africa'. My focus is on more recent white German immigrants, all of whom experienced their primary socializations in 'postwar' Germany before settling in Namibia as adults. Unlike the Namibian-born Germans, this group had no experience of life in southern Africa prior to their arrival and found themselves re-locating to a radically new cultural and political

environment. This included witnessing Namibia's historical transformation from a South-African occupied apartheid society to national independence in 1990 and an unprecedented personal confrontation with
Germany's colonial past. It is the encounter with these historical trajectories that I am particularly concerned with and the ways in which individuals situate themselves, through acts of biographical narration, within
them. Using a postcolonial lens to interpret these narratives, I explore
how being 'German' becomes an ambiguous narrative act of racial and
historical self-positioning.

Research Context

The empirical research informing this discussion was conducted in 2006
and addresses the socio-historical context of the time. I conducted biographical interviews and ethnographic research among German immigrants who had settled in Namibia since the 1950s.[10] The study was
carried out over four months, particularly in the two urban centres of
German settlement, Windhoek, the capital, and Swakopmund, a coastal
town whose German colonial history is still visible today, not least
through the quaint Wilhelmine buildings that line its central streets. My
main aim was to explore the relationship between a postcolonial route of
emigration and processes of identity among German newcomers. They
settled in a country which was colonized by Germany between 1884 and
1915, became mandated to South Africa in 1920 and gained its independence in 1990. Social and economic relationships among the country's
multi-ethnic population had been forged by the politics of colonialism
and apartheid in ways which systematically disadvantaged the black
population in all spheres of life, from employment to education and welfare. This accounted for one of the world's starkest income disparities on
the eve of independence and enduring socio-economic inequality since.[11]
While the post-independence period saw the rise of a new black middle
class, the majority of black Namibians remain impoverished. Politically
the white minority became disempowered, yet it remained economically
influential and saw little challenge to its lifestyle.

  Given these circumstances I expected these immigrants to re-interpret
what it meant to be German from a radically different geopolitical vantage point. In the course of this research I interviewed about fifty first-
generation immigrants, about half of whom had arrived during the 1950s
and 1960s and the others in the 1980s and 1990s. While German immigration numbers to Namibia were small, newcomers were able to benefit from established social and economic German networks.[12] Namibia's

multi-ethnic population of about two million included an estimated 75,000 whites of whom 20,000 were German, comprising both native 'Southwesters' and immigrants, 50,000 Afrikaners and about 5,000 citizens of British and Portuguese descent.[13]

In searching for willing participants and benefitting from being 'snowballed' among acquaintances, it soon became clear that social affiliations within the German-speaking networks were closely related to immigrant generations: Germans who had arrived at a similar point in time often belonged to the same age group and had met each other through the schooling of children or other socializing activities. The 'new' Germans frequently set themselves apart from the native German 'Southwesters', named after the German colony 'Southwest Africa', who considered themselves descendants of the late nineteenth century colonial settlers and often derived a claim to indigeneity and sense of pride from that history.

This discussion will focus on the more recent arrivals, as they had spent less time in the country and were still often negotiating their migration biographies. They had settled in Namibia between the late 1980s and late 1990s and were mostly born between the 1950s and 60s. Most were West Germans even though a small number of East Germans had arrived since unification. As the social networks I got to know overwhelmingly consisted of West Germans this article focuses on them only. It would be misleading to claim that these Germans united more than their shared language and origin. They had different backgrounds and varying motives for migration. However, a few common characteristics are worth mentioning. Notably many arrived as individuals who were later joined by partners, married locally, stayed single, or came with partners, but rarely as part of a larger family. A sizeable number among this cohort developed careers in tourism, which represented breaks with their pre-migration careers.

After independence, tourism became a significant economic sector – capitalizing on Namibia's wildlife, natural beauty and ethnic diversity.[14] It is important to note in this context that the Namibian tourist industry reflected the racialized economic and social divisions created under colonialism and apartheid. Research in the 2000s found that both the ongoing unequal distribution of land and the assets and skills required to develop tourism disproportionally advantaged Namibian whites. These actors were in a position to create viable links with international tour operators and to accumulate capital. As Papen observed: 'The lion's share of the income derived from tourism goes to privately owned hotels, lodges, guest-farms and tour operators remaining in the hands of the predominantly German-, Afrikaans- and English-speaking, white Namibians'.[15]

The sector offered a unique niche in post-independence Namibia in which an immigrant white and 'German' identity could be used as an asset. Many Germans were involved in mid- to up-market tourism, catering to a European and specifically German clientele in ways that capitalized on tourist desires for 'Africa's wildlife' and 'exotic' vestiges of German colonialism. The German-speaking tour guides and safari operators I met often stated that they offered a 'safe space' to German tourists and simultaneously prided themselves on contributing to Namibia's struggling post-independence economy.[16]

The skilled crafts and trade sector represented the second economic niche opportunity for German immigrants. Long before 1990 Germans entered Namibia to work in skilled professions, often following specific offers of employment under South African governance which encouraged white immigration into skilled labour. A number of those who had arrived between the 1950s and 1970s had followed job offers in the German press, and later became self-employed in different trades: from engineering and construction to carpentry and plumbing. After independence many of these self-employed German traders still catered largely for the better economically endowed white sector of the population.

All research participants lived in what were historically white neighbourhoods, and within different degrees of securitized 'gatedness'. While this chapter's main focus is on narratives, it will be seen below how 'gated' spatial practices inform language about identity.

Researching White Migrations in a Postcolonial Context

As Pauline Leonard puts it, '[n]either colonial, nor postcolonial, experiences and histories can be understood in homogenised or essentialised terms. The abstract needs to be made particular through attention to the specific and the local'.[17] I focus on the local through life stories, drawing on the epistemological premise that larger social and historical landscapes are articulated in the micro-spheres of local lives and everyday stories. While a full account of the (post)colonial history that links Germany and Namibia cannot be given here, I seek to trace some of the legacies of this relationship as they became expressed in conversations held at a specific point in time, and within a white German immigrant enclave. Two larger long-term effects of colonial rule and knowledge formation can be looked at through these local cases. The first addresses the historical geography of power that was formed through colonial relations and became mirrored in the trajectories and subjectivities of these individuals as 'migrants'. The second relates to the racial position of whiteness, which became recontextualized in Namibia, as individuals became part of a demographic minority and a specific history of racial hierarchy. I address each in turn.

Local and global relations of inequality are routinely inscribed in the universal figure of the 'migrant' whose actual degree of control over her or his mobility and the cultural, economic or ethnic capital she or he can invest or accrue in the migration process can differ vastly. Over the past few years migration scholars have recognized this by expanding their traditional emphasis on the disadvantaged labourer who moves from global south to north to include 'privileged migrants' whose routes of travel map on reverse or other and emerging geographies. 'Mobile professionals', 'expatriates' and 'lifestyle migrants' represent the most popular labels for migrants associated with privilege and, often, a Western identity. In fact, these terminologies have attracted critical commentary on their own, as they have been seen to mask both an implicit racial discourse and a wider politics of migration: while 'migrant' is readily associated with the non-privileged and non-white subject, their white Western and more privileged counterpart is frequently known as 'expat' – a term far less politicized and associated with 'problems' of migration – despite the fact that both may be 'economic migrants'.[18] As popular and scholarly discourses criss-cross the field, migration terminologies become imprecise and difficult to reify empirically. However, for purposes of reflection on my case, the debate around 'lifestyle migration' is useful. Scholars initially developed this category around research on inter-European migrations to Spain, France or Portugal.[19] They placed a strong conceptual emphasis on migration motivations associated with 'lifestyle' and the economic, political and cultural privilege that enabled relocation on quality of life grounds.[20] As Benson and O'Reilly argue, lifestyle migrants are typically attracted by the promise of different geographies and 'can mobilise capital, assets and resources in ways that make their aspirations for a better way of life possible within the destination. ... In other words, the capitals that they possess have an enhanced currency when they move'.[21] The authors rightly imply that such privilege can be 'relative' in the sense that it does not need to be attached to great personal wealth, yet still offer structural advantages in 'global and historical relations of power'.[22] Lifestyle migration has also been associated with tourism, for the romantic and self-enhancing desires typically involved in both, or the fact that tourist visits can prepare for more permanent forms of migration.[23] This was certainly the case for some of the Germans I met in Namibia.

While the 'lifestyle' literature foregrounds migration as a spatial practice and often focuses on the significance of 'place' to the construction of migrant identities,[24] an interest in colonial relations conjures questions about history. Scholars have begun to infuse migration studies with a historical perspective that takes a particular interest in the relationships of Western 'expats' to the colonial pasts of their destination countries, or their family or community implications in colonial histories.[25] This involves intriguing questions about the historical genealogies between the colonial emigrant and their present-day 'successors', or, more generally, about the ways in which empire survives in contemporary practices of mobility, race and identity.

Looking at postcolonial migrations suggests that the boundaries between career and lifestyle mobility are more fluid than what is sometimes assumed.[26] As will be seen further below, the groups of migrants I knew in Namibia occupied a continuum between these poles. All of them were economically active after relocating to Namibia, often developing new careers. However, lifestyle considerations were an integral part of the picture. Unlike what the scholarly literature suggests, though, these did not always drive the 'motivation' to emigrate but could be assimilated post-migration. Lifestyle, as it turned out, could be both alluring and ensnaring, particularly as people assessed the options of return against the comforts they had become habituated to. As will be seen below, at a narrative level, lifestyle became manifest in the everydayness of consumption, leisure, domesticity and work, whose routines, practices and materialities were structured by historically shaped relations of gender, race and class.

This brings me to the notion of whiteness, the second lens to inform my analysis. Being a white immigrant in southern Africa was not only a visible marker of identity but a form of capital that could safeguard or enhance a newcomer's opportunities. Migration scholars have only recently begun to draw more analytical attention to whiteness as a structuring factor in shaping transnational mobilities, or to the dynamics of migrant incorporation in local matrices of race.[27] Critical whiteness studies have exposed whiteness as a social construction underpinning race privilege in white dominated societies. In these contexts awareness of white cultural norms is often skewed: while it is visible to those they hurt and exclude, whites often remain ignorant of the effects of race privilege in their lives.[28] Critical race scholars have argued that one of the articulations of contemporary Euro-American whiteness lies in its historic links to colonial discourses which have conflated white identities with European identities and constructed whiteness in opposition to the racially and culturally inferior 'Other' to underpin claims to power and ruling.[29] At the same time, white identity constructions are not fixed but have been lived and articulated alongside different historic and geographic configurations. In Namibia whiteness was not an invisible hegemonic force but historically politicized as part of a racist colonial project. Ideologically and institutionally forged as dominant in a hegemonic racial system, the principle of white superiority first served colonialism and later the ideological and political interests of an apartheid state. The South African scholar Melissa Steyn pointed out that under apartheid 'white South Africans knew they were racialized', took the '"naturalness" of being thus privileged' for granted and 'held on to many of the colonial assumptions that helped to underwrite the social construction of whiteness with particular tenacity'.[30] Similar legacies of white subjectivity have been observed for Namibia.[31]

The political disempowerment of whites inaugurated with Namibian independence in 1990 raised questions about the changing status of whiteness in the post-apartheid, postcolonial state, and the ways in which whites negotiated their relationship to a newly empowered black majority. The Namibian government introduced affirmative action and Black Economic Empowerment programmes to redress the stark legacies of racial inequality.[32] This process of political transformation also represented the 'historical present' for the Germans I met and in relation to which they assumed positions in Namibian society. While only a few of those who figure in this article had a significant pre-1990 Namibian experience, themes of change and Black political empowerment were present in most stories. Moreover, all had experienced becoming part of a politically marginal but economically powerful minority, and assumed new forms of awareness of their own subjectivities as 'white'. Negotiating what it means to be 'German' in the Namibian environment, thus, did not simply revolve around cultural attributes but included negotiating 'structural advantage' in an environment that was deeply unequal and still offered privileges to economically resourceful white subjects. In what follows I shall explore how Germans negotiated their migrant experience at a narrative level and inscribed themselves into a space called 'Africa' whilst both articulating and detracting from the unequal relations of race and class.

Narratives – Framing Germanness

The extracts below are taken from larger biographical stories which were produced in interview situations. In placing these stories interpretively, I draw on wider principles in narrative theory which suggest that acts of storytelling are acts of meaning making which are fundamental to human sociability.[33] In storytelling a 'narrator explicitly links actors, motives, acts, and consequences in a causal chain'.[34] As such, narrative acts engage both the individual and the social, in that narrators draw on culturally acquired scripts to interpret and morally charge the world they live in. As Cheryl Mattingly puts it, narrative practice is not simply peculiar to the individual but is 'a form of cultural thinking'.[35] 'Narrative epistemology'[36] places considerable interpretive emphasis on the contexts of narrative production. Whilst the manifold contextual vantage points from which someone tells a story may not be easily accessible to the researcher, the following factors contextualized the narratives I collected in tangible ways: the historical present from which biographers related their experience; the themes and experiences they chose to or were invited to address; the social worlds they were part of; the historical and 'cultural meta-narratives'[37] they related to; and the dynamic of the interview context itself. To interpret some of these contextual ways of speaking, I draw, in a broad sense, on what sociolinguists call 'positioning'. Positioning is based on the idea that individuals actively perform relational work through storytelling. Narrators not only situate themselves in relation to their own experience, but people their story worlds with significant others, address present or absent audiences, and relate to dominant ideologies and discourses.[38] Exploring relational practices at the level of narrative, thus, aids in the understanding of how individuals construct themselves as agents in the world who position themselves socially, politically and ideologically.

My own identity as a white German researcher involved mutual 'positioning' which became reflected in the ensuing stories. Being relatively close in age to many of those I interviewed facilitated access as well as linguistic exchange and involved a shared knowledge about our country of origin. I became acutely aware of shifting positions in the 'gray zone'[39] of whiteness, partly through the troubling ways in which some whites shared 'uncensored' racism with me, partly through taking advantage myself of the racialized spaces of entitlement which I had come to study.

In what follows I present a series of interview extracts. They provide a flavour of the collected material and illustrate ways in which speakers positioned themselves in personal migration stories (as requested by me), and in wider social and historical relations. While only a small number of interviews can be presented here, the selection represents narrative tropes and rhetorical styles which were found in the material at large. The interpretive focus is on how interviewees crafted a sense of being German in their Namibian environments. Principally 'being German' became constructed as narrative emplotment in three areas which I call 'comfort zones', 'contact zones' and 'conflict zones'. The notion of storied 'zones' highlights that these constructions were predicated on characterizations of social spaces in which different groups of people interacted, and across varying types of mental and physical boundaries. Whilst such 'zonal' constructions of 'Germanness' often figured in one and the same conversation and frequently overlapped, I separate them heuristically to highlight a culture of compartmentalization which was narratively and socially observable.

Being German in the Comfort Zone

Many of the Germans I interviewed displayed remarkably confident narrative stances, positioning themselves as active agents in control of their own biographies. While some were still trying to secure permanent residence permits, many research participants routinely claimed an entitlement to international mobility. All conceded that the lifestyles they could afford in Namibia would not be transferable to Germany or anywhere else, and while this held a certain ambiguous force over their futures, the majority emphasized they were determined to stay or entertained ideas of moving elsewhere only if things should become difficult for whites politically. Most were holding on to their German passports as 'safety nets'. Whilst this immigrant group rarely displayed ignorance about their positions of privilege in Namibian society, they still often constructed their own history of immigration as a seamless transposition from one 'German' space into another. Migration was hardly interpreted as a culturally dislocating experience but more often as a career break, a route to self-realization, or, in some cases, even a 'homecoming'. The following examples illustrate this.

Christa

Christa was a trained nurse who had always had a strong desire to live in Africa and spoke of her immigration as a 'homecoming'. She found a German Namibian employer's job advert and encouraged her husband to apply. He was offered the post and the family left their southern German town for Namibia in 1987. She was in her mid-forties when we met and had just given up nursing to retrain as a tour guide, a profession she embraced enthusiastically.

> C: Everything was German here. You could buy everything. It was simply a matter of price, whether it was food or shampoo, coffee, whatever it was, you could get it. You just noticed that this is a German colony, it had a strong German influence and it still has it today. Namibia CANNOT[40] deny that it used to be German, wherever you go, especially in Swakopmund, which is still today, I always say to my guests [tourists] when you enter Swakopmund

you get the feeling that you are in Germany of a hundred years ago. I believe that the ties between Germans have been very strong, then as well as now. And if someone comes over, like you and you call and say 'I am Heidi and I have such and such a problem'. You help without fail, you just do it, you are part of the German family. Here you make friends much more easily than in Germany. People are simply more open. They are not so reserved, they place more importance on being human ... . Look, here we have these 75,000 whites, the 1.8 million live on 82, 83 million hectares. And how is it over there? Very small and many many more people. Namibia is two and a half times bigger and much fewer people, you simply have space to breathe and yes you really cherish social contacts here, much much more. Maybe because you are a foreigner.

H: Do you often feel like a foreigner?

C: No, no absolutely not. It is home [Heimat] for me. It would be a nightmare if they said 'you have to leave'.

Christa's story is one of a regained 'Heimat' where a welcoming German community, German consumer products, a nostalgic German colonial heritage and Namibia's wide open spaces provide a framework for personal renewal and contentment. A number of individuals echoed this sentiment, comparing the hectic pace of stressful jobs and time-pressured home lives in Germany to a slower, more humane and sociable one in Namibia. As she positions me as a hypothetical immigrant in the shared German world and eventually situates Germans in the minority of 'whites', she actively aligns the comfort of the Namibian experience with white German insularity. The insular perception is also present in the following extract where the speaker constructs Windhoek's city space as 'German'.

Frank

Frank's quotation starts this chapter. Having worked for a big multinational company for twenty-three years, he visited Namibia on an extended southern African tourist trip in 1993, seeking respite from work-related 'burnout'. Attracted by the country's natural beauty and the 'German' enclave in Windhoek, he moved to Namibia in 1994. By the time we met he had married a Namibian-born German and expressed pride in his upwardly mobile achievements and affluent lifestyle.

H: How did you experience the social environment when you arrived here?

F: Well look, as a tourist I had already seen the Post Mall, which is the pedestrianized street in Windhoek, and I had constantly noticed hands going up 'Hello Willi, hello Katrin, hello Peter!' Everybody knows each other here, everybody knows everybody else. And I was sitting there watching this and thought to myself, 'oh my God what a village! It's just like a village.' Through my profession in tourism my contacts have grown from Katima to Lüderitz, particularly in tourism, and when I walk through town today it is exactly the same, 'Hello Frank' here and 'hello Frank' there and well yes, it is like a village and I feel totally comfortable and safe here.

H: Are the people you know mainly Germans?

F: I would perhaps put it this way, 70% German, 25% white English, Afrikaner and 5% Blacks. I have relatively little contact with the black population here because there is hardly a black person in tourism. As lodge owner ... that is why I live in a relatively white world here but I don't have a problem with the guys ['Jungs'].

Frank's visual image of Windhoek as populated by Germans mirrors the city's apartheid heritage with its territorial separation between a 'white' urban centre and spatially removed 'townships' for 'blacks' and 'coloureds'. Whilst these territorial racializations were still evident during my research, representing the central Windhoek street as 'German' relied on rendering the black urban demographic invisible. As if to assert the 'German' cultural presence he described in the story, he made a point of speaking German to the black staff in the Windhoek café where we were holding our conversation. 'I want to reinforce German here, I only speak English if they don't understand me', he explained. Positioning the black majority as 'Jungs', or 'guys', who might cause 'problems', constructed the black population as male and potentially troublesome. It reinforced the association of immigrant wellbeing with 'white only' spaces. This confident self-emplacement in a racialized comfort zone was frequently paired with the claim that Namibia was 'not really' Africa, as the following extracts show.

Katrin

Katrin, in her mid-forties when we met, had arrived shortly before independence in 1988. She had been seconded by her employer, a German bank, which was establishing business links in South Africa and Namibia. She said she knew nothing about the country before departure: 'German TV news always showed Namibia as the dotted line because it was still a South African protectorate'. A year later her husband followed, immediately 'fell in love' with the country, and they later had children. Katrin's story revolved around the ambivalence of enjoying a highly comfortable lifestyle which also trapped her in what she described as social and professional provincialism. Here she aligns everyday comfort and material success with 'non-African' Namibia:

What makes life in Namibia totally easy for us, we used to call Namibia 'Africa for beginners', because it is Africa and you can get by in your language, you get your German food, you have infrastructure, everything is totally easy, it is not Africa at all! We don't get what you may have to bear in a country like Angola where you have to boil the salad leaves, like our friends who we have just visited there, we don't even have a clue of what that means! You can't compare it, this is a German life in Africa. We really have butter on both sides of the toast! The sun, a job, the money, and well yes it's just brilliant, you would actually be stupid to leave.

The narrative removal of Namibia from 'Africa' was a recurring motif. Comparable to the participants above, the following speaker invokes a tourist gaze to describe her environment. Aged thirty-nine at the time, Tina explained that a strong desire to leave Germany had given rise to a year spent travelling which preceded her settling down in Namibia. Married to an Afrikaans-speaking white Namibian, she was self-employed, running a bed and breakfast business and working as a tour operator.

Tina

T: I always call Namibia Africa for beginners, because actually it is not an African a typical African country. Typical for me is Central Africa, West Africa, that is for me very black Africa ['Schwarzafrika'] that is typically African for me. Everything in southern Africa, such as Botswana, Zimbabwe, South Africa, Namibia, is very civilized, Europeanized. And because there are a lot of immigrants here who have mixed with each other, a distinctive culture has emerged. And it is very close to the European or American or Australian world view. And if you grew up like that it makes it easier to live here.

H: Really, Africa for beginners?

T: (laughs) Yes, the road system is good. Everybody here has email, everybody has a phone, if you have to make a payment for anything here you know exactly it will arrive at the destination and you get what you have paid for. Somewhere in Central Africa I would never pay for anything in advance … it's like Europe but with an African <touch> [English] (laughs) you know. The masks hang on some wall or the drums beat somewhere but really you are still at home.

Tina's typologies of 'Africanness' derive from a discourse of 'civilization' and common ideological tropes of 'development'. As she describes the former southern African settler colonies as cultures of mixing formed by 'many immigrants' and a western 'worldview', she actively excludes a black African agency and the history of colonialism and apartheid from the story. Namibia's Africanness is relegated to a mere 'touch', evoked as a clichéd ambience of 'masks and drums'. The unreflective use of terminology loaded with colonial ideology such as 'Schwarzafrika' and 'civilized'[41] points at the linguistic normalization of stereotypes, and the ongoing force of colonial discourses in the construction of relations between Europe and Africa.

As these descriptions of seamless integration into a familiar cultural and professional space reflected privileged forms of mobility, they equally worked as distancing devices to the cultural and political fabric of Namibian society.[42] 'Being German' became overwhelmingly contextualized in communities of lifestyle actively constructed as white spaces and a self-identification with European norms against which 'Africa' became an exotic or deficient Other. The material and historical relations underpinning these racialized insularities become more visible in the following section.

Being German in the Contact Zone

Beyond the boundaries of their personal networks these immigrants varyingly situated themselves in relation to three main camps: native-born Germans; Afrikaans-speaking whites of South African origin; and black Namibians. Contact as negotiated in biographical narratives took place across explicit and assumed boundaries of ethnicity, race, class, gender, language and political attitude. For instance, Namibian Afrikaners, or Boers, were largely referred to as descendants of the 'poor whites' that South Africa had exported to Namibia. Both native and immigrant Germans distinguished themselves from them as figures of both excess and deficit. In 'German' stories Boers were excessively racist and held responsible for apartheid, yet they had also tainted their whiteness and Europeanness through a longer historical presence in Africa and the 'primitivization' of their ways of life. Informed by class prejudice, these views included the charge that Boers lacked a decent work ethic, were 'primitive' and 'backward', and cultivated deeply conservative gender relations and 'hypocritical' religious practices.[43] Very few of the people I met, however, had any close social contact with the Afrikaner community. Other Germans, however, as well as black Namibians, were part of people's everyday lives. During colonialism and apartheid work places and white homes were paradigmatic 'contact zones'[44] between black and white populations in which racial inequality was continuously forged. These structures had ongoing relevance following independence. All German immigrants I met employed black domestic staff, and many had black employees; very few socialized with black individuals as friends, and even fewer had black partners. Black Namibians thus, were over-whelmingly positioned as a social group with whom the speaker had an employer-employee or emerging co-employee relationship. As I explored elsewhere, the world of work and attitudes to work represented a major topic of self-distinction for these 'new' Germans.[45] Compared with those Germans and other whites who were 'already here for too long', they often claimed both 'an advantage in modern liberalism' and 'a more per-fected self-enterprising spirit'.[46] Individuals often claimed authenticity as 'German Germans' by positioning themselves as brokers of a European capitalist rationality whose work ethic and 'know how' was superior to that of other whites and to that of black Namibians who were often constructed as resistant to principles of the 'German' work ethic. The following extracts are typical in presenting contact across such bounded ethno-spatial frames. First Carla evokes ambivalent boundary crossings to native German and black Namibians.

Carla

Aged thirty-nine when we met, Carla identified herself as a cosmopolitan who had followed her husband, 'who always wanted to go to Africa', to Namibia in 1994. Both were scientists. By the time we met they had had two children and were divorced. She had become self-employed in tour-ism, offering specialist tours to Namibia's distinctive geological sites. In this part of her narrative, she distances herself from native Germans:

> I think you can compare it really well with the Ossis in Germany. Just by look-ing at the situation. The Ossis lived their whole lives behind the wall and all of a sudden the wall is gone. And here people grew up under Apartheid and have the corresponding attitudes to blacks and that is SO entrenched in their thinking that they don't really have the aptitude to see society with an open mind or they can't or won't do it you know [relates stories about white moth-ers in Kindergarten discriminating against black children]. And when those topics come up and they start talking about the Kaffir and so on I simply shut my mouth. Because if you say something they just brush you off and tell you 'oh you Deutschländer', you know, they don't take you seriously, 'what do YOU know, you don't have a clue, no matter how long you have lived here.' That's what they say.

West Germans of this generation occasionally compared Namibian-born Germans to 'Ossis' (East Germans), usually for what they observed as a strong sense of community or parochial mentality. Carla positions the Namibian Germans as backward isolationists, incapable of adapt-ing to post-1990 Black rule. In a constructed dialogue which dramatizes their antagonistic relationship, she becomes dismissed as an ignorant 'Deutschländer'[47] for her avowedly anti-racist attitude. However, in the same story this antagonistic relationship is also relativized:

> I know especially older farmers who one would normally decry as the TOTAL racists. Actually they have an immensely generous heart for their farmworkers, you know erm but they would never accept blacks as equals, they treat them as immature children. On the other hand I mean I also know black tour guides, I know good black tour guides but even those who are good you often see, those who have really already made something of themselves and have potential and everything you know, it often happens that they turn up at some stage and are either totally arrogant 'Well I am somebody now and have made it' and kick those below, their own people, or they say, 'Well we are poor blacks and you have to help us now' and who think it's normal to take on an attitude of taking, just because they are black.

The unresolved tension between distance to, and partial sympathy for, the patriarchal white farmer becomes echoed in a similar oscillation between sympathy for, and critical distance to, the 'black employee'. As Carla integrates her description of 'black tour guides' into a subtext of post-1990 Black Economic Empowerment, she draws a picture of a figure who abuses their newly won professional status and social empowerment by either maltreating 'their own people' or placing undue demands on whites on the basis of 'being black'. Using one's black identity as a new form of racial capital to gain undue benefit from or advantage over whites was an often used white response to post-1990 changes and figured in most of these interviews.

Marianne

Marianne, in her mid-forties when we met, arrived in Namibia's independence year of 1990, following a job advert she found in Germany. She said she had ended up in Namibia 'more by chance than by choice', as preferred options of emigration to Canada or Australia did not work out. Much less economically secure than Katrin, she alluded to a similar sense of entrapment, as future options of return looked financially implausible ('I neither have health nor pension insurance'). She married a native-born German with whom she ran a retail business and they had several black employees. At this point in her story, Marianne discusses employing cheap domestic labour by engaging both a critique and a defence of white privilege. Whilst men rarely recognized their gendered privilege in the household, women often explained that Namibia had freed them from the chores of domesticity in unprecedented ways. Many suggested that the accessibility of cheap black labour allowed them to reconcile careers with children and housework and negotiated tensions of privilege around this subject. This is also displayed below where Marianne addresses the lifestyle she adapted post-migration as an ambiguous process of enculturation into gendered and racialized norms of everyday domesticity:

> Well in Germany you are used to doing everything yourself. And here you have everything done for you. Even so you actually claim 'I did my garden yesterday'. And in the beginning I believed what people said. I went 'wow the woman gardened in a 2000 square meter plot yesterday', and I thought 'respect!' But she didn't do it, she had it done. Until I actually realized it, it took me years to fully grasp that people here have everything done for them … I picked up pretty quickly that you HAVE TO wear ironed clothes because everybody has a cleaner at home who does the ironing. Everything is being done. If you have the money you hardly do any work yourself. But people don't really see it that way. They don't notice it anymore, they lack the awareness. Like him [points to her husband who is sitting nearby] he grew up with it, they had a male cleaner in the house every day. He was there every single day from morning till night doing everything. This is a totally different assumption that you don't need to do any work in your household. [Elaborates on contradictions of Südwester Germans whose racism did not deter them from leaving their children in the care of black nannies]. For me it was also that there was a black cleaner, that she does everything in my house, well they know the house better than I do. She knows, even today she probably knows my house better than I do. But actually, it is not really manageable anyway. Because houses here are not made like in Europe, so easy to clean, you don't have the cleaning devices which you have in Germany. For instance, it's only now that dishwashers have become more available. And for the price of a dishwasher I can afford a cleaner for five months or longer.

Similarly to Carla, Marianne navigates tensions between being critical of historical race relations, on the one hand, and maintaining positions of authority in interracial domestic and economic spaces, on the other. Like in Carla's case, she confronts historical racism through a critique of native Germans – in this case her own husband – and claims to be different whilst also relativizing the injustices of the old order.

As inhabiting these white subjectivities became in part a reflective awareness of a history structured by racism, these immigrants did not inscribe themselves into this history, but preferred to identify as Germans from Germany who had had no involvement in the difficult Namibian past and its present implications. This distancing stance included German colonialism, insofar as it represented a history of violence, rather than a spectre of heritage conservation as promoted by the local tourist industry. Contrary to my expectations, research participants rarely included the topic in their stories, and offered views only after prompting – which could be regarded as a form of distancing in itself. Unsurprisingly, many of these 'postwar' Germans explained that they had only had marginal knowledge about Germany's colonial history or relevant information about Namibia prior to arrival, and often shared memories of incredulous amazement at their first encounter with the country's German heritage in the shape of colonial memorials, Imperial era architecture or linguistic landscapes. While a few individuals claimed that living in Namibia had motivated further interest in the German colonial period, there was a nearly unanimous denial of its importance for contemporary society, in both Germany and Namibia. As the following section will show, this stance was in part a response to the Herero reparation claims in the early 2000s.

Being German in the Conflict Zone

Many historians recognize the massacre of the Herero and Nama peoples by German colonial troops between 1904 and 1907 as the first genocide of the twentieth century.[48] It is estimated that 80 per cent of the Herero were killed in a campaign that followed their uprising against German colonial oppression.[49] In 2001 Herero leaders lodged a lawsuit in a US court against three German companies and the German government, demanding reparations for their historical losses.[50] This generated a debate about German colonialism in Germany and Namibia, which was taken up again in 2004, the centenary of the massacres, when a number of commemorative events were held in both countries.[51] These debates also drew some renewed attention to a stance of 'colonial revisionism' which had long been observed among sections of the German minority in Namibia.[52] At bottom, revisionist arguments reject the 'genocide thesis' or relativize colonial violence, weighing up ills against so-called 'achievements'.[53] Many of my research participants drew on these stances despite the often self-confessed lack of information or interest. Two relativizing discourses were commonly present and often intermingled: first, the long time span that had passed and could allegedly no longer implicate present-day Germans in historical guilt, a claim which was often associated with veiled or explicit references to the Holocaust; and second, an association of colonial violence with an 'early form of development aid' as Böhlke-Itzen ironically puts it.[54] This broadly followed the argument that German colonialism may have been violent, but that it introduced technological innovations such as roads and railways which literally paved a route to modernity for Africans. Often the relativizing argument included claims that Germany paid exceptional sums in development aid, and had no obligation to offer separate reparation payments, an argument which the German government itself has persistently used to reject Herero and Nama claims.[55] The question of German colonialism exposed political rifts in the struggle for collective memory in independent Namibia which came to the fore in conflicts over public memory in 2004, and, as will be seen below, still animated opinions during my fieldwork. Thus, for instance, the Namibian government did not support the Herero campaign, arguing that litigation claims would undermine the 'special relationship' between Germany and Namibia.[56] While the Herero considered their historical suffering under German colonialism central to collective identity, other ethnic groups, most notably the demographically stronger and politically more powerful Oshivambo, regarded the long liberation struggle against South Africa as a foundational historical event.[57] In the shadow of these struggles for a unifying national memory, most Germans I spoke to – both native and immigrant – exonerated themselves from the historical crimes of their forebears. Amongst the individuals introduced here, Frank was most outspokenly revisionist. Claiming to have researched the subject, he went so far as to reject the term 'colonialism' for Germany's imperial politics in Namibia, relying on revisionist historians and elderly Southwesters as sources of authority. Below we return once more to Christa, Carla and Marianne who conceded German 'guilt' yet engaged strongly relativizing discourses.

Christa

> It's not my fault, it's not your fault, our generation is not to blame, this happened a hundred years ago, you have to get to the point and say, 'let bygones be bygones, live in the present and make the best of it.' It doesn't make sense to keep rubbing salt in the same old wound and keep going on about the same old stuff. I have had it up to there with this topic, honestly, I can't hear it anymore. And as far as the Hereros are concerned, they are trying to distort things as if the fault had only been with the Germans, and that is wrong, OK, one has to see things from both sides and there were mistakes on both sides, on the German and the African side, many many things were out of order.

Christa makes veiled references to historical guilt without articulating what happened. The phrase 'there were mistakes on both sides' obscures the role of Germans as aggressors. She assumes a defensive stance, claiming to be continuously charged, as a German, with the responsibility for a historical calamity she had no involvement in. The exhortative address to a generic 'you' enacts a dialogue not just with me but with a larger audience that takes a different view to her own. The argumentative mode she assumes in demanding 'to let bygones be bygones' is reminiscent of some Holocaust debates in Germany which may have served as a subtext in this case.[58] The link between these two twentieth-century genocides was explicitly articulated by Carla.

Carla

Well personally I can neither be blamed for the Herero campaign nor for the extermination of the Jews, as a German I feel no obligation of culpability. And now this, this erm this centenary of the Herero campaign has been splashed all over the press here. The lawsuit of the Herero against the German government in an American court, all I am telling myself is, 'Well better be careful dear Hereros you had better be quiet, because if you push through that charge some-one should quickly support the Bushmen and get you drawn into the courts.'

Carla confidently repudiates moral responsibility for the Holocaust[59] and for what she judiciously calls the 'Herero Campaign'. Comparably to Christa, she argues with a wider audience, in this case the Herero them-selves whose lawsuit is denounced as illegitimate because they too, she suggests, have been oppressors. Such references to pre-colonial conflicts among Africans were common and frequently used to relativize colonial aggression or present it as a pacifying force. As Carla moved on in her narrative, she drew a link to contemporary EU development aid and its alleged embezzlement by corrupt Namibian politicians. As far-fetched as these argumentative chains seemed to be, they forged an association of meanings which relativized historical violence and juxtaposed the essen-tially historically vindicated German to the still to-be-developed African. Marianne brings this to the point, linking the Herero claims to her own status as a post-independence immigrant.

Marianne

This is far away for me. And hearing about the Herero case now, that they are still bringing their charges, I really don't get it. All this has to do with me is that I am still waiting for my residence permit and if I am thinking about the German state donating 60 Million Euros development aid, which is a legacy of colonialism that Namibia gets most development aid from Germany out of ALL countries, and on the other hand they build palaces for the president, the corruption and also the work ethic of the blacks, the way in which they don't accept responsibility [at work]. The way in which after all is said and done the boss or the white man becomes the scapegoat.

Marianne combines a remarkable chain of meanings which dismiss colonialism as violence, and conclude in her own 'victimization' as a German
immigrant still waiting for a residence permit, and a white employer disadvantaged by changing labour relations in post-independence Namibia.

Conclusion

To conclude we glance back at Frank's quotation at the beginning of
this chapter. In recognizing that Namibia's history enabled him to get
off to an easy start, Frank invoked the bigger picture within which these
migrations have to be read. To be sure, Frank was a colonial revisionist.
However, this did not detract from the fact that his migration and successful incorporation in Windhoek was contextualized in an imperial
legacy and postcolonial global hierarchy. These migrant trajectories were
empowered by, and revelatory of, historical and geographical maps of
interconnection (e.g. between Germany-Namibia, South Africa-Namibia,
Europe-Africa) and the hierarchies and politics of violence which had
shaped them. Unsurprisingly some of these Europe-African mobilities
intersected with trajectories of North-South tourism, displaying what
Doreen Massey calls a 'power-geometry'[60] which included post-independence Namibia into larger circuits of tourism. The majority of these
Germans had been in a position to choose emigration for reasons associated with lifestyle and could mobilize their skills and capitals as assets in
the process. 'Privileged migration' involved passports, access to visas and
immigration lawyers, continued membership in a powerful European
nation state, savings, educational qualifications, the capital of whiteness
that paved routes to employment (particularly pre-1990), and a range of
social, cultural and economic resources in the host country which were
inherited from the previous system. Participants addressed the everyday through negotiations of lifestyle which included, for instance, gated
neighbourhoods, the availability of German or international schools
and culture clubs, the opportunity to manage daily life in German and
English, the availability of imported consumer goods, and the access to
cheap domestic, industrial and service industry labour. Without wishing
to claim that people lived carefree lives, it is important to note that these
migrants settled in new relations of power which they were assimilating
in the post-migration process.

I have tried to explore how the individuals I met negotiated these
simultaneously personal, geographical and historical trajectories at a narrative level, and re-positioned themselves as 'German' in the process.
Using the analytical notion of narrative 'positioning', I identified three

'story zones' – comfort, contact and conflict – to interpret the identity work that was performed in these interviews. This 'work' was intricately involved in negotiating the symbolic and material status of Germanness as whiteness and a form of ethnic 'authenticity' whose geographical reference point was Germany as opposed to Africa. Narrators constructed the 'comfort zone' largely in historical reference to their own migration biographies and immersion in 'German' communities of lifestyle. Stories of comfort demarcated everyday social, symbolic and material spaces where whiteness was deemed secure, black Namibians kept out of focus, and 'Africa' subject to a tourist gaze. Narrations of the 'contact zone' referenced the historical present of a post-apartheid, post-independence society and its complex boundaries of race, class and gender. Here research participants claimed to be 'new' or 'German' Germans whose membership in 'modern' Germany underpinned their distinctiveness, not least in contrast to the 'retrograde' Southwesters. Being 'German German' was also about displaying the ability to engage in biographical re-invention in which professional skills, resourcefulness and a strong work ethic were represented as a key to immigrant success. Black Namibians, who remained vital for, yet invisible in, stories of immigrant wellbeing and success, appeared as a wayward 'Other' in the 'contact zone' whose ambition for post-independence equality was misdirected, if not an expression of misunderstood capitalist modernity and the knowledge and norms of behaviour it required. Such interpretive positioning of black Namibians became particularly exposed in the 'conflict zone' which referenced German colonialism. Here interviewees addressed the Herero lawsuit which told history from a victim's point of view and positioned Germany as liable for imperial aggression. Narrators removed themselves from positions of moral accountability to advocate forms of active forgetting and radically re-framed the relationship between the two parties: what the Hereros constructed as an exchange between the formerly colonized and the colonizer was turned into an exchange between the to-be-developed African and a European benefactor.

Looking at these narrative practices as instances of 'identity work' suggests that these immigrants did not simply situate themselves as 'Germans' but as white Germans who negotiated, at times with defensiveness and ambiguity, white subjectivities in Namibian society in the midst of a post-independence political process. The significance of the 'colonial' in meanings of whiteness was striking: a deep-seated assumption of Euro-Western superiority, the desire to tell history from the vantage point of denial, and the consistent 'othering' of the black subject. These stances were, to a considerable extent, testament to a socialization into prevailing cultures of whiteness in Namibia. However, they also reflected the cargo of colonial amnesia in the luggage of these immigrants. They had, after all, grown up in a society which had erased its imperial past from its geographical and historical imaginations of national identity.

Heidi Armbruster is a Social Anthropologist and Associate Professor in German Studies at the University of Southampton. She has a long-standing interest in the anthropology of migration, and her research has focused in particular on how identity and collective history are negotiated and transformed through processes of migration. A study on diasporic communities of Syrian Christians in Germany and Austria has looked at the post-migration negotiation of a traumatic history. It has been published as *Keeping the Faith: Syriac Christian Diasporas* (Sean Kingston, 2013). She has also been involved in interdisciplinary research on German and European border communities and on multicultural transformations in provincial regions of Europe. She is director of the Centre for Transnational Studies at the University of Southampton.

Notes

1. See, for example, Thomas, *Colonialism's Culture*, 77; Young, *Postcolonialism*, 2–3.
2. See also Burton, *After the Imperial Turn*.
3. Wildenthal, 'Notes on a History of "Imperial Turns" in Modern Germany'.
4. E.g. Zimmerer, 'Colonialism and Genocide'; Perraudin and Zimmerer, *German Colonialism and National Identity*.
5. See also Forum, 'The German Colonial Imagination', 251–71.
6. Friedrichsmeyer, Lennox and Zantop, 'Introduction', 24.
7. The German Historical Museum (Deutsches Historisches Museum) in Berlin showed its first major exhibition on German colonialism in 2016. See http://www.dhm.de/ausstellungen/archiv/2016/deutscher-kolonialismus.html (accessed 20 August 2017).
8. Wildenthal, 'Notes on a History', 144.
9. A full reference list cannot be offered here. See, e.g., Ayim, *Blues in Schwarz Weiß*; Oguntoye, Opitz and Schultz, *Farbe bekennen*; Sow, *Deutschland Schwarz Weiss*. For an East German perspective, see Piesche, 'Black and German?'; Lauré al-Samarai, 'Unwegsame Erinnerungen'.
10. I would like to thank the research participants for sharing their experiences with me. All personal names are pseudonyms.
11. See Jauch, Edwards and Cupido, 'Inequality in Namibia'; Diener and Graefe, *Contemporary Namibia*.
12. The German Federal Statistical Office registered between 200 and 300 German emigrations to Namibia every year between 1991 and 2005 (personal information). The Namibian authorities did not maintain immigration statistics at the time.
13. These numerical estimates can be found in a range of publications and were also mentioned by interviewees.

14. Before independence tourism was under South African government control and built around game reserves, national parks and private guest farms. Most tourists were South Africans (Novelli and Gebhardt 2007: 450).
15. Papen, 'Exclusive, Ethno and Eco', 83.
16. A recent report by the Namibian Ministry of Tourism shows that German tourists lead the overseas visitor statistics by far (Ministry 2015).
17. Leonard, 'Work, Identity and Change?', 1249.
18. See also Lundström, *White Migrations*, 1–2.
19. See e.g. Benson, 'The Context and Trajectory of Lifestyle Migration'; Casado-Diaz, 'Retiring to Spain'; O'Reilly, *The British on the Costa del Sol*; Torkington, 'Place and Lifestyle Migration'.
20. Benson and O'Reilly, 'From Lifestyle Migration'.
21. Benson and O'Reilly, 'From Lifestyle Migration', 29.
22. Ibid.
23. Cohen, Duncan and Thulemark, 'Lifestyle Mobilities', 160.
24. Benson and O'Reilly, 'From Lifestyle Migration', 23.
25. See e.g. Fechter and Walsh, 'Examining "Expatriate"; Knowles, 'Making Whiteness'.
26. As, for example, in Cohen, Duncan and Thulemark, 'Lifestyle Mobilities', 162.
27. See e.g. Conway and Leonard, *Migration, Space and Transnational Identities*; Lundström, *White Migrations*.
28. For pioneering studies see Frankenberg, *White Women Race Matters*; Dyer, *White*; Tyler, *Whiteness, Class and the Legacies of Empire*.
29. See Frankenberg, *White Women*, 17; Tyler, *Whiteness*.
30. Steyn, '"White Talk"', 122.
31. E.g. Schmidt-Lauber, *Die abhängigen Herren*; Schmidt-Lauber, *'Die verkehrte Hautfarbe'*; Schmidt-Lauber, 'Die ehemaligen Kolonialherren'. For a work on the pre-1945 period, see Walther, *Creating Germans Abroad*.
32. Jauch, Edwards and Cupido, *Inequality*, 225.
33. E.g. Bruner, *Acts of Meaning*.
34. Mattingly, 'Reading Minds', 137.
35. Mattingly, 'Reading Minds', 138.
36. Spector-Mersel, 'Narrative Research'.
37. Spector-Mersel, 'Narrative Research', 212.
38. Bamberg, 'Positioning between Structure and Performance'; De Fina, Schiffrin and Bamberg, 'Introduction'.
39. Back, 'Guess Who's Coming to Dinner?'.
40. These transcriptions are translations from the German. Capitals indicate emphasis. Brackets enclose comments by the author, '…' indicates untranscribed sentences.
41. For an analysis of colonial stereotypes in the German language, see Arndt and Hornscheidt, *Afrika und die deutsche Sprache*.
42. This discursive distancing from black Namibia reminds one of the cultural dynamics of white self-insulation observed by both literary and scholarly writers in settler cultures of southern Africa (e.g. Hughes, *Whiteness in Zimbabwe*, 1–12).
43. See also Armbruster, '"With Hard Work and Determination"', 624. For a historical perspective on the German 'blackening' of Afrikaners, see Aitken, 'Looking for the Besten Boeren'. British or other European whites rarely figured in the identity claims I heard among Germans.
44. This term is inspired by Pratt, 'Arts of the Contact Zone'.
45. The field material used in the present chapter is also the basis of Armbruster, '"With Hard Work and Determination"' and Armbruster, '"Realising the Self"'. While the first publication compares narratives of incorporation among two different generations of

German immigrants, the second explores cultural models of personhood which revolve around the work ethic and tropes of Western modernity.

46. Armbruster, "'With Hard Work and Determination'", 623.
47. A term Namibian Germans used for Germans from Germany, often with irony.
48. See Gewald, *Herero Heroes*; Melber, 'Ein deutscher Sonderweg?'; Zimmerer, 'Krieg, KZ und Völkermord in Südwestafrika'.
49. Drechsler, *'Let Us Die Fighting'*, 214.
50. The lawsuit failed eventually but brought international attention to the issue. For more detail, see Cooper, 'Reparations for the Herero Genocide'.
51. See Förster, Henrichsen and Bollig, *Namibia – Deutschland*; Zeller, 'Genozid und Gedenken'; Morgan, 'Remembering Against the Nation-state'.
52. See Böhlke-Itzen, 'Die bundesdeutsche Diskussion'.
53. Böhlke-Itzen, 'Die bundesdeutsche Diskussion', 104–10.
54. My translation. Böhlke-Itzen, 'Die bundesdeutsche Diskussion', 109.
55. Buser, 'German Genocide in Namibia before U.S. Courts'.
56. Cooper, 'Reparations for the Herero Genocide', 115.
57. For more detail, see Kößler, 'Im Schatten des Genozids'.
58. Calls to 'draw a line' under the past have long been part of the wider discourse about Holocaust commemoration in Germany. In a study published in 2015 the Bertelsmann Stiftung found that a majority of Germans would prefer 'to let the past rest'. See Hagemann and Nathanson, *Deutschland und Israel heute*, 22–26.
59. The links these individuals draw between these two campaigns of genocide evoke a broader context. The question of dis/continuity between German colonialism and Nazism has not only preoccupied historians (see Langbehn and Salama, 'Introduction: Reconfiguring German Colonialism') but also been mobilized by Herero leaders who referred to the massacres as their 'Holocaust' and suggested that Germany's rejection of reparation claims was rooted in racism (Böhlke-Itzen, 'Die bundesdeutsche Diskussion', 111). German governments which have rejected reparation claims to the present have also brought the 'singularity' of the Jewish Holocaust into play. Some observers suggested that this served to reinforce the impression that Germany's responsibility for genocide remained limited to the 'exceptional' period of 1933–1945 (ibid., 112). At a commemorative event in Namibia in 2004, a German government minister formally apologized for the colonial atrocities. Since then official Germany has changed its stance. Since 2012 both countries have engaged in negotiations regarding reconciliation, and German officials have begun to call the campaigns against the Herero and Nama 'genocide' and 'war crimes'. Yet, the German government has also insisted that this 'could not entail any legal consequences', preferring to negotiate further development aid with Namibia (Buser, 'German Genocide in Namibia before U.S. Courts'). The Herero and Nama lodged a new lawsuit for reparations in January 2017.
60. Massey, *For Space*, 64.

Bibliography

Aitken, R. 'Looking for the Besten Boeren: The Normalisation of Afrikaner Settlement in German South West Africa, 1884–1914'. *Journal of Southern African Studies* 33(2) (2007), 343–60.

Armbruster, H. '"Realising the Self and Developing the African": German Immigrants in Namibia'. *Journal of Ethnic and Migration Studies* 36(8) (2010), 1229–46.

_____. '"With Hard Work and Determination You Can Make it Here": Narratives of Identity among German Immigrants in Post-Colonial Namibia'. *Journal of Southern African Studies* 34(3) (2008), 611–28.

Arndt, S. and A. Hornscheidt (eds). *Afrika und die deutsche Sprache: Ein kritisches Nachschlagewerk*. Münster: Unrast Verlag, 2004.

Ayim, M. *Blues in Schwarz Weiß*. Berlin: Orlanda, 1995.

Back, L. 'Guess Who's Coming to Dinner? The Political Morality of Investigating Whiteness in the Gray Zone', in V. Ware and L. Back (eds), *Out of Whiteness: Color, Politics, and Culture* (Chicago: The University of Chicago Press, 2002), 33–59.

Bamberg, M. 'Positioning between Structure and Performance'. *Journal of Narrative and Life History* 7(1–4) (1997), 335–42.

Benson, M. 'The Context and Trajectory of Lifestyle Migration – The Case of the British Residents in Southwest France'. *European Societies* 12(1) (2010), 45–64.

Benson, M. and K. O'Reilly. 'From Lifestyle Migration to Lifestyle *in* Migration: Categories, Concepts and Ways of Thinking'. *Migration Studies* 4(1) (2016), 20–37.

Böhlke-Itzen, J. 'Die bundesdeutsche Diskussion und die Reparationsfrage: Ein "ganz normaler Kolonialkrieg"?', in H. Melber (ed.), *Genozid und Gedenken. Namibisch-deutsche Geschichte und Gegenwart* (Frankfurt am Main: Brandes & Apsel, 2005), 103–19.

Bruner, J.S. *Acts of Meaning*. Cambridge, MA: Harvard University Press, 1990.

Burton, A. (ed.). *After the Imperial Turn: Thinking with and through the Nation*. Durham, NC and London: Duke University Press, 2003.

Buser, A. 'German Genocide in Namibia before U.S. Courts: Ovaherero and Nama Sue Germany over Colonial Injustices – Again'. *Völkerrechtsblog*, 11 January 2017. Retrieved 14 July 2017 from https://voelkerrechtsblog.org/german-genocide-in-namibia-before-u-s-courts/.

Casado-Diaz, M. 'Retiring to Spain: An Analysis of Difference among North European Nationals'. *Journal of Ethnic and Migration Studies* 32(8) (2006), 1321–39.

Cohen, S.A., T. Duncan and M. Thulemark. 'Lifestyle Mobilities: The Crossroads of Travel, Leisure and Migration'. *Mobilities* 10(1) (2015), 155–72.

Conway, D. and P. Leonard. *Migration, Space and Transnational Identities: The British in South Africa*. Basingstoke: Palgrave, 2014.

Cooper, A.D. 'Reparations for the Herero Genocide: Defining the Limits of International Litigation'. *African Affairs* 106(422) (2007), 113–26.

De Fina, A., D. Schiffrin and M. Bamberg. 'Introduction', in A. de Fina, D. Schiffrin and M. Bamberg (eds), *Discourse and Identity* (Cambridge: Cambridge University Press, 2006), 1–23.

Diener, I. and O. Graefe (eds). *Contemporary Namibia: The First Landmarks of a Post-Apartheid Society*. Windhoek: Gamsberg Macmillan, 2001.

Drechsler, H. *'Let Us Die Fighting': The Struggle of the Herero and Nama against German Imperialism (1884–1915)*. London: Zed Press, 1980.

Dyer, R. *White*. London: Routledge, 1997.

Fechter, A.-M. and K. Walsh (eds). 'Examining "Expatriate" Continuities: Postcolonial Approaches to Mobile Professionals'. Special Issue. *Journal of Ethnic and Migration Studies* 36(8) (2010).

Förster, L., D. Henrichsen and M. Bollig (eds). *Namibia – Deutschland: Eine geteilte Geschichte.* Wolfratshausen: Edition Minerva, 2004.

Forum. 'The German Colonial Imagination'. *German History* 26(2) (2008), 251–71.

Frankenberg, R. *White Women Race Matters: The Social Construction of Whiteness.* London: Routledge, 1993.

Friedrichsmeyer, S., S. Lennox and S. Zantop. 'Introduction' in S. Friedrichsmeyer et al. (eds), *The Imperialist Imagination: German Colonialism and its Legacy* (Ann Arbor: The University of Michigan Press, 1998), 1–29.

Gewald, J. *Herero Heroes: A Socio-political History of the Herero of Namibia 1890–1923.* Oxford: James Currey, 1999.

Hagemann, S. and R. Nathanson. *Deutschland und Israel heute: Verbindende Vergangenheit, trennende Gegenwart?* Gütersloh: Bertelsmann Stiftung, 2015.

Hughes, D. McD. *Whiteness in Zimbabwe: Race, Landscape, and the Problem of Belonging.* Basingstoke: Palgrave Macmillan, 2010.

Jauch H., L. Edwards and B. Cupido. 'Inequality in Namibia', in H. Jauch and D. Muchena (eds), *Tearing Us Apart: Inequalities in Southern Africa* (Johannesburg: Open Society Initiative for Southern Africa, 2011), 181–255.

Knowles, C. 'Making Whiteness: British Lifestyle Migrants in Hong Kong', in C. Alexander and C. Knowles (eds), *Making Race Matter: Bodies, Space and Identity* (Basingstoke: Palgrave Macmillan, 2005), 90–110.

Kößler, R. 'Im Schatten des Genozids: Erinnerungspolitik in einer extrem ungleichen Gesellschaft', in H. Melber (ed.), *Genozid und Gedenken. Namibisch-deutsche Geschichte und Gegenwart* (Frankfurt am Main: Brandes & Apsel, 2005), 49–77.

Langbehn, V. and M. Salama. 'Introduction: Reconfiguring German Colonialism', in V. Langbehn and M. Salama (eds), *German Colonialism. Race, the Holocaust, and Postwar Germany* (New York: Columbia University Press, 2011), ix–xxxiv.

Lauré al-Samarai, N. 'Unwegsame Erinnerungen: Auto/biographische Zeugnisse von Schwarzen Deutschen aus der BRD und der DDR', in M. Bechhaus-Gerst und R. Klein-Arendt (eds), *AfrikanerInnern in Deutschland und schwarze Deutsche – Geschichte und Gegenwart*, (Münster: Lit Verlag, 2004), 197–210.

Leonard, P. 'Work, Identity and Change? Post/Colonial Encounters in Hong Kong'. *Journal of Ethnic and Migration Studies* 36(8) (2010), 1247–63.

Lundström, C. *White Migrations: Gender, Whiteness and Privilege in Transnational Migration.* Basingstoke: Palgrave Macmillan, 2014.

Massey, D. *For Space.* London: Sage, 2005.

Mattingly, C. 'Reading Minds and Telling Tales in a Cultural Borderland'. *Ethos* 36(1) (2008), 136–54.

Melber, H. 'Ein deutscher Sonderweg? Einleitende Bemerkungen zum Umgang mit dem Völkermord in Deutsch Südwestafrika', in H. Melber (ed.), *Genozid und Gedenken: Namibisch-deutsche Geschichte und Gegenwart* (Frankfurt am Main: Brandes & Apsel, 2005), 13–21.

Ministry of Environment and Tourism, Republic of Namibia. *Tourist Statistical Report 2015.* Windhoek, 2015. Retrieved 23 July 2017 from https://www.namibiatourism.com.na/uploads/file_uploads/MET%20Tourist%20Statistical%20Report%202015_017.pdf.

Morgan, K.L. 'Remembering Against the Nation-state: Hereros' Pursuit of Restorative Justice'. *Time & Society* 21(1) (2012), 21–38.

Novelli, M. and K. Gebhardt. 'Community Based Tourism in Namibia: "Reality Show" or "Window Dressing"?' *Current Issues in Tourism* 10(5) (2007), 443–79.

Oguntoye, K., M. Opitz and D. Schultz (eds). *Farbe bekennen: Afro-deutsche Frauen auf den Spuren ihrer Geschichte*. Frankfurt am Main: Fischer Verlag, 1992.

O'Reilly, K. *The British on the Costa del Sol: Transnational Identities and Local Communities*. London: Routledge, 2000.

Papen, U. 'Exclusive, Ethno and Eco: Representations of Culture and Nature in Tourism Discourses in Namibia', in A. Jaworski and A. Pritchard (eds), *Discourse, Communication and Tourism* (Clevedon, Buffalo and Toronto: Channel View Publications, 2005), 79–120.

Perraudin, M. and J. Zimmerer (eds). *German Colonialism and National Identity*. New York: Routledge, 2010.

Piesche, P. 'Black and German? East German Adolescents before 1989: A Retrospective View of a "Non-existent Issue" in the GDR', in L. Adelson (ed.), *The Cultural After-Life of East Germany: New Transnational Perspectives* (Washington DC: American Institute for Contemporary German Studies, 2002), 37–59.

Pratt, M.L. 'Arts of the Contact Zone'. *Profession* (1991), 33–40.

Schmidt-Lauber, B. *Die abhängigen Herren: Deutsche Identität in Namibia*. Münster and Hamburg: Lit Verlag, 1993.

——. 'Die ehemaligen Kolonialherren: Zum Selbstverständnis deutscher Namibier', in L. Förster, D. Henrichsen and M. Bollig (eds), *Namibia, Deutschland: Eine geteilte Geschichte. Widerstand, Gewalt, Erinnerung* (Wolfratshausen: Edition Minerva, 2004), 226–43.

——. *'Die verkehrte Hautfarbe': Ethnizität deutscher Namibier als Alltagspraxis*. Berlin and Hamburg: Dietrich Reimer Verlag, 1998.

Sow, N. *Deutschland Schwarz Weiss: Der alltägliche Rassismus*. Munich: C. Bertelsmann, 2008.

Spector-Mersel, G. 'Narrative Research: Time for a Paradigm'. *Narrative Inquiry* 20(1) (2010), 204–24.

Steyn, M. '"White Talk": White South Africans and the Management of Diasporic Whiteness', in Alfred J. Lopez (ed.), *Postcolonial Whiteness* (New York: State University of New York Press, 2005), 119–35.

Thomas, N. *Colonialism's Culture: Anthropology, Travel and Government*. Cambridge: Polity Press, 1994.

Torkington, K. 'Place and Lifestyle Migration: The Discursive Construction of "Glocal" Place-Identity'. *Mobilities* 7(1) (2012), 71–92.

Tyler, K. *Whiteness, Class and the Legacies of Empire: On Home Ground*. Basingstoke: Palgrave Macmillan, 2012.

Walther, D.J. *Creating Germans Abroad: Cultural Policies and National Identity in Namibia*. Athens, OH: Ohio University Press, 2002.

Wildenthal, L. 'Notes on a History of "Imperial Turns" in Modern Germany', in A. Burton (ed.), *After the Imperial Turn: Thinking with and through the Nation* (Durham, NC and London: Duke University Press, 2003), 144–56.

Young, R.J.C. *Postcolonialism: A Very Short Introduction*. Oxford: Oxford University Press, 2003.

Zeller, J. 'Genozid und Gedenken: Ein dokumentarischer Überblick', in H. Melber (ed.), *Genozid und Gedenken: Namibisch-deutsche Geschichte und Gegenwart* (Frankfurt am Main: Brandes & Apsel, 2005), 163–88.

Zimmerer, J. 'Colonialism and Genocide', in M. Jefferies (ed.), *The Ashgate Research Companion to Imperial Germany* (Farnham: Ashgate, 2015), 433–51.

———. 'Krieg, KZ und Völkermord in Südwestafrika: Der erste deutsche Genozid', in J. Zimmerer and J. Zeller (eds), *Völkermord in Deutsch-Südwestafrika: Der Kolonialkrieg (1904-1908) in Namibia und seine Folgen* (Berlin: Ch. Links Verlag, 2004), 45–63.

Chapter 3

'Ich bin parteilich, subjektiv und emotional'

Eigensinn and the Narrative (Re)Construction of
Political Agency in Inge Viett's *Nie war ich furchtloser*

Katharina Karcher

It is easy to present Inge Viett's life as a story of violence, ideological illusions and political defeats. Born in 1944 into extreme poverty, she experienced neglect and abuse in the West German foster care system. In the early 1970s, she joined the armed leftist group 'Movement of June Second' (MJ2), which failed to win popular support. In the course of the 1970s, she was involved in two abductions and a range of other violent attacks. After the dissolution of the MJ2 in 1980, Inge Viett joined the 'Red Army Faction' (RAF) to continue her armed struggle against the West German state. Whilst working for the RAF in Paris, she was caught in a traffic control, which led to her shooting a police officer, who survived but was paralysed. To avoid arrest, Viett went into hiding in East Germany in the early 1980s and became a fervent supporter of state socialism at a point in time when the German Democratic Republic (GDR) was at the brink of collapse. Shortly after reunification, Viett was arrested in Magdeburg. Up to this day, she publicly defends the social and political values of the GDR. An article in the lifestyle magazine *Tempo* from the early 1990s described her as 'a freedom fighter, who took the liberty to deprive others of their freedom, and who was happy in a country that wasn't free. A communist who remained committed to communism although it had clearly failed',[1] Viett has rejected this reading of her life and has published an autobiography that she considers to be a 'piece of authentic counterhistory'.[2]

In August 1992, the Higher Regional Court of Koblenz sentenced Inge Viett to thirteen years in prison.[3] She experienced the prison system as a machine that threatened to destroy her sense of self by imposing its space, concept of time and hierarchical authority onto her. In this situation, life writing became both a survival strategy and a way of constructing and defending a sense of political agency. While in prison, Viett wrote two books, and further publications followed after her imprisonment.[4] In an interview that she gave shortly after her early release in January 1997, she claimed that writing had helped her to come to terms with the past and to cope with the overwhelming emptiness of prison.[5] Viett's openly 'biased, subjective and emotional'[6] account of her life can be read as a radical act of self-affirmation in a hostile environment and as a manifestation of *Eigensinn*. According to Alf Lüdtke, *Eigensinn*, which is commonly used to refer to a stubborn insistence on an opinion, can be a creative 'act of (re)appropriating alienated social relations' and of developing a sense of self and meaning in an environment characterized by significant power asymmetries.[7] Yet, *Alltagsgeschichte*, as practiced by Lüdtke and other historians, has shown that *Eigensinn* should not simply be equated with resistance against prevailing powers. Rather, it can be understood as a dynamic process of relating to the world that challenges 'the pattern of thought of one-dimensional bipolarity'.[8] To explore the dynamics and contradictions in Viett's ideas, actions and narrative, we need to avoid judging her based on dichotomies such as resistance/ political conformism and ethical behaviour/immoral conduct that feature prominently in Viett's autobiography and in previous research on political prison writing.

In his analysis of South African political prison writing in the apartheid era, Paul Gready argues that prison writing can function as a means of self-empowerment and as a form of political resistance.[9] His analysis shows that autobiography 'is one of a series of weapons which although potentially available to use to undermine the prisoner … is primarily a weapon of redress, a means of reducing pain and returning power to the prisoner'.[10] Gready's study focuses on the accounts of political activists who were part of a broad struggle against a system of institutionalized racism and oppression. While these men and women are commonly understood to be political prisoners, it is disputed whether this label can and should be applied to Viett and other members of armed leftist groups in West Germany. According to Kim Richmond, a political prisoner can be defined as one 'who has been charged with crimes pertaining to his or her political beliefs or activities'.[11] In her recent study *Women Political Prisoners in Germany: Narratives of Self and Captivity, 1915–91*, Richmond does not consider self-representations by Viett or other members of armed leftist groups in West Germany, because she refuses to see their 'violent, dangerous actions' as political.[12]

The aim of this chapter is not to assess whether Viett is morally entitled to claim that she is a revolutionary and/or political prisoner. Rather, it discusses her narrative as a means to gain control over her experience and to (re)create a sense of self and meaning against the background of the changing political landscape of postwar Germany. Whether she succeeded in conveying this image to her readership is another question. I agree with Richmond that there is a negotiation between how writers see themselves and how their readers see them.[13] Viett knows that many people consider her a terrorist. Despite or because of her public image, she claims the right to tell the story of her life as she experienced it.[14] Rather than trying to overcome the distance between her and her readers, Viett wants to confront them with a different perspective.

This chapter on Viett's autobiography *Nie war ich furchtloser* is based on *Anteilnahme* (empathy) – an affirmative yet critical involvement with her narrative. *Anteilnehmen*, as discussed by Lüdtke, 'does not aim at a naïve "nestling up" to the subject. Rather, what it facilitates is greater awareness of the shape of that *distance* separating "them" from "us"'.[15] As a political dissident, who has been involved in attacks that have hurt and killed people, Viett wrote her autobiography at least in part to explain and justify her actions. Although it is thus crucial not to mistake her subjective constantly evolving sense of authenticity for factual accuracy, Viett's narrative offers fascinating insights into the ways in which she constructed herself as a historical agent in a divided country and how she made sense of the reunification process. Throughout the book, Viett emphasizes her opposition to the Federal Republic of Germany (FRG). The FRG, as she understands it, is the product of a 'history of lost revolutions and repressed resistance' and a fascist, imperialist and authoritarian state.[16] By writing herself into the history of an ongoing revolutionary struggle against fascism and for a socialist society, Viett gave meaning to her life and imprisonment.

In her book *Terror and Democracy*, Karrin Hanshew argues that the left-wing political violence carried out by Viett and others was a 'litmus test for German democracy, where the responses of the state and populace were taken as evidence for the lessons West Germans had or had not learned from the past'.[17] While this is a widely accepted position, scholars come to different conclusions regarding the legitimacy and appropriateness of the state response to this perceived threat. According to Hanshew, the confrontation between the West German state and the RAF and other militant leftist groups led to a normalization of resistance to anti-democratic forces and established the state as a 'militant democracy' (*wehrhafte Demokratie*) – literally a democracy that can defend itself. Donatella Della Porta, by contrast, argues that political violence in the FRG was at least in part triggered by the reluctance of the existing political elite to integrate demands for reform. She criticizes the fact that state repression in the FRG 'created martyrs and myths' and contributed significantly to the radicalization of left-wing radicals such as Inge Viett.[18] As Viett's case shows, radical protest and political violence against the West German state cannot be examined in isolation from the GDR, because it led to alliances and divisions beyond the German-German border.

Rewriting a Traumatic Childhood

Inge Viett was born in Stemwarde in Schleswig-Holstein. In her autobiography, she notes that her entire knowledge about her early childhood stems from police reports.[19] Apparently, Viett's mother gravely neglected her seven children and lost custody of them shortly after the war. A report by the Federal Criminal Police Office from the late 1970s describes Viett's early childhood in drastic terms: 'Viett was born into dreadful circumstances. The mother is described as a slut. After two years of neglect by her mother, Viett is put into care and given to foster parents in 1950'.[20] The report does not mention a father or any other family members. After spending four years in an orphanage, Viett was adopted by a foster family in a small village in Schleswig-Holstein. Here, she experienced repeated abuse and an attempted rape by a local resident.[21] After she managed to avoid him and fight him off on numerous occasions, the man tried to rape her in the moorlands. The only reason he eventually let her go was, according to Viett, that she whispered: 'We're drowning'.[22] Rather than stating an objective truth or being a deceptive manoeuvre, this claim was a genuine expression of Viett's subjective experience and her *Eigensinn*. During the attempted rape, she could hear the gurgling sound of the muddy swamp water and felt that she was sinking into the earth, even though she realized soon afterwards that the ground was perfectly stable.[23]

At the age of fourteen, Viett fell in love with a female teacher. Although she mentions on several occasions that she feels attracted to women, her sexual identity plays a minor role in her narrative. In Viett's autobiography, lesbianism is not an 'exclusive and continuous ground of identity and politics'.[24] Rather, it seems that the author's sexual orientation was one of many reasons why she felt different from her peers and why she rejected a conventional lifestyle. As soon as she was old enough, Viett ran away from her foster family.[25] After completing her basic education at school, with a focus on domestic science, she studied to become a gymnastics teacher. She left college without a degree. In the following years, she worked as a stripper, courier, maid and in a range of other jobs in different cities in West Germany.[26]

There can be no doubt that Viett's belief in the socialist project has helped her to come to terms with the neglect, violence and discrimination that she had experienced in her childhood and adolescence. Although she has never tried to find her mother, Viett emphasizes that she holds no grudge against the woman 'who had to give birth to seven children that she could not protect and love'.[27] Retrospectively, she sees her mother as a victim of a class-based society shaped by fascist ideology, and she claims that the people in the village where her foster family lived were influenced by the same worldview. Apparently, villagers greeted each other with 'Heil Hitler' and the recent past was a taboo topic in the local school.[28] According to Viett, the fascist ideology in the village led to a hatred against everything and everyone different.[29] Since she was different from other children in the village, Viett experienced discrimination and violent attacks. By presenting herself as a victim of the fascist ideologies that have led to the Holocaust, Viett aligns herself with the victims of the Nazi regime and distances herself from the generation of perpetrators and followers.

Viett's narrative suggests that she understood the full extent of the problem of *Vergangenheitsbewältigung* in the Federal Republic only after spending some time in the GDR. In the early 1980s, she and other RAF members spent several weeks in the GDR to receive military training. As part of a 'political education' programme for the participants in this training, Stasi officers organized a guided tour at Buchenwald concentration camp. Viett describes the trip to this 'place of horror' (*Stätte des Grauens*) as a deeply upsetting and eye-opening experience. She notes that she was appalled to see 'with how much cowardice and deception' the generation of her parents in the FRG had 'covered the stinking morass of the past with a volcanic eruption of consumption'.[30] Here and elsewhere in the book, Viett establishes a strong link between fascism and capitalism, which enables her to portray the self-declared anti-fascist and anti-capitalist GDR as the better German state. Apparently, she and her comrades felt overwhelmed by a sense of shame and guilt after their trip to Buchenwald – feelings which their hosts found difficult to understand. Viett reasons that this can be explained by the fact that people in the GDR were living in a different history.[31] In more than one way, Viett's autobiography can be read as an attempt to write herself into this different history.

Politicization and Radicalization in West Berlin

Although Viett mentions the 'Easter Marches' against nuclear weapons and other West German protest movements in the early and mid-1960s, she openly admits that she took little notice of these groups. While many young people in West Berlin and other university cities took to the streets, Viett showed no interest in politics.[32] This changed in 1968, when she left her partner in Wiesbaden and quit her job. Attracted by the vibrant student culture and the subcultural scene in West Berlin, she moved into one of the first communes in Kreuzberg. The house was located close to the Berlin Wall, where rents were particularly low. At this point in time, Viett had no desire to explore the world on the other side of the wall. Retrospectively, she criticizes the fact that the 'blurred mosaic picture' (*verschwommenes Mosaikbild*) of East Germany that she and other young people in West Germany had was based on bias rather than a real engagement with the GDR.[33]

In the 1960s, West Berlin was a hotbed of student protests and a hub of counter-cultural activity. Initially, Viett showed little interest in the theory and politics of the New Left in West Berlin. Rather than discussing revolutionary violence in the 'Republikanische Club', as Rudi Dutschke and other student activists did, she experimented with drugs and alternative forms of living. In this period, the people who inspired her were thus not Herbert Marcuse and Frantz Fanon but counter-cultural icons such as the actor Magdalena Montezuma and the film maker and gay rights activist Rosa von Praunheim. In her autobiography, Viett describes her commune in Kreuzberg as follows:

> This was the place where men and women met to discuss the newest exciting events in the 'political scene', smoke good pot, listen to records, drink Chinese tea, maybe to take some LSD, or simply to show off a little – to be hip – when the conversation turned to Andy Warhol or the 'Kommune 1', or Che Guevara, or Ravi Shankar.[34]

Viett identified with a part of the subcultural scene in West Berlin that became known as the 'Berlin Underground'. According to Anja Schwanhäußer, the Berlin Underground was a broad cultural movement in the 1960s and 1970s, whose followers rejected the traditional bourgeois norms and experimented with a range of alternative lifestyles.[35] Even if there were numerous intersections and overlaps between the Berlin Underground and the student movement, the two subcultures should be distinguished for three reasons. First, the lifestyle of most students at the time differed considerably from that of the individuals and groups associated with the Berlin Underground. Only parts of the anti-authoritarian wing in the student movement led similarly unconventional lives to many people in the drug scene, the *'Gammler'* movement or in the first communes.[36] Second, groups in the Berlin Underground tended to be less intensely intellectual and more accessible to young people from lower-class backgrounds than many student organizations.[37] Third, similar to other hedonistic youth subcultures in the 1950s and early 1960s, the individuals and groups associated with the Berlin Underground had – at least initially – no political agenda. Rather, the young people in this diverse subcultural scene shared a desire to experience a life outside existing social norms and constraints.

Viett's narrative suggests that her politicization in the late 1960s was not the result of intellectual analyses but of specific bodily experiences and social perceptions. A road trip to Northern Africa left a lasting impression on her. Viett notes that she had seen poverty and exploitation in Germany, but she was horrified by the extent of suffering in Third World countries. She writes: 'What I saw on this and other trips to disadvantaged, pillaged and colonized parts of the world was the result of centuries of the predatory lust for property and power in the "civilized" Western world'.[38] Viett claims that after her trip to Northern Africa she read Fanon and understood immediately what he meant.[39] Like many student activists, she came to the conclusion that oppressed people in the Third World were left with no alternative but to use violence to fight against colonial oppression. After her return to West Berlin, she felt appalled by the consumerism in West Germany. She began to avoid shopping malls and avenues with luxury shops in West Berlin, and gave away antique furniture and other personal property.

In the late 1960s, West Berlin became a hotbed of leftist political violence. In this period, Viett and others in the Berlin Underground began to 'fight back' against police brutality during drug raids.[40] Initially, their activities limited themselves to vandalism, arson and bombings directed against property.[41] Viett and her friends smashed the windows of porn shops, carried out arson attacks against the cars of Springer employees and tried to defend squatted social centres with Molotov cocktails.[42] As Klaus Weinhauer highlights, the recourse to violence in the Berlin Underground was mostly spontaneous and defensive, but some of the actors involved radicalized further and turned to more organized forms of violence.[43]

In 1969, a loose network of occupants and visitors of two radical leftist communes in West Berlin formed the militant groups 'Hash-Rebels' and the 'Tupamaros West-Berlin' (TW). Both groups are direct predecessors of the Movement of June Second, which Viett joined in 1972. In February 1969, more than a year before the RAF committed its first attack, members of the TW made plans to kill US president Richard Nixon during a visit to West Berlin.[44] On 9 November in the same year, they planted a bomb in a Jewish community centre.[45] Although these and other attacks in the late 1960s did not claim any lives, they illustrate that some groups in the Berlin Underground no longer shied away from violence against people.

While members of the Berlin Underground formed the first militant leftist group in the FRG, the first armed attack in West Berlin was carried out by a group led by former student activists. In May 1970, the student Gudrun Ensslin, the lawyer Horst Mahler, the journalist Ulrike Meinhof and several other people liberated Andreas Baader by force of arms from prison in West Berlin and founded the Red Army Faction (RAF). As the name indicates, the group wanted to form the military wing of a not yet existing communist party. The RAF understood itself as an avant-garde expediting a revolution, which it expected to be carried out by the working class and other oppressed groups all over the globe. Due to their ideology and theoretical background, the founding members of the RAF quickly earned the reputation of 'Leninists with guns'.[46] Soon, the group realized that their attacks were not mobilizing the masses in West Germany nor in the Third World. Facing a lack of support by the working class, the RAF drew on theories of revolution that did not make proletarian participation a precondition. The group found this theoretical framework in the 'foco theories'[47] proposed by Che Guevara, Fidel Castro and Régis Debray. According to this theoretical framework, the support of the masses was no longer a crucial precondition for an armed struggle.

Initially, the founding members of the RAF hoped that the enemy of their enemy would be their friend. Shortly after the RAF's formation in 1970, founding member Meinhof urged the GDR authorities to support the group's armed struggle. While Stasi officials allowed RAF members to use the GDR as a transit country, they rejected the group's request to plan attacks from East Germany. Previous research suggests that this decision was as much the result of diplomatic considerations as of political disagreements.[48] The RAF's ideological stance deviated from the Marxist-Leninist position of the GDR authorities. Amongst other things, Stasi officials criticized the fact that the RAF pursued a strategy of 'individual terror' and disapproved of the fact that the group had abandoned the notion of the working class as the revolutionary subject. Despite these ideological differences, the Stasi not only tolerated but actively supported armed leftist groups in West Germany. According to Martin Jander, this can be attributed to the fact that they had common enemies: the Federal Republic of Germany and its allies, in particular the

United States.[49] As Jander highlights, the RAF and the Stasi even used similar terms to describe these enemies: fascism, imperialism and predatory capitalism. These concepts feature prominently in Viett's narrative and provide a link between her life as an urban guerrilla fighter in West Berlin, her exile in the GDR and her imprisonment and political activism in the post-reunification period.

Although Viett and others in the Berlin Underground shared the RAF's anti-imperialist, anti-fascist and anti-capitalist stance, they rejected the vanguardist position of the RAF. In January 1972, some of the remaining TW and several other small militant leftist groups in the Berlin Underground founded the MJ2 as a militant alternative to the RAF. Most group members identified as anarchists, at least in the broad sense of the term, others as Stalinists, but all were clearly more interested in practising the armed struggle than theorizing about it. They wanted to be a 'fun guerrilla' and hoped to mobilize revolutionary forces in the working class by adopting a more populist line than the RAF. Also, the internal structure of the group differed from that of the RAF. The RAF was a hierarchical and centralist organization and, after Baader's rescue in 1970, operated almost entirely underground. The founding members of the MJ2, in contrast, wanted to avoid going underground for as long as possible. Moreover, they aimed to create a less hierarchical, horizontally connected network of local groups.[50]

Viett joined the MJ2 soon after its formation in 1972. One of her first tasks for the group was to help carry out a series of attacks against the British yachting club in Berlin against two cars belonging to the Allied forces. The attacks were a rather spontaneous and ill-prepared response to the events during Bloody Sunday on 30 January in Northern Ireland.[51] One civilian died whilst trying to deactivate one of the explosive devices. To avoid arrest, the actors involved in the attacks went underground. In the course of the 1970s, Viett was involved in two abductions and a range of other violent attacks. Stasi officials took a similar stance to the MJ2 as to the RAF: although they distanced themselves from the group's approach,[52] they allowed group members to use the GDR as a country of transit.[53]

Until the dissolution of the MJ2 in 1980, Viett was a driving force in the group. Although she lived in constant fear of arrest, Viett experienced this period of her life as liberating and fulfilling:

> At no point in my life have I been less scared than during this time in the underground, a place which allowed me a new, different existence outside of the ugly world. I have never been freer, never been less tied to my own

responsibility than in this state of complete detachment from state authority and from social norms.[54]

According to Viett, her involvement in the Berlin Underground and in the MJ2 opened the door to a utopian social space that was free from authoritarian structures and oppressive gender norms.

While Viett and other women in the MJ2 wanted to be equal to their male comrades in every regard, they did not identify as feminists. In an interview in 1997, she stressed this point clearly: 'None of us had a background in the feminist scene … We did not deliberately choose to go through a process of liberation as women … We simply made a decision and then we fought and did the same things as men. For us, that was no man-woman question. Underground, the old role models were irrelevant to us'.[55] Although Viett distances herself from feminism, her narrative can be read as an attempt to write herself into a history of revolutionary women.[56] It is interesting in this context to note how she compensated for a lack of female role models in her own life by creating narrative links to Rosa Luxemburg and to women partisans. The way in which Viett describes one of her guns in her autobiography illustrates this point: 'Maybe this gun had once protected a woman partisan. It was an excellent fit for a woman's hand. I cherished it like a precious heirloom'.[57] This imagined bond with revolutionary women is another manifestation how Viett developed and maintained a sense of political agency and historical continuity that was radically different from those of most other women of her generation.

Even in their utopian clandestine world, the members of the MJ2 could not escape the quickly changing political reality in the FRG. In the late 1970s, political differences among group members became an increasing source of tension. The trigger for the internal conflict was a falling out over the events during the 'German Autumn'[58] in 1977. In an interview in 1978, some members of the MJ2 openly criticized the hijacking of an airplane in October 1977 and other RAF attacks during the German Autumn as 'anti-grass roots' (*volksfeindlich*).[59] They defended the idea of the 'fun guerrilla' (*Spaßguerilla*) and insisted that the armed struggle in West Germany could succeed only with humour and provocation. Viett and other group members, by contrast, criticized a lack of seriousness in the group. They formed the 'internationalist wing' of the MJ2, which gravitated increasingly towards the course of the RAF. The internal discord in the MJ2 reached a peak in June 1980, when a part of the group declared the end of the MJ2, and Viett and a few others joined the RAF.

Reconfiguring a Revolutionary Identity in the GDR

Throughout the 1970s, the Stasi had followed the activities of the MJ2 and other armed leftist groups in the FRG closely. Archived interview transcripts suggest that state authorities in the GDR had been aware of Viett's involvement in the MJ2 at least since November 1973, when MJ2 founding member Michael Baumann had provided Stasi officers with detailed information about her and other group members.[60] Viett's narrative suggests that she and other members of armed leftist groups in West Germany used the GDR as a transit country without caring much about its culture and people.[61] On one occasion, she was stopped by GDR border guards and interrogated by a Stasi officer. Apparently, her interrogator 'Harry' welcomed her as a 'comrade'. According to Viett, he emphasized that, whilst rejecting terrorist tactics, the GDR had no intention of betraying her and her fellow fighters to the common enemy.[62] One of the most striking features of Viett's narrative is her portrayal of her interactions with the State Ministry for State Security. Since she has only good things to say about the Stasi and provides no critical details about her agreements with East German state authorities, Viett has repeatedly been accused of being a Stasi collaborator.[63]

In May 1978, Viett and other MJ2 members liberated a fellow group member from prison in West Berlin. As on other occasions, the group managed to escape via East Berlin. When trying to travel to Czechoslovakia, they were arrested in Bulgaria, and Viett had to make use of her connections to the Stasi to avoid extradition to West Germany.[64] Despite her increasingly close collaboration with the Stasi, Viett stresses that she remained sceptical of secret services in socialist states, because she considered them to be as 'obscure and unpredictable' as their Western counterparts.[65] The facts tell a different tale: in the following years, Viett acted as a key link between the Stasi and the militant Left in West Germany. Soon after joining the RAF in 1980, she acted as a mediator when eight fellow fighters wanted to lay down their arms and make a fresh start in the GDR.[66] While Stasi officials rejected requests for direct financial support, they agreed to provide military training for Viett and other RAF members in the GDR.

A few months after participating in this training, Viett told the Stasi officials that she, too, wanted to make a fresh start in East Germany. It is difficult to assess whether this decision was primarily the result of the growing isolation of the militant Left and of an existential crisis triggered by the shooting of the police officer in Paris, as her narrative suggests, or whether there were other factors at play.[67] To prepare for her new life, Viett had to participate in Stasi training. Here she learned to speak like GDR citizens and worked her way through a local library: 'GDR literature, socialist history, socialist economics, poetry'.[68] Despite all her efforts, she found it difficult to familiarize herself with culture and everyday language in the GDR. Small mistakes and misunderstandings were tell-tale signs of her background in the FRG. She used the term *Supermarkt* (supermarket) rather than *Kaufhalle* (shopping hall), she struggled with abbreviations that were obvious to GDR citizens and she found it difficult to relate to the concerns and aspirations of people who had grown up in the GDR.

One of the first things that Viett noticed in East Germany was the constant presence of political banners and slogans. She recalls seeing slogans such as 'I am a worker, but who is more?' and 'Build socialism' on walls and signboards in the GDR.[69] Unlike many other people, Viett found this state propaganda straightforward and convincing. Not without reason, she argues that many Western critics of the GDR would conveniently ignore the ideologically charged nature of public spaces in the Western world, which manifested itself in ubiquitous advertising campaigns, the commercialization of everyday life and the privatization of the public sector.[70] According to Viett, the crucial difference between political propaganda in the FRG and in East Germany was that the former promoted consumerism while the latter endorsed humanitarian values.

After months of intensive preparation by the Stasi, Viett moved to a small flat in a *Neubaugebiet* (new development) in Dresden. Here, she introduced herself as Eva Maria Sommer – a forty-year-old woman from West Germany who had moved to the GDR from West Germany because she considered it a better political system. Although she tried to adapt to her environment in Dresden, Viett never managed to allay the mistrust of her neighbours and colleagues. Her life narrative met with incomprehension, and she found it difficult to make friends. Unlike Susanne Albrecht and other former RAF members who had gone into hiding in the GDR, Viett refused to marry and did not want to have a family. This position distinguished her from most of her co-workers in Dresden, who she describes as 'typical GDR women: qualified, married, one child, facing a double burden'.[71] In a recent study of German gender politics, Myra Marx Ferree emphasizes that '[a] woman in the GDR had been defined as a "worker-mother" who was a full-time employee as well as responsible for children and housework'.[72] The norm in the FRG, by contrast, was a 'wife mother', who remained 'economically and socially subordinate' to her husband.[73]

Although Viett paints a rosy picture of life in the GDR, she struggled to fit in. This was partly because she found it difficult to avoid West German figures of speech and gestures and adopted a Stasi narrative that left many people in her environment unconvinced, and partly because she refused to enter a marriage of convenience and rejected the model of the 'worker-mother'. To calm down her nerves after the first day at work as Eva-Maria Sommer, Viett went to a bar and ordered 'Cognac' (French brandy) – a request to which the waitress responded with disbelief and sarcasm. After the second 'Weinbrand' (local brandy), Viett started to feel more positive about her situation, and soon she began to see the run-down photo laboratory where she worked as a space of creative improvisation and anarchic joy.[74] She writes: 'after a long period of social isolation, I felt a profound willingness to embrace everything in a posi-tive and constructive manner, a feeling which had emerged like a flying albatross spreading its wings'.[75] This emotional state and the actions resulting from it were not primarily gestures of compliance or resistance in relation to the existing political powers. Rather they were manifesta-tions of *Eigensinn* that have affected her status and prospects in complex and at times contradictory ways.

Apart from her marital status and naïve enthusiasm for the GDR, Eva Maria Sommer fed suspicions with her Lada. Viett notes that she learned only later that her Russian car had probably excited a similar amount of envy as a fancy sports car in the FRG.[76] After three and a half years in Dresden, an acquaintance recognized her on a wanted poster in the FRG. Once again, Inge Viett had to go into hiding and once again, she asked the Stasi to help her make a fresh start. In 1987, she moved to Magdeburg, where she rented a flat under the name Eva Maria Schnell. According to her new 'Legende' (life story), she had been born on 15 January 1946 in Moscow and was a widow with a degree in economics. Viett's new life story was not only closer to the biographies of her colleagues in the GDR, it also allowed her to rewrite her traumatic childhood. She made up a father who joined the Red Army to fight against Nazism, and set her birthday on the day on which Rosa Luxemburg was shot in Berlin.[77] By creating a symbolic link to Luxemburg, Viett associated herself with a revolutionary thinker and activist who was immensely popular in East Germany. Up to this day, thousands of people gather on 15 January in Berlin to commemorate the murder of Luxemburg and her fellow cam-paigner Karl Liebknecht.[78]

Viett found it much easier to settle into her life in Magdeburg than in Dresden. After several years in the GDR, she was more confident in eve-ryday life situations and found it less difficult to build relationships with neighbours and colleagues. Her new job was to organize summer camps for the children of the 6,500 employees of the Schwermaschinenkombinat Karl Liebknecht.[79] Apparently, she liked this job and was popular with her colleagues.[80] At no point does Viett mention how her life in the

GDR relates to that of her heroine Rosa Luxemburg, but this, too, can be understood as an expression of *Eigensinn*. Viett openly acknowledges the subjective and emotional nature of her narrative, and she makes no effort to fill the gaps and to reconcile contradictions in her account.

In Magdeburg, Viett lived in a two-room apartment in a new housing development in Magdeburg Nord. In 1991, the journalist Christoph Scheuring described this part of Magdeburg as a 'dormitory town – a sad place during the day and a cemetery at night'.[81] Viett considers such negative depictions of life in the GDR as symptomatic of the 'intellectual arrogance' (*intellektuelle Hochmütigkeit*) of the bourgeois Left in the FRG.[82] In her autobiography, she emphasizes that her experience of life in the GDR was profoundly different: 'The eight years that I spent in the GDR were too short to be bored for a single day; but they were long enough to develop a sense of shared responsibility for the heights and pitfalls, for the failures and achievements in the historically unique struggle for an alternative to the capitalist society'.[83]

Although Viett's conformist behaviour in the GDR could be seen as a clear break with her revolutionary past, her narrative presents it as a continuation and extension of her revolutionary socialist politics in West Germany. Kim Richmond rightly emphasizes that '[a]utobiography creates the impression of a consistent identity over time and therefore it can, in many cases, represent the author's pursuit of continuity and wholeness of self'.[84] According to this approach, Viett's narrative can be read as an attempt to create a consistent revolutionary socialist identity, which evolved over time from an armed struggle against fascism, imperialism and capitalism to a non-violent but no less committed struggle for an anti-fascist, anti-imperialist and anti-capitalist society.

Viett's blatant disregard for political repression in the GDR shows how strongly she identified with the East German state. Even the fact that social and political structures around her were disintegrating in the late 1980s could not undermine her faith that the GDR was the 'better half' of Germany.[85] In autumn 1989, she attended one of the Monday prayers in the Cathedral of Magdeburg. In an internal newsletter at her workplace, Viett warned colleagues in Madgeburg that this and other gatherings in churches were part of a counter-revolution that jeopardized the only chance of building a 'truly democratic, humanist, social and antifascist society'.[86] While many of her fellow workers were trying to leave the country, Inge Viett put all her energy into the next summer camp.[87] In the wake of the victory of the 'Alliance for Germany' in the elections to the People's Chamber on 18 March 1990, she was finally willing to accept that the population would not stand up for state socialism. She notes in her autobiography 'I feel as if the era that I have been part of is coming to an end'.[88] Although she knew that this political change meant that her arrest was imminent, she made no attempt to escape.[89] After positioning herself as an opponent of the political and economic system of the FRG and supporter of the East German state socialism, Viett saw the reunification of Germany not as a positive development but as a hostile takeover.

Viett's arrest on 12 June 1990 was the result of concerted efforts by East and West German police authorities. Apparently, neighbours had recognized her on a wanted poster and reported her to West German police authorities who passed the message on to their East German colleagues. At a press conference on 13 June, a spokesman from the Federal Criminal Police Office praised the cooperation of police officers in the new and old states. The minister of the Interior of the GDR Peter-Michael Diestel raised hopes for further arrests of former terrorists and condemned the '"unimaginably diabolical collaboration" between the dissolved Ministry for State Security and the West German terrorists' in the strongest terms.[90] By distancing themselves emphatically from their former 'comrades' in the RAF and MJ2, GDR authorities emphasized a new unity with their former enemy West Germany and underlined their commitment to the democratic principles of the FRG.

Conclusion: (Re)Constructing a Militant Life in Reunited Germany

According to Christian Davenport, repression is present in all nation states but is perceived differently in different political contexts.[91] Indeed, while there is now a broad consensus that state repression in Nazi Germany and in the GDR was illegitimate, a certain degree of state repression in the FRG and other democratic states tends to be considered necessary and legitimate in the fight against terrorism – even if it involves measures that restrict the freedom of individual citizens and/or inflicts bodily pain on them. Inge Viett's narrative challenges this widely accepted view of state repression in twentieth-century Germany in two ways. Firstly, she argues that the West German state was a fascist, imperialist, authoritarian and thus illegitimate political regime, in which revolutionary violence was a necessary response to state repression. Secondly, she refuses to condemn state repression in the GDR and portrays political protest against the regime as counter-revolutionary. Following this logic, she claims that her trial had a double function for the newly reunified German state: to persecute and denunciate the urban guerrilla in West Germany and to discredit the GDR by criminalizing the Stasi.[92]

In prison, the 'narrative (re)construction of [her] revolutionary self' became a central project for Inge Viett.[93] In this context, life writing was both a survival strategy and a form of resistance. Her narrative illustrates that autobiographical accounts do not merely document historical events. As the author of her own life story, Viett could select, structure, hide and resignify events in ways that allowed her to develop a sense of self and meaning in a changing political landscape. Which events and developments are considered meaningful by the author (and her critics) tells us as much about her as an individual as about the political contexts in which the book was written and read.

Gready rightly emphasizes that even 'within autobiography the written word is not completely one's own, control is always incomplete and it remains to some extent a compromise, the self and the self-image do not coincide, they can never coincide in the written word'.[94] In 2000, Inge Viett threatened legal action against the film maker Volker Schlöndorff, who had used material from her autobiography for his film *Die Stille nach dem Schuss* (The Legend of Rita) without seeking her permission.[95] Schlöndorff countered that the film plot was inspired by Viett's life rather than based on her book, and it was not his intention to tell the story from her point of view.[96] However, for Viett there was more at stake than her rights as an author. As this chapter has shown, her narrative allowed her to relate differently to the poverty and neglect that she experienced as a child and to create an imaged bond with Rosa Luxemburg and other revolutionary women. Most importantly, it enabled her to create a consistent revolutionary socialist identity in a period marked by drastic political changes.

Lütdke's notion of *Eigensinn* can help to complicate this image in a productive way. Although Viett's narrative neatly divides most of her actions into acts of resistance against the FRG and activities in support of socialism, her views and actions do not always fit into this bipolar model. While Viett claims to be a committed anti-fascist who was deeply moved by the plight of Jewish-German citizens during the Third Reich, her political activity does not include a single attempt to show solidarity with the victims of the Holocaust or to protest against anti-Semitism. For the most part, Viett's actions as a member of armed leftist groups in West Germany focused on the release of imprisoned comrades and/or sought to secure the financial survival of the groups. A number of attacks seem to have hurt or killed people for the sole reason that they happened to be in the wrong place at the wrong time. Lüdtke writes about everyday life at the workplace during German fascism that the 'preferred way of displaying Eigensinn was not resistance against "above" but distance from everyone including your own work-mates'.[97] Viett's decision to go underground and to stay in hiding for so many years was at least in part related to a desire to avoid a long prison sentence and to live an unconventional life that was neither that of the 'wife-mother' in the FRG nor that of the 'worker-mother' in the GDR. Viett experienced her life underground as free from authoritarian structures and oppressive gender norms and tried to keep up aspects of this lifestyle after she had made a fresh start in the GDR, even if that was clearly not advantageous.

Katharina Karcher is Lecturer in German at the University of Birmingham. Her research focuses on feminist theory, European women's movements and the history and memory of political protest, extremism and violence. Her monograph *Sisters in Arms? Militant Feminisms in the Federal Republic of Germany since 1968* (Berghahn, 2017) analyses the role of confrontational and violent tactics in three major feminist struggles in post-Second World War Germany: the movement against the abortion ban, the struggle against violence against women and a solidarity campaign for women workers in the Third World. A German edition of the book was published in 2018 by Assoziation A.

Notes

1. 'eine Freiheitskämpferin, die sich die Freiheit genommen hatte, anderen Menschen die Freiheit zu nehmen, und die danach in einem unfreien Land glücklich war. Eine Kommunistin, die dem Kommunismus die Treue hielt, obwohl dieser sich schon selbst beerdigt hatte'. Scheuring, 'Schuld und Sühne'.
2. 'ein Stück authentische Gegengeschichte'. Viett, *Nie war ich furchtloser*, 8.
3. Rosenkranz, 'Offene Rechnung'.
4. Publications by Inge Viett include autobiographical books and travelogues. See, e.g., Viett, *Einsprüche*; *Nie war ich furchtloser*; *Cuba Libre bittersüss*; *Morengas Erben*.
5. Radio Interview with Inge Viett in the programme *SWR 3 Leute*, 1 April 1997.
6. 'parteilich, subjektiv und emotional'. Viett, *Nie war ich furchtloser*, 249.
7. Lüdtke, *The History of Everyday Life*, 313.
8. Lüdtke, 'Alltagsgeschichte: Aneignung und Akteure: Oder – es hat kaum begonnen!'. *Werkstattgeschichte* 17 (1997), 84.
9. Gready, 'Autobiography and the "Power of Writing"', 493.
10. Ibid., 521.
11. Richmond, *Women Political Prisoners in Germany*, 5–6.
12. Ibid., 169.
13. Ibid., 12–13.
14. Ibid., 8.
15. Lüdtke, *The History of Everyday Life*, 24. Editors' note: 'empathy' is used by Lüdtke in the sense of compassion – feeling with an other – as opposed to the notion of *Einfühlung* as

deployed by early twentieth-century empathy theorists including Theodor Lipps. For Lipps, 'empathy' was a process of finding oneself in the other; in Lüdtke, the emphasis is on how empathy facilitates insight into the subjective integrity of the other as an entity beyond the self. See Lipps, *Ästhetik*.

16. 'die Geschichte verlorener Revolutionen und niedergeschlagenen Widerstands'. Viett, *Nie war ich furchtloser*, 7.

17. Hanshew, *Terror and Democracy in West Germany*.

18. Della Porta, *Social Movements*, 191.

19. Viett, *Nie war ich furchtloser*, 16.

20. 'Die VIETT wird in unmögliche häusliche Verhältnisse hineingeboren. Die Mutter wird als Schlampe bezeichnet. Mit 2 Jahren wird die VIETT wegen völliger Verwahrlosung durch die Mutter in Fürsorgeerziehung untergebracht und 1950 Pflegeeltern übergeben'. Hamburger Institut für Sozialgeschichte (HIS), KOK 08/002.

21. Viett, *Nie war ich furchtloser*, 36, 44–45.

22. 'Wir versinken'. Ibid., 44–45.

23. Ibid., 45.

24. Martin, 'Lesbian Identity', 390.

25. Viett, *Nie war ich furchtloser*, 50.

26. Ibid., 68.

27. 'die sieben Kinder gebären musste, die sie nicht ernähren, behüten und lieben konnte'. Ibid., 17.

28. Ibid., 33, 21.

29. Ibid., 21.

30. 'Mit welcher Feigheit und Täuschung hat diese Generation im westlichen Teil Deutschlands ihren Morast mit dem vulkanischen Konsumausbruch nach dem Krieg bedeckt'. Ibid., 232.

31. Ibid., 233. For a detailed discussion of the legacy of the Nazi past in the two Germanys, see Herf, *Divided Memory*.

32. Viett, *Nie war ich furchtloser*, 61.

33. Ibid., 252.

34. 'Hier trafen Frau und Mann sich, um über die neusten aufregenden Ereignisse in der "Politszene" zu sprechen, guten Shit zu rauchen, die neusten Platten zu hören, chinesischen Tee zu trinken, vielleicht einen gemeinsamen LSD-Trip zu unternehmen, oder auch nur um ein bisschen anzugeben, "in" zu sein, wenn es um Andy Warhol oder Kommune I oder Che Guevara oder Ravi Shankar ging'. Ibid., 73.

35. Schwanhäusser, *Stilrevolte Underground*, 19.

36. Grob, *Das Kleidungsverhalten jugendlicher Protestgruppen*, 203.

37. Siegfried, *Time Is on My Side*, 402.

38. 'Was ich auf dieser und späteren Reisen in die benachteiligten, vom Kolonialismus ausgeplünderten Regionen der Welt sah, … waren Ergebnisse von einer jahrundertealten räuberischen Besitz- und Machtgier der "zivilisierten" westlichen Welt'. Viett, *Nie war ich furchtloser*, 78.

39. Ibid., 79.

40. Fritzsch and Reinders, *Die Bewegung 2. Juni*, 22–23.

41. Neidhardt, 'Linker und rechter Terrorismus', 438.

42. Viett, *Nie war ich furchtloser*, 83–85.

43. Weinhauer, Requate and Haupt, *Terrorismus in der Bundesrepublik*, 225.

44. Wunschik, 'Die Bewegung 2. Juni', 542–43.

45. On the anniversary of the Jewish pogrom in 1938, the TW carried out an attack against a Jewish community centre and painted pro-Palestinian slogans on Jewish memorials in Berlin. Whilst distancing itself emphatically from the anti-Semitism of the Third Reich, the group considered Israel a fascist state and wanted to show solidarity with the

Palestinian people. For a detailed discussion of anti-Semitism in the West German Left, see Weiss, '"Volksklassenkampf"'.

46. Schildt and Siegfried, *Deutsche Kulturgeschichte*, 384.

47. 'Foco' is Spanish for focus. 'Foco theories' or focalism is a form of guerrilla warfare that focuses on operations by small and mobile groups of fighters that are supported by larger parts of the population.

48. Jander, 'Differenzen im antiimperialistischen Kampf', 699.

49. Ibid., 697.

50. Wunschik, 'Die Bewegung 2. Juni', 557.

51. On 30 January 1972, British soldiers killed and wounded twenty-six unarmed protesters during a demonstration in Derry, Northern Ireland. For a detailed discussion of the events, see Walsh, *Bloody Sunday*.

52. In an internal document from 1978, a high-ranking member of the armed forces stated: 'Die Handlungen dieser Personen [three members of the MJ2] werden ausgehend von unserer grundsätzlichen Position ... nicht gebilligt. Aber – ausgehend vom Klassenstandpunkt – ist dies absolut kein Grund, den Imperialisten, insbesondere in der BRD, in irgendeiner Weise gegen diese Personenkreise Unterstützung zu geben' (Stasi Archive Berlin, MfS HA XXII 19188, 18).

53. Detailed descriptions of many of these trips can be found in the Stasi Archive. See, e.g., MfS HA XX AIG 496, MfS XV 17463/91, MfS HA XXII 19188.

54. 'Nie in meinem Leben war ich sicherer und furchtloser als in dieser Zeit im Untergrund, dem Ort, der ein neues, anderes Sein außerhalb der häßlichen Welt gestattete. Nie war ich freier nie war ich gebundener an meine eigene Verantwortung als in dem Zustand völliger Abnabelung von der staatlichen Autorität und von gesellschaftlichen Vorgaben. Kein Gesetz, keine äußere Gewalt bestimmte mehr mein Verhältnis zur Welt, zu meinen Mitmenschen, zum Leben zum Tod'. Viett, *Nie war ich furchtloser*, 114–15.

55. 'Wir sind alle nicht aus der feministischen Bewegung gekommen ... Wir haben nicht bewusst so einen Frauenbefreiungsprozess für uns durchleben wollen ... Wir haben uns einfach entschieden, und wir haben dann gekämpft und dieselben Dinge getan wie die Männer. Es war für uns keine Frage Mann-Frau. Das alte Rollenverständnis hat für uns in der Illegalität keine Rolle gespielt'. Diewald-Kerkmann, 'Frauen in der RAF'.

56. Viett, *Nie war ich furchtloser*, 239.

57. 'Vielleicht hatte sie bereits einer Partisanin Schutz gegeben. Sie war für eine Frauenhand vortrefflich geeignet. Ich pflegte sie wie ein kostbares Erbstück'. Ibid., 119.

58. The German Autumn (*Deutscher Herbst*) refers to a dramatic peak in the escalating conflict between the RAF and the West German state. It began with the abduction of the business executive Hanns-Martin Schleyer in September 1977 and ended with the death of the detained RAF founder members in October of the same year.

59. Fritzsch and Reinders, *Die Bewegung 2. Juni*, 122.

60. HIS, MfS 73/022 KOPIE BStU Archiv Nr.: 2984/74.

61. Viett, *Nie war ich furchtloser*, 225.

62. Ibid., 179–80.

63. For details, see, e.g., Kanonenberg and Müller, *Die RAF-Stasi Connection*.

64. Viett, *Nie war ich furchtloser*, 206.

65. 'auch sie sind undurchschaubar und unberechenbar'. Ibid.

66. Jander, 'Differenzen im antiimperialistischen Kampf', 711.

67. In September 1981, the French police officer Francis Violleau wanted to fine Viett for a traffic offence. After a wild chase, Viett found herself cornered and shot Violleau to escape. Paralysed since the attack, he died in 2000 at the age of fifty-four. Moréas, 'Un nom sur une porte'.

68. Viett, *Nie war ich furchtloser*, 255.

69. 'Ich bin Arbeiter, wer ist mehr?', 'Den Sozialismus aufbauen'. Ibid., 253.

70. 'Wohin du in der kapitalistischen Gesellschaft den Blick auch wendest, die Schritte lenkst, die Sinne richtest, stößt du an ihre Propaganda'. Ibid., 254.
71. 'typische DDR-Frauen: qualifiziert, verheiratet, ein Kind, doppelt belastet'. Ibid., 268.
72. Marx Ferree, *Varieties of Feminism*, 142.
73. Ibid.
74. Viett, *Nie war ich furchtloser*, 258–60.
75. 'Nach der langen Zeit sozialer Isolation hattte die Bereitschaft, alles positiv aufzunehmen, sich in meinem Inneren ausgebreitet wie der fliegende Albatros seine Schwingen'. Ibid., 259.
76. Ibid., 270.
77. 'Große Freiheit, kleine Freiheit', documentary, 83 min, directed by Kristina Konrad, 1:04.
78. Hollstein, 'Gedenkfeier für Rosa Luxemburg spaltet die Linke'.
79. Kriener, 'Den Totschläger auf dem Nachttisch'.
80. Ibid.
81. '"Schlafburg" – ein Trauerspiel am Tage und ein Friedhof bei Nacht'. Scheuring, 'Schuld und Sühne'.
82. Viett, *Nie war ich furchtloser*, 248.
83. 'Meine acht Jahre in der DDR waren zu kurz, auch nur einen Tag Langeweile zu haben ... Aber sie waren lang genug, ... mitverantwortlich zu sein für alle Höhen und Abgründe, für Mißlungenes und Gelungenes im geschichtlich einzigartigen Kampf für und um die Alternative zur kapitalistischen Gesellschaft'. Ibid.
84. Richmond, *Women Political Prisoners in Germany*, 91.
85. Viett, '"Daß der Kampf sinnlos ist"'.
86. Viett, *Nie war ich furchtloser*, 298.
87. Ibid., 293.
88. 'Mir ist, als ginge ein Zeitalter unter, zu dem ich gehöre'. Ibid., 303.
89. 'Wohin auch? Und wofür noch? Der Kapitalismus ist überall'. Ibid.
90. '"unsäglich teuflische ... Zusammenarbeit" zwischen dem aufgelösten Staatssicherheitsministerium und den westdeutschen Terroristen'. Baum, 'Über ihr wohnte ein Bevollmächtigter der Polizei'.
91. Davenport, *State Repression*, 35.
92. Viett, *Nie war ich furchtloser*, 309.
93. Bielby, 'Narrating the Revolutionary Self', 237.
94. Gready, 'Autobiography and the "Power of Writing"', 507.
95. 'Schlöndorff vs. Inge Viett: Streit um Urheberrecht beigelegt', *Spiegel Online*, 14 September 2000. Retrieved 25 January 2017 from http://www.spiegel.de/kultur/gesellschaft/schloendorff-vs-inge-viett-streit-um-urheberrecht-beigelegt-a-93321.html.
96. 'Grillparty mit der Stasi', *Spiegel Online*, 14 February 2000. Retrieved 25 January 2017 from http://www.spiegel.de/spiegel/print/d-15680709.html.
97. Lüdtke, 'People Working', 83.

Bibliography

Baum, K.H. 'Über ihr wohnte ein Bevollmächtigter der Polizei'. *Frankfurter Rundschau*, 15 June 1990.
Bielby, C. 'Narrating the Revolutionary Self in German Post-Terrorist Life-Writing: Gender, Identity and Historical Agency'. *German Life and Letters* 67(2) (2014), 219–41.

Bruner, J. 'The Autobiographical Process'. *Current Sociology* 43(2–3) (1995), 161–77.

Davenport, C. *State Repression and the Domestic Democratic Peace*. New York: Cambridge University Press, 2007.

Della Porta, D. *Social Movements, Political Violence, and the State: A Comparative Analysis of Italy and Germany*. Cambridge: Cambridge University Press, 1995.

Diewald-Kerkmann, G. 'Frauen in der RAF'. *BPB Spezial: 'Wer wenn nicht wir'*. Retrieved 25 January 2017 from http://www.bpb.de/gesellschaft/kultur/filmbildung/43364/frauen-in-der-raf?p=all.

Fritzsch, R. and R. Reinders. *Die Bewegung 2. Juni: Gespräche über Haschrebellen, Lorenzentführung, Knast*. Berlin: Edition ID- Archiv, 1995.

Gready, P. 'Autobiography and the "Power of Writing": Political Prison Writing in the Apartheid Era'. *Journal of Southern African Studies* 19(3) (1993), 489–523.

'Grillparty mit der Stasi'. *Spiegel Online*, 14 February 2000. Retrieved 25 January 2017 from http://www.spiegel.de/spiegel/print/d-15680709.html.

Grob, M. *Das Kleidungsverhalten jugendlicher Protestgruppen in Deutschland im 20. Jahrhundert: Am Beispiel des Wandervogels und der Studentenbewegung*, Beiträge zur Volkskultur in Nordwestdeutschland 47. Münster: F. Coppenrath, 1985.

'Große Freiheit, kleine Freiheit', directed by Kristina Konrad, documentary, 83 min, release date 23 January 2001.

Hanshew, K. *Terror and Democracy in West Germany*. Cambridge and New York: Cambridge University Press, 2012.

Herf, J. *Divided Memory: The Nazi Past in the Two Germanys*. Cambridge, MA: Harvard University Press, 1999.

Hollstein, M. 'Gedenkfeier für Rosa Luxemburg spaltet die Linke'. *Die Welt*, 12 January 2013. Retrieved 10 August 2017 from https://www.welt.de/politik/deutschland/article112725362/Gedenkfeier-fuer-Rosa-Luxemburg-spaltet-die-Linke.html.

Jander, M. 'Differenzen im antiimperialistischen Kampf: Zu den Verbindungen des Ministeriums für Staatssicherheit mit der RAF und dem bundesdeutschen Linksterrorismus', in W. Kraushaar (ed.), *Die RAF und der linke Terrorismus* (Hamburg: Hamburger Edition, 2006), 696–713.

Kanonenberg, M. and A. Müller. *Die RAF-Stasi Connection*. Berlin: Rowohlt, 1992.

Kriener, M. 'Den Totschläger auf dem Nachttisch'. *die tageszeitung*, 15 June 1990.

Lipps, T. *Ästhetik: Psychologie des Schönen und der Kunst*. Hamburg and Leipzig: Leopold Voss, 1906.

Lüdtke, A. 'Alltagsgeschichte: Aneignung und Akteure: Oder – es hat kaum begonnen!'. *Werkstattgeschichte* 17 (1997), 84.

_____. *The History of Everyday Life: Reconstructing Historical Experiences and Ways of Life*. Princeton, NJ: Princeton University Press, 1995.

_____. 'People Working: Everyday Life and German Fascism'. *History Workshop Journal* 50 (2000), 74–92.

Martin, B. 'Lesbian Identity and Autobiographical Difference(s)', in S. Smith and J. Watson (eds), *Women, Autobiography, Theory: A Reader* (Madison: University of Wisconsin Press, 1998), 380–92.

Marx Ferree, M. *Varieties of Feminism: German Gender Politics in Global Perspective*. Stanford, CA: Stanford University Press, 2012.

Moréas, G. 'Un nom sur une porte: mémorial pour un flic'. *le monde blog*, 18 April 2000. Retrieved 10 August 2017 from: http://moreas.blog.lemonde. fr/2010/04/18/un-nom-sur-une-porte-memorial-pour-un-flic/.

Neidhardt, F. 'Linker und rechter Terrorismus: Erscheinungsformen und Handlungspotentiale im Gruppenvergleich', in W. von Bayer-Katte, et al. (eds), *Gruppenprozesse, Analysen zum Terrorismus* (Opladen: Westdeutscher Verlag, 1982), 433–76.

Richmond, K. *Women Political Prisoners in Germany: Narratives of Self and Captivity, 1915–91*. Bithell Series of Dissertations 43. London: Institute of Modern Languages Research, 2016.

Rosenkranz, G. 'Offene Rechnung'. *Die Zeit*, 4 September 1992.

Scheuring, C. 'Schuld und Sühne'. *Tempo*, December 1991, 28–31.

Schildt, A. and D. Siegfried. *Deutsche Kulturgeschichte. Die Bundesrepublik: 1945 bis zur Gegenwart*. Bonn: Bundeszentrale für Politische Bildung, 2009.

'Schlöndorff vs. Inge Viett: Streit um Urheberrecht beigelegt'. *Spiegel Online*, 14 September 2000. Retrieved 25 January 2017 from http://www.spiegel. de/kultur/gesellschaft/schloendorff-vs-inge-viett-streit-um-urheberrecht-beigelegt-a-93321.html.

Schwanhäusser, A. *Stilrevolte Underground: Die Alternativkultur als Agent der Postmoderne*. Münster: LIT, 2002.

Siegfried, D. *Time Is on My Side: Konsum und Politik in der westdeutschen Jugendkultur der 60er Jahre*. Hamburger Beiträge zur Sozial- und Zeitgeschichte. Göttingen: Wallstein, 2006.

Viett, I. *Cuba Libre bittersüss*. Hamburg: Edition Nautilus, 1999.

———. '"Daß der Kampf sinnlos ist": Inge Vietts Abschiedsbrief an ihr Magdeburger Arbeitskollektiv'. *die tageszeitung*, 14 July 1990.

———. *Einsprüche: Briefe aus dem Gefängnis*. Hamburg: Edition Nautilus, 1996.

———. *Morengas Erben: Eine Reise durch Namibia*. Hamburg: Edition Nautilus, 2004.

———. *Nie war ich furchtloser: Autobiographie*. Hamburg: Edition Nautilus, 1997.

———. Radio interview in the programme *SWR 3 Leute*, 1 April 1997.

Walsh, D. *Bloody Sunday and the Rule of Law in Northern Ireland*. New York: St. Martin's Press, 2000.

Weinhauer, K., J. Requate and H.G. Haupt (eds). *Terrorismus in der Bundesrepublik: Medien, Staat und Subkulturen in den 1970er Jahren*. Frankfurt am Main: Campus, 2006.

Weiss, V. '"Volksklassenkampf" – Die Antizionistische Rezeption des Nahostkonflikts in der militanten Linken der BRD'. *Tel Aviver Jahrbuch für deutsche Geschichte* (2005), 214–38.

Wunschik, T. 'Die Bewegung 2. Juni', in W. Kraushaar (ed.), *Die RAF und der linke Terrorismus* (Hamburg: Hamburger Edition, 2006), 531–61.

Chapter 4

Asymmetrical (Be)Longing
Villagers, Spatial Practices and the German 'Other'

Marcel Thomas

Introduction

E pitomized by the border fortifications of the Berlin Wall, the division of Germany was permanent and quite literally set in concrete. The separation of the FRG and the GDR produced very real spatial divides, restricting the movement of people and disrupting links between families and friends. Over the last decade, however, scholars have begun to understand division as an '"experience" rather than just a brute fact'.[1] In particular for border communities, historians have explored how ordinary Germans gave meaning to the Cold War partition of Germany in their everyday lives. The work of Edith Sheffer, Sagi Schaefer and Jason Johnson has provided important insights into how the 'mundane attitudes and actions' of individuals in frontier communities along the inner German border shaped the physical and imagined border that separated East and West.[2] In addition, Daphne Berdahl and Jan Palmowski have analysed the local practices through which border communities responded to fractured local identities and severed ties between neighbouring localities.[3] Much less, however, is known about how Germans who did not live in the vicinity of the border engaged with division in their everyday lives. While we now have a detailed understanding of the ways in which the inhabitants of border communities helped to make the Iron Curtain, Germans outside the border regions continue to be seen as passive observers to the brute reality of division.

This chapter uses oral history interviews with twenty residents each in two case-study localities to explore how East and West Germans who lived far away from the border imagined and responded to the division of the country. It focuses on the locals' spatial imaginations of the other Germany and analyses how these were embedded in a range of everyday cultural practices. Life history narratives are thus used as a window into the embodied and affective practices which constituted the peculiarly German Cold War experience in East and West. In recent years, a number of oral histories have emphasized that the spatiality of life history narratives can reveal how individuals have situated themselves in the larger political context of their time. For instance, Werner Holly has shown how Germans and Czechs in the border region between both countries have used 'distancing strategies' when talking about the problematic twentieth-century history of their communities.[4] Tim Cole's study of the spatiality of Holocaust survivor testimony has highlighted that survivors take control of their narratives by choosing where to place themselves in their stories.[5] Similarly, Andrew S. Bergerson, in his oral history research on the Nazi era in a German town, found that his interviewees described the spaces of their locality in the past in a way that allowed them to remove themselves from Nazi crimes.[6]

Of course, personal memories are always shaped by present concerns and searches for identity and can thus not be taken as authentic representations of the past. As Lutz Niethammer has put it, life histories have to be seen as 'texts produced in a certain moment from a selection of experiences that are woven into an overall construction of meaning'.[7] While we can thus not rely on memory as a depository of facts, life history narratives can open a window into the shifting ways in which individuals have made sense of their world in the past and present. As Alistair Thomson has stressed, 'our opportunity in oral history is to study both the unchanging past and the changing uses and meanings of that past in the present'.[8] Rather than seeing the shifting narratives of oral history as a weakness, they can be used as a strength of the approach. The very attempts of interviewees to present themselves in a positive light in the interviews often offer insights into long-standing tensions in their identity or contentious issues in their past. Moreover, past self-understandings often remain at the heart of oral testimonies, even if they are dressed in the language of the present. As Bergerson has pointed out, the present context shapes narratives of the past 'rarely out of whole cloth', since 'inside these narratives lies the same style of self-cultivation by which one shaped that identity in the first place'.[9] Therefore, oral histories can serve as a tool to lay bare the ways in which ordinary Germans have imagined and narrated themselves into the Cold War division of their country.

This chapter argues that Easterners and Westerners developed a set of cultural practices of the spatial imagination – 'spatial practices', as they will be called in the following – through which they engaged with the division of Germany. The notion of 'spatial practices' was initially introduced by Michel de Certeau in his classic study *The Practice of Everyday Life*. De Certeau defines spatial practices as the everyday thoughts and actions through which individuals appropriate the rationally planned spaces of their urban environments.[10] His prime example of a spatial practice is the act of walking in the city, which subverts and manipulates the spatial layout put in place by the powerful.[11] In de Certeau's understanding, spatial practices can refer to material or physical ways of using and appropriating spaces (such as going where you are not supposed to) as well as imagined ones (such as thinking about crossing a boundary).[12] Both are equally 'real' and important, as both shape self-understandings and undermine the layout of the modern city. As this chapter will show, different spatial practices in East and West became vehicles of asymmetrical feelings of longing and belonging which separated but also closely linked the two Germanies.

The analysis first demonstrates that the inhabitants of the two case-study localities distanced themselves from the other Germany for different reasons: while the Easterners tried to mitigate unsatisfied feelings of longing, the Westerners sought distance from the GDR to render themselves citizens of the one and only legitimate Germany. It then shows that Germans on both sides of the Iron Curtain also dealt with the inner German border in very different ways. While the Easterners challenged or avoided the border, the Westerners stressed its permanence to ward off uncomfortable uncertainties about national identity in a divided nation. Therefore, the chapter reveals that the division of Germany was an experience shaped in the lived and embodied practices of everyday life, not just a fixed reality which Germans passively accepted. Far beyond border communities, Easterners and Westerners had a degree of agency in shaping this experience of division.

A Distant Place? Village Life and the Other Germany

The interviews on which this chapter relies were gathered in the small localities of Neukirch (Lausitz) in Saxony and Ebersbach an der Fils in Baden-Württemberg between April 2013 and April 2016.[13] Neukirch, located about forty kilometres east of Dresden, and Ebersbach, located about thirty-five kilometres east of Stuttgart, were chosen as part of a larger project which explores experiences of social change in villages in the divided Germany.[14] Both were distant from the Iron Curtain: Ebersbach was 254 kilometres away from the inner German border, Neukirch 179 kilometres.[15] Neither had any special link to the other Germany. In fact, it is likely that the inhabitants of the two villages had never heard of the other. Both localities were large industrial villages which experienced a thorough transformation in the postwar era. Ebersbach benefited from the economic boom in West Germany and developed into a diverse commuter town of nowadays 15,000 inhabitants, almost tripling its population in the first two decades after the war.[16] Neukirch, on the other hand, was redesigned into a 'socialist village' by the regime and stagnated, shrinking from just over 7,000 inhabitants in the mid-1950s to just over 5,000 today.[17] With these diverging developments, the two villages were fairly typical of small localities in postwar Germany. Of course, this does not mean that the residents' views of the other Germany can be seen as representative of East and West German perspectives.

The focus of the interviews was on the interviewees' experiences of social change in their locality rather than their relationship to the state on the other side of the Iron Curtain. In the interviews, I first explained to my conversation partners that I was particularly interested in their individual life histories and their personal experiences of the transformation of their locality throughout their lifetime. I also informed them that my project was a comparative study of East and West, which in some cases certainly encouraged references to the other Germany. I then asked the interviewees to talk about their biographies and their memories of life in the villages as freely as possible. Once they had finished their initial discourse, I followed this up with specific questions about themes which had sprung up, points that needed clarification or tensions I noticed in the narrative. In addition, I also had a set list of questions about various aspects of village life from which I brought in a few as the interview progressed. The interviewees were selected following recommendations from local contacts or previous interview partners. I decided not to advertise for interviewees and instead approached potential interviewees myself in order to stay in control of the make-up of the sample. This also meant that I was careful to follow multiple chains of recommendation to avoid replicating narratives or being pushed to interview several individuals with similar views. No matter how 'balanced' the sample is in terms of age, gender and social status, it does not claim to be representative of the population of Neukirch or Ebersbach during the postwar era. It was not my goal to find the 'typical' cross-section of the local community, but rather to obtain a diverse sample and analyse a range of experiences in depth.

The interviews revealed very different views of the other Germany in East and West. In Ebersbach, the GDR hardly featured in the life history narratives, and the interviewees in most cases only brought it up when prompted by my questions or remarks about the comparative nature of the project. This silence about the East can be traced back to the removal of discussion about the GDR from everyday life in West Germany for much of the postwar period. Particularly in the 1950s, West German politicians publicly lamented the undemocratic nature of the GDR and, following the official policy of non-recognition, denied its legitimacy by referring to it as 'the zone' (*die Zone*). However, discussions of life in the GDR were soon reduced to news reports and ritualized expressions of solidarity.[18] In the local media in Ebersbach, occasional references to the East were made by local politicians until the early 1960s, but faded soon after the construction of the Wall. For instance, the first report of the local council after the war still ended with the wish that 'we can soon live in a reunited Germany', but later editions are devoid of any references to the East.[19] Only when reunification became foreseeable in 1989 did the GDR once again become a prominent concern for the locals.[20] Unlike in border localities, the East thus remained mostly absent from local media in Ebersbach.

The Ebersbachers described the East not as a place of longing, but as a distant country that was clearly separated from the 'here' in which they lived their lives. When asked about the GDR, most interviewees expressed a marked disinterest in East German life and culture. None of them watched Eastern TV or were particularly interested in aspects of East German society. Instead, most interviewees stressed that they had no contact with the GDR, as in the case of Walter Hertle (born 1934): 'No, I didn't have anything to do with the GDR. ... No, *Wessi* or *Ossi* or whatever, those are words that were only created later. We were busy here and lived our lives here and had nothing to do with the GDR politically'.[21] Later in the same interview, Hertle was more explicit about the spatial distance he experienced in his relationship to the GDR. When discussing reunification, he stated that 'of course we saw on TV how great this was for the people in the GDR, but here this didn't really touch anyone, that was far away'.[22] Similarly, Volker Philipp's (born 1944) answers revealed that separation from the East was accepted as a fact among the Ebersbachers, despite ritualized expressions of compassion for the Germans on the other side of the Wall: 'As I said, until '89 there were two blocs. That's simply how it was. And the further you went away from the border, the more distant this became. You still had this old hope that one day reunification might happen, but that it then fell into our lap so quickly and surprisingly – no one would have expected that'.[23] Like Hertle, Philipp stressed that geographical distance from the East translated into emotional distance. This claim was striking: while the East was certainly less present in everyday life in Ebersbach than in border communities, the locals still had substantial exposure to the GDR through national TV or their relatives in the East. Volker Philipp and his wife Gudrun (born 1947) personally remembered learning about the GDR at school and sending parcels to relatives in the East.[24] Therefore, the interviewees' emphasis on distance from the other Germany has to be seen at least partly as a narrative strategy. In Philipp's case, highlighting remoteness from the East allowed him to justify his growing disinterest in the GDR and the gradual 'withering away' of contact with acquaintances in the East.

In addition, the interviews suggested that the Ebersbachers distanced themselves from the East to firmly situate themselves on the more advanced side of the Iron Curtain. The interviewees almost exclusively used the term *drüben* or even *dort drüben* ('over there') when talking about the GDR, a phrase that created a sense of otherness and spatial distance.[25] On the one hand, the use of the term can be traced back to the West German refusal to properly name the GDR, which continued to influence public discourse even after the shift of official policies in the *Neue Ostpolitik*.[26] 'Drüben' in this context served as a commonly understood shorthand for the other German state that was not to be talked about. On the other hand, the interviewees in Ebersbach used the term to assure themselves of their superiority over the socialist East. Life in the GDR was often looked down upon, as in the case of Gilbert Kübler (born 1955), who referred to the famous wood carvings from the Saxon Ore Mountains – a scarce and much-appreciated export good – merely as 'that Ore Mountain stuff' which his relatives from 'over there' packed in every parcel.[27] Those who had visited the GDR portrayed it as an oddly familiar but also notably backward place. This was particularly striking in the case of Martin Hafner (born 1941), who described his first visit to the GDR in late 1989 as time travel to the Ebersbach of his youth:

> When I went over there for the first time … I felt like I was in the forties or fifties here. There were these piles of coal on the pavement and they then shovelled them down like they used to do here, making our eyes tear from the soot. … For me, that was like walking through a memory from my youth.[28]

Hafner's narrative clearly posited the West as the more advanced Germany, revealing a common tendency among the interviewees to emphasize difference for a positive self-assurance. In a particularly telling response to the question of whether she had felt West German at the time, Inge Haller (born 1935) remarked that 'of course we were happy that we were living in the West!'.[29] Describing the GDR as a strange 'over there' allowed the Ebersbachers to assure themselves that they were on the 'right' side of the Iron Curtain.

These distancing strategies also served to frame the West as the one and only legitimate Germany. Especially those who did not have relatives or personal contacts on the other side of the Wall stressed that the other Germany had seemed just like any other foreign country to them. As Wolfgang Scherr (born 1955) pointed out:

> Well as long as the Wall stood … they really only became humans at the end. Before that, it was … well, it was 'population'. Only then I met people here who had relatives [in the GDR] and so on. Then I also met people who were visiting here …. And only then you perceived them as humans. It was the same view like on Luxemburg or so, just 'population'.[30]

However, Scherr's use of the term 'drüben' later in the interview demonstrated that the GDR was precisely not just like Luxemburg: only the other Germany could be referred to under this commonly understood shorthand. Instead, such attempts to describe the GDR as a normal other state served to exclude Easterners from the German nation. This was also evident in a number of other interviews. For instance, when asked whether she identified as West German before 1989, Helena Huber (born 1963) responded: 'We felt German and the others were the exotics, that's how it was. They were … "those from the GDR"'.[31] Stefan Schmid's (born 1938) answer to the same question was even more revealing: 'We were the Germans, and those over there, you basically didn't notice them. That was just "over there" and so on'.[32] By rendering East Germany a distant and exotic place, the Ebersbachers were able to claim ownership over the German nation and reinforce their self-understanding as citizens of the 'true' German state. Ironically, by defining their national identity directly against the East, they also firmly linked themselves to the GDR.

The Neukirchers engaged with the other Germany through a set of very different spatial practices. In the life history narratives of the Neukirchers, the FRG was highly present and was often mentioned without my prompting. On the one hand, this significance of the West as an important reference point can be traced back to the official line of the regime. Throughout the postwar era, local media and propaganda publications in Neukirch referred to the West as the reactionary German 'other' which had to be overtaken.[33] At times, this rhetoric of Cold War competition was still evident in the language used by the interviewees. For example, Helmuth Richter (born 1935) compared the conditions in Neukirch in the early 1950s with those in the FRG and pointed out that at the time he genuinely believed that 'we really, if things would have gone on like that, could have overtaken the FRG'.[34] More importantly, however, the West was present in the Neukirchers' narratives due to its significance as a place of longing. For instance, Stephan Albert (born 1952), who left the GDR on an exit visa in late 1989, kept returning to the FRG in his memories, stressing his yearning for the place where his relatives lived and where a life without shortages and political discrimination seemed possible.[35] Petra Mrosowski (born 1958) repeatedly commented on her perception of the West as an attractive place of consumer happiness where goods such as fridges or TVs seemed to be abundant.[36] This association of the FRG with the affluent material culture of the 'Western' lifestyle was particularly demonstrated by the fact that the interviewees normally referred to the FRG as 'the West'.[37] For the Neukirchers, the other Germany was an attractive alternative to the shortage economy they lived in – a perception which only intensified in the 1980s as the difference in living standards grew wider.

In the interviews, the villagers described how this longing for the West found expression in a range of everyday practices. Several interviewees reminisced about how they had craved Western consumer goods such as Levi's jeans or had anxiously waited for parcels from their Western relatives.[38] They also recalled listening to West German radio stations or using their connections to obtain records of Western bands – even if this meant risking conflict with the law.[39] Unlike most East Germans, the Neukirchers were not able to watch West German TV due to the village's location in the so-called 'Valley of the Clueless' (*Tal der Ahnungslosen*), the area between Dresden and the Polish border which was cut off from Western TV signals. Nonetheless, many interviewees recalled, in poignant detail, their usually vain attempts to receive a TV signal from the FRG, which was only possible under rare weather conditions.[40] The prestige linked to watching Western TV was illustrated by the comments of Jürgen Thomas (born 1950), who remembered that his neighbour often boasted about watching West German TV but never had a signal when Thomas went over to see for himself.[41] Similarly, Hannelore Schubert (born 1947) recalled how she always pressed visitors from other parts of the GDR about what they had recently seen on Western TV, which usually sent her back to her own TV set, desperately (but unsuccessfully) searching for a signal.[42] Schubert's example also shows how the Neukirchers stayed informed about the West without TV: through radio, newspapers and word of mouth from family and friends in other parts of Germany.

Nonetheless, many interviewees commented on the lack of West German TV in the village and stressed that their location in the 'Valley of the Clueless' made them feel particularly distant from the West. As

Ingrid Köhler (born 1952) pointed out, geographical distance to the West materialized into a frustrating feeling of remoteness:

> We didn't have Western TV here anyway. ... I think we were missing out on quite a bit. People who lived around Berlin and had more of these comparisons certainly were better informed. My sister [who lived in East Berlin] always said that, she said you can tell that I am from the deepest East, I didn't know anything [laughs].[43]

Similarly, Andreas Buchert (born 1960) stressed that it was a constant struggle to get more information about the West: 'There was a blank spot in our knowledge and that was the Federal Republic. You had to read or enquire about it all by yourself. That was kept secret from us. But of course you had the urge to establish links, to see this as a whole again'.[44]

There is no doubt that Neukirch's geographical distance from the West had a very real impact on the villagers' views of the other Germany. However, some interviewees also used this remoteness to distance themselves from the West and explain their private happiness in a dictatorial system. For instance, Mrosowski asserted that Neukirch's remoteness meant that the locals had no chance to reflect on the dictatorial nature of the GDR and the opportunities they were missing out on compared to the West: 'You knew: *Bezirk* Dresden, Valley of the Clueless. And here we were even further away, we were close to Poland and the Czech Republic [*sic*]. Yeah, you were far away from it all [*weit ab vom Schuss*]. And perhaps a lot passed us by that might have been quite different somewhere else. That's my impression'.[45] In striking contrast to her detailed comments about the affluence of the West, Mrosowski distanced herself from the FRG in order to side-step difficult questions about why she did not develop a more critical perspective on the dictatorial system in which she grew up.

Other Neukirchers distanced themselves in similar ways from the West in their narratives to moderate feelings of longing for the West and protect the modest sphere of happiness they had carved out for themselves. Several interviewees, who otherwise compared Neukirch to the West in detail and were fascinated by Western culture, stopped themselves at a certain point in their narratives and claimed that they 'didn't know' how much better living standards in the FRG were and thus could have not felt like they were missing out.[46] For example, when discussing issues that frustrated him about life in the GDR, Thomas stated: 'We didn't have relatives in the West with whom you could have started any big conversations. At the beginning, you didn't realize all this. Those who had connections to the West and knew that they could travel to all these places ... I mean, we knew that too, but we didn't care that much'.[47]

Thomas, who in the same interview shared recollections of talking to West German visitors in his neighbourhood and recalled listening to radio programmes about the West German football league, seemed anxious to maintain a rather forced narrative of lacking knowledge about the West. Similarly, Schubert remarked that she did not feel like she was missing out compared to the FRG because 'what we didn't have, we simply didn't have – and we didn't know [about it]'. Her case in particular reveals that this was a narrative strategy rather than a real gap of knowledge, as only a few seconds later she added that she had been able to visit West Germany twice during the GDR era and had seen the difference in living standards with her own eyes.[48] These narrative strategies were certainly retrospective attempts to defend precious personal memories of life in the GDR. However, it seems likely that they relied on distancing strategies which the Neukirchers used during the GDR era to protect their modest happiness under socialism from uncomfortable comparisons with the affluence of the West.

This strategy of avoiding self-critical comparisons was also evident in the Neukirchers' memories of visits to the FRG. The majority of the interviewees in Neukirch had in fact been to West Germany at least once before reunification, and their memories of these visits predominantly focused on the material wealth of the other Germany.[49] Employing a common narrative trope, Hannelore Venus (born 1942) remembered her first visit to the FRG as a physically overwhelming experience:

> I was lost for words. When I arrived at the station in Berlin, there were these flower shops. You didn't get that here at all. I pressed my nose against the windows of the flower shops, it was overwhelming. ... Then I went to Kassel, where my sister-in-law lived. 'What would you like to have?' [she asked]. I said, 'I would like to have a nice blouse, we don't have any here!' [laughs]. Then we went through the shopping centres, and I couldn't make up my mind. I had never seen so many blouses in one place [laughs]. Yeah, I had to go outside, I felt sick. ... That was too much.[50]

Albert constructed a very similar narrative of bodily exhaustion in the face of Western affluence when he visited his aunt and uncle in the 1980s: 'And we went through the shops in town there. And the first thing was that I got diarrhoea [laughs]. Everything literally overwhelmed me. ... To see this stark difference [in living standards] with your own eyes basically knocked me off my feet'.[51] Almost all interviewees who had been to the West before reunification framed their visits in a similar narrative of how 'overwhelmed' they had been.[52] On the one hand, their memories testify to the stark difference they perceived between life in the West and the East. On the other, describing their visits as physically overwhelming allowed the Neukirchers to avoid a thorough and uncomfortable reflection on what was missing from their lives in the GDR. Refusing to rationally engage with the reality of life in the West allowed the Neukirchers to protect their own sphere of modest happiness in the GDR.

Like the Ebersbachers, the Neukirchers stressed German-German estrangement and rendered the West a distant country to avoid painful thoughts about their separation from this place of longing. In her interview, Mrosowski used an anecdote from her childhood to distance herself from the West and relieve herself from the burden of comparing:

> [As a child I once] asked my mum whether they speak a different language in West Germany. That they speak German too ... for me that was foreign, that was a different country. That's how stupid we were basically, but we were also kept that stupid. ... But also because you didn't have any connections there, for me that was a different country just like Poland, Czechoslovakia, Russia.[53]

Placing herself into the divided Germany as her childhood self, Mrosowski tried to argue that she hardly knew anything about the West – a claim that was clearly disproved by her other memories, which show that she was well-informed about life in West Germany. That the FRG was precisely not just any other country for the Neukirchers was revealed by the fact that Mrosowski and many other interviewees used the word 'drüben' when referring to it. Like the Ebersbachers, they used this term as a shorthand for the country that was always on people's minds: the capitalist alternative to the socialist 'here'. Therefore, Mrosowski's attempt to describe the FRG just like any other country has to be seen as a longstanding narrative strategy for dealing with frustrated feelings of longing for the consumer affluence of the West.

A Permanent Disconnect? Confronting the Inner German Border

Different spatial practices in East and West were even more evident regarding the border that separated the GDR and the FRG. For the Neukirchers, the inner German border had fundamental relevance as the marker of their lifeworld and as a painful boundary that restricted them in their movement. Many interviewees lamented that they were unable to travel where they wanted and expressed a feeling of spatial confinement.[54] When explaining the reasons for applying for an exit visa in 1989, Albert pointed out that 'You were basically imprisoned. You were certainly able to go to the Black Sea or Lake Balaton, but not more, and many things only under heavy regulations. When I wanted to go to Hungary, I was only allowed to exchange … so and so many Forints there, which was enough for one week of holiday at best'.[55]

Even interviewees who were not as clearly opposed to the SED regime stressed that they felt 'imprisoned' by the border.[56] Moreover, several Neukirchers recalled being confronted with the painful reality of division. For example, Richter described how he often had to drop off his boss, who was allowed to travel to the West, at the so-called 'Palace of Tears', the border checkpoint Friedrichstraße in Berlin. Richter vividly remembered the 'terrible' scenes of crying relatives who were separated by the Wall, noting how these moments had brought home the cruel reality of the Iron Curtain.[57] Although the inner German border was hundreds of kilometres away, the Neukirchers sensed it very strongly in their lives – not only because it separated them from the West, but also because it quite literally walled them in in the Eastern bloc.

In their narratives, the Neukirchers developed two distinct strategies to deal with this painful spatial confinement. The first and most common way of coming to terms with the border was to avoid it. Although many Neukirchers admitted that they felt restricted by the Wall, they claimed that they had not cared about it because they had never wanted to go further anyway. This was particularly evident in the case of Thomas, who recalled how the visits of his neighbour's West German cousin had painfully brought home the reality of his spatial confinement:

> He told me: 'The weekend before last, we went to Milan, where Bayern [Munich] played.' Yeah, quickly going from Munich to Milan, for us that was … I don't know how much of it he made up. Yeah, but you were astonished, you were wondering. But it was not like 'I need to get there whatever it takes', that feeling didn't come up. I was too modest for that. I mean, of course you desired that, and whenever you got in contact … what opportunities we had [compared to that]! Oh well.[58]

Thomas was fascinated by the mobility the West Germans enjoyed, but he was anxious to stress that he did not care because he was 'too modest'. His spatial confinement clearly did bother him, but in his narrative he turned away from the freedom of the West Germans to avoid facing the painful limitations of his own lifeworld. Such narratives were common among the Easterners. For instance, Lothar Dietrich (born 1954) admitted that it frustrated him that he could not travel far, but he quickly asserted that he was not a 'travel person' (*Reiseonkel*) and therefore did not mind so much after all.[59] Similarly, Sabine Buchert (born 1963) instantly qualified her husband's remark that he felt 'imprisoned' in the GDR by adding that this feeling came up 'only when you wanted to go somewhere'.[60]

It seems likely that this was not just a present-day attempt to defend memories of private happiness in the GDR, but a long-standing strategy used by the Neukirchers in dealing with the painful limitation of their lifeworld.

The other strategy revealed in the interviewees' narratives was to take control of the border. In their interviews, a number of Neukirchers dealt with the border by playing with the idea of crossing it in their mind, thereby gaining agency over their spatial confinement. Again, Thomas was a particularly striking example. In both interviews conducted with him, he briefly brought up the same anecdote from his time as a border guard. As he recalled, while on duty at the border in Thuringia in the late 1960s, he was often able to walk along the actual border behind all border fortifications, so close to the West that the West German officers were walking right next to him. Only a simple step separated him from the FRG in those moments. In almost identical words in both interviews, he pointed out that 'I had the opportunity in 1969/70, when I was with the army, I could have made that step across that famous line. I didn't do it, because I said: I am staying here'.[61] Asked about his reason for staying, he explained that otherwise he would never have been able to see his family again, as he expected the Wall to be there for many more decades. Even more than forty years later, the fascination which 'that famous line' exercised upon Thomas could be grasped in his words. The way he brought up this anecdote in both interviews suggests that it is a story he has often told since his duty at the border and a story which has for many years been central to his self-understanding. On the one hand, this feeling of getting literally one step close to the border and still not being able to cross it painfully epitomized the significance of the Iron Curtain as the powerful divide between two worlds. On the other hand, by placing himself in a situation in which he was actually able to make that step in his story, Thomas gained agency over the border. Telling himself that he could have made that step and that it was his decision not to, Thomas imagined the border as crossable – although his experience demonstrates that it was impossible to make that final step without sacrificing his whole existence. Crossing this boundary in his imagination was a spatial practice which helped him to regain control over his movement and his life choices.

Thomas's fantasy of stepping over the border was not the only one. Helmuth Richter recalled with fascination the story of how he had walked through Brandenburg Gate on a trip to Berlin just hours before the border was sealed in August 1961, completely clueless about the events that were about to unfold.[62] Similar to Thomas's anecdote, Richter told this story on several occasions, indicating that he has re-walked this short stroll through Brandenburg Gate in the quiet of an August summer night countless times in his memory.[63] Crossing the border in their memories in such ways was a spatial practice which helped the Neukirchers deal with the painful reality of their confinement. As Brigitte Hipfl, Anita Bister, Petra Strohmaier and Brigitta Busch have shown in their interviews with residents at the Austrian-Slovenian border, playing with the thought of crossing borders is a significant act of asserting power over these boundaries and disputing their political significance.[64] Although the practices of avoiding and challenging the border at first glance seem contradictory, they in fact complemented each other: they allowed the Neukirchers to confront the border on their own terms and gain agency over these boundaries. The villagers were not able to change the reality of the border, but many of them continued to challenge the Wall in their minds and thereby refused to come to terms with their spatial confinement.

For the West Germans, on the other hand, the inner German border had much less relevance. The Ebersbachers hardly discussed the border in the interviews, and when asked about it, they merely described it as a lamentable but unchangeable reality. For instance, Hertle detailed the many journeys he undertook for his wheelchair sports club and the various connections he made with similar clubs all over Europe. He pointed out that he 'came around a lot, yeah. But not to the GDR. There was a disconnect (*Trennung*). There was nothing. ... They had wheelchair sports too, but just no connection to us'.[65] For Hertle, the Wall really disconnected the East from the West – a lamentable fact, but also a reality that he hardly questioned. Since the Westerners had much less interest in the East than vice versa, they did not feel personally restricted by the border. Scherr summed this up in his remark that 'I myself had hardly any connections to people who came from the GDR or who had relatives there. Therefore the border was not a real conflict for me'.[66] Even those who had Eastern relatives or were genuinely concerned about the plight of the East Germans were only able to view the Wall with the passive gaze of the Western perspective. Lothar Böllinger (born 1937) was one of the few Ebersbachers who described the separation of the country as painful, as he had relatives in the East and had always dreamed of visiting Thuringia. He recalled how he once flew to West Berlin for work and decided to see the Wall in order to make sense of it: 'And I stood up there on these wooden stairs in front of Brandenburg Gate, looked over to the other side and I could barely comprehend it'.[67] Böllinger was able to see the Wall from the superior gaze of the elevated Western perspective, thereby challenging its purpose of prohibiting views across the border. Nonetheless, looking at the Wall from the viewpoint by Brandenburg Gate in the end became nothing more than a voyeuristic act that left him speechless and powerless. Böllinger's experience epitomizes how, in one way or the other, the Westerners quietly accepted the inner German border as a permanent divide that separated the East from them.

Unlike the Neukirchers, the Ebersbachers did not feel restricted by the Wall and therefore did not challenge its existence. Instead, their narratives suggested that in some ways they found its permanence reassuring. As Hertle's and Scherr's perception of the border as an unproblematic 'disconnect' indicate, the Wall made it easy to forget about the East and gave an almost comforting permanence to the unresolved German question.[68] As the comments of Kübler showed, the construction of the Wall signalled that the separation of East and West was set in stone:

> You just have to see it like that: the Federal Republic was firmly integrated into the West, the GDR was firmly integrated into the Eastern part of the world. These two worlds were divided, East and West. And in between, there was the Wall. So of course the Wall was a signal for people to say 'oh well, that's how it is now'.[69]

Kübler was only six years old when the Wall was built, and he could hardly have experienced it personally as a turning point in the relationship to the other Germany. Rather, his comments show how the Ebersbachers used the permanence of the Wall to explain their fading interest in the East. This was also demonstrated by the fact that the Ebersbachers who had actually been to the GDR recalled not the journey into the East but the return to the West as the happiest moment in their memories. They vividly remembered the harassment by East German border police and their very real fear in the face of East German state authority. It was not the moment of overcoming separation and visiting the GDR that was perceived as comforting or liberating, but the moment of return into the safety of the FRG.[70] Their memories suggest that the reassurance of being on the 'right' side of the Wall was in many ways a more pressing need for the Ebersbachers than challenging the division. As the very different imaginations of the Wall in Ebersbach and Neukirch demonstrate, there was a fundamental difference between the experience of being merely separated from the other Germany and the experience of being walled in in the Eastern bloc.

These contrasting views became particularly evident in the interviewees' memories of the opening of the border in 1989. The Neukirchers recalled overcoming spatial confinement as a very powerful moment, and several of them drove across the border to explore the West in the last two months of 1989.[71] They remembered the moment of walking across the border as a profoundly liberating act, such as in the case of Köhler:

> Well, we drove over there straight away, I had my sister in Berlin. And we
> went to 'the West', as you say, for the first time. In this euphoria, that was emo-
> tionally impressive. That you could really say, you can walk across the border.
> ... This freedom! That you can really say now, we can maybe go anywhere and
> ... Those were the things that were quite moving.[72]

The Ebersbachers, by contrast, mostly recalled watching the events unfold
on TV from the perspective of a distant observer in a foreign country.[73]
While several of them stressed that they had been highly moved by the
fall of the Wall, they had no urge to explore the East.[74] Böllinger, who had
years earlier stood on the wooden platform by Brandenburg Gate, was
the only one who recalled walking across the border as a very powerful
moment.[75] Unlike the Neukirchers, the Ebersbachers did not experience
the opening of the border as a liberation, but rather as an event that took
away the certainty the Wall had offered. As Huber recalled, when the
first Easterners came to Ebersbach in late 1989, the locals were forced
to directly engage with the other Germans who they had pushed out of
their lives for so long: 'When our first colleague from the East came here,
that was strange. You really had fears of contact, you didn't know what
to talk to him about or how they generally were. So it was much stranger
(*viel fremder*) than with people from other European countries'.[76] With the
Wall gone, there was no more excuse to avoid the uncomfortable German
question – a moment of profound mutual estrangement which foreshad-
owed the growing tensions between East and West Germans in the years
following reunification.

Conclusion

The life history narratives of the Ebersbachers and Neukirchers offer
a window into the spatial practices through which Germans on both
sides of the Iron Curtain situated themselves in the Cold War division
of the nation. Different spatial practices became vehicles of asymmetrical feelings of longing and belonging, which separated but also closely
linked the two Germanies. Citizens in the FRG and the GDR distanced
themselves from the other Germany, although for very different reasons.
While the Easterners tried to balance their longing for the West with
protecting the modest sphere of happiness they had carved out under
socialism, the Westerners tried to absolve themselves of the burden of
caring and positioned themselves as the citizens of the 'better' Germany.
Moreover, Easterners and Westerners also had contrasting experiences
of the boundary that separated them. The Easterners' attempts to gain

agency over the border that confined them to the Eastern bloc stood in contrast to the Westerners' quiet acceptance of the Wall.

These contrasting perceptions of life beyond the Iron Curtain among the Neukirchers and Ebersbachers illustrate the asymmetrical nature of German-German relations in the Cold War era. Despite their different perceptions of the other Germany, however, Easterners and Westerners shared a parallel history of estrangement and othering in their daily engagement with the division of the nation. This demonstrates that the constant glance across the Wall, which Thomas Lindenberger describes as central to life in the 'divided, but not disconnected' country, found meaning not only in cultural artifacts, but also in a range of everyday practices.[77] As Sheffer has shown, the inner German border 'became a product of the people who lived it, whose daily hopes, fears and motives gave form to, and continued to be formed by, the line that divided them'.[78] While the residents of communities outside the border regions did not directly contribute to shaping the nature of the actual border, they nonetheless negotiated its meaning in their everyday lives. Villagers in the GDR and the FRG used the other Germany to assess the development of their own communities and assure themselves of their place in the Cold War world. Therefore, understanding how Easterners and Westerners narrated themselves into the political landscape of division sheds light on the making of the Cold War experience in East and West. The spatial practices through which postwar Germans engaged with division allow us to explore 'asymmetrical entanglement' through the bottom-up perspective of everyday life.[79]

In fact, the villagers' memories emphasize the very 'everydayness' which defined division. The personal life histories of the Ebersbachers and Neukirchers remain closely linked with the Cold War. Just like their different memories of life in the divided country continue to shape their self-understandings today, the asymmetrical gaze across the Wall also linked past and present during the forty years of division. For the Westerners, distancing themselves from the East was an expression of a shared sense of achievement and postwar recovery, and thus a central part of being West German. For the Easterners, an ambiguous engagement with the FRG constituted a quiet acknowledgement of the shared experience of getting by under socialism. As a consequence, division became a product of these entangled searches for identity on both sides of the Wall. Albert, who had lived in both the FRG and the GDR before reunification, pointed towards this shared German history of estrangement and othering in his interview. Explaining that his acquaintances in the distant Baden-Württemberg knew much less about the GDR than his relatives who lived near the inner German border in Lower Saxony, he emphasized that real and imagined distance from the border shaped engagement with division on both sides of the Iron Curtain:

> All those who had no direct border with the GDR and who hardly ever watched GDR TV had completely skewed ideas about the GDR, just like it was for us. In the GDR era I didn't know where the Black Forest was. Is it cutting across or going up [on the map]? Where is Baden-Württemberg, what does it border on? You didn't know any of that. And it was the same for them.[80]

Albert's comments revealed a recognition that Easterners and Westerners had relied on simplistic images of the other Germany and shared a long history of estrangement and mutual misunderstandings. As the examples of Neukirch and Ebersbach demonstrate, asymmetrical notions of longing and belonging defined the unique German experience of the Cold War and lay at the heart of what it meant to be East or West German.

Marcel Thomas is Departmental Lecturer in Twentieth-Century European History at St Antony's College, University of Oxford. He completed his PhD at the University of Bristol in 2017. His thesis 'Local Lives, Parallel Histories: Villagers and Everyday Life in the Divided Germany' is the first comparative study of how East and West German villagers experienced and navigated social change in their localities in the postwar era. His research interests include the history of the divided Germany, space and place, memory and oral history. He has previously published in the *Journal of Urban History* and the *European Review of History*, and he is the co-editor of *The GDR Today: New Interdisciplinary Approaches to East German History, Memory and Culture* (Peter Lang, 2018).

Notes

1. Lindenberger, 'Divided, But Not Disconnected', 11.
2. Sheffer, *Burned Bridge*; Schaefer, *States of Division*; Johnson, *Divided Village*. The quotation is from Sheffer, *Burned Bridge*, 6. See also Patrick Major's notion of the 'invisible frontiers of power' in East German society: Major, *Behind the Berlin Wall*, 2–11.
3. Berdahl, *Where the World Ended*; Palmowski, *Inventing a Socialist Nation*, 229–39.
4. Holly, 'Traces of German-Czech History'.
5. Cole, '(Re)Placing the Past'.
6. Bergerson, 'The Devil's Horn in Hildesheim', 250–51.
7. Niethammer, 'Glasnost privat 1987', 29.
8. Thomson, 'Anzac Memories Revisited', 26.
9. Bergerson, *Ordinary Germans in Extraordinary Times*, 240.

10. De Certeau, *The Practice of Everyday Life*, 92–101.

11. Ibid., 97–101.

12. Ibid., 97–107.

13. The interviews were semi-structured and therefore gave the interviewees room to guide the conversation to aspects of life in the village which they perceived as important. The sample of interviewees comprised altogether twenty-three men and seventeen women, born between 1922 and 1963. All interviewees consented to the use of their testimony for research publications. Ethics approval for this project was granted by the University of Bristol in February 2015.

14. Thomas, 'Local Lives, Parallel Histories'.

15. Data from Google Earth, measured as the shortest distance to the inner German border.

16. Geiger, *Ebersbach an der Fils*.

17. Ortschronisten Neukirch, *Aus der Geschichte unseres Heimatortes Neukirch/Lausitz*, 14–65.

18. Sheffer, *Burned Bridge*, 213–22.

19. Stadtarchiv Ebersbach, Zeitgeschichtliche Sammlung, Box 5.7, Gemeinde Ebersbach an der Fils, 'Tätigkeitsbericht der Gemeindeverwaltung für die Jahre 1948-1953', 30.

20. See in particular the 1989 and 1990 editions of the *Ebersbacher Weihnachtszeitung*, an annual magazine published by the local council, which comments on events of importance for the local community, in the Stadtarchiv Ebersbach, Zeitungssammlung.

21. Interview with Walter Hertle, Ebersbach, 2 May 2014. See also: interview with Inge Haller, Ebersbach, 16 June 2014; interview with Dorothea Liebisch, Ebersbach, 18 June 2014; interview with Stefan Schmid, Ebersbach, 4 March 2015.

22. Interview with Hertle.

23. Interview with Volker and Gudrun Philipp, Ebersbach, 27 April 2016.

24. Interview with the Philipps.

25. See in particular: interview with Martin Hafner, Ebersbach, 29 April 2014; interview with Renate Wild, Ebersbach, 17 June 2014.

26. Sheffer, *Burned Bridge*, 214–17.

27. Interview with Gilbert Kübler, Ebersbach, 30 April 2014.

28. Interview with Hafner.

29. Interview with Inge Haller, Ebersbach, 16 June 2014. See also: interview with Schmid.

30. Interview with Scherr. See also: interview with Hertle; interview with Liebisch.

31. Interview with Helena Huber (pseudonym), Ebersbach, 2 May 2014.

32. Interview with Schmid.

33. See in particular the socialist village chronicle: Arbeitsgruppe Ortschronik/ Heimatgeschichte, 'Neukirch im Spiegel der 40-jährigen Geschichte unserer Deutschen Demokratischen Republik' (1989), Heimatmuseum Neukirch, Zeitgeschichtliche Sammlung.

34. Interview with Helmuth and Inge Richter, Steinigtwolmsdorf, 11 April 2014.

35. Interview I with Stephan Albert, Steinigtwolmsdorf, 19 June 2013; interview II with Stephan Albert, Steinigtwolmsdorf, 17 April 2014.

36. Interview III with Petra Mrosowski, Neukirch, 14 April 2014.

37. Interview III with Mrosowski; interview with Frank Pötter, Neukirch, 18 July 2013; interview with Bernd Harig, Neukirch, 12 August 2014; interview I with Jürgen Thomas, Neukirch, 3 April 2013; interview with Hannelore Schubert and Erika Böhme, Neukirch, 19 August 2014.

38. See for example: Interview II with Albert; interview III with Mrosowski; interview with Andreas and Sabine Buchert (pseudonyms), Neukirch, 24 July 2013.

39. For instance, Albert, who became a fan of the Beatles and the Bee Gees, was caught listening to Western radio as a teenager and was banned from studying at the university in Dresden: interview I with Albert.

40. Interview I with Thomas; interview with Harig; interview with Lothar Dietrich (pseudonym), Neukirch, 8 April 2013; interview with Schubert and Böhme.
41. Interview I with Thomas.
42. Interview with Schubert and Böhme.
43. Interview with Ingrid Köhler (pseudonym), Neukirch, 22 July 2013. See also: interview with Hans-Henning von Kleist, Neukirch, 12 August 2014; interview with Karl-Louis Lehmann, Neukirch, 20 August 2014.
44. Interview with the Bucherts.
45. Interview II with Petra Mrosowski, Neukirch, 4 April 2013. See also: interview with von Kleist; interview with Pötter.
46. Interview I with Thomas; interview with Schubert and Böhme; interview with Köhler; interview III with Mrosowski.
47. Interview I with Thomas.
48. Interview with Schubert and Böhme.
49. See, for example: interview with Pötter; interview with the Bucherts; interview with the Richters. See also: Sheffer, *Burned Bridge*, 225.
50. Interview with Hannelore Venus, Neukirch, 22 April 2016.
51. Interview II with Albert.
52. Interview with the Bucherts; interview with Lehmann; interview with Klaus and Christiane Bergmann (pseudonyms), Neukirch, 22 April 2016.
53. Interview II with Mrosowski.
54. Interview I with Thomas; interview with Lehmann; interview with the Richters; interview with Köhler; interview with von Kleist.
55. Interview I with Albert.
56. Interview with the Bucherts.
57. Interview with the Richters. See also: interview with the Bucherts; interview with Walter Pfützner, Polenz, 24 June 2013.
58. Interview II with Jürgen Thomas, Neukirch, 22 April 2014.
59. Interview with Dietrich.
60. Interview with the Bucherts.
61. Interview II with Thomas.
62. Interview with the Richters. See also: interview with Pötter; interview with Lehmann.
63. Interview with the Richters; unrecorded conversation with Helmuth Richter, Steinigtwolmsdorf, 12 July 2015.
64. Hipfl, Bister, Strohmaier and Busch, 'Shifting Borders', 57–63.
65. Interview with Hertle.
66. Interview with Scherr.
67. Interview with Lothar and Inka Böllinger (pseudonyms), Ebersbach, 5 March 2015.
68. Interview with Hertle; interview with Scherr.
69. Interview with Kübler.
70. Interview with Huber; interview with Schmid; interview with the Philipps.
71. Interview with Lehmann; interview with Köhler; interview II with Mrosowski; interview II with Thomas.
72. Interview with Köhler. See also: interview with Lehmann; interview II with Mrosowski.
73. Interview with Hertle; interview with Kübler; interview with Huber; interview with Wild.
74. Interview with Manfred Neumann, Süßen, 6 March 2015; interview with Wild; interview with Schmid.
75. Interview with the Böllingers.
76. Interview with Huber.
77. Lindenberger, 'Divided, But Not Disconnected', 29.
78. Sheffer, *Burned Bridge*, 9.

79. Kleßmann, *Zwei Staaten, eine Nation*, 11–15.
80. Interview II with Albert.

Bibliography

Berdahl, D. *Where the World Ended: Reunification and Identity in the German Borderland*. London: University of California Press, 1999.
Bergerson, A.S. 'The Devil's Horn in Hildesheim, or The Space and Time of Everyday Life', in B. Davis, T. Lindenberger and M. Wildt (eds), *Alltag, Erfahrung, Eigensinn: Historisch-anthropologische Erkundungen* (Frankfurt am Main: Campus, 2008), 249–63.
_____. *Ordinary Germans in Extraordinary Times: The Nazi Revolution in Hildesheim*. Bloomington: Indiana University Press, 2004.
Cole, T. '(Re)Placing the Past: Spatial Strategies of Retelling Difficult Stories'. *Oral History Review* 42(1) (2015), 30–49.
De Certeau, M. *The Practice of Everyday Life*. London: University of California Press, 1984.
Geiger, U. *Ebersbach an der Fils: Bilder im Wandel der Zeit*. Horb: Geiger, 2013.
Hipfl, B., A. Bister, P. Strohmaier and B. Busch. 'Shifting Borders: Spatial Constructions of Identity in an Austrian/Slovenian Border Region', in U.H. Meinhof (ed.), *Living (with) Borders: Identity Discourses on East-West Borders in Europe* (Aldershot: Ashgate, 2002), 53–74.
Holly, W. 'Traces of German-Czech History in Biographical Interviews at the Border: Constructions of Identities and the Year 1938 in Bärenstein-Vejprty', in U.H. Meinhof (ed.), *Living (with) Borders: Identity Discourses on East-West Borders in Europe* (Aldershot: Ashgate, 2002), 95–118.
Johnson, J. *Divided Village: The Cold War in the German Borderlands*. Abingdon: Routledge, 2017.
Kleßmann, C. *Zwei Staaten, eine Nation: Deutsche Geschichte 1955–1970*. Göttingen: Vandenhoeck & Ruprecht, 1988.
Lindenberger, T. 'Divided, But Not Disconnected: Germany as a Border Region of the Cold War', in T. Hochscherf, C. Laucht and A. Plowman (eds), *Divided, But Not Disconnected: German Experiences of the Cold War* (Oxford: Berghahn, 2010), 11–33.
Major, P. *Behind the Berlin Wall: East Germany and the Frontiers of Power*. Oxford: Oxford University Press, 2010.
Niethammer, L. 'Glasnost privat 1987: Reportage über eine Befragung unter den Zeitgenossen Honeckers zu Zeiten Gorbatschows', in L. Niethammer, A. von Plato and D. Wierling (eds), *Die volkseigene Erfahrung: Eine Archäologie des Lebens in der Industrieprovinz der DDR. 30 biographische Eröffnungen* (Berlin: Rowohlt, 1991), 9–73.
Ortschronisten Neukirch. *Aus der Geschichte unseres Heimatortes Neukirch/Lausitz*. Herrnhut: Gustav Winter, 2009.
Palmowski, J. *Inventing a Socialist Nation: Heimat and the Politics of Everyday Life in the GDR, 1945-1990*. Cambridge: Cambridge University Press, 2009.

Schaefer, S. *States of Division: Border and Boundary Formation in Cold War Rural Germany*. Oxford: Oxford University Press, 2014.

Sheffer, E. *Burned Bridge: How East and West Germans Made the Iron Curtain*. Oxford: Oxford University Press, 2011.

Thomas, M. 'Local Lives, Parallel Histories: Villagers and Everyday Life in the Divided Germany'. PhD thesis, University of Bristol, 2017.

Thomson, A. 'Anzac Memories Revisited: Trauma, Memory and Oral History'. *Oral History Review* 42(1) (2015), 1–29.

Chapter 5

Everyday Displacements in Cold War Berlin

Short Prose from East and West

Áine McMurtry

> In this everyday, the Strange Gaze came into being. Gradually, quietly, merci-
> lessly in the familiar streets, walls and objects. The powerful shadows prowl
> about and occupy. And you follow them with all senses flickering incessantly
> and burning from inside. That just about sums up the stupid word persecu-
> tion. And that's the reason why I can't get over the STRANGE GAZE, as it's
> attributed to me in Germany. The Strange Gaze is old, imported from a famil-
> iar context. It has nothing to do with my migration to Germany. Strange, for
> me, is not the opposite of something familiar, but the opposite of something
> trusted. The unfamiliar is not necessarily strange but the familiar can become
> strange.
>
> —Herta Müller, *Der Fremde Blick oder Das Leben ist ein Furz in der Laterne*[1]

In her 1999 essay, *Der Fremde Blick*, the Romanian-German Nobel
Laureate Herta Müller identifies everyday life in Ceaușescu's Romania
as that which has defined the strange gaze on the world that informs
her textual practice. Herta Müller was born into the German-speaking
minority in the Romanian Banat and, after years of political persecution
at the hands of the *Securitate*, she left for West Berlin in 1987 at the age of
thirty-four.[2] Müller's German-language oeuvre is centrally preoccupied
with the lived experience of totalitarianism and, with the award of the
Nobel Prize for Literature in 2009, she was acclaimed by the Swedish
Academy as a writer 'who, with the concentration of poetry and the
frankness of prose, depicts the landscape of the dispossessed'.[3] In recent
years, Müller has been one of the foremost literary voices in Germany

to speak out publicly in support of refugees, invoking those who fled abroad under National Socialism to make a historical case for Germany's contemporary humanitarian obligations.[4]

Her 1999 essay describes how it was the everyday experience of surveillance that generated the 'Strange Gaze' that is widely understood to define her writing. Müller is categorical that the insidious familiarity of everyday persecution, not the mere fact of physical displacement to another country, is what generates radical dislocation. The German adjective 'fremd' can be translated variously into English as 'strange', 'foreign', 'alien' and, in English-language discussions of Müller's 1999 essay, scholars have often chosen to render the word as 'alien', emphasizing experiences of subjective isolation and psychic fracture that drive the author's production.[5] The extreme dislocation suggested by this translation, however, potentially re-inscribes linguistically the othering experienced during persecution, and the word is also at odds with Müller's insistence in the above lines on the material imbrication of self and environment. Her essay presents the everyday in terms of insidious invasion, drawing attention to a threatening collapse of the familiar into the strange, and evoking the implications for the self in spatial and temporal terms of gradual occupation.

The quotidian character of the English word 'strange' comes closest to Müller's meaning in the essay; but it also foregrounds the inextricability of material reality and subjective experience. The everyday is experienced materially in streets, walls and objects, all of which provoke a sensory response that both warns and injures, as well as giving rise to a 'Strange Gaze' that assumes an agency of its own which – writ large – determines the author's perception of the world. In the context of this volume's focus on the role of cultural production in figuring human experience of social agency, analysis of the strange gaze in Müller's fictional work also reveals the highly political character of her unconventional portrayal of the relationship between self and society.[6]

In her 1989 novel *Reisende auf einem Bein*,[7] Herta Müller casts her strange gaze on West Berlin. The novel appeared in English translation as *Traveling on One Leg*[8] and it is the only work from Müller's oeuvre to date to be set in Germany. To this volume's consideration of entangled histories and shared experiences between East and West in the postwar period, Müller's novel adds a radicalized portrayal of everyday experience in divided Berlin that throws up complex interrelations and parallels between West Berlin and the Eastern Bloc as figured through its oblique portrayal of Ceauşescu's Romania. The novel was published in autumn 1989 just two years after Müller's arrival in the West and it charts the emigration of its traumatized female protagonist from a state in the

Eastern Bloc to West Berlin before the fall of the Wall. This chapter examines everyday West Berlin in Müller's novel alongside a consideration of
the textual figuration of East Berlin in writings by Emine Sevgi Özdamar,
which take as their primary setting the Eastern half of the city after the
speaker's escape from right-wing extremism in Turkey. A writer, play-
wright and actor, Özdamar is one of the most significant artists of her
generation and, in 1991, she was the first German-language writer of
Turkish origin to win the prestigious Ingeborg Bachmann Prize.[9] My
concern in what follows is to consider the displaced vision of Berlin in
texts by two multilingual writers who came from countries on either
side of the Cold War divide to reside in the respective halves of the city.
West and East Berlin offered Müller and Özdamar refuge following their
persecution under opposing political regimes and their texts fictionalize
aspects of these real-life experiences. Both writers engage with divided
Berlin as a place of resettlement and new beginnings, yet are simultaneously concerned to reveal parallels between the regimes they had left
behind and the German context, as well as to highlight historical continuities between the two Cold War Germanys. In their portrayals of the
divided city, their texts depart from realist and conventional memoir
forms to develop instead 'strange' literary modes generated from the
material encounter with everyday Berlin.

As Müller suggests in interview comments about her Berlin novel,
'Fremdheit' constitutes a constructive creative strategy rather than a condition to be overcome: 'I don't think that the ideal is to not be strange. The
ideal relationship to an environment is – in my view – a strangeness that
you get used to. Strangeness is not something that can be implemented
because it is a mode of perception. Conscious perception and critical
vision will always have strangeness as their consequence'.[10] My concern
is to probe this 'strange' figuration of Berlin in prose by Emine Sevgi
Özdamar and Herta Müller. The political implications of the two writers'
aesthetic programme can be drawn out through writings by several commentators on the political aesthetics of the everyday, and specifically on
the prose works of Özdamar and Müller. Jacques Rancière offers a first
insight into political art in *The Politics of Aesthetics*, which highlights the
need to ensure 'a double effect: the readability of a political signification
and a sensible or perceptual shock caused, conversely, by the uncanny,
by that which resists signification'.[11] At the close of his text, Rancière
advocates the prose of Virginia Woolf over Émile Zola's 'social epic'
for the ability of the former to establish 'a grid that makes it possible to
think through the forms of political dissensuality', which he attributes to
Woolf's 'way of working on the contraction or distension of temporalities,
on their contemporaneousness or their distance, on her way of situating

events at a much more minute level'.[12] For Rancière, political dissensus is a process that serves to challenge the dominant framework of perception, identification and classification. As he points out, the aesthetic is what enables perceptions of the urban everyday. By writing about East and West Berlin, Müller and Özdamar can thus be seen through the lens of Rancière as actively reconfiguring the two halves of the city, employing a textual politics that provokes a reconceptualization of the German capital and its Cold War status as the symbolic site of East-West division.

Rancière's insights are reinforced by critics writing on the specific relation between German-language literary fiction and political sub-ject formation. In the context of reunified Germany, Andreas Huyssen was one of the first critics to identify issues of citizenship, asylum, and immigration as crucial to any new democratic understanding of German national identity.[13] Huyssen called explicitly for greater attention to the relationship between 'diasporic memory and the memory formations of the national culture within which a given diaspora may be embedded'.[14] Leslie Adelson was arguably the foremost German Studies scholar to respond to Huyssen's call. Her groundbreaking 2005 monograph, *The Turkish Turn in Contemporary German Literature,* emphasized the 'cultural labour' performed by Turkish-German texts in contributing to a new understanding of modern German history and public memory. Adelson, however, questions the validity of Huyssen's use of the term diaspora to refer to German literature written in the 1990s and born out of the Turkish migration that began in the 1960s.[15] In her view, loosening 'an exaggerated attachment to identity as an analytical category' permits 'new questions about the nature of cultural contact in literary texts'.[16] Her readings of German-language writing by Özdamar and Zafer Şenocak, amongst others, highlight the contribution of literary works to new kinds of subject formation at historical moments of structural transformation in which the former East-West coordinates of Cold War division and the binaries of Orient and Occident are no longer valid.[17]

A similar understanding of textual production by writers who migrated to Germany as an imaginative cultural archive for rethinking the reuni-fied nation drives my analysis below. The imaginative engagement in each of the works with quotidian experience is shown to enable literary figuration of human entanglement in material and historical realities. As Michael Sheringham suggests, 'the relational, performative aspects of the *quotidien* – a dimension that emerges through the act of being appre-hended – are enacted in the way a film, play, or artwork "stages" an interaction between human subjects and social structures'.[18] Following Sheringham in focusing on how Müller and Özdamar's texts perform their speakers' material situation in everyday Berlin, I offer an alternative to dominant interpretations that emphasize their status as responses to subjective experiences of historical trauma, cultural otherness and social alienation. My approach is particularly indebted to Margaret Littler's Deleuzian interpretations of Özdamar's writings, which stresses the relevance of the philosopher's materialist thought for an understanding of the transformative potential of literature to imagine alternative worlds.[19] In her reading of Özdamar's 1998 novel *Die Brücke vom Goldenen Horn*, Littler outlines her understanding of 'material, historical reality and individual protagonist, as inextricably connected in the novel, the personal life entirely continuous with and externalized onto the forces permeating the world she inhabits; the self as an unfolding of the outside, rather than the interiority of a psyche'.[20] Instead of looking for subjective stories and individual psychologies, Littler attends to cinematic techniques and parodic moments in the novel, arguing that it 'both thematizes and enacts a non-representational aesthetic ... building to a collective enunciation not localizable in any individual subject'.[21]

My analysis similarly relates the 'strange' vision of everyday Berlin to an undoing of the conventional subject that gives expression to the imbrication of personal and socio-historical reality. Rather than focusing on the portrayal of an individual psychology, the texts are seen to develop strange focalizers that generate new perspectives on the experience of everyday Berlin. Ultimately, my comparative readings of these imagistic textual engagements by writers from countries on different sides of the former Cold War divide move towards interpretations that are not determined by identity politics or ethnic and national difference, but rather investigate the potential of cultural production to generate a more radical rethinking of the nation post-1989.

Mein Berlin

The imaginative relationship between divided city and self stands at the centre of 'Mein Berlin', a text that looks back on Berlin during its years of partition. Özdamar wrote her text in the years following German reunification and it was first published in the 2001 German-language collection *Der Hof im Spiegel* (*The Courtyard in the Mirror*) alongside a sister-text, 'Mein Istanbul'. Liesbeth Minnaard's rich account of these two city texts has established their significance in offering 'an exceptional perspective on (German and Turkish) history and public memory' in 'a subtle rewriting of dominant national history ... from the perspective of Turkish-German migration'.[22] As Minnaard highlights, the two cities share a history of division between East and West – partitioned by a wall in one case, and by a waterway in the other. Minnaard's analysis demonstrates how 'Özdamar's literary cartography unites these two problematic histories of division in a transnational comparison', revealing '[t]he "geographic" variables "East" and "West" as locally specific, ideological constructs'.[23] But Minnaard's compelling interpretation of 'Mein Berlin' as 'a particular kind of "Wende" literature' can be further developed by paying heightened attention to the relational aspects of the quotidian as enacted in Özdamar's prose. This everyday focus casts light on how the artwork figures the relation between human subjects and social structures.[24] Right from its opening lines, 'Mein Berlin' highlights the intersection of personal experience with wider history: the first-person, female speaker identifies the year as 1976, nine years after her first stay in the German city and following her arrest after the 1971 military coup in Turkey, when – through Amnesty International – friends have intervened to bring her back to Berlin. The speaker's biography bears striking parallels to that of Özdamar herself, who came to West Berlin from Turkey as a foreign worker in the 1960s and then studied acting in Istanbul, before returning to East Berlin to work with the Brecht director, Benno Benson, at the Volksbühne.[25] Throughout the short text, references to experiences of political persecution in Turkey, including her own imprisonment and the murder of friends at the hands of fascists, give clear sociohistorical contours to the situation that has been left behind. The narrative play with time and space, however, as well as the frequent use of irony, disrupt straightforward identification of the speaker as Özdamar and any clear-cut sense of textual order and stability. Özdamar's speaker identifies with the city, claiming it as her own. Indeed, the first-person vision of animated Berlin presents the reunion as something mutually welcomed by both speaker and city. The city is figured through a series of vignettes whose haphazard inclusion reflects the shifting character of everyday perception and human memory:

> At Bahnhof Zoo, I waved to all the busses driving past. I was free and rejoiced at the rain. I thought: Berlin has been waiting nine years for me. It was as though, way back when I had left for Istanbul, Berlin had freeze-framed into a photograph in order to wait for me with its long, towering trees, with the Gedächtniskirche, the double-decker busses, the corner taverns. Berliner Kindl, the checkmarks they put on the coasters to keep a running tab. Walls. Checkpoint Charlie. U-Bahn. S-Bahn. Bockwurst. The Brecht Theater 'Berliner Ensemble.' *Arturo Ui*. Canals. Pfaueninsel. Bums at the train stations. Pea Soup. Lonely women in Café Kranzler. Schwarzwälder Kirschtorte. Workers from foreign countries. Spaghetti. Greeks. Scumbag Turks, Café Käse. Telefon Tanz. Bullet pocks on the walls of buildings. Cobblestone. Currywurst. White bodies waiting for the sun at Wannsee. Police dogs. Searchlights of the East

> Berlin Police. Dead railroad tracks with grass growing between the rails. ... Ducks on the Wannsee. A neighbourhood tavern with music from the Forties, elderly women dancing with women. Broiled chicken.[26]

At first glance, this train-of-thought sequence appears to be an account of everyday impressions of a city streetscape. The breathless sequence of names, places and images has the character of a children's game of word association and it works rhythmically to combine personal memories of double-decker buses and Black Forest gateau with snapshots of bullet holes, border guards and dogs, signalling a narrative refusal to comment explicitly on the obvious sociohistorical context for these uncomfortable impressions. The above sequence of images defies the attempt to ascribe the portrayal to either East or West. Whilst the lines could evoke the image entertained by a West Berliner of the city, as most images are of West Berlin, the portrayal is in fact a tripartite one with images of the West, a few specific images of the East which refer to border fortifications and culture, as well as a number of everyday scenes that bring the two together. This complicates any account of the text as an East Berlin narrative, since it is also a text on all of Berlin from the perspective of a figure who is able to cross the border.

Özdamar has in the past been accused of downplaying political injustice, particularly in the context of the GDR, through her non-committal observational style, which focuses on everyday details and occurrences. In the author's defence, Claudia Breger has suggested that this 'faux naïveté' playfully critiques the stereotype of the naïve Oriental woman,[27] whilst Liesbeth Minnaard identifies a 'narrative mode of tactful wondering that often touches upon the sad and tragic absurdities of the situations of separation described'.[28] In my view, however, these readings do not go far enough in acknowledging the political provocation of Özdamar's engagement with Berlin. In fact, the juxtapositions which define the structure of Özdamar's impressionistic narrative call out to be read as images that register the everyday in textual form. Their imagistic character, first signalled in the reference to the freeze-frame photograph of Berlin with which the sequence begins, appear derived from the realm of everyday perception and recollection. No obvious logic links the impressions and, instead, their disconnection from one another is made apparent in the narrative cuts which are reminiscent of cinematic montage techniques. In this light, the images of the fortified border and historical bullet holes, which feature in the textual montage alongside references to pea soup and Wannsee bathers, draw out with devastating clarity the everyday character of the signs of past and present violence that scar the urban landscape.

Özdamar's narrative foregrounding of the freeze-frame within imagistic everyday impressions can be further illuminated by the second
volume of Gilles Deleuze's *Cinéma* work, *The Time-Image*, where modern
cinema is explicitly associated with unexceptional images of the quotidian. According to this philosophical account of post-war cinema, which
Deleuze terms 'a cinema of the seer and no longer of the agent', cinema
helps its viewers to think by filming our relation to the world. In his discussion of everydayness in the work of the twentieth-century Japanese
filmmaker Yasujiro Ozu, Deleuze suggests: 'In everyday banality, the
action-image and even the movement-image tend to disappear in favour
of pure optical situations, but these reveal connections of a new type,
which ... bring the ... senses into direct relation with time and thought'.[29]
In the shift from the 'movement-image' to the 'time-image' in modern
cinema, Deleuze identifies an autonomy in the act of reading the everyday image, which renders both character and viewer visionaries: 'The
purely optical and sound situation gives rise to a seeing function, at once
fantasy and report, criticism and compassion'.[30] The anticipatory quality of this vision is therefore seen to break beyond the known to register
what Margaret Littler terms 'an outside, an unthought, a non-linear time
and a non-homogeneous space, not limited to its historical "setting"'.[31]
Foregrounding the capacity of modern cinema to record radical shifts at
the level of their everyday impact, Deleuze identifies the political character of this cinema in 'precisely the weakness of the motor-linkages ... that
are capable of releasing huge forces of disintegration'.[32]

Deleuze's reading helps to draw out the wider politics of Özdamar's
imagistic montage of animated Berlin, which also calls on the reader
to respond to the contrasting images it accumulates, drawing together
diverse social groups and historical sites within a non-hierarchical narrative frame that signals their fundamental equality and basic difference simultaneously. The deliberate and often comic juxtapositions in
Özdamar's observation of the Berlin streetscape open a narrative space
in which attention can be directed towards those things that are not said.
The speaker contextualizes her move to East Berlin with a description of a
final walk through the Western part of the city and of the array of graffiti
slogans daubed on West German walls. The textual ellipsis signals to the
reader-observer the need to read between the lines: 'GDR ... German Dirt
Republic ... Attention! You are entering the Axel Springer sector ... Send
the commies to the gas chamber ... It's time to live high on the hog – so
get a job! ... USA Army go home'[33] – which suggest the political diversity and activism of the populace. In East Berlin, the speaker appears to
identify more with the intellectual figures memorialized in the names of

underground stations, which she contrasts with her knowledge of persecution in Turkey:

> The name of the subway station at the Volksbühne always made me smile: Rosa-Luxemburg-Platz. And I liked the name of the subway station Marx-Engels Platz, too. In Turkey, people were arrested for having books by Marx, Engels and Luxemburg. And I also liked the fact that cucumbers cost the same no matter where you bought them: 40 pfennigs. Unlike West Berlin, there weren't any slogans scrawled on the walls of buildings or on the Wall itself.[34]

The everyday juxtapositions included in the shifting narrative, which moves from fond recognition of left-wing intellectuals in the context of bad memories of the Turkish regime, to allusion to fixed prices in the GDR economy and the conspicuous absence of graffiti in East Berlin, enable a politicized narrative that nonetheless circumvents the fixed articulation of an ideological stance. The bleak reality for free speech in the GDR – signalled in the pointed contrast of the graffiti-free walls in East Berlin – provokes simultaneous reflection on the prohibitions that accompany more positive aspects of the Socialist order. The correspondences created through Özdamar's shifting first-person narrative that weaves together memories, anecdotes, fragments of conversations and dream, enable a relational mode that figures the narrator's past and present experience between Berlin and Istanbul as part of an imaginative space in which alternative forms of identification are presented to those defined in terms of nation or political allegiance. The text closes with an encounter between the speaker and a young boy she meets at the cemetery in East Berlin, to whom she must explain that Turkey is a country near Bulgaria. The contrast between the official GDR map of history and the complex reality of lived experience reproduced in the narrative web is left to speak for itself.

Reisende auf einem Bein

The ambivalent figuration of Berlin also defines Herta Müller's engagement with the city in *Traveling on One Leg*. Like Özdamar, Müller employs an imagistic poetic prose that is unconcerned with plot development, and instead engages with the minutiae of everyday experience to offer an unconventional view of the divided city. In contrast to the animated vision of 'My Berlin', however, Müller's is a fractured portrait that narrates the emigration of her protagonist Irene from an unnamed but recognizable Romania under military surveillance to the West Berlin of the late 1980s. As has been frequently pointed out in scholarly discussions of the novel, so strange was its portrait of the Western half of the city that the text perturbed early reviewers, foremost amongst whom was Christian Huther, who went so far as to question 'whether the protagonist Irene really finds herself in Federal German territory'.[35] Instead of portraying well-known central Berlin districts or locations, Müller's fragmentary narrative plays out in the northern district of Wilhelmsruh, a poor suburb of the city populated by down-and-outs, child prostitutes and workers from Eastern Europe, who – like Irene – appear stranded in inhospitable and unexceptional terrain.

In their reading of the novel published in 2004, Brigid Haines and Margaret Littler convincingly suggest that the text's ambivalent portrayal of West Berlin calls into question late twentieth-century myths of the city as a free bastion during the Cold War, which 'tended to erase the earlier history of the city, deny what was common to both halves of the city and of Germany, and present the success story of West Berlin as the whole story'.[36] Their discussion draws together central strands from existing scholarship on the novel, combining aspects of trauma theory with Rosi Braidotti's work on nomadic subjectivity to interpret 'der Fremde Blick' not as 'marker of separation between Irene and what she sees' but rather 'a continuing estrangement of the self and of the very relationship between self and other, arising from trauma but sustained by postmodern city life'.[37] The dual foci – trauma theory and nomadic subjectivity – are said to share certain preoccupations, 'not least their theorizing of the viability of an identity based on aporia and of the desirability of giving expression to unique experience'. This narrative foregrounding of the fragmented and isolated female self leads Haines and Littler to acknowledge Müller's rejection of organized politics, but also to qualify the wider political implications of her novel. They suggest that – unlike Braidotti – Müller's nomadic subject does not seek to 'reinvent politics, empower women and enable new forms of interrelatedness'.[38]

If Müller's prose is seen through the lens of the strange everyday, it becomes possible however to reconceptualize the political significance of her prose. Irene's position as onlooker allows her to record aspects of her precarious existence in the city and to establish linkages between the intersectional experience of the female migrant and others who exist at the fringes of society. The political implications of Irene's onlooker status emerge for instance in a passage towards the end of the novel where she travels to Marburg by train. Here, Irene contrasts her sense of living at a remove from her environment with the automatic responses of those close to her, who lose no opportunity to perform their own closeness to those towns and cities in which they reside:

Irene had the feeling, through her gaze on these towns, the people close to her, of becoming distanced from the towns. She made an effort not to show her estrangement,

But the people close to Irene never missed a chance to show her how close they were to these towns.

They always knew exactly what to do wherever they were.

... Then Irene saw that the people close to her carried the city in which they were living on their backs.

In those moments Irene knew that her life had run into observations. The observations made her unable to act.

The actions Irene forced herself to undertake weren't even that. They got stuck in their beginnings. They were beginnings that fell apart. Not even individual gestures would remain whole.[39]

Irene's recognition of her position as observer in these lines recalls Deleuze's comments in *Cinema II* on the relation between the everyday realm and the new observer status of the filmic subject in modern cinema. As is the case for Özdamar's prose vision of Berlin, the textual politics at work in Müller's portrait can be illuminated by Deleuze's conception of the character as

> a kind of viewer ... the situation he is in outstrips his motor capacities on all sides, and makes him see and hear what is no longer subject to the rules of a response or an action. He records rather than reacts. He is prey to a vision, pursued by it or pursuing it, rather than engaged in an action.[40]

For Deleuze, then, the everyday forms neither the mere backdrop to individual action, nor the site of automatic responses. It sets the scene instead for the emergence of exactly that viewer-character whom Irene recognizes in herself: a protagonist who 'records rather than reacts, ... is prey to a vision, pursued by it or pursuing it, rather than engaged in an action'.[41] Rather than voicing any interior perspective, Müller's text thus employs an image of material burden to evoke the forces weighing down on the inhabitants of the city. In its closing description of Irene's aborted actions, Müller's strange prose further undermines Irene as a subject capable of taking individual action, stressing the abortive and fragmented character of her attempts to do so.

Like the Italian neo-realist film that is the object of Deleuze's interpretation, Müller's strange vision of Irene might similarly be understood to convey a general process of social disintegration. The politics of Müller's prose are therefore to be located in how it performs Irene's situation in everyday Berlin, giving literary figuration to human entanglement in changing sociohistorical circumstances. This performative emphasis is strengthened by a marked tendency in Müller's narrative to avoid explicit sociopolitical commentary, particularly in relation to the German situation. Instead, her text focuses on her protagonist's experience of isolation and otherness. This is the aspect of *Reisende* that has provoked comment on the novel's status as a form of trauma narrative, in interpretations that foreground Irene's alienation and powerlessness.[42] Whilst many of these readings offer productive and convincing accounts of the symptomatic character of Müller's dislocated, imagistic prose, their focus on long-term psychological disturbance resulting from persecution often neglects the context of the novel's pointed use of the strange gaze to generate oblique modes of reflection on insidious power relations and modes of surveillance and sociopolitical exclusion. One of the most striking evocations of the subjective implications of the strange gaze occurs in chapter two of the novel, when Irene looks at passport photographs of herself as she prepares to leave the 'other country'. The everyday bureaucracy of the emigration process forms the trigger for a moment of estrangement. A shift in perspective displaces the reader, relocating him or her as focalizer of the action:

> Then Irene had wanted to hold the passport pictures in the rain, and hadn't done it. Had gone under the roof of the first house entrance. Had taken a photo out of the envelope and looked at it.

> A familiar person, but still not like her. And, there, where it mattered, where it mattered to Irene, the eyes, the mouth, and there the groove between nose and mouth, had been a strange person. A strange person had crept into Irene's face.

> The strangeness in Irene's face had been the other Irene.[43]

The process of narrative displacement performed in this passage begins with the omission of the subject from the second and third sentences, which disturbs textual coordinates. The ambiguous auxiliary verb forms which begin both sentences resist the possibility of distinguishing between first and third person, and issue an implicit challenge to reader assumptions about their situation in relation to the events described. In this way, the reader's situation shifts towards the place inhabited by Irene, merging their respective viewpoints until the subsequent paragraph break, which asserts the process of textual transfer. The passage's sudden focus on the familiar yet estranged object of the gaze, who stands alone in a sentence stripped of verb and agency, moves the reader into the place of Irene, as her self-image fractures into a series of facial parts.

As the strange gaze takes in the dislocated eye, mouth and nose, the fragments are then reconstituted as an estranged Other, which results in a moment of disembodiment, doubling and disassociation. The moment of looking at the official photograph might therefore be understood to figure a sudden recognition of those othering processes inherent to power structures that establish their control through the monitoring of individuals and the production of groups of insiders and outsiders.

In subsequent chapters set in West Berlin, the strange narrative gaze established in this passage persists, recording everyday scenes from the city's backstreets and second-hand shops, at one point describing a flea market as 'one of the many places forgotten by the city where poverty disguised itself as business'[44] in a rare instance of explicit critique of the free market economy. For the most part, Irene herself is also observed to be taking a position amongst other impoverished subjects on the fringes of society:

> All the spaces were taken in the hostel. Irene lived in the home for asylum seekers. It was on Flottenstraße. Flottenstraße was a dead-end street.
>
> The railway embankment was on one side of the street, the barracks on the other.
>
> Flottenstraße had the hardness of large ports, of iron bars that double in the water's reflection.
>
> Unused tracks lay rusting on the railway embankment.
>
> … The barracks was a brick building. Had two storeys. But seemed too tall due to the red bricks. One half belonged to the police. The other half was a home for asylum seekers.
>
> … Clothes were alms on Flottenstraße. Scarves yawned between necks and shoulders.
>
> Irene knew the cheap shoes in supermarket boxes. She had seen men and women shoving each other away and digging through the boxes. And among them children trying to pull their mothers and fathers away. And crying.[45]

In a discussion of the novel that foregrounds its status as 'a story of migration' that compiles 'everyday scenes without sketching any kind of development', Sigrid Grün interprets the home on Flottenstraße as 'a symbol for the lives of refugees in the Federal Republic', highlighting the dead-end character of the street that lies between abandoned railway tracks.[46] Sanna Schulte concurs with Grün's symbolic reading, suggesting that the militarized character of the scene where police and soldiers dominate the streetscape is to be interpreted as a comment on Irene's ongoing persecution.[47] Such universalizing interpretations, however, can themselves be seen to strip the female migrant of agency by relegating her to a permanently excluded other of the system. Instead, the strange everyday detail of the scene militates against any simplified symbolic interpretation. Despite the fact that there are few rooms or resources going spare, West Berlin appears emptied of human presence and contact. Müller's prose gives stark articulation to those everyday juridical and economic exclusions that isolate and contain the solitary female migrant who lives in a building shared with the West Berlin police. The short sentences provide a matter-of-fact summary of the bleak situation; the pared-down narrative style is stripped of adjectives and its sentences are often missing the subjects of verbs, which compounds the impression of stasis and struggle for human agency. As Sabine Egger has highlighted, classical tropes of the journey – the street, railway tracks and ports – are presented in unconventional terms as disused and blocked off.[48] Müller's language and imagery thus reduplicate the state of disconnectedness in which Irene finds herself, living in temporal suspension as she awaits a decision from the immigration authorities.

Notably, references to others and othering also occur at points in the narrative when expression is sought for experiences of disassociation explicitly related to the structures and mechanisms of the political orders through which the protagonist passes. In the opening lines of the novel, for example, the attempt to name a militarized border zone marked by radar screens and soldiers provokes the first of many critical references to 'the other country'. Similarly, in Berlin, fleeting allusion to the little cloud that passes over the German-German border permits implicit comment on the artificiality of the political divide: 'A cloud was thin and broken. It came from the other part of the city. Over from the other state'.[49] The choice of the same descriptor to refer to both East-West and inner-German divisions points towards shared othering practices through which apparently opposing political orders construct their self-definitions. Throughout the narrative, textual links are established between West Berlin and the anonymous country Irene left behind; grimy locations in the West are portrayed in comparable terms to the drinking dens and comfortless rooms that Irene frequents at the beginning of the narrative and the same weeds grow on Berlin wasteland.[50] As in Özdamar's text, where the narrator makes repeated reference to her surprise that the East and West parts of the city experience the same weather conditions, Irene contemplates the cloud[51] and swifts – or 'Mauersegler'[52] – that sail freely over the Wall, gesturing towards a natural state which shows up the artificiality and man-made character of the political divide that defines human experience in the city. The relational mode of her narrative thus establishes connections and contrasts without providing explicit commentary. The Wall features obliquely in the text; its presence is acknowledged without being endowed with symbolic significance. Rather, in its banal everydayness, the Wall stands in the background, contributing to the sense of containment in the city, as well to the unreality of a political system that lends the strange scene the character of a theatre set.

Critics including Moray McGowan have affirmed this view of Müller's text by pointing out how it goes beyond the re-inscription of straightforward ideological binaries, instead establishing a complex web of relations between West Berlin and Communist Romania:

> Instead of a complacent polarity that views Berlin as a microcosm for the encounter of two systems, *Reisende* constructs complex patterns of parallel and difference between West Berlin and the East European dictatorship, and, within these patterns, it constructs moments that resist resolution altogether. *Reisende* is not a text of longing to transcend the Wall, not one of anticipation of its fall.[53]

McGowan offers convincing readings of Müller's prose in a wide-ranging discussion of the symbiotic relationship between city and self in the novel. His analysis, however, omits to reflect on the wider significance of the parallelism at work throughout the text, suggesting instead that 'Müller replaces one predictable dichotomy – the East-West binary – with another, less predictable though perhaps no less schematic one, that between the city ... and the state'. Yet this assumes that West Berlin can somehow be divorced from the wider political order of the Federal Republic. Rather than searching for predictable binaries in the novel, it seems crucial to acknowledge the text's more complex commentary on societies of control and their mechanisms, which consistently reflects a web of power relations from which there is no escape. Especially in her interviews with officials from the Federal Intelligence Service, Irene experiences a strong sense of déjà vu, as the material features of the West German official's wardrobe, demeanour and speech patterns bring to mind past interrogations:

> The official wore a kind of dark blue suit that Irene recognized from the other country. The colour between brown and grey. Only the shadows were that colour. And that shade of blue-white was only for shirts that belonged to the shadows. Let me worry about the differences. After all that's what I'm paid for. The angle of the head with the face half in profile glancing down, Irene recognized that too. The chin always just over the shoulder without touching it whilst speaking.[54]

Here, Müller's strange gaze suggests the extreme anonymity of interroga-
tion in which the official becomes a mere mouthpiece of interchangeable
systems, signalled in his narrative erasure as the agent of speech. Instead
he is figured in material terms as the blind spot at which a certain type
of clothing, formulaic turns of phrase and contrived gestures converge.

There is a strong narrative suggestion, in sum, that the figure of the
anonymous official is to be found in both East and West. Müller can be
seen here to be making a wider comment on modern political systems
and the transnational character of their social organization. As Patricia
Hill Collins points out in a discussion of the politics of empowerment in
black feminist thought, 'capitalist and socialist countries alike depend
on bureaucracies – this style of organization becomes highly efficient
in both reproducing intersecting oppressions and masking their effects.
Bureaucracies, regardless of the policies they promote, remain dedicated
to disciplining and controlling their workforces and clientele'.[55] In its
focus on everyday oppressions, Müller's prose establishes a means of
making links and connections between precisely those different forms of
coercion and exclusion that Hill Collins identifies as common to socialist
and capitalist systems.

Irene's experience of migration is particularly crucial here. As is
true for the first-person account of passing through animated Berlin in
Özdamar's text, Müller's novel is consistently preoccupied with charting the implications of the migrant's non-automatic movement throughout the city, establishing connections and contrasts without providing
explicit commentary. Throughout the text, Irene's interactions with those
around her also reflect the multiple levels on which expulsion and othering take place – political, territorial, juridical and economic. In the novel's
closing lines, unenthusiastic about the letter informing her that she has
been awarded German citizenship, Irene continues to reflect on others
still moving through the city: '[p]eople who no longer knew whether
they were travellers in thin shoes in these cities. Or inhabitants with hand
luggage. Irene was lying in the dark thinking of the city. Irene refused
to think goodbye' (*Reisende*, 176). With this ambivalent counter-vision
to national citizenship, Müller's text can be seen to conclude with an
unsteadying of established political categories and subject positions that
at least partially valorizes mobility and transit over more conventional
modes of belonging.

In this respect, the novel can be seen to share Thomas Nail's project to
'reinterpret the migrant first and foremost according to its own defining
feature: its movement'.[56] Rejecting the dominant conceptualization of
the migrant as failed citizen, Nail's study sets out to develop a political theory that 'allows us to *diagnose the capacity of the migrant to create*

an alternative to social expulsion'.[57] Clearly Irene – as someone who can both speak the language and apply for German citizenship in the FRG – enjoys certain rights and privileges unavailable to other migrants. But the achievement of the novel is to be located in its sustained – and highly political – refusal to render Irene a representative figure or social type. Rather, by focusing on the material experience of West Berlin, it works to undermine easy distinctions and to suggest the ambiguous realities of Irene's situation, where spatial and temporal boundaries blur and the displaced female migrant's experience instead offers a surface onto which intersecting oppressions – political, territorial, juridical, economic – may begin to be mapped.

One example is Irene's queer relationship with Thomas, a bisexual man who sleeps with Irene, which offers the context for a rare instance of explicit commentary on Irene's understanding of the difference between East and West. Throughout the text Irene interacts with three male figures who at times are presented as interchangeable, Franz, Stefan and Thomas, yet it is Thomas with whom she appears most intimate.[58] Referring to Thomas as a prefiguration of Leo Auberg in *Atemschaukel* (2009), Karin Bauer has suggested that Müller's writing constructs homosexuality as 'an alternative third position that breaks open the binaries of gender and exchange'.[59] With Thomas, Irene appears able to articulate her sense of impasse when, towards the end of the novel, she describes to him the difference between the two social orders that she has experienced: 'In the other country, said Irene, I understood what wore people down. The reasons were obvious. It was really painful to see the reasons every day. ... And here, Irene said. I know there are reasons. I can't see them. It's painful not to see the reasons every day'.[60] In these lines, a tension between different forms of hegemony finds articulation, which might simultaneously shed light on the strange literary mode devised in the text. Everyday experience of totalitarianism has made Irene sensitive to hidden power structures and their human consequences, which is further reflected in her simultaneously intimate and distrustful exchanges with Thomas. The textual refusal to identify causal relations responsible for the damage forms a further acknowledgment of the insidious character of their invisible stranglehold and influence on aspects of existence, which cannot, in any straightforward sense, be named or counted. Instead, the relational mode of the narrative establishes connections and contrasts without providing explicit commentary. The exchanges between Irene and Thomas identify a shared fear related to the experience of Eastern dictatorship which is communicated and understood in corporeal terms: 'I know the Kings of the East, said Irene. I'm afraid. And you're afraid, you don't know them. Sometimes, said Thomas, when you talk and gesture with your hands, I know them too. Perhaps they're the Kings of the West then, if I talk about the Kings of the East here'.[61] These lines point towards the relativity of spatial demarcations and categorizations, as well as the transmutability of systems of oppression. Following Irene's comments, Thomas suggests that the movement of people through transit spaces in the city enables an appreciation of the material potential of human existence to break beyond rational constraints:

> Thomas raised his head. Sometimes you could think we don't have any powers of reason. And don't need any either. Only sensual force to live. Do you know where you realize it – on windy streets, on railway platforms outside and on bridges. So lightly and shamelessly do people move there that they almost touch the sky. Sometimes I see that the people passing me by are feeling well, said Irene. They don't have a goal, only sensual steps driving them through the streets, carrying them forward. Air hits my face. It's as though the leaves of all the trees are rustling between my thighs. I become unsure. Who knows what will become of me if I feel well.[62]

This articulation of potentiality generated by the material movement through the city, in which steps – not human subjects – take on self-perpetuating agency, gestures towards forms of becoming that are closely aligned with the position of the migrant as a dynamic force for social change. Throughout the narrative, Müller's strange depiction of everyday Romania and Berlin lays bare the debilitating othering mechanisms through which social orders exclude individuals in states of static containment. In Irene's counter-image of people streaming through the city on foot, a figuration of what the political philosopher Thomas Nail has termed 'pedetic social force' might be identified:

> Pedetic motion is the force of the foot – to walk, to run, to leap, to dance. As a social force of motion, it is defined by its autonomy and self-motion. It is different from the social forces of centripetal, centrifugal, tensional, and elastic power because it has neither center nor surplus. Instead its movement is irregular and unpredictable. It is turbulent. It does not expand by social expulsion but by inclusive social transformation.[63]

Conclusion

Nail's comments suggest that the strange vision of precarious arrival and multiple belonging on the final pages of Müller's novel, which carries particular resonance in our contemporary era of mass flight and displacement, might also be seen to cast migration as the primary phenomenon by which new societies come into being – in this case, a new German social

order that transcends the dualism of East and West. In the years immediately following German reunification, antagonism towards foreigners
and migrant communities in both former East and West Germany grew
rapidly. There were notorious outbreaks of violence in the early 1990s,
when Turkish homes were firebombed in Mölln and Solingen, and Roma
and Vietnamese residents were attacked in Rostock.[64] Andreas Huyssen
gives a striking interpretation of this growing tide of xenophobia as 'a
complex displacement of an inner-German problematic', suggesting
that old hostilities relating to 'the other Germany' were projected onto
non-Germans.[65] Calling for a new democratic understanding of German
national identity, Huyssen identifies issues of citizenship, asylum and
immigration as crucial for redefining the German nation.[66]

This chapter has attempted to demonstrate that it is the work of cultural production that permits expression, where conventional forms of
language falter, of the political entanglements, lived realities and social
possibilities towards which Huyssen gestures. Herta Müller herself has
indicated that such new possibilities also depend on abandoning notions
of German particularity. At a public forum entitled 'Berlin – tolerant
and open' that was held in the reunified city during April 1993, Müller
delivered a speech that challenged the popular conception of tensions
between East and West as being somehow particular to the German
national situation:

> The way that East and West Germans encounter each other is not a conse-
> quence of unification, rather it's as old as the first flight from East to West.
> What people characterize – in terms of whinging in the East and arrogance in
> the West – as *typically German*, is elsewhere typically Hungarian, when people
> from Transylvania who'd like to be part of Hungary meet straightforwardly
> Hungarian people from Hungary. And when Romanians from Romania and
> Moldova meet, then it's typically Romanian. Relations between East and
> West Germans are as *typical* as anywhere, where there's a difference between
> two people who speak the same language. To say these relations are *typically
> German* is simply not the case.[67]

Müller's words highlight the inevitable relation between apparently
stable categories of identity and those conflicts that ensue in the face of
unequal power relations and material conditions. Oppositional subject
positions based on territorial boundaries and borders are acknowledged
as universally problematic but – in the language of the public speech –
they are presented as irresolvable binaries tied to concrete historical
and territorial contingencies. In both Özdamar and Müller's prose
narratives, however, a strange literary gaze on everyday experience
moves towards a linguistic overthrow of these categories. Set in the

period immediately before the fall of the Berlin Wall, the two texts pre-empt Andreas Huyssen's urgent call to reconceive the city through the lens of migration. Through the portrayal of everyday migrant experience in Cold War Berlin, the texts enable implicit critical questioning of the city's infamous symbolic status as the fractured meeting point of East and West. Whilst Müller casts her strange gaze on West Berlin to offer an ambivalent portrait of its status as a free enclave, Özdamar fashions a first-person vision of animated East Berlin. Coming from different sides of the Cold War divide, the two writers configure the respective halves of the divided city as ambivalent spaces of renewal. Using innovative textual means, the works indicate the relative and arbitrary character of spatial alignments and national allegiances. The focus on material aspects of everyday experience enables entangled histories to be traced, and intersecting oppressions to be mapped on a minute level. By suggesting experiential affinities between figures on either side of the East-West divide, these dissenting works of cultural production can be seen to challenge dominant conceptual frameworks and gesture towards possibilities for solidarity and forms of perceptible community in the reunified capital which are as yet unthought and unimagined.

Áine McMurtry is Lecturer in German at King's College London. Her teaching and research concentrate on German literature from the twentieth century to the present with an emphasis on experimental modes of writing. Her current work employs materialist and postcolonial perspectives to explore textual strategies in contemporary multilingual writings. She is the author of *Crisis and Form in the Later Writing of Ingeborg Bachmann*, which appeared in the MHRA's Bithell Series in 2012.

Notes

A version of this chapter was published in *German Life and Letters* 71(4) (2018), 473–94; I thank the editors and publisher of *German Life and Letters* for their permission to reprint this material.

1. 'In diesem Alltag ist der Fremde Blick entstanden. Allmählich, still, gnadenlos in den vertrauten Straßen, Wänden und Gegenständen. Die wichtigen Schatten streifen herum und besetzen. Und man folgt ihnen mit einem Sensorium, das immerzu fla-ckert und einen von innen verbrennt. So ungefähr sieht das dumme Wort Verfolgung aus. Und dies ist der Grund, weshalb ich es beim FREMDEN BLICK, wie man mir ihn in Deutschland bescheinigt, nicht belassen kann. Der Fremde Blick ist alt, fertig

mitgebracht aus dem Bekannten. Er hat mit dem Einwandern nach Deutschland nichts zu tun. Fremd ist für mich nicht das Gegenteil von bekannt, sondern das Gegenteil von vertraut. Unbekanntes muß nicht fremd sein, aber Bekanntes kann fremd werden'. Müller, *Der Fremde Blick*, 11–12. Unless otherwise referenced, translations from the German are my own.

2. 'Herta Müller Biographical', 2009. Retrieved 28 January 2018 from http://www.nobel-prize.org/nobel_prizes/literature/laureates/2009/muller-bio.html.

3. 'The Nobel Prize in Literature 2009 – Press Release', 2009. Retrieved 28 January 2018 from http://www.nobelprize.org/nobel_prizes/literature/laureates/2009/press.html.

4. 'Das Flüchtlingsdrama: Hört uns zu!', *Bild*, 20 August 2015. Retrieved 28 January 2018 from http://www.bild.de/politik/inland/fluechtling/hoert-uns-zu-42375908.bild.html.

5. C.f. Eke, '"Macht nichts, macht nichts, sagte ich mir, macht nichts"'; Gunew, 'Estrangement as Pedagogy'; Marven, 'An Alien Gaze'.

6. C.f. 'Texte Herta Müllers ... sind Nachklang eines politischen Alltags, der sich durch Verhören und Verstecken regelte, durch Ausgefragtwerden und Flucht'. Köhnen, 'Terror und Spiel', 19.

7. Müller, *Reisende auf einem Bein*.

8. Müller, *Traveling on One Leg*.

9. 'Der Ingeborg-Bachmann-Preis', 2007. Retrieved 28 January 2018 from http://archiv.bachmannpreis.orf.at/bachmannpreis.eu/de/information/30/.

10. 'Ich glaube nicht, daß es das Ideale ist, nicht fremd zu sein. Die ideale Beziehung zu einer Umgebung ist aus meiner Sicht eine Fremdheit, an die man sich gewöhnt. Fremdheit kann nicht ausgetragen werden, weil sie eine Modalität der Wahrnehmung ist. Bewußte Wahrnehmung und kritische Sicht werden immer Fremdheit zur Folge haben'. Haines and Littler, 'Gespräch mit Herta Müller', 20.

11. Rancière, *The Politics of Aesthetics*, 59.

12. Ibid., 61.

13. Huyssen, *Twilight Memories*, 82.

14. Huyssen, 'Diaspora and Nation', 151.

15. Adelson, *The Turkish Turn in Contemporary German Literature*.

16. Adelson, 'The Turkish Turn in Contemporary German Literature and Memory Work', 327.

17. Ibid.

18. Sheringham, *Everyday Life*, 334.

19. Littler, 'Intimacy and Affect in Turkish-German Writing', 334–35.

20. Littler, 'Machinic Agency', 292.

21. Littler, 'Machinic Agency', 293.

22. Minnaard, *New Germans*, 74.

23. Ibid., 75.

24. My interpretation moves away from reading the text's 'disruptive quality' (ibid., 79) in the protagonist's 'outsider status' (ibid., 85) against a Brechtian tradition of artistic estrangement. Instead, the comparative treatment of Özdamar and Müller's prose figuration of felt encounter with divided Berlin offers an understanding of their non-identitarian textual politics that enables – following Rancière – a creation of 'forms of perceptible community (that) unite people within living ties'. Rancière, *The Politics of Aesthetics*, 55–56.

25. Yildiz, *Beyond the Mother Tongue*, 146.

26. Özdamar and Friedberg, 'My Berlin', 227. 'Am Bahnhof Zoo begrüßte ich alle Busse, die vorbeifuhren. Ich war in Freiheit und freute mich über den Regen. Ich dachte: Berlin hat neun Jahre auf mich gewartet. Es war, als wäre Berlin damals, als ich nach Istanbul zurückgegangen war, zu einem Foto erstarrt, um auf mich zu warten – mit den langen, hohen Bäumen, mit der Gedächtniskirche, mit den zweistöckigen Bussen, mit

den Eckkneipen, Berliner Kindl, die Kreuze auf den Bierdeckeln. Mauern. Checkpoint Charlie. U-Bahn. S-Bahn. Kino Steinplatz. Abschied von gestern. Alexander Kluge. Bockwurst. Das Brecht-Theater Berliner Ensemble. Arturo Ui. Kanäle. Pfaueninsel. Bahnhofspenner. Erbsensuppe. Einsame Frauen im Café Kranzler. Schwarzwälder Kirschtorte. Arbeiter aus anderen Ländern. Spaghetti. Griechen. Kümmeltürken. Café Käse. Telefon Tanz. Einschußlöcher an den Hauswänden. Kopfsteinpflaster. Currywurst. Am Wannsee auf die Sonne wartende weiße Körper. Polizeihunde. Scheinwerfer der Ost-Berliner Polizei. Tote Bahnschienen, zwischen denen Gras wuchs. … Enten am Wannsee. Ein Lokal mit Musik aus den 40er Jahren, alte Frauen tanzen mit Frauen. Broiler'. Özdamar, 'Mein Berlin', 56. Hereafter cited as *MB*.

27. Breger, '"Meine Herren spielt in meinem Gesicht ein Affe?"', 30–59.
28. Minnaard, *New Germans*, 80.
29. Deleuze, *Cinéma II*, 18.
30. Ibid., 19.
31. Littler, 'Machinic Agency', 292.
32. Deleuze, *Cinéma II*, 19.
33. Özdamar and Friedberg, 'My Berlin', 228. 'DDR: Deutscher DReck … Attention! You are entering the Axel Springer sector … Alle Roten in die Gaskammer … Wird Zeit, daß wir leben – Geh erst mal arbeiten … USA Army go home'. *MB*, 58.
34. Özdamar and Friedberg, 'My Berlin', 229. 'Jedesmal freute ich mich über den Namen der Haltestelle an der Volksbühne: "Rosa-Luxemburg-Platz". Ich freute mich auch über die U-Bahn-Haltestelle "Marx-Engels-Platz". Wegen der Bücher von Marx, Engels und Luxemburg hatte man in der Türkei Menschen verhaftet. Ich freute mich auch, daß eine Gurke in jedem Land gleich viel kostete: 40 Groschen. Im Gegensatz zu West-Berlin gab es an den Hauswänden oder an der Mauer keine Sprüche'. *MB*, 59.
35. 'eine Strafexpedition in die lebensgeschichtlich längst bewältigten frühen Fünfziger'. Franzen, 'Test the West'.
36. Haines and Littler, 'Herta Müller', 102.
37. Ibid., 116.
38. Ibid., 113.
39. 'Irene hatte das Gefühl, durch ihren Blick auf diese Städte, die Menschen, die ihr nahestanden, von den Städten zu entfernen. Sie gab sich Mühe, ihre Fremdheit nicht zu zeigen. Doch die Menschen, die Irene nahestanden, ließen keine Gelegenheit aus, ihr zu zeigen, wie nahe ihnen diese Städte standen. Sie wußten sehr genau, was sie an jedem Ort tun sollten. … Dann sah Irene, daß die Menschen, die ihr nahestanden, die Stadt, in der sie lebten, auf dem Rücken trugen. In diesen Augenblicken wußte Irene, daß ihr Leben zu Beobachtungen geronnen war. Die Beobachtungen machten sie handlungsunfähig. Wenn sich Irene zu Handlungen zwang waren es keine. Sie blieben in den Anfängen stecken. Es waren Anfänge, die zusammenbrachen. Nicht einmal die einzelnen Gesten blieben ganz'. Müller, *Reisende auf einem Bein*, 139. Hereafter cited as *Reisende*. All translations are my own.
40. Deleuze, *Cinéma II*, 3.
41. Deleuze, *Cinéma II*, 20.
42. For readings of the engagement with trauma in the novel, see especially Haines, '"The Unforgettable Forgotten"'; Marven, *Body and Narrative*, 53–114.
43. 'Dann hatte Irene Lust gehabt, die Paßphotos in den Regen zu halten, und hatte es nicht getan. War unters Dach vor den ersten Hauseingang gegangen. Hatte ein Photo aus dem Umschlag genommen und es angeschaut. Eine bekannte Person, doch nicht wie sie selbst. Und da, worauf es ankam, worauf es Irene ankam, an den Augen, am Mund, und da, an der Rinne zwischen Nase und Mund, war eine fremde Person gewesen. Eine fremde Person hatte sich eingeschlichen in Irenes Gesicht. Das Fremde an Irenes Gesicht war die andere Irene gewesen'. *Reisende*, 18–19.

44. 'einer der vielen, von der Stadt vergessene Orte, wo sich die Armut tarnte als Geschäft'. *Reisende*, 68.
45. 'Im Übergangsheim waren alle Plätze belegt. Irene wohnte im Asylantenheim. Es lag in der Flottenstraße. Die Flottenstraße war eine Sackgasse. Der Bahndamm lag auf der einen Straßenseite. Die Kaserne auf der anderen Seite. Die Flottenstraße hatte die Härte der großen Häfen, der Eisenstangen, die sich in der Spiegelung des Wassers verdoppelten. Auf dem Bahndamm rosteten die stillgelegten Gleise. ... Die Kaserne war ein Backsteingebäude. Hatte zwei Stockwerke. Schien doch zu hoch, wegen der roten Steine. Die eine Hälfte gehörte der Polizei. Die andere Hälfte war ein Asylantenheim. ... Die Kleider waren in der Flottenstraße Almosen. Zwischen Hals und Schultern klaffte das Tuch. Irene kannte die billigen Schuhe aus den Kisten der Supermärkte. Sie hatte Männer und Frauen gesehen, die sich drängten und in den Kisten wühlten. Und Kinder dazwischen, die ihre Mütter und Väter wegziehen wollten. Und weinten'. *Reisende*, 30.
46. 'Die Erzählung *Reisende auf einem Bein* ist eine Migrationsgeschichte, die sich jenseits einer Identitätssuche entwickelt. Eine Episode reiht sich an die nächste – Alltagsszenen –, ohne dass sich eine Entwicklung abzeichnen würde. ... Das Flüchtlingslager in der Flottenstraße scheint ein Symbol für das Leben der Flüchtlinge in der Bundesrepublik zu sein. Die Straße ist eine Sackgasse zwischen stillgelegten Bahngleisen', *Reisende*, 29. Grün, *'Fremd in einzelnen Dingen'*, 101.
47. Schulte, *Bilder der Erinnerung*, 29.
48. Egger, 'Der Raum des Fremden als "fahrender Zug"', 44.
49. 'Eine Wolke war dünn und zerbrochen. Sie kam aus dem anderen Teil der Stadt. Aus dem anderen Staat herüber'. *Reisende*, 32.
50. *Reisende*, 68.
51. *Reisende*, 32.
52. *Reisende*, 130.
53. McGowan, '"Stadt und Schädel"', 67.
54. 'Der Beamte trug einen dunklen Anzug, wie Irene sie kannte aus dem anderen Land. Die Farbe zwischen braun und grau. Nur der Schatten hatte diese Farbe. Und das Blauweiß hatten nur die Hemden, die zum Schatten gehörten. Lassen Sie das Differenzieren vorläufig meine Sorge sein. Dafür werde ich schließlich bezahlt. Auch die Haltung des Kopfes, das Gesicht halb im Profil, ein wenig nach unten gewandt, kannte Irene. Das Kinn immer knapp über der Schulter, ohne sie beim Sprechen zu berühren'. *Reisende*, 27.
55. Hill Collins, *Black Feminist Thought*, 281.
56. Nail, *The Figure of the Migrant*, 3.
57. Ibid., 7.
58. C.f. Haines and Littler, 'Herta Müller', 115.
59. Bauer, 'Gender and the Sexual Politics of Exchange', 155–56.
60. 'In dem anderen Land, sagte Irene, hab ich verstanden, was die Menschen so kaputtmacht. Die Gründe lagen auf der Hand. Es hat sehr weh getan, täglich die Gründe zu sehn. ... Und hier, sagte Irene. Ich weiß, es gibt Gründe. Ich kann sie nicht sehn. Es tut weh, täglich die Gründe nicht zu sehn'. *Reisende*, 138–39.
61. 'Ich kenne die Könige des Ostens, sagte Irene. Ich habe Angst. Und du hast Angst, du kennst sie nicht. Manchmal, sagte Thomas, wenn du redest und mit den Händen zeigst, was du erzählst, kenn ich sie auch. Vielleicht sind es dann die Könige des Westens, wenn ich von den Königen des Ostens hier erzähl'. *Reisende*, 140.
62. 'Thomas hob den Blick: Manchmal könnte man meinen, wir haben keinen Verstand. Und brauchen auch keinen. Nur sinnliche Kraft, um zu leben. Weißt du, wo man das merkt, auf windigen Straßen, auf Bahnsteigen im Freien und auf Brücken. Dort bewegen die Menschen sich so schamlos und leicht, daß sie den Himmel fast berühren. Manchmal sehe ich, sagte Irene, daß es den Menschen, die an mir vorbeigehen, gut geht. Sie haben kein Ziel, nur sinnliche Schritte treiben sie durch die Straßen. Die übertragen

sich. Luft schlägt mir über das Gesicht. Es ist mir, als rauschten die Blätter aller Bäume zwischen meinen Schenkeln. Ich werde unsicher. Wer weiß, was aus mir wird, wenn es mir gut geht'. *Reisende*, 141.
63. Nail, *The Figure of the Migrant*, 125.
64. '20 Jahre Brandanschlag in Solingen', *Bundeszentrale für politische Bildung*, 28 May 2013. Retrieved 28 January 2018 from http://www.bpb.de/politik/hintergrund-aktuell/161980/brandanschlag-in-solingen-28-05-2013.
65. Huyssen, *Twilight Memories*, 82.
66. Ibid.
67. 'Wie Ost- und Westdeutsche einander begegnen, ist keine Folge der Vereinigung, ist so alt wie die erste Flucht von Ost nach West. Was man am Lamentieren im Osten und an der Überheblichkeit im Westen als *typisch deutsch* bezeichnet, ist anderswo typisch ungarisch, wenn sich wunschzugehörige Ungarn aus Siebenbürgen und "selbstverständliche Ungarn" aus Ungarn begegnen. Und wenn sich Rumänen aus Rumänien und Moldawien begegnen, ist es typisch rumänisch. Der Umgang zwischen Ost- und Westdeutschen ist so *typisch* wie überall, wo es zwischen zwei Gleichsprachigen ein Gefälle gibt. *Typisch deutsch* ist dieser Umgang nicht'. Müller, 'Und noch erschrickt unser Herz', 27.

Bibliography

Adelson, L. *The Turkish Turn in Contemporary German Literature: Toward a New Critical Grammar of Migration*. New York and Basingstoke: Palgrave Macmillan, 2005.
———. 'The Turkish Turn in Contemporary German Literature and Memory Work'. *The Germanic Review: Literature, Culture, Theory* 77(4) (2002), 326–38.
Bauer, K. 'Gender and the Sexual Politics of Exchange in Herta Müller's Prose', in B. Haines and L. Marven (eds), *Herta Müller* (Oxford: Oxford University Press, 2013), 153–71.
Breger, C. '"Meine Herren spielt in meinem Gesicht ein Affe?" Strategien der Mimikry in Texen von Emine S. Özdamar und Yoko Tawada', in C. Gelbin, K. Konuk and P. Piesche (eds), *AufBrüche: Kulturelle Produktionen von Migrantinnen, Schwarzen und jüdischen Frauen in Deutschland* (Frankfurt am Main: Helmer, 2000), 30–59.
Deleuze, G. *Cinéma II: The Time-Image*, H. Tomlinson and R. Galeta (eds). London and New York: Bloomsbury, 2013.
Egger, S. 'Der Raum des Fremden als "fahrender Zug" in Herta Müllers *Reisende auf einem Bein*'. *Zeitschrift für interkulurelle Germanistik* 7(2) (2016), 35–54.
Eke, N.O. '"Macht nichts, macht nichts, sagte ich mir, macht nichts": Herta Müller's Romanian Novels', in B. Haines and L. Marven (eds), *Herta Müller* (Oxford: Oxford University Press, 2013), 99–116.
Franzen, G. 'Test the West: Herta Müllers Prosa *Reisende auf einem Bein*'. *Die Zeit Online*, 10 November 1989. Retrieved 28 January 2018 from http://pdf.zeit.de/1989/46/test-the-west.pdf.
Grün, S. *'Fremd in einzelnen Dingen': Fremdheit und Alterität bei Herta Müller*. Stuttgart: ibidem, 2010.

Gunew, S. 'Estrangement as Pedagogy', in R. Braidotti, P. Hanafin and B.B. Blaagaard (eds), *After Cosmopolitanism* (Abingdon and New York: Routledge), 132–48.

Haines, B. '"The Unforgettable Forgotten": The Traces of Trauma in Herta Müller's *Reisende auf einem Bein'*. *German Life & Letters* 55(3) (2002), 266–81.

Haines B. and M. Littler. 'Gespräch mit Herta Müller', in Brigid Haines (ed.), *Herta Müller* (Cardiff: University of Wales Press, 1998), 14–24.

_____. 'Herta Müller, *Reisende auf einem Bein* (1989)', in B. Haines and M. Littler (eds), *Contemporary Women's Writing in German: Changing the Subject* (Oxford: Oxford University Press, 2004), 99–117.

Hill Collins, P. *Black Feminist Thought: Knowledge, Consciousness and the Politics of Empowerment*. New York and London: Routledge, 2000.

Huyssen, A. 'Diaspora and Nation: Migration into Other Pasts'. *New German Critique* 88(4) (2003), 147–64.

_____. *Twilight Memories: Marking Time in a Culture of Amnesia*. New York and London: Routledge, 1995.

Köhnen, R. 'Terror und Spiel: Der autofiktionale Impuls in frühen Texten Herta Müllers', in H. L. Arnold (ed.), *Herta Müller: Text + Kritik* (Munich: edition text+kritik, 2002), 18–29.

Littler, M. 'Intimacy and Affect in Turkish-German Writing: Emine Sevgi Özdamar's "The Courtyard in the Mirror"'. *Journal of Intercultural Studies* 29(3) (2008), 331–45.

_____. 'Machinic Agency and the Powers of the False in Emine Sevgi Özdamar's *Die Brücke vom Goldenen Horn* (1998)'. *Oxford German Studies* 45(3) (2016), 290–301.

Marven. L. 'An Alien Gaze'. *Red Pepper* (2010). Retrieved 28 January 2018 from http://www.redpepper.org.uk/an-alien-gaze/.

_____. *Body and Narrative in Contemporary Literatures in German: Herta Müller, Libuše Moníková, and Kerstin Hensel*. Oxford: Oxford University Press, 2005.

McGowan, M. '"Stadt und Schädel", "Reisende", and "Verlorene": City, Self, and Survival in Herta Müller's *Reisende auf einem Bein'*, in B. Haines and L. Marven (eds), *Herta Müller* (Oxford: Oxford University Press, 2013), 64–83.

Minnaard, L. *New Germans, New Dutch: Literary Interventions*. Amsterdam: Amsterdam University Press, 2008.

Müller, H. *Der Fremde Blick oder Das Leben ist ein Furz in der Laterne*. Göttingen: Wallstein, 1999.

_____. *Reisende auf einem Bein*. Berlin: Rotbuch, 1989.

_____. *Reisende auf einem Bein*. Frankfurt am Main: Fischer, 2010.

_____. *Traveling on One Leg*. Trans. V. Glajar and A. Lefevere. Evanston, IL: Northwestern University Press, 1998.

_____. 'Und noch erschrickt unser Herz', in *Hunger und Seide: Essays* (Reinbek bei Hamburg: Rowohlt, 1995), 19–38.

Nail, T. *The Figure of the Migrant*. Stanford: Stanford University Press, 2015.

Özdamar, E.S. 'Mein Berlin', in *Der Hof im Spiegel*. Cologne: Kiepenhauer & Witsch, 2001.

Özdamar, E.S. and L. Friedberg. 'My Berlin'. *Chicago Review* 48(2/3) (2002), 226–230.

Rancière, J. *The Politics of Aesthetics*. London and New York: Bloomsbury, 2004.

Schulte, S. *Bilder der Erinnerung:* Über *Trauma und Erinnerung in der literarischen Konzeption von Herta* Müllers *Reisende auf einem Bein und Atemschaukel.* Würzburg: Königshausen & Neumann, 2015.

Seyhan, A. *Writing Outside the Nation.* Princeton and Oxford: Princeton University Press, 2001.

Sheringham, M. *Everyday Life: Theories and Practices from Surrealism to the Present.* Oxford: Oxford University Press, 2006.

Yildiz, Y. *Beyond the Mother Tongue: The Postmonolingual Condition.* New York: Fordham, 2012.

Chapter 6

DEFA's 'Home-Made' Experiment
Traces of GDR Reality and International Avant-Garde Film in Jürgen Böttcher's *Transformations* (1981)

Franziska Nössig

The only experimental film ever produced at *DEFA*, Jürgen Böttcher's trilogy *Verwandlungen* (*Transformations*, 1981), was filmed in and around a private rental flat – Böttcher's home – in a large, ten-storey concrete slab in Berlin-Friedrichsfelde.[1] Against the background of daily life in the GDR in its last decade, Böttcher and his cameraman Thomas Plenert shot a non-narrative and aesthetically unconventional project that combined over-painting onto art postcards, stop-motion animation and multiple projections. Within the DEFA studio tradition, the trilogy's short individual parts *Potter's Stier, Venus nach Giorgione* and *Frau am Klavichord* (*Potter's Bull, Venus by Giorgione, Woman at the Clavichord*) stand out as unparalleled examples of avant-garde art film.

The trilogy's prominent position is particularly noteworthy given the fact that avant-garde art and especially international experimental art influences were viewed critically, or were even censored, in the GDR. As curator Christoph Tannert has pointed out, renowned experimental artists 'Andy Warhol, Stan Brakhage or Kenneth Anger were not even discussed in art history classes at university'; moreover, underground film, or avant-garde movements were generally taboo.[2] Nevertheless, Böttcher's trilogy reveals both explicit and implicit aesthetic and conceptual links with the international experimental film scene. This raises a number of questions: what sources inspired Böttcher? Did state officials grant him exclusive access to otherwise censored material on, for instance, underground art movements? Did they perhaps even commission *Transformations* as a Cold War project to appeal especially to

Western audiences, and to present the GDR as a culturally advanced, art-appreciating nation on the international (film) stage?

Born in 1931, Jürgen Böttcher is a highly significant, if not the most significant GDR documentarist, and widely acknowledged visual artist. Nationally as well as internationally acclaimed films such as *Wäscherinnen* (*Laundry Women*, 1972), *Martha* (1978) and *Rangierer* (*Shunters*, 1984) are among more than forty films he directed and co-directed for the state-owned film production company DEFA (Deutsche Film-Aktiengesellschaft) between 1961 and 1990. Following his studies of fine art in Dresden in the mid-1950s, Böttcher moved on to studying film-making in Berlin after two of his paintings were dismissed as 'primitive' and 'formalist' by SED culture critics at his first official exhibition in 1961, resulting in his exclusion from the *Verband Bildender Künstler der DDR* (VBKD), the Association of Visual Artists of the GDR, that same year. Notwithstanding official criticism and rejection, and unlike many artists and intellectuals at the time, Böttcher chose to stay in the GDR. While he was making a living and a career in the state-regulated film industry, he continued to be active as an artist privately, working independently from home and outside of both state structures and the GDR's underground art scene.

To a large extent, the rejection Böttcher experienced as an artist was due to his paintings not adhering to the doctrine of socialist realism prescribed by East German cultural policy. Put simply, according to conventional socialist realist aesthetics, acceptable or desired subjects of GDR art were monumental, often heroic depictions of optimistic workers and marching party supporters. Apart from this cliché, socialist realism indeed demanded that all GDR artists contribute to and help to shape socialist society with their art. In contrast to the Western notion of 'art for art's sake', this understanding assigns a clear purpose and social function to (any) cultural production. As the foreword in an art catalogue published in 1970 explains, 'A high socialist quality of any piece of art is unthinkable without deep ideological substance ... It is the question of one's personal relation to the idea of man, of one's decision for the societal theme and its diversity, of responsibility towards socialist community and its expectations'.[3] Without any such trace of ideological foundation, Böttcher's paintings and drawings clearly come nowhere near the concept of socialist realism. *Transformations* in particular is an example to what extent, on the contrary, the artist film-maker foregrounds self-reference and self-referential practice. Indeed, all three parts of the trilogy bear the hallmarks of a self-referential film, i.e. a film which refers to itself as a production and makes its audience aware of the film-making process.

This chapter shows how Böttcher imaginatively extended his everyday boundaries – the walls of the apartment that also served as his studio – into the cultural space of the international film avant-garde. I will examine the cultural, political and social circumstances that both shaped and facilitated the production of such an unconventional DEFA film. I call it unconventional because this trilogy – commissioned by DEFA's documentary studio, filmed by its employees with studio equipment, and eventually distributed by DEFA – captures an experimental art practice which, influenced, in particular, by the avant-garde scene of the United States, was carried out within the domestic space of a typical home in 1980s East Berlin. As I will argue, Böttcher's set of cultural practices, such as fragmentation or layering and ranging from collage to the production of self through performance, allows us to understand cultural space within the GDR as both rooted in the everyday and transnationally connected. To help the reader grasp a first understanding of the nature of *Transformations*, I will open this chapter with a discussion of the imagery and composition of select scenes from the trilogy. An overview of the political situation as well as the GDR's cultural policy in the late 1970s and early 1980s will then provide the necessary production context. Put simply, following the expatriation of Wolf Biermann in 1976, initially strict regulations concerning artistic expression were relaxed, which gave rise to innovative projects both in official and underground cultural production. What is striking is that Böttcher's *Transformations*, as this chapter explores, does not fit straightforwardly into either category.

Against this important background of experimental development, Böttcher's trilogy ended up influencing non-conformist GDR artists who made avant-garde film their main focus. This stood in contrast to his day-to-day role as an employee of DEFA, in which capacity he also collaborated in the documenting of party congresses, state jubilees and industrial progress. Alongside such contributions, he acquired the freedom to make films such as *Im Pergamon-Museum* (*In the Pergamon Museum*, 1962) or the above mentioned *Shunters*, which emphasize his enthusiasm for both the aesthetics of the everyday and work as a subject matter, and in which he walks a fine line between artistic autonomy and state-sanctioned propaganda. In *Transformations*, the everyday serves as both backdrop and stage for artistic experiments, which cause different boundaries to oscillate, namely those between public and private, film and fine art, and between the avant-garde and the quotidian and allegedly mundane.

Everyday Art Practice

Three sets of over-painted art postcards with motifs ranging from
the Renaissance to Romanticism are the cornerstone and *leitmotif* of
Transformations. Also employing live action footage, photographs, TV
recordings and stop animation, Böttcher sensuously experiments with
traditions of European art as well as with a repertoire of stage gestures,
cinematic close-ups and projections, shadow play and performance. Each
of the three films is introduced with a set of hand-written title cards: first,
a Roman numeral defines each short as one part of a series of three, while
the second title card displaying the title is decorated with ornaments and
scrawls characteristic of the artwork by Strawalde, Böttcher's adopted
pseudonym as a painter (fig. 6.1). But while both numerals and film titles
seem to imply a system of organization and rigorous serial structure,
the trilogy's overall character is spontaneous and unstructured. Despite
thematic or organizational repetitions and references between sequences
across all three films, there is no definitive linking pattern between them
and no discernible narrative or development either across the three films
or within them individually.

Figure 6.1. Hand-drawn title card for *Potter's Bull*. Credits: Jürgen Böttcher,
Transformations (screenshot from DVD, Edition Filmmuseum). Published with
permission.

The visual and material basis for Böttcher's experiments is a stack of off-the-shelf art postcards, which depict paintings from the sixteenth through to the nineteenth century. The films' titles, *Potter's Stier* (17 min), *Venus nach Giorgione* (22 min) and *Frau am Klavichord* (17 min), refer to three works by Dutch and Venetian artists, which, although not the only images subject to over-painting, are at the centre of Böttcher's artistic reinterpretations in this trilogy: Paulus Potter's *De Stier* (*The Bull*, 1647), *Interieur met vrouw aan het virginal* (*Interior with a Woman at the Clavichord*, c. 1665-1670) by Emanuel de Witte, and *Venere dormiente* (*Sleeping Venus*, 1508/10) by Giorgione. Throughout the films, Böttcher playfully modifies these art postcards as well as other artworks by applying stripes, dots or ornaments with pastels, black or coloured ink. He decorates Potter's bull for instance with a set of wings and encases it into a bluish cuboid shape resembling an aquarium (*Potter's Bull*), and he covers Giorgione's Venus in layers of dripping paint (*Venus by Giorgione*). Asked about his motivation for this playful practice, Böttcher explained in an interview, 'I would never over-paint Vermeer, or Picasso, or Rembrandt, but rather works which, although fantastic, have a little something about them that, as I think, one simply cannot do, like Giorgione's "Sleeping Venus"… With her, I have always felt irritated by the red cushion, and by the fact that this nude is literally lying on the doorstep'.[4] Expressed in Böttcher's statement is not primarily a wish to engage with art history by means of experimentation, but rather to evaluate and, in some cases, explicitly reject other painters' conceptions of art. Moreover, his small-scale intervention is mischievous rather than disgruntled, that is, it is not a negation of anything in principle. Furthermore, despite being light-heartedly judgmental, Böttcher's assessment is not intended to shake up artistic conventions. Rather, as art historian Karin Thomas states, it conveys his particular skill, 'to transform art historical quotations into a personal expression of his own mental state'.[5]

Several scenes in *Transformations* show Böttcher's nimble brushstroke adding scrawls, ornamental structures, or even new figures, shifting existing constellations of characters and image composition (fig. 6.2). Moreover, by projecting these manipulated artworks onto both fabrics and people, the film-maker deconstructs each work into its constituent colours, signs and structures, but also creates from these elements new associations and spontaneous connections. According to film historian Lutz Haucke, Böttcher is in pursuit of precisely such 'invention of imagery' and is interested in engaging in playful narratives of symbols and gestures, rather than words.[6] For this purpose, Haucke explains, Böttcher breaks down the existing image compositions into their component parts. Focusing on the underlying layers of meaning in each picture rather than on their previously established lines of perspective, he thus exposes new associations, signs and potential narratives. Similarly to its diverse imagery, the trilogy's audio track combines a variety of sounds consisting of tonal classical music, dissonant piano and string chords and experimental sound fragments, as well as faint ambient noise. There is no explanation of what is shown; however, Böttcher's own vocal experiments, ranging from whistling to singing and rhythmic growling, could be considered a consistent, non-verbal commentary.

At the beginning of both *Potter's Bull* and *Venus*, the domestic location is introduced in a shot sequence viewed from the balcony: in the background is a residential area, a small square with trees, surrounded by three identical blocks of flats. The block containing Böttcher's flat forms the implied fourth side of this rectangle, but except for the balcony, it remains invisible to the viewer. Rather like the three 'walls' limiting a proscenium stage, the three buildings thus frame the balcony in the foreground, which, facing the spectator, represents an invisible fourth 'wall'. While the composition of these shots reduces external reality to a backdrop – a backdrop, however, that is constitutive to the idea of

Figure 6.2. Böttcher overpainting a postcard in *Potter's Bull*. Credits: Jürgen Böttcher, *Transformations* (screenshot from DVD, Edition Filmmuseum). Published with permission.

personal expression and subjectivity – the role of the domestic domain as the facilitator of creative impulse and preserver of artistic self-realization is emphasized, and the contrast between both spheres is heightened. Within a setting characteristically associated with private, everyday life in the GDR, the underlying imaginary structure of a conventional pro-scenium arch stage, which is normally associated with public cultural performance, may seem out of place. However, its incongruity is coun-tered by Böttcher's use of his balcony, after all a liminal space, which can be understood as serving a double function: a private space as part of Böttcher's flat, it is also a public stage where characters perform in front of a camera and for the audience behind it.

According to Haucke, Böttcher's withdrawal from the public into the private sphere enabled him to envision and compose such imagery, and thus preserved his sensual productivity and sensitivity.[7] It is important to keep in mind, however, that the home, or the private sphere, was an ambivalent space in GDR socialism. In fact, as Paul Betts has pointed out, 'private life and state socialism have long been assumed to be antithetical by definition, insomuch as that the private person has no legal identity or political standing outside the socialist community'.[8] However, as Betts explains, while most social interaction, including political activity, 'was heavily monitored, the private sphere functioned for many citizens as an outpost of individuality, potential dissent, and alternative identity-for-mation'; in other words, the domicile 'acted as a semi-permeable refuge from public life and prescribed collective identities, as well as giving form to more private understandings of the self'.[9]

To an extent, Betts's comments can be applied to Böttcher in *Transformations*. While filming in his flat, Böttcher indeed explores his individuality by acting out the roles of artist, film-maker and performer, amongst others, to form and present his alter egos to his audience. Moreover, by painting and projecting in his own living room, Böttcher displays a private understanding of his self, as Betts puts it, in the sense that he develops in private what he is not allowed to show in public. As mentioned above, without membership in the VBK, Böttcher's art-making had been relegated to the private sphere since the early 1960s, resulting in his public reputation as 'only' a film-maker for several years. Interestingly, by filming his private artistic practice for DEFA, Böttcher makes this aspect of his career public again, thus blurring the lines between inside and outside, public and private.

As Betts argues, private life 'was never a world apart, but was always shot through by the forces of state and society', which is why, as he explains, people in the GDR 'constructed and staged a private sphere for various purposes'.[10] While Böttcher indeed puts on a performance in his home in *Verwandlungen*, he does not portray socialist everyday life at home. In other words, he is neither a chronicler of the domestic interior, nor does he portray family collectivity. On the contrary, he stages his artistic individuality – but not for the purpose of being subversive. As Betts states, 'private life possessed no determinate political meaning in itself, but very much depended on the situation and inhabitant'.[11] Filming himself in his rental flat as an artist at work, Böttcher uses his everyday artistic practice, I would argue, in an attempt to be daring and experimental while working within DEFA structures.

If one were to assign any 'political meaning' at all to Böttcher's private sphere as presented in *Transformations*, it would be that the film playfully asserts the existence of an artist (i.e. Strawalde) who was not an artist, at least not an officially registered one. Significantly, the liminal space of the balcony, as discussed above, seems to provide a corresponding stage for Böttcher to perform his ambiguous status as an artist. Moreover, not dissimilarly from the underground artists who were at this point in GDR history turning studios and flats in Prenzlauer Berg into showrooms for their film experiments, Böttcher's balcony in Friedrichsfelde serves as an independent arts venue: an art gallery for sculptures, a platform on which Böttcher presents his art postcards and a performance space for Böttcher and his wife, the actress Erika Dobslaff (fig. 6.3). By including his wife as his co-performer, Böttcher emphasizes once more that his art practice is rooted in the everyday and, more significantly, in his own personal experience and private life. Again, the amateur and experimental practice of self-referentiality is employed here, heightened even more by the fact that Dobslaff already had a supporting role as the muse of one of the main characters in Böttcher's documentary portrait *Drei von Vielen* (*Three of Many*, 1961).

Moreover, this significant autobiographical aspect of Böttcher's preamble to *Transformations* underlines the home-made character of the trilogy. These films are 'home-made', and thus part of everyday cultural production and practice, both in the literal sense – they are 'made at home' rather than at an artist's studio or on a DEFA film set – but also figuratively, since they derive from an artisanal labour of love, and thus contain spontaneous idiosyncrasies rather than industrially manufactured perfection, which in turn foreground the films' improvised and playful nature. A brief sequence in *Clavichord* juxtaposing supposedly mundane, ordinary shots of an aquarium with a jar of bottled yellow plums, and the projection of one of Böttcher's over-paintings gliding over his pet cat, for instance, accentuate this light-hearted experimentation within the realm of the domestic.

Böttcher's home-study is ostensibly detached from external events in its self-sufficient, concentrated experimentation with light, colour, textures and patterns. However, some images evoke the iconography of the avant-garde and locate *Transformations* within the traditions of international experimental film. For instance, the moving projection of de Witte's painting onto a naked female torso (*Clavichord*) brings to mind the naked woman's body turning under curved shadows and reflections at the end of Man Ray's *Le retour à la raison* (*Return to Reason*, 1923). Böttcher's animation practice and overlapping of colours and forms further bears some resemblance with the works of Stan Brakhage (1933–2003), especially his early experimental films, including his *Dog Star Man* cycle (1961–1964). Böttcher remembers meeting Brakhage, the pioneer of the so-called New American Cinema, during the Holland Experimental Film festival in Amsterdam in the late 1970s in his hotel room where he showed Brakhage his over-painted postcards: 'He kept bouncing on his bed like on a trampoline while shouting "Great! Great! You must make a film about them!"'[12] As Claus Löser mentions, Brakhage's Super 8 films, which Böttcher had seen at the time, were one impetus for his

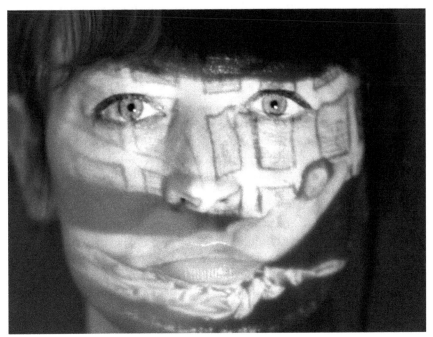

Figure 6.3. Projection onto Dobslaff's face in *Venus*. Credits: Jürgen Böttcher, *Transformations* (screenshot from DVD, Edition Filmmuseum). Published with permission.

use of postcards in *Transformations,* and also laid the foundations for his use of projections.[13] One can further detect West German imagery as de Witte's painting is superimposed onto a television recording of a dancing sequence featuring West German entertainer Peter Kraus. Moreover, in its focus on the poetry of the everyday through the lens of an artist's living and working conditions, *Transformations* further recalls the avant-garde genre of American diary film, especially Jonas Mekas's portrayal of the 1960s New York avant-garde scene in *Walden: Diaries, Notes and Sketches* (1969), or Marie Menken's *Notebook* (1963) with its combination of real-life shots and animated scenes. However, *Transformations* feels less structured than these earlier films. Instead, Böttcher's trilogy self-referentially focuses on experimenting with a layering of materials and media while playfully repeating and varying the processes involved in the making of film and art. Above all, the artist/film-maker's practice happens within the borders of the domestic while, as I have mentioned above, being filmed for a public audience as a regular, if highly unconventional, DEFA production.

In addition to witnessing the creation of film art unfolding directly in front of the camera, the spectator thus also watches the artist himself at work. This involves Böttcher taking on multiple roles simultaneously, acting at once as film-maker, painter, collage-maker, animation and performance artist. In *Potter's Bull* for instance, he presents his collection of over-painted postcards to the camera with the mannerisms of a slapstick comedian: with half a cigarillo between his lips, his face half-covered by the pack of postcards he holds at head-height in front of him, he occasionally peeps over the pack while quickly leafing through the motifs (fig. 6.4). His glance back at the camera, his raised eyebrows and momentarily enlarged eyes draw the spectator in, suggesting that the cards and what is about to follow are worth seeing. In *Clavichord* Böttcher employs artisanal strategies as he draws a round shape centrally in the background of the image with what looks like black chalk or pastel, and then rubs away some colour with his fingernail; or, dipping his brush into a jar full of water, he causes ink and water to mingle, which results in a brief, yet poetic image of a murky, rolling underwater wave. The artist at work, as Böttcher presents him, is self-sufficient and spontaneous. Able to choose from a repertoire of innovative techniques and to turn any device or reference into an integral part of his art, he produces a piece of creative work that is not tied to any specific purpose.

Böttcher's lighthearted playfulness, his method of collage and the production of self through his performance in front of the camera – as painter, film-maker, comedian – constitute fundamental aspects of his everyday artistic practice: taking on a multitude of roles, he presents not only his over-paintings and his films, but also visualizes the process and the production conditions of his art- and film-making. The avant-garde practices mentioned above are developed in the quotidian, intimate sphere of a pre-fabricated flat in East Berlin. In line with experimental film practices as demonstrated by Brakhage or Ken Jacobs, who would film in their private apartments or neighbourhood capturing friends and family, Böttcher, too, employs his domestic sphere as a space of subjective and self-referential artistic productivity. His practice thus helps to shape the cultural space of the GDR as still embedded in the everyday, while also tethered to an international experience through the film festivals.

Signs of Renewal

Contrary to Erich Honecker's famous claim from 1971 that there could be no taboos in art and literature, an assertion which seemed to suggest boundless freedom for literature and the arts, the 1970s were marked by vicissitudes in state cultural politics that were not dissimilar to those of

Figure 6.4. Böttcher on his balcony in *Potter's Bull*. Credits: Jürgen Böttcher, *Transformations* (screenshot from DVD, Edition Filmmuseum). Published with permission.

previous decades.[14] Despite prior concessions, the regime still adhered to the aesthetic doctrine of socialist realism with the result that, as Daniela Berghahn asserts, '[t]he Party's insistence on the artists' *Parteilichkeit* (partisanship), however, remained uncontested'.[15] After a period of relative relaxation during the early years of the Honecker era, political and economic circumstances caused a re-tightening of state control as well as an increase of censorship. This renewed restrictive cultural policy culminated in the forced expatriation of East German singer-songwriter Wolf Biermann in November 1976. As Biermann's friend, and as a film-maker and artist, Jürgen Böttcher signed the petition alongside prominent GDR writers, film-makers and actors in support of the songwriter. However, in contrast to Armin Mueller-Stahl, Eva-Maria Hagen, Thomas Brasch, Frank Beyer or Sarah Kirsch, to name but a few who left the GDR in protest at the Biermann affair, Böttcher was part of the group of artists and intellectuals who chose to stay – a decision which would shape his artistic output as well as his reputation within both the East German and the international art scene.

Especially in art and literature, those boundaries between official and independent cultural production were pushed even more from the mid-1970s onwards and some restrictions were lifted. Galleries and museums, for instance, began to renew their interest in contemporary as well as early twentieth-century art. After decades of neglecting modernist movements in favour of socialist realist state doctrine, museums in Berlin (1978), Dessau and Weimar (annually from 1976) began to break up the rigid grid of canonical works stipulated by the regime with newly curated exhibitions about, for instance, the Bauhaus or avant-garde movements.[16] A growing number of predominantly younger artists also began to create their own gallery spaces, thus undermining the strictly licensed trade with GDR artworks as well as the official exhibition regulation, which was overseen by the VBK. Alongside a number of new state-owned art galleries, from 1974 onwards a total of around 450 so-called *Kleine Galerien* (small galleries) were set up in city districts and municipalities. Although formally sponsored by the state, these galleries were officially encouraged to provide an alternative space for the presentation and reception of art. Showrooms such as the *Galerie Nord* (Gallery North) and *Galerie Mitte* (Gallery Central) in Dresden thus managed to both create their own distinct profile and extend their programme to include artists and projects that had not (yet) been included in the canon: Böttcher's works, for instance, were exhibited in the Galerie Mitte in 1981.[17] As informal art spaces, these galleries blurred the boundaries between official and underground art presentation and trade because despite their 'specialist' portfolio of lesser known or not yet established artists, they remained open to the general public. They are thus testament to the fundamental difference in approach to art reception in East and West, as April Eisman describes in her chapter in this volume: while art was generally aimed at an elite in West Germany, East German art was first and foremost art created for the people.[18]

A few years before presenting his works in the Galerie Mitte, Böttcher had his first major public exhibition at the Leonhardi-Museum in Dresden in 1978. In the early 1970s, the museum famously set about renewing its 1960s reputation as an acclaimed forum for contemporary local art, including installations, expressionist and abstract works. Although officially overseen by the VBK and the Dresden district council, the group of painters, graphic artists and sculptors responsible for the museum's programme remained over the next twenty years independent in their choice of artists to exhibit.[19] To be precise, the first ever public, yet much smaller presentation of Böttcher's works since his exclusion from the VBK had taken place even earlier, in 1975 at the independent gallery *Erfurter Atelierbund* (Erfurt studio union). This unique collaborative association of painters, photographers, metalwork and graphic designers had existed since 1964 and had held forty-five exhibitions by such non-conformist artists as Hermann Glöckner, Gerhard Altenbourg and Werner Schubert-Deister.[20] However, it was in Dresden that the entire scope of Böttcher's artistic oeuvre became clearly visible through a broad selection of drawings, paintings, collages and over-paintings. This is highly significant because the majority of these works, the painterly and graphic output of the film-maker Böttcher, had been created outside of the official institutions for artistic production, without artistic licence, so to speak, since Böttcher had been excluded from the VBK since 1961.

In practice, this had meant that Böttcher's works were not considered for national or regional art fairs and exhibitions. Even more defining was the fact that he had been denied access to the very materials of his practice, since the relevant supplies were assigned only to associated VBK members. While his film-making was continually gaining public attention, Böttcher's art production during those years was largely restricted to the private sphere. This is also reflected in his pseudonym Strawalde, which derived from the village of Strahwalde where he grew up and which he first used when signing his works for the Leonhardi show.[21] Yet, as the exhibited range of artworks demonstrated, Böttcher had made use of this relegation to develop an approach that naturally incorporated private everyday experience into his art practice. The Leonhardi exhibition changed Böttcher's status, and also began to mark him out as a figure capable of shifting the boundaries of everyday experimentation in legitimate GDR art practice.

Amongst the works presented at the Leonhardi-Museum were a number of over-painted art postcards, precisely the medium still accessible for Böttcher who, since he was no longer a member of the VBK, was excluded from the association's art supplies such as paper, canvas or paint. His artistic practice was thus crucially affected by the conditions of the everyday: the party's ideology determined the structures for artistic support and access to material. Consequently, these circumstances affected how art was produced, and what types of art were made, as artists navigated and jostled for their own artistic expressions. For Böttcher, this meant that he was employing both amateur techniques and his professional skills as a painter to create art from everyday materials. He had experimented with postcards since the mid- to late 1970s and had thus created a sizeable collection of small-scale over-paintings, collages and illustrated poems. As film historian Günter Agde points out, 'in the beginning, these playful acts were intended as witty greetings for friends (Böttcher's style of mail-art)'.[22] Moreover, they represented an everyday form of communication that required hardly any of the tools and materials the VBK had reserved exclusively for artistic members. Thus, essentially, these everyday materials and the artistic practices that Böttcher developed around the postcards made him autonomous in his production of art. With the release of *Transformations* nationally and internationally, and following the development of an independent art scene that provided a context for his work, this engagement with the everyday entered the GDR public (art) sphere. In a state which had always had, for some people at least, permeable borders, Böttcher's practice renegotiated the boundaries between the domestic and the public while also incorporating influences from the international avant-garde.

Independent Experiments

As a result of the developments from the mid-1970s onwards described above, restrictions on the official cultural production of art, literature, music and film in the GDR relaxed, or at least shifted in favour of projects and venues that existed outside the well-established boundaries of institutionalized artistic practice. As Löser explains: 'By the early 1980s the formerly impenetrable legitimating system for the cultural policy of the state began to erode... A uniquely interdisciplinary character distinguished the independent GDR art scene: painters performed improvised music, poets transposed their own texts into graphics, musicians became performance artists'.[23]

Löser's comment highlights the ways in which previously clearly defined boundaries between media and disciplines, as well as spaces and activities, were all of a sudden blurred by these artists. After the revived Leonhardi-Museum and the newly established smaller galleries, which – although still state-owned – ran far less canonical exhibition programmes, galleries with a truly independent structure were also set up in subsequent years. They mainly exhibited politically or aesthetically problematic artists, including those who were not accepted as members of the VBK, or who were preparing to leave the GDR for West Germany. Most importantly, in this context 'independent' meant that, technically, their exhibition activity had not yet been officially approved and was therefore only semi-legal.[24] However, as the interesting example of the Leipzig gallery *Eigen+Art* shows, this in-limbo state did not necessarily result in state sanctions. Because neither the Leipzig gallery owner nor his predominantly young artists were subversive, and also because most of them were still members of the VBK, no official efforts were made to close the gallery. Opened in a workshop space in a former factory in 1985, the gallery had quickly surrounded itself with a circle of loyal visitors who, had they been confronted with the closure of their venue, would presumably not have sat in silence.[25] Simultaneously, staunchly preserved boundaries in other areas of cultural production began to relax as well. Within the publication sector, literature and magazines that had not previously gained state approval were now self-published in very small editions. Publisher Gerhard Wolf even managed to include works by previously suppressed authors in the programme of the Aufbau Verlag, the GDR's leading publishing house. Between 1988 and 1991, Wolf's series *Außer der Reihe* (Out of Order) thus provided a platform for those young, independent writers who were predominantly part of Berlin's oppositional literary community in Prenzlauer Berg. Moreover, suddenly newly-formed punk bands emerged for one concert or two, and vanished again without even applying for an official licence to perform publicly.[26] By performing in less clearly defined, often liminal spaces, these punk bands as well as the independent galleries, writers and publishers explored entirely new practices, which, up to this point, had been unheard of within GDR cultural production.

Interestingly, while DEFA documentarist Böttcher moved towards rediscovering the practice of presenting his artworks publicly in the late 1970s, independent painters, photographers, poets, musicians and even puppeteers went the other way: in an attempt to seek new, contemporary modes of artistic expression, they began to experiment with the then readily available Super 8 film format.[27] The small community of GDR underground film-making artists, which developed over the next decade counted seventy-five active participants.[28] The group's centres of activity were Dresden and especially East Berlin, and film-making painters such as Christine Schlegel and Cornelia Schleime moved cities to join the creative community already established by the independent writers and musicians in the Prenzlauer Berg district.[29] Subsequently, artists' studios and flats served regularly as screening venues for members' experiments, events through which these primarily personal spaces were turned into both semi-private and semi-public liminal spaces occupied not by the general public, but by a selected, pre-approved 'public of insiders'. It is worth pointing out that these underground painters, graphic designers or performance artists sought to explore the specific technical qualities of both film stock and camera by deliberately refusing to attain proficiency and instead embracing their role as amateurs.[30] In fact, they were using layman, everyday film-making equipment as a basis for an experimental practice, which, similar to Böttcher's, claims a place for everyday experience in the arena of international art. The notable difference, of course, is that Böttcher was clearly neither an amateur nor an underground film-maker, but a professional documentarist.

A precursor of this underground movement, and inspirational figure for visual artists such as Helge Leiberg, Schleime and Schlegel, was independent Dresden painter A.R. Penck, who had become increasingly famous in West Germany in the 1970s, a decade before relocating there following his expatriation from the GDR in 1980. Since founding the artist group *Lücke frequentor* in Dresden in 1971, Penck had documented the group's collaborative painting sessions and performances on small gauge film stock.[31] Further inspiration for those young film-making artists came from influential, often taboo-breaking performance artists who rejected conventional art practices and whose works were known in East Germany only through books and *Westfernsehen* (West German television): artists such as Viennese Actionist Günter Brus, who explored the human body as both artist tool and canvas during public performances in the 1960s, Andy Warhol, or Fluxus-artists such as Wolf Vostell, who created his art through *décollaging* or tearing apart.

In translating these influences into film, underground artists not only blurred the boundaries between art and film, but also challenged the film-making state monopoly of DEFA and GDR television. As Löser points out, they not only explicitly turned to 'officially disdained "late-bourgeois" art' and contemporary Western modernity; they actively subverted state channels of production, distribution and communication by relying on 'an autonomous network … that operated parallel to or below the official organs'.[32] Moreover, underground artists circumvented other established cultural structures as well, such as the state-funded hobby art circles, which since the early 1960s had offered amateurs a platform to engage publicly with their interests in, for instance, theatre, dance, photography and film. Their predominant purpose, however, was to engage the working population in *künstlerische Selbstbetätigung* (artistic activity) as a way of helping to establish a socialist community.[33] By rejecting institutional structures such as these nearly a decade later to allow the production of their own amateur films autonomously, these underground artists attracted critical attention from the authorities. This forms an important context for Böttcher's art practice; eschewing the label of the amateur, he demonstrated instead that experimental artistic production and performance rooted in the everyday could well be recognized as legitimate art by the party, albeit not without reservations.

DEFA's Own Avant-Garde Film

When trying to gauge Böttcher's status within the GDR's artistic scene in the late 1970s, it is important to remember that he was DEFA's most prolific documentarist, a professional and, by the early 1980s, well-established director who was employed to work within the state-controlled documentary studio where he regularly worked with 35mm film. To be clear, in contrast to Super 8, 35mm film is not an amateur or home-movie format as it cannot be edited or projected at home; it requires instead professional film-making, editing and projection equipment. This was of course at Böttcher's disposal. Although he had re-entered the art world in the mid-1970s, he approached avant-garde film not as an underground painter or designer, but from the stance of a trained film-maker, albeit with a background in fine arts. Moreover, as he was already nearly fifty in the early 1980s, he was not part of the generation of artists in their early thirties and younger who had only just begun to explore the film medium. Although these artists did not belong to the underground scene per se, they saw their future as non-conformist painters, film-makers and performance artists in West Germany rather than in Dresden, Leipzig or East Berlin. As an employee of DEFA, Böttcher worked entirely independently of this group's structures. Nevertheless, its members referred to him as an 'insider tip' ('Geheimtipp'), a reputation he gained from his being a fairly unknown painter as a result of the state's selective cultural policy.[34]

Thus connected to the underground scene and aware of the productions within, Böttcher's avant-garde trilogy as well as the experiments in feature film by other directors of DEFA were, as Reinhild Steingröver points out, 'not created from a vacuum'.[35] Nevertheless, *Transformations* stands out as an unparalleled example of experimental film art made within the DEFA studios. Despite tentative signs of renewal taking place within the documentary and essay film genres at DEFA, avant-garde experiments by DEFA directors were virtually non-existent. Elke Schieber notes that, 'after Jürgen Böttcher's trilogy, located between animation and real film, no further such examples of short film followed'.[36] Although Böttcher never established his own 'school' of avant-garde film, his highly individual *Transformations* did however directly influence the artist Cornelia Schleime, for instance, in her use of over-paintings; according to curator Tannert, her films as well as those by several underground artists would be unimaginable 'without this unprecedented piece of work within GDR film'.[37] That is to say, *Transformations* influenced projects by independent artists made in the early 1980s: they began experimenting with stop-/ slow-motion and acceleration effects and explored fragmented montage, performance and absurd theatre. They also engaged in practices such as 'painting, scratching, puncturing, burning and gluing of the celluloid'.[38] From about the mid-80s onwards, these predominantly formal studies gave way to more content-orientated experiments, resulting in films which lacked, on the one hand, a clear narrative and classic plot, and, on the other hand, a clear documentary approach.

Essentially, *Transformations* is a true exception to DEFA filmmaking: the GDR's only state-funded experimental film produced by the DEFA documentary studio, apparently able to defy its generally strictly observed rules. According to an anecdote Böttcher told, he may have outwitted the documentary film studio by initially proposing *Transformations* as a children's animation film, and gaining the Ministry of Culture's approval under that category.[39] An experimental film upon completion, however, *Transformations* bore no resemblance to a project tailored for a young audience. Although it was not banned, the Ministry of Culture withheld authorization of its distribution for public release in GDR cinemas until 1985. When these restrictions were lifted, possibly in reaction to Böttcher's highly acclaimed documentaries *Shunters* and *Ein kurzer Besuch bei Hermann Glöckner* (*Hermann Glöckner: A Brief Visit*) (both 1984), the Ministry released the trilogy to be sent to international as well as West German retrospectives and film festivals in Amsterdam and Paris (both 1986), Edinburgh (42nd International Film Festival, 1988), Wunschsiedel / Selb (Grenzlandfilmtage, 1986), Hamburg (1986) and Berlin (Forum, 37th Berlinale, 1987).[40] For a GDR audience in the early 1980s, however, the number of public screenings was kept to a minimum and prevented *Transformations* from becoming more widely known. It should be noted that, while the film's approval status was in limbo for a whole year, the trilogy was nevertheless screened at least four times in official film clubs and art-house cinemas in Berlin, Dresden, Leipzig and Neubrandenburg.

With regard to the state-regulated cultural production, it hardly comes as a surprise that Böttcher was not included in the decision-making process that preceded the export of *Transformations* to festivals in the West. Instead, the Ministry of Culture selected films for competitions and screenings, appointed the delegation of culture functionaries and journalists to represent GDR film culture and decided which directors and actors were to be permitted to accept the festivals' invitations. Unless they were officially assigned by the Ministry, film-makers were not able to attend such events abroad and usually were not even aware that they had been invited. On its own soil, the GDR attracted film-makers from all over the world from the 1960s onwards to attend the International Leipzig Documentary and Short Film Week: an annual industry fair – and essentially a political affair – whose reputation abroad grew following the GDR's international acceptance as a sovereign state in 1973.[41] In turn, festivals in Oberhausen and Mannheim screened DEFA documentaries and short films as early as the mid-1950s; however, this exchange was not without conflict. As Andreas Kötzing explains, by choosing films with politically provocative topics, the *Club der Filmschaffenden* (Club of film-makers), the GDR film-maker's official representative body abroad, aimed to instrumentalize West German festivals as international fora to discuss GDR politics, thus attempting to fuel conflicts that epitomized the relationships between East and West Germany.[42] For instance, for the IX Mannheim film festival in 1960 the association entered the documentary ...*Du und mancher Kamerad* (*The German Story*, 1956) by Andrew and Annelie Thorndike, which presents itself as delivering a factual report of German history between 1893 and 1956 based on archival footage, but which openly employs the SED's perspective in line with Marxist historiography. Detecting 'anti-constitutional' tendencies, the West German censors initially banned the film in Mannheim, but later suggested a screening for a select audience comprising journalists, politicians and educators. Offended by these restrictions and the overt discrimination, a number of GDR delegates immediately left the festival.[43]

Years later, those 'test-screenings' of Böttcher's trilogy at festivals in West Germany and abroad continue the GDR's cultural diplomacy, however, on different terms and less provocatively. They highlight a crucial transnational, as well as trans-German, dimension to an intrinsically East German story, which could easily be overlooked. Such test-runs – employed as a 'soft' tool in the state's foreign relations strategy – exported the state's self-image as a place where liberal and open-minded cultural production prospered. In the case of *Transformations*, the practice of showing the trilogy first outside its country of origin before distributing it within influenced not only how East Germans thought about their documentaries, but also explains why the party did not pan this example of East German avant-garde film. For once it was made it could be utilized precisely for the state's cultural diplomatic ambitions: the reception and prestige earned in the West reflected positively on the East German state and its eager pursuit of international recognition. Moreover, it helped to protect the highly idiosyncratic *Transformations* from falling into oblivion in the GDR.

Conclusion

Unparalleled within the history of DEFA film, *Transformations* represents the only experimental art film produced by DEFA. In the tradition of avant-garde practice, Böttcher creates a non-narrative collage of fragments including everyday observations, atmospheric scenes, repetition and experimentation with both vision and sound. Everyday artistic practices are carried out within the domestic sphere: performance, over-painting and projection all take place in the space of the home. This home, located within a block of flats, represents the epitome of everyday living experience for the majority of GDR citizens in the 1980s.

For Böttcher, this apartment is also his temporary artist's studio; for *Transformations*, it even becomes his private film set. Excluded from the VBK as early as 1961, and thus unable to obtain artist materials let alone a studio, Böttcher's work as a graphic artist and painter was confined to the private realm while he gained public acclaim as a film-maker for DEFA. But Böttcher uses this restriction to his advantage by incorporating precisely this private everyday experience into his art practice. Making art at home, Böttcher employs his professional skills yet amateur techniques and other cultural practices that help him to mischievously explore the artistic quality of the quotidian. While refusing the label of amateur for himself, he develops a strong case for creating a new understanding and re-evaluation of profane everyday artistic production as legitimate aesthetics: not inferior, but with an equal right to exist alongside socialist realist art.

With the release of *Transformations* nationally and internationally, Böttcher's private engagement with the everyday enters the GDR public sphere, renegotiating within the state's already permeable borders the boundaries between the domestic and the public. This private engagement thus manages to remain, on the one hand, rooted in the everyday, while on the other hand, GDR cultural practice reaches out to and incorporates influences from both its own underground art scene and the international avant-garde.

Interestingly, for both Böttcher and the GDR, *Transformations* represents part of their self-image. For the artist film-maker, the experimental trilogy is his most self-referential film, combining his background as a non-conformist painter with his profession as a documentarist and poetic film-maker. For the GDR, the films helped to build the image of an open-minded and liberal state where free artistic expression was not only possible but officially supported. With its detour via film festivals in the West, the distribution history of *Transformations* demonstrates how the party utilized even cultural productions that were initially frowned upon as being non-representative of socialist realist art to promote the GDR as a culturally diverse state on an international stage.

Franziska Nössig's PhD thesis, 'Artists and Artworks in the Films of Jürgen Böttcher', is based on research at King's College London on the representation of art and artistic labour in the films of GDR documentary film-maker and artist Böttcher. She has interviewed the film-maker in Berlin and has presented his films at the German Embassy in London and at the Weimarer Kunstgesellschaft. She is currently conducting research on Stanley Forman and his ETV archive as part of the DAAD-funded project 'Circulating Cinema'. She has also given conference papers on Böttcher's films *Im Pergamonmuseum*, *Ein Weimarfilm* and *Kurzer Besuch bei Hermann Glöckner*.

Notes

1. Interview with the author, February 2015 (transcribed from recording). Several building blocks formed the large estate on Mellenseestraße, which is partly used for senior housing today. Böttcher lived in number 42 during the 1970s and 1980s. See Flügge and Penndorf, *STRAWALDE Jürgen Böttcher*, 231 (see image caption on that page).
2. '[v]on Andy Warhol, Stan Brakhage oder Kenneth Anger wurde selbst in den kunstwissenschaftlichen Seminaren der Universitäten nicht gesprochen'. Tannert, 'Von Vortönern und Erdferkeln', 25.
3. 'Eine hohe sozialistische Qualität des Kunstwerkes ist undenkbar ohne einen tiefen ideologischen Gehalt .... Es ist die Frage nach dem persönlichen Verhältnis zum Menschenbild, nach der Entscheidung für das gesellschaftliche Thema in seiner Vielfalt, nach der Verantwortung gegenüber der sozialistischen Gemeinschaft und ihren Erwartungen'. *Weggefährten*, 6–7.

4. 'Ich würde nie van Delft oder Picasso oder Rembrandt überzeichnen, sondern Sachen, die zwar großartig sind, aber die ein klein bisschen so etwas haben, dass ich meine, das kann man nicht machen, wie diese "Schlummernde Venus" von Giorgione... [B]ei der hat mich immer das rote Kissen geärgert, und dass die gleich so vor der Haustür liegt, die Nackte'. Molitor, 'Jürgen Böttcher/Strawalde', 144.
5. 'die Umwandlung kunsthistorischer Zitate in ein persönliches Ausdrucksvermögen der eigenen Befindlichkeit'. Thomas, 'Utopie und Menetekel des bildnerischen Eigen-Sinns', 115–16.
6. 'Erfindung von Bildwelten'. Haucke, 'Jürgen Böttchers Verwandlungen (1981)', 127.
7. Ibid., 131.
8. Betts, *Within Walls*, 5.
9. Ibid., 6.
10. Ibid., 13 and 15.
11. Ibid., 14–15.
12. 'Der sprang auf dem Bett wie auf einem Trampolin und schrie immer "Great! Great! You must make a film about them!"' Interview with the author, February 2015 (transcribed from recording).
13. Löser, *Strategien der Verweigerung*, 105.
14. Honecker, 'Die Hauptaufgabe umfaßt auch die weitere Erhöhung des kulturellen Niveaus', 287–88.
15. Italics in original. Berghahn, *Hollywood behind the Wall*, 196–97.
16. Grundmann, 'Selbstbestimmte Kunst'.
17. Ibid.
18. See Chapter 9 in this volume.
19. Grundmann, 'Selbstbestimmte Kunst'.
20. Michael, 'Die Erfurter Ateliergemeinschaft'. The founding group of the *Ateliergemeinschaft* (Erfurt studio collective) existed until 1974; the gallery then continued under the name *Erfurter Atelierbund* until 1977.
21. Flügge and Penndorf, *STRAWALDE Jürgen Böttcher*, 230.
22. '[a]nfangs ... waren diese Spiele nur als originelle Grüße an Freunde gedacht (mail-art nach Böttchers Art)'. Agde, 'Zwei Künstler in einem', 26.
23. Löser, 'Media in the Interim', 95.
24. Ibid., 95.
25. Grundmann, 'Die Galerie Eigen+Art'.
26. Löser, 'Metamorphosen', 58.
27. The affordable Russian Super 8 camera model Quarz and three-minute reels were readily available in stores in the GDR. Moreover, second-hand stores in the GDR sold small-gauge film stock and portable cameras from West Germany where video had replaced Super 8. See Löser, 'Media in the Interim', 104–5; Steingröver, 'Blackbox GDR', 110.
28. Löser, 'Media in the Interim', 98.
29. Like many other artists, Schleime and Schlegel left the GDR during the mid-1980s to pursue their artistic careers in West Germany.
30. Löser, *Verweigerung*, 221.
31. Tannert, 'Von Vortönern und Erdferkeln', 36.
32. Löser, 'Media in the Interim', 95, 104.
33. Von Richthofen, *Bringing Culture to the Masses*, 161.
34. Löser, *Verweigerung*, 104–5.
35. Steingröver, 'Blackbox GDR', 111.
36. 'Jürgen Böttchers zwischen Animation- und Realfilm angesiedeltem Triptychon ... folgten keine weiteren Beispiele in dieser Richtung des Kurzfilms'. Schieber, 'Im Dämmerlicht der Perestroika 1980 bis 1989', 217.

37. '[o]hne diese für den DDR-Film beispiellose Bildarbeit'. Tannert, 'Von Vortönern und Erdferkeln', 29. See also Löser, *Verweigerung*, 105.
38. Löser, 'Media in the Interim', 105.
39. Interview with the author, February 2015.
40. Haucke, 'Jürgen Böttchers Verwandlungen (1981)', 121.
41. The festival was first founded in 1955, but due to government restrictions was suspended during the following years until 1960.
42. Kötzing, 'Provozierte Konflikte', 382.
43. Ibid., 379–80.

Bibliography

Agde, G. 'Zwei Künstler in einem: der Maler Strawalde und der Dokumentarfilmregisseur Jürgen Böttcher', in Leipziger Dokfilmwochen GmbH (ed.), *Seismogramm(e) des Augenblicks. Texte zu Jürgen Böttcher* (Leipzig: Leipziger Dokfilmwochen GmbH, 2001), 24–27.
Berghahn, D. *Hollywood behind the Wall: The Cinema of East Germany*. Manchester and New York: Manchester University Press, 2005.
Betts, P. *Within Walls: Private Life in the German Democratic Republic*. Oxford and New York: Oxford University Press, 2010.
Flügge, M. and J. Penndorf (eds). *STRAWALDE Jürgen Böttcher: Maler und Regisseur*. Altenburg and Nuremberg: Lindenau-Museum / Verlag für moderne Kunst: 2012.
Grundmann, U. 'Die Galerie Eigen+Art'. *Dossier: Autonome Kunst in der DDR, Bundeszentrale für politische Bildung*. Retrieved 8 September 2018 from http://www.bpb.de/geschichte/deutsche-geschichte/autonome-kunst-in-der-ddr/55832/eigen-art.
_____. 'Selbstbestimmte Kunst in offiziellen Ausstellungsinstitutionen 1970–1990'. *Dossier: Autonome Kunst in der DDR, Bundeszentrale für politische Bildung*. Retrieved 8 September 2018 from http://www.bpb.de/geschichte/deutsche-geschichte/autonome-kunst-in-der-ddr/55788/selbstbestimmte-kunst-in-offiziellen-ausstellungsinstitutionen-1970-1990?p=all.
Haucke, L. 'Jürgen Böttchers Verwandlungen (1981): Infragestellungen der Zentralperspektive der europäischen Maltradition in einem DDR-Experimentalfilm', in J. Paech (ed.), *Film, Fernsehen, Video und die Künste: Strategien der Intermedialität* (Stuttgart: J.B. Metzler, 1994), 118–31.
Honecker, E. 'Die Hauptaufgabe umfaßt auch die weitere Erhöhung des kulturellen Niveaus: Schlußwort auf der 4. Tagung des ZK der SED, Dezember 1971', in G. Rüß (ed.), *Dokumente zur Kunst-, Literatur- und Kulturpolitik der SED 1971–1974* (Stuttgart: Seewald, 1976), 287–88.
'Internationale Festivals'. *DEFA-Stiftung*. Retrieved 8 September 2018 from http://www.defa-stiftung.de/internationale-festivals.
Kötzing, A. 'Provozierte Konflikte: Der Club der Filmschaffenden und die Beteiligung der DEFA an der Mannheimer Filmwoche 1959/60', in M. Wedel (ed.), *DEFA international: Grenzüberschreitende Filmbeziehungen vor und nach dem*

Mauerbau, Film, Fernsehen, Medienkultur (Wiesbaden: Springer VS, 2013), 369–84.

Löser, C. 'Media in the Interim: Independent Film in East Germany before and after 1989', in R. Steingröver and R. Halle (eds), *After the Avant-Garde: Contemporary German and Austrian Experimental Film* (Rochester: Camden House, 2008), 95–108.

———. 'Metamorphosen: Lutz Dammbeck und die Ansätze eines unabhängigen Animationsfilms in der DDR'. *Filmdienst* (19) (2003), 58–61.

———. *Strategien der Verweigerung: Untersuchungen zum politisch-ästhetischen Gestus unangepasster filmischer Artikulationen in der Spätphase der DDR*. Schriftenreihe DEFA-Stiftung. Berlin: DEFA-Stiftung, 2011.

Michael, K. 'Die Erfurter Ateliergemeinschaft'. *Dossier: Autonome Kunst in der DDR, Bundeszentrale für politische Bildung*. Retrieved 8 September 2018 from http://www. bpb.de/geschichte/deutsche-geschichte/autonome-kunst-in-der-ddr/55824/ erfurter-ateliergemeinschaft.

Molitor, D. 'Jürgen Böttcher/Strawalde: Brüderlichkeit hatte die größte Bedeutung in meinem Leben', in I. Poss et al. (eds), *Das Prinzip Neugier: DEFA-Dokumentarfilmer erzählen*, Schriftenreihe der DEFA-Stiftung (Berlin: Neues Leben, 2012), 121–56.

Schieber, E. 'Im Dämmerlicht der Perestroika 1980 bis 1989', in G. Jordan and R. Schenk (eds), *Schwarzweiß und Farbe: DEFA-Dokumentarfilme 1946–92* (Berlin: Filmmuseum Potsdam & Jovis, 1996), 181–233.

Tannert, Ch. 'Von Vortönern und Erdferkeln. Die Filme der Bildermacher', in K. Fritzsche and C. Löser (eds), *Gegenbilder: filmische Subversion in der DDR, 1976–1989: Texte, Bilder, Daten* (Berlin: Janus Press, 1996), 24–59.

Thomas, K. 'Utopie und Menetekel des bildnerischen Eigen-Sinns', in G. Muschter and R. Thomas (eds), *Jenseits der Staatskultur: Traditionen autonomer Kunst in der DDR* (Munich: Hanser, 1992), 108–36.

von Richthofen, E. *Bringing Culture to the Masses: Control, Compromise and Participation in the GDR*, Monographs in German History, vol. 24. New York: Berghahn Books, 2009.

Weggefährten: 25 Künstler der Deutschen Demokratischen Republik. Dresden: VEB Verlag der Kunst, 1970.

Chapter 7

Style Identities and Individualization in 1980s East and West Germany

Alissa Bellotti

In the summer of 1983 West German journalists Wolfgang Büscher and Peter Wensierski travelled to East Berlin to find and interview young East Germans living alternative lifestyles. In West Germany, there was apprehensive talk of a second wave of youth protest as alongside the squatters, peace activists and environmentalists, new and aggressively visible style-based youth subcultures proliferated. In Prenzlauer Berg the journalists found a scene that was surprisingly familiar to them from their time reporting in West German cities. Prenzlauer Berg had a similar mix of punks, provos, avant-garde artists, and peaceniks. However, when they began to dig deeper into the lives, beliefs, fashions and socio-economic circumstances of this East Berlin alternative community, they saw small but significant differences. Among punks in the German Democratic Republic (GDR), one of the first differences Büscher and Wensierski noticed were the symbols they irreverently wore. GDR punks had the same propensity for leather jackets with studs, safety pins and torn up t-shirts and trousers but they decorated the fabric between the holes with the detritus of their socialist childhoods: badges for good studying, sashes celebrating the achievements of their collectives, the small red-gold emblems from national holidays and medals of German-Soviet friendship.[1] Were these East German teens simply aping Western cultural trends with the only materials they had at hand? Or had they turned an international youth culture into one that reflected their own, GDR-specific priorities, worries and values?

In this chapter, an examination of the 'small things' that young East and West Germans used in their subcultural styles helps us to understand the process of making global pop culture meaningful in local contexts.[2] This particular analysis of small things is an analysis of consumption. Concern with how physical items were used, inscribed with meanings, and re-inscribed with new or additional meanings emphasizes the productive aspects of consumption; they are productive of social relations and political meanings. Decoding meanings inscribed on ordinary objects by subcultural German youths lays bare some of the values and desires that were important to young people in the 1980s, and that often differed from those of older generations.

In the context of divided Germany, an analysis of everyday items and their uses has the added advantage of allowing us to see how local interpretations of international youth culture were similar and different in the two German societies. Since the practices of these German youth were parallel but not identical, they provide an opportunity to untangle cultural ruptures and continuities in the histories of both German states through local, everyday experiences. Disparate political and economic conditions caused the local forms of punk, new wave, heavy metal and other subcultures to differ in East and West Germany. Yet, many of the concerns, values and problems articulated by young East and West Germans were similar. In the late 1970s and early 1980s, despondency over the future and dissatisfaction with the present combined in both German states to lead a subset of the youth to search for meaning in carefully curating their own lifestyles. This was a search for self-determination that was part of a broader, ongoing process of individualization in the West and, to a lesser extent, the East.

This chapter also contributes to the growing historiography of everyday life in the 1970s and 1980s GDR. Scholarly work on East German punks has concentrated on a handful of consciously political acts against the GDR state made by a small number of punks using highly charged political language.[3] This is important work but the emphasis on repression obscures some of the other uses and meanings that ostentatious styles and alternative youth cultures had in young East Germans' everyday lives. When one digs into interviews done in the 1980s it becomes clear that the majority of punks, *Gruftis* and heavys embraced these styles because they fulfilled specific needs for them, such as self-expression and self-determination. The extreme subcultural styles they developed were more than an aesthetic transgression that allowed them to push back against a gerontocratic, unresponsive regime. Pursuing their own self-fulfilment was enough to bring East German punks into conflict with some of the GDR's core principles. By constructing their own, creative, non-conformist styles with the consumer goods meant to shore up support for the SED regime, they undermined and transformed the meanings of these everyday goods.

Why Style?

Why focus on style when subcultures revolve just as much around music and attitude? Style is the most visible aspect of subcultural expression and the vector through which subcultures engage with everyday objects. One of Dick Hebdige's primary insights was to appreciate that subcultures are not separate from the dominant culture but are busy reworking the dominant culture's norms and values, often responding to some of the same concerns and socio-economic conditions as the rest of society. Subcultures do this through bricolage – or hybridizing – the material culture available to them. Common objects are thus appropriated into new networks of symbolic meanings. One way of disentangling the meanings of style in 1980s East and West Germany is to examine the 'small things' young people used to craft their styles and to contextualize them.

International youth cultural trends like punk, new wave, goth and hip-hop certainly brought their own collections of internationally recognizable symbols to Germany. A leather jacket with metal studs, tight trousers and a ripped-up t-shirt with safety pins made one just as identifiable as a punk in Budapest as it did in London. However, universally recognized subcultural symbols also took on more local meanings through small additions made to the subcultural uniform or by being embedded in new social contexts. In this way, many of the symbols and style elements used in the new youth styles of the 1980s can be thought of as empty signifiers, ready to be filled with locally pertinent meanings.

The 1980s saw a proliferation of extreme youth styles, the diversity of which exceeded anything either German state had seen before.[4] Commercial and media overexposure drove young Germans, like their counterparts in other developed countries, to constantly push subcultural styles in new directions. This process resulted in a large and colourful array of subcultural styles. In the early 1980s, punks began to split into different subgroups, each with their own style, music, attitude and politics (or lack thereof). The Ur-punks begat hardcore punks, leftist skinheads, ska-punks, fun punks and racist skinheads. Following punks were other subcultural groups including new romantics and goths (called Gruftis in the GDR), small groups of teds (teddy boys) and mods, poppers (preppies), hip-hoppers, more extreme forms of heavy metal (heavys) and, at the end of the decade in West Germany, skaters. The process continued into the 1990s with ravers, death metal-heads, straight-edge and riot grrrls. This brief overview demonstrates the diversity of subcultures. However, the borders between these groups were also exceptionally fluid. Young Germans often 'tried on' different subcultural lifestyles, commonly cycling through many in quick succession, or coming up with their own combination of styles and music by taking elements from different styles. I therefore refer to style-scenes in this chapter. The term is meant to encompass the dynamic relationships between subcultures and the overlap between groups created by their fluid participants.

This chapter draws primarily on interviews with subcultural youths conducted during the 1980s. A great deal of memory work has occurred in Germany in the past twenty years with numerous exhibitions, documentaries and retrospective reports on the glories of the subcultures of the 1980s, especially punk. I therefore rely on contemporary interviews when possible, being careful to consider whether interviews were conducted in groups with peers, by other young people or adults, or by West or East Germans. I supplement these with retrospective interviews and quality memoirs, photographs and fanzines where available and appropriate.

Setting the Scene: German Youth Cultures in the 1970s

The youth subcultures of the 1980s were not the first stylistically exuberant youth subcultures to be seen in the postwar Germanys. West Germans had witnessed the short-lived but conspicuous *Halbstarke*, exis, and rockers in the 1950s followed by hippies in the 1960s and smaller groups of teds and mods.[5] West German youth culture during the early and mid-1970s was dominated by commercial rock and pop music but heavily influenced by what Sven Reichardt and Detlef Siegfried have called the 'alternative milieu'. This milieu was a loose collection of politically left-leaning projects, communes, local advocacy, music and local publications that together constituted an accessible, anti-bourgeois cultural and political scene in many West German cities. Long, flowing hair – especially on men – blue jeans and the ubiquitous parka jacket went hand in hand with the pursuit of communality and warmth that characterized the left-alternative lifestyle. The alternative milieu's political activism helped to create the feminist, ecological and anti-nuclear New Social Movements, which lasted into the 1980s.[6]

By the late 1970s however, the careful observer would have noticed more and more variation in mainstream West German youth cultures.

Rock music had diversified into different subgenres like progressive rock, underground rock, hard rock and metal driven by a sense that rock's powers of political and cultural critique had been sapped by the genre's commercialization and the growth of the star cult.[7] An extremely pessimistic mood was gripping the youth of West Germany by this time. Rising unemployment, greater awareness of environmental degradation and renewed nuclear proliferation led many young West Germans to fall into disappointment and anger. By 1984, when the widely respected Shell Study surveyed teens and young adults, approximately 80 per cent of them thought that unemployment was the biggest problem they faced.[8] It was onto this volatile tinder that punk landed like a spark in the late 1970s. As Sven Reichardt recently observed, it was in this youth culture that the left utopias of the 1970s found their end.[9] The new style-based youth cultures of the 1980s marked a break with the optimistic, change-oriented, politically left youth cultures that had dominated West German alternative scenes since the mid-1960s.

East German youth culture in the 1960s and 1970s was dominated by a series of freezes and thaws in accordance with the fluctuating cultural policies of the ruling Socialist Unity Party (SED). Erich Honecker's ascension to General Secretary of the SED in 1971 was accompanied by one such thaw that included the successful staging of the international World Festival of Youth and Students in East Berlin in 1973. Under Honecker in the early 1970s there was a new push for more youth clubs and resources for hobbies such as composing and performing rock music and theatre. Beloved bands like Die Puhdys and Karat were founded (and licensed by the state) at this time. But Honecker soon began to have doubts about these relatively magnanimous policies. Activities within the youth clubs, especially in cities, came under tighter control of the Free German Youth (FDJ), the SED's powerful youth organization. The new freeze culminated in the infamous expulsion of singer-songwriter and dissident Wolf Biermann on 16 November 1976. Shocked that the SED had gone so far, this incident proved to many young East Germans that any overtures the SED made towards greater freedom in youth culture, and especially in music, would not last.[10] Increasing numbers of young East Germans donned parkas and climbing shoes, grabbed a rucksack and went hitch-hiking – or *trampen* – to the next blues or rock concert. The *Blueser* or *Kundenszene* was a homegrown subculture, specific to the GDR and its longest lasting subculture. Blueser and other 'long-hairs' were persecuted by security services for their unkempt appearance and unwillingness to settle into sensible jobs and take their responsibilities to society seriously. With the beginning of the 1980s peace movement, the Blueser subculture was firmly intertwined in oppositional politics.[11]

Symbols for a New Age of Youth Style-Scenes

Slowly at first, propelled by travel accounts in the first (West) German punk fanzines, and then in a great rush, punk made its way from London to West German cities in 1976 and took hold by 1977. This first foray into the new wave of subcultures that would change 1980s youth culture was one of the most dynamic and would become one of the most diverse.[12] In both Germanys, the young participants in this new subculture used everyday objects and actions – safety pins, ripping holes in trousers, using super-concentrated sugar water to fashion extreme hairstyles – to mount an aesthetic critique of the worn-out youth rebellion of the 1970s and to rebel against threats to their futures. Many of the same symbols and mundane objects were re-appropriated in both German states. But can it be said that this constituted a symbolic language intelligible to punks on both sides of the Wall?

A perusal of early German punk photos from both German states suggests that there were very few individual stylistic elements that were essential to practising a punk style. Early photos in both East and West show a variety of suit jackets worn over t-shirts, leather trousers worn with respectable overcoats and heavily graffitied jeans jackets worn with completely normal jeans.[13] However, those few style elements that were shared by nearly all early punks were common to punks in East and West Germany: irreverent, aggressive postures; clothing transformed through ripping/tearing, the addition of handwritten slogans or by mismatching pieces of an outfit; and short, spikey hair, especially on young men.

Short, spikey hair seems to have had a special power to signal a young man's transformation into a punk. When three young apprentices in Leipzig in 1982 wanted to play punk music, they knew their 'long hair had to go'.[14] Xao Seffcheque, an early Düsseldorf punk, was inspired to develop a punk style for himself when he was shocked by other young men's short hair. He remembered that:

> When I was 17 I had a full beard. Totally idiotic. I looked like I was 60, well let's say 40. Until 1976 Mike Hentz and his group at the time *Padlt Noidelt* were in Graz. When I met them for the first time at the beginning of 1975 they looked like us. And then came 1976 and they all had super short hair, dyed blond, ridiculously *straight* [orig. in English]. I thought, 'What's going on now? That's totally crazy.' It came across so fascistic (*faschomäßig*). But it was only an affirmation of their *straightness*. I thought only, 'Boys, I'm with you.' I got myself some *straighter* clothes… And I got my hair cut. I really had the feeling that I was getting more oxygen to my noggin.[15]

Short hair was such an effective punk signifier in both Germanys because, in both places, long hair on young men had been socially accepted since the mid-1970s and was wholly unremarkable.[16] To cut one's hair short disrupted the norms of youthful style that had grown out of the hippie and left-alternative movements of the late 1960s and 1970s.[17] In addition, the relative irrevocability of shorn hair signalled a commitment to the subculture made by altering one's own body.

However, most common punk symbols had a variety of meanings, or no meanings at all. The circle-A, long a symbol of anarchist movements, was employed by punks in East and West Germany as a component of punk style from the earliest days of the subculture. In West German fan-zines and photos, the circle-A appears sporadically next to other symbols that have also been ripped from their contexts. The circle-A was used to mark pubs and concert venues friendly to punks, like 'the Korn', a pub in Korn Street, Hannover, but was only one symbol among a collection of graffitied names, slogans, grotesque cartoons and the occasional swastika. The circle-A's usage among punks in West Germany began to change through the early 1980s as punk split into many sub-genres. Increasingly, it was used to mark out anarcho-punk fanzines, a sub-genre begun by the English band CRASS, whose name was written with the circle-A as the third letter.[18] It is difficult to know if the circle-A's usage and meanings also shifted at this time in East Germany. With no option to print fanzines and fewer available photos we can draw only on interviews from the 1980s and memoirs where the circle-A is discussed. These sources reveal a symbol that, as in the early days in West Germany, signified different meanings to different people. According to one GDR punk's recollection, it was the 'symbol of symbols' and stood for true anarchy, not the dysfunction of the authoritarian GDR government, which, he specified, was chaos.[19] To three other East Berlin punks asked in the summer of 1982, the circle-As they wore on their leather jackets meant no authority and no laws (15, young woman), no cops, no borders and not always doing what is directed from above (18, young man) and 'just to be hanging around and then suddenly to drive over there [to West Germany] and wherever else' (20, young man).[20]

The disparate meanings of the circle-A, both within each German state and between them, points to the nature of punk's symbolic language. Punk relied not on individual symbols to signify meanings but on the juxtaposition of many symbols with each other and with the other style elements of the subculture. There was no universal symbolic punk language that would make meanings equally clear to punks in either German state. It is questionable whether a West German punk would understand the East German punk slogan 'Anti Nazi League' as mocking the GDR's official anti-fascist ideology. However, a West German punk who saw East German punks with 'Anti Nazi League' emblazoned on a leather jacket among circle-As, band names and a jumble of pins would infer this slogan was derisive in some way because it was part of the assemblage. East and West German punks did not participate in a shared network of symbols with specific signifiers, but they did participate in a shared homology of chaos. The fact that symbols were ripped from their common meanings and contexts, that they were placed into a cacophony of 'bad' taste, unconventional clothing and collaged texts meant that they could be understood collectively as signifiers of chaos, even if their individual meanings could not always be deciphered.[21]

The adaptation of internationally relevant subcultural symbols to fit national and local conditions was not limited to punks. Though the symbolic regimes of other style-based subcultures in this decade were less chaotic than punk's, each of them adapted internationally popular subcultural styles by re-appropriating everyday objects, spaces and behaviours to disrupt the norms and expectations of their teenaged lives. East German Gruftis wore their gothic crosses upside-down to ward off the friendly advances of an expanding Christian movement, not to worship Satan. West German racist skinheads appropriated the simple braces, work trousers and sturdy boots from the originally left-leaning working-class skinhead subculture, using it as a non-uniform signifying right-wing hyper-masculinity.[22]

'No Future' Attitudes

Alongside the circle-As and other punk symbols, the slogan 'no future' was a part of the punk style in East and West Germany. Originally used by English punks to decry their lack of economic opportunity, early West German punks regarded the slogan as an ironic joke or as signifying the future as a blank slate. It was taken increasingly seriously by later iterations of punk as the mood in many West German sub-genres of punk darkened.

As with the circle-A and similar symbols, the 'no future' slogan signified a variety of meanings for early West German punks. One early punk, Moritz R, used 'no future' ironically. For him, 'no future', 'no fun' or 'I'm bored', all used in English, were hyperbole akin to using a swastika or other Nazi symbol. Another early West German punk, Peter Hein, attributed his later musical success to his belief in his particular version of 'no future'. For Hein, the slogan signified his ambivalent attitude towards planning a future and building a career. Instead, he credits his come-what-may attitude with making him open to new musical opportunities despite working at the Xerox corporation throughout the 1980s.[23] 'No future' was part of a limited use of English in punk, a musical style that mostly adopted German-language lyrics to set itself apart from the beat and rock music of the 1960s and 1970s, which were primarily sung in English. Despite the various meanings ascribed to 'no future', the use of this and a handful of similar phrases in English linked the nascent West German punk scene to the international youth culture of punk.

As new sub-genres like hardcore, new wave and polit-punk were developed in the first half of the 1980s, 'no future' came to signify a pessimism about the future that was closer to the original English meaning in the Sex Pistol's 'God Save the Queen'. The new wave band Ideal's song 'Eiszeit' tapped into these despondent feelings both through its lyrics and the style portrayed in the music video. A massive hit in 1981, the singer describes her alienation and isolation; her phone has not rung in years but she also has no desire to talk with anyone else. The only thing of any importance to her is the reflection she sees in the mirror. The music video shows the four-member band in an ordinary but completely black and white room with a chequered floor and little decoration other than the windows, which have been sketched in behind them. Everything in the frame is stark black or white with the exception of the lead singer's head and bright red vinyl jacket. The band stands facing straight ahead, feet planted firmly on the floor, with their heads tilted somewhat downwards. When the camera zooms in they glower slightly from underneath their eyebrows, moving as little as possible during their performance. The lead singer Annette Humpe's red jacket makes her stand out from the rest of the scene, visually isolated in a cold world. The aggressive way in which she delivers the lyrics signals little hope for change as do the band members' slumping heads and sagging shoulders as the song ends abruptly. There were good reasons why this pessimistic mood resonated so widely with West German youth. The relatively new phenomenon of youth unemployment threatened to limit young West Germans' career options and the achievement of personal goals, while environmental destruction and renewed nuclear tensions threatened the future itself.[24]

East German punks also used 'no future' to signal a discontent particular to the GDR. By 1982, the punk style had everywhere become more colourful through the influence of new wave and fun punk. In the GDR, punks used riotous displays of colour as a bulwark against the grey sameness of life and the limits young East Germans perceived for their futures. In Magdeburg in the summer of 1982, a small group of fifteen-year-olds sat in a basement crafting their first punk clothes while listening to Ideal's song 'Eiszeit' on the radio. Shanghai Drenger later remembered that 'we made ourselves colourful'. They did this by turning golden yellow potato nets into t-shirts, wearing any outrageous sunglasses they could find and sewing colourful bits of cloth salvaged from other garments onto tight, black trousers. Drenger recalled that he and his friends did this expressly to differentiate themselves from the shift workers that they saw each day commuting back and forth to work. The group scorned the workers who, in their words, 'stupidly dragged themselves to work every morning [in their] thin chequered shirts, knit trousers, pomaded hair and crudely-dyed synthetic leather jackets'.[25]

These young punks showed such contempt for shift workers because the workers very probably represented a window into the young men's own futures. Even if these particular punks were destined for university or to learn advanced skills like machine repair, they would have to conform to both the socialist sensibilities of their company's hierarchy and a pervasive petty-bourgeois culture. It was this imagined future, not the anticipation of a life spent working, that so bothered punks and other subcultural youths through the 1980s. Despite taunts from hostile adults that suggested otherwise ('You should be put in a work camp'), punks in the GDR nearly all had jobs or apprenticeships and spoke freely about them in group interviews. The work ethic among young East Germans remained strong for the rest of the GDR's existence and beyond, and in the mid-1980s Gruftis defended themselves against media attacks by emphasizing the fact that they had jobs and contributed to East German society through their work.[26]

Rather than a lack of opportunities, East German punks used the 'no future' slogan to decry a future that was all too clear, one laid out for them by the policies of the SED state and the petty-bourgeois GDR culture. In a 1982 interview, three punks turned the meaning of the classic punk slogan on its head while still retaining the hopelessness that the original British slogan conveyed:

Kaiser: ... Over there [West Germany] they're all no-future-punks, keine Zukunft [he repeats it in German after saying it in English]. Maybe they have a reason for it if there's no work.
Lade: it's good, no future, still good.
Kaiser: I don't think so.
Lade: Well yeah, but it depends what you mean.
Kaiser: Nah, I mean, here with us, maybe for everyone, for everyone their development...
Micha: ... already too much future.

Kaiser: … yeah, maybe too much future. When you're born, already…
Micha: … the path is all planned out.
Kaiser: That's it, it's really like that.[27]

The dialogue shows with surprising clarity punks' anxieties about being on a collision course with a future over which they had no say. They could make themselves colourful to distinguish themselves from the socialist worker (both real and imagined) but were apprehensive about what their lives would be like after they gave up their punk personas and became adults. Punks' colourful protests were directed as much at the sclerotic petty-bourgeois norms of GDR society as they were at state policies. A son of two East German diplomats, who could have very reasonably expected something better than shift work for his future, told an interviewer in 1983 that 'the *Spießbürgertum* [philistinism] pisses me off. I'm against being German. Germans are by nature petty bourgeois and total squares. This whole fuss, these masks that no one takes off, they bother me'.[28]

Searching for Meanings in a New Modernity

The increased value that young participants in the style-scenes placed on their outward appearances and lifestyles was part of a trend that extended to other youth cultural milieus in East and West Germany. West German youth sociologist Dieter Baacke identified a similar emphasis on lifestyle among the more politically oriented groups of squatters, feminists, peace activists, anarchists, Young Democrats and polit-rock groups living in communal flats (*Wohngemeinschaften*) in West German cities in the 1980s. He wrote that, 'The search for new lifestyles in the Wohngemeinschaften [of these groups] was just as important as political engagement. The search for happiness and warmth and the acknowledgement of one's own lifestyle came before the wish to 'change society'.[29] The trend had also begun to affect more mainstream political engagement. Youth participation in West German party politics in the 1980s had decreased compared to the participation of young people in the 1970s. A pair of surveys conducted by the Social Science Research Institute of the Konrad Adenauer Stiftung, the foundation of the Christian Democratic Parties (CDU/CSU), found that the disinterest in politics among West German youth that the first survey identified in 1974 had continued to increase through 1980 when the second survey was conducted. However, the reason for political apathy in the two youth generations was completely different. The youth of the 1970s increasingly stayed away from formal politics due to feelings of powerlessness. Researchers attributed these feelings to the failure of the previous youth rebellion and continued efforts in the early 1970s to effect meaningful political change. The youth of the 1980s did not primarily see themselves as powerless – in fact they were surprisingly happy with the FRG's parliamentary democratic system. They simply did not prioritize political activity over expending energy on projects that would provide them with a better everyday lifestyle. In 1980, only 10 per cent of 14 to 17-year-olds and 25 per cent of 18 to 21-year-olds responded that they were 'very strongly' or 'strongly' interested in politics. Reporters covering the results of the study summarized as follows: 'Evidently they [young people] believe in shaping their lives outside of politics, in realizing their own interests and fulfilling their own wishes'.[30]

Sociologists and pedagogues in West Germany also documented how memberships in organized youth groups in churches, unions and local civic organizations – all types of groups other than sporting associations – decreased during the 1980s. These organizations had long shaped young West Germans' free time, but the Shell Studies found that self-chosen friend groups were now more influential during free time than these more traditional organizations led by adults.[31] Time spent with friends was often time spent consuming and 'trying on' different lifestyles. The style-scenes are again an excellent illustration of this trend. The processes of stylistic innovation that drove the development of so many style-scenes in the 1980s rested on fine distinctions between styles such as fun punk and new wave. Very few adults would have had the depth of knowledge required to differentiate between closely related styles, especially since they were constantly evolving. The constant construction and re-construction of styles was intended just as much for the consumption of young people's peers as it was to shock adults.

Some youth sociologists at the time found the proliferation of new style-scenes to be the product of a process of individualization taking place among young West Germans. Sociologist Ulrich Beck argued that in Western welfare states, as barriers to mobility, communal ties and traditional class-based institutions began to break down, individuals were increasingly forced to construct their own biographies based on their choices 'between different lifestyles, subcultures, social ties and identities'. Though still influenced by class background and family connections, young people were increasingly learning how to use the conditions and materials at hand to more actively shape their public and self-identities.[32] Sociologists other than Beck, those who worked specifically on youth, examined the ways in which particular character traits were constructed. In reference to youth cultural bricolage, Dieter Baacke wrote that 'Individuality, a highly prized commodity in light of growing social-ization, is increasingly not developed but *appropriated*'.[33] By cobbling together their own styles, young West Germans created something new, something unique to them as individuals. This new way of constructing an identity was, Baacke explained, in contrast to older, bourgeois notions of identity formation through making one's mark upon the world. His analysis of youth cultures during the 1980s also suggested that the out-ward appearances of young people had become increasingly important indicators of what lay inside them, a concept he called *die Wahrheit der Oberfläche* (truth of the surface). Young West Germans, struggling in a society that was filled with arbitrary meanings (*Sinn-Beliebigkeit*), came to understand that what was on the surface was an accurate represen-tation of the person underneath.[34] The subcultures of the 1980s were the most extravagant manifestation of this new way of thinking. Goths represented their inner melancholy with re-appropriated funerary attire. Poppers identified with and flaunted their privilege by pairing brand name clothing with a refusal to take anything seriously, even study that might help them perpetuate their status once adults.

East German youth researchers did not produce such holistic expla-nations for the equally great changes in youth behaviour underway in the GDR. However, they did document changes similar to those in West Germany through surveys. By the mid-1980s it was becoming clear to researchers at the East German Central Institute for Youth Research (ZIJ) that the various kinds of punks, Gruftis, heavys and poppers were the most visible part of a larger shift in the young generation's satisfaction with everyday life in the GDR.

Outside of the subcultures and style-scenes, the mass of East German youth had begun to view Western countries more favourably than they had in the past. When researchers at the ZIJ asked GDR pupils to rate the populations of capitalist and socialist countries on traits like intel-ligence, modernity and friendliness in 1968 and again in 1988, the results changed markedly. Both the United States and the FRG were perceived as less intelligent, less modern and less friendly than the Soviet Union in 1968 but had surpassed the USSR in each of these traits by 1988. What is perhaps even more telling is that East German pupils had come to view the populations of the US and FRG as more intelligent and more modern than their own population in the GDR.[35] East German young people were also becoming more unabashed in their admiration of Western bands. Whereas in 1979 just under half (49 per cent) of young men surveyed told researchers their favourite song was by an East German band, by 1984 only 31 per cent named a song by an East German band and the year after the figure fell to only 22 per cent. Even more galling to FDJ functionaries and GDR youth workers was that more and more of these favourite songs were in English: 24 per cent in 1979, 37 per cent in 1984 and 59 per cent in 1985.[36]

The internationalization of unofficial youth culture in the GDR had been underway since the Rock 'n' Roll wave of the 1950s. However, the frustrations and disappointments of East German life in the late 1970s and 1980s were leading young people to increasingly look West for inspiration and entertainment. Since the 'golden period' of homegrown GDR rock music in the mid-1970s, the appeal and quality of East German pop music, feature films and some television genres had decreased markedly.[37] This, according to a report that finally reached members of the Politburo in 1987, meant that East German stars had shrinking influence over 'the fashion and the lifestyles of the young generation'.[38] Western stars, on the other hand, had been steadily gaining influence for at least a decade.

Likewise, after thirty years of socialism, the lacklustre appeal and quality of consumer goods – to say nothing of chronic shortages – was unacceptable. When, in 1988, East German youth were asked what a good reason would be for a young person to leave the GDR, 45 per cent replied, 'unhappiness with the range of goods on offer, especially consumer goods and fashionable clothing for young people'.[39] Further investigation by the ZIJ revealed to researchers why clothing was such a sticking point for young East Germans. The results of a study of young peoples' relationship to fashion in 1986 suggested that, rather than using clothing styles to differentiate themselves from adults as researchers had expected, young East Germans were primarily interested in using clothing to fashion self-identities. The study concluded that 'young people certainly do not want to look uniform. In their conception of self, they attach great importance to the development of their individuality, especially the girls'. Tellingly, the study concluded by noting that young people would accomplish this goal using whatever types, colours or designs of clothing were available to them.[40]

The punks and other stylistically 'decadent' young East Germans were at the forefront of a critique that resonated with many other East German youths. Why could one not be an upstanding citizen and pursue one's own goals and shape one's own destiny? The great majority of these stylistically adventurous young people wanted to be productive members of their society but wanted to do it on their own terms. But there were no indications that conditions in the GDR would change, even after Mikhail Gorbachev began to liberalize Soviet policies. Style was an avenue open to East Germany's young generation and they seized the opportunity for self-expression and self-determination. Adults who worked closely with alternative youth in the GDR recognized that their lifestyles and behaviours fulfilled such needs. For example, four youth workers in a protestant church in Jena who reached out to subcultural groups throughout the 1980s noted with approval that punks' pogo (a dance of jumping up and down energetically in time with fast punk music) at church events underscored the importance of individuality to punks. One of them remembered that 'This style of dancing demonstrated that individuality was more important than sociability... They danced out their aggression and then happily got drunk'.[41] By the mid-1980s other youth workers had begun to notice the same need for self-actualization among the young people they worked with, including those not in a subculture. A youth worker at an East Berlin church told a West German reporter, '[Young East Berliners of high school age] certainly have the feeling that lifelong conformity just isn't worth it'.[42]

Within the repressive GDR state, the self-expression practised by punks and other members of the style-scenes had even greater significance. By flaunting their ostentatious styles in public spaces, young East German members of the style-scenes were breaking the state monopoly on control of legitimate cultural capital. Three elements of the East German iterations of the style-scenes made this possible. First, to an even greater extent than in the FRG, style-scenes in the GDR constructed their styles and associated identities by using small, everyday items and materials that were available to anyone. This left the GDR state with less control over the materials needed for this type of cultural production. Second, the common, everyday nature of these items and materials meant that the meanings assigned to them by the style-scene participants were easily transformed and re-transformed. To stay current in one's understanding of this shifting symbolic world required immersion in the scenes. Indeed, Stasi documents of this period reveal how difficult it was for agents to prevent, or even interpret, symbolic messages they knew must be subversive. This remained an obstacle despite the many informants the security agency had within the scenes. This leads to the third element: the style-scenes began to reverse, in a very public and visible way, the SED state's control of cultural criticism. The style-scenes existed outside of the reach of the cadre of trained, ideologically dependable cultural critics tasked with shaping public opinion of new types of cultural production. These critics claimed in newspaper articles, paperback books and public lectures that punk and the other decadent styles were symptoms of a crisis of capitalism. But the actual presence of punks in the GDR trumped the critics' imagined capitalist crisis.

Conclusion

The wave of subcultural activity that traversed the developed world in the 1980s proved to be an amazingly adaptable vehicle for self-expression. It was the 'small things' that allowed the subcultural youths of East and West Germany to adapt an international youth cultural trend to have meaning within their own lives. The results were a complex mixture of internationally recognizable style and locally readable symbols.

Despite the fact that material and political conditions did not allow for a common network of intelligible symbols to develop between East and West German style-scenes, the meanings the scenes assigned and reassigned to small, everyday things can help us to identify ruptures and continuities in each state. Gradual change in cultural and social norms is notoriously difficult to pin down. Studying everyday things as they were used in youth cultures allows one to combine cultural and semiotic analysis with concepts of generational change.

In the context of our current subject, the local interpretations of internationalized youth culture make it clear that the purposes of these subcultural statements extended beyond vague attempts at anti-consumerist or anti-conformist protest in the West. In communist Germany, the attraction of the new style-scenes was about more than criticizing a repressive government or a mindless desire to ape the fashions and trends of the West. In both German states, the flamboyant styles were the most visible manifestations of a broader turn towards lifestyles as a mode of identity construction and an emergent location of social value among a new generation of teenagers and young adults in the 1980s. Unlike gender, class or family background, which were identity elements over which one had little control, lifestyle offered young people some choice in the identities they 'wore' in public. In East and West German contexts, youth had a lot of control over what they consumed and how they consumed it. This may be one reason why, in an era of disgruntlement and anxiety, developing one's own lifestyle held such appeal to youth in both German states.

Alissa Bellotti is a PhD candidate at Carnegie Mellon University in Pittsburgh, Pennsylvania. Her research on the entangled social and cultural histories of East and West Germany focuses on popular culture and the evolution of social values in late modernity. She is currently finishing her dissertation on the politics of youth culture in divided Germany during the 1970s and 1980s.

Notes

1. Büscher and Wensierski, *Null Bock auf DDR*, 11.
2. Many thanks to Erica Carter, Katrin Schreiter and Donna Harsch for their excellent comments, the participants in the GSA Seminar 'Experience and Cultural Practice: Rewriting the Everyday History of Postwar Germany' for their probing questions and Alex Simmith for pointing me towards the concept of empty signifiers.
3. Lenski, *Zwischen Utopie und Resignation*; Hayton, '"Härte Gegen Punk"'; Dale, *Popular Protest in East Germany*; Dennis and LaPorte, *State and Minorities in Communist East Germany*; Pehlemann and Galenza, *Spannung, Leistung, Widerstand*; Hahn, *Pogo im Bratwurstland*; Robert-Havemann-Gesellschaft, e.V. and Bundeszentrale für politische Bildung, 'Alternative Jugendkultur in Der DDR', Jugendopposition in Der DDR, retrieved 1 January 2017 from http://www.jugendopposition.de/index.php?id=1. An exception is Peter Wurschi's monograph *Rennsteigbeat: jugendliche Subkulturen im Thüringer Raum 1952–1989*, where he analyses subcultures in Suhl as cultural revolt.
4. See also Michael Schmidt's analysis on the postwar West German jazz scene in this volume.
5. I refer here only to these subcultures' first appearances in West Germany. Rockers, teds, mods and hippies all have very different histories in the United Kingdom and United States than they do in German-speaking lands.
6. Reichardt and Siegfried, *Das Alternative Milieu*.
7. Wicke, 'Music, Dissidence, Revolution, and Commerce', 121; Shahan, *Punk Rock and German Crisis*, 10.
8. Jugendwerk der Deutschen Shell, *Shell Jugendstudie*, 13.
9. Reichardt, *Authentizität und Gemeinschaft*, 37.
10. Grünbaum, *Wolf Biermann 1976*.
11. See Rauhut and Kochan, *Bye Bye Lübben City*.
12. Hayton, 'Culture from the Slums', 88–119.
13. At the time of writing, a wide variety of photos arranged by year and place are available on Karl Nagel's online punk archive, www.punkfoto.de.
14. Friedrich, 'Die Leipziger Bands', 35.
15. Teipel, *Verschwende deine Jugend*, 18–19.
16. Horschig, 'In der DDR hat es nie Punks gegeben', 34.
17. See Büsser, *If the Kids are United*, 22.
18. See the West German anarcho-punk fanzines *Der Falschmelder*, No. 3–7, 1983–1984 and *Der Tiefschlag*, No. 2, 5 and 6, 1980–1981.
19. Horschig, 'In der DDR hat es nie Punks gegeben', 35.
20. Furian and Becker, *'Auch im Osten trägt man Westen'*, 13.
21. Early West German punks Peter Hein and Jäki Eldorado discuss the impossibility of deciphering the swastika as a punk symbol in Teipel, *Verschwende deine Jugend*, 40. Dick Hebdige was also forced to conclude that the meaning of the swastika 'evaporates' in his study of English punks. Homology is Hebdige's term for the way in which chaos contributed to the coherence of the punk style in England in the late 1970s. See Hebdige, *Subculture: The Meaning of Style*, 117 and 113–17, respectively.
22. Stock and Mühlberg, *Die Szene von innen*, 61.
23. Teipel, *Verschwende deine Jugend*, 89, 175, 361.
24. Ideal, 'Eiszeit', *Der Ernst des Lebens*, WEA Musik GmbH, 1981.
25. Drenger, 'Vitamin A in Magdeburg', 325–26.
26. See the interviews with *Gruftis* in Stock and Mühlberg, *Die Szene von Innen*.
27. Furian and Becker, *Auch im Osten*, 36. 'Too much future' resonated with many other GDR punks and was chosen by Carsten Fiebeler and Michael Boehlke as the title for

their 2006 documentary chronicling GDR punk (*Ostpunk! Too Much Future,* Good! Movies, 2006).
28. Büscher and Wensierski, *Null Bock auf DDR,* 27.
29. Baacke, *Jugend und Jugendkulturen,* 21.
30. Hansen and Veen, 'Auf Der Suche Nach Dem Privaten Glück', *Die Zeit,* 5 September 1980.
31. Zinnecker, *Jugendkultur,* 348.
32. Beck, *Risk Society,* 51, 131. Originally published as *Risikogesellschaft: Auf dem Weg in eine andere Moderne* (Frankfurt am Main: Suhrkamp, 1986).
33. Baacke, *Jugend und Jugendkulturen,* 240; emphasis in original.
34. Ibid., 194–97, 240–41.
35. Friedrich and Schubarth, 'Ausländerfeindliche und rechtsextreme orientierungen bei ostdeutschen Jugendlichen', 1059.
36. BArch, DC 4/705, 'Tendenzen der Beliebtheit von Formen populärer Musik aus dem Hitlistenvergleich 1979/1984/1985 – Expertise des ZIJ', 1985. In 1985, survey participants were given the choice of 'other' country of origin for the first time. 7 per cent of respondents chose a song from neither the GDR nor a capitalist country. Even after adjusting for this discrepancy, the decreasing popularity of GDR-made pop music is still evident.
37. See Jan Palmowski's contribution in this volume (chapter 1).
38. BArch, DY 30/IV 2/2.039/233. 'Jugendpolitik der SED' 14.7.1987, 23.
39. Förster, 'Weltanschaulich-politisches Bewußtsein', 137.
40. Günther, *Modespezifische Verhaltensweisen von Jugendlichen in der DDR,* 69.
41. Lenski, *Zwischen Utopie und Resignation,* 23.
42. Büscher and Wensierski, *Null Bock auf DDR,* 26.

Bibliography

Baacke, D. *Jugend und Jugendkulturen: Darstellung und Deutung.* Weinheim: Juventa, 1993.
Beck, U. *Risk Society: Towards a New Modernity.* Translated by M. Ritter. London: Sage, 1992.
Brück, W. 'Jugend als soziales Problem', in W. Friedrich and H. Griese (eds), *Jugend und Jugendforschung in der DDR: Gesellschaftspolitische Situationen, Sozialisation und Mentalitätsentwicklung in den achtziger Jahren* (Opladen: Leske + Budrich, 1991), 191–200.
Büscher, W. and P. Wensierski. *Null Bock auf DDR: Aussteigerjugend im anderen Deutschland.* Reinbek bei Hamburg: Rowohlt, 1984.
Büsser, M. *If the Kids are United …: von Punk zu Hardcore und zurück.* Mainz: Dreieck-Verlag, 1995.
Dale, G. *Popular Protest in East Germany, 1945–1989.* London: Routledge, 2005.
Dennis, M. and N. LaPorte. *State and Minorities in Communist East Germany.* New York: Berghahn Books, 2013.
Drenger, S. 'Vitamin A in Magdeburg', in R. Galenza and H. Havemeister (eds), *Wir wollen immer artig sein: Punk, New Wave, HipHop, Independent-Szene in der DDR, 1980–1990* (Berlin: Schwarzkopf & Schwarzkopf, 2005).
Fenemore, M. *Sex, Thugs and Rock 'N' Roll: Teenage Rebels in Cold-War East Germany.* New York: Berghahn Books, 2007.

Förster, P. 'Weltanschaulich-politisches Bewußtsein', in W. Friedrich and H. Griese (eds), *Jugend und Jugendforschung in der DDR: Gesellschaftspolitische Situationen, Sozialisation und Mentalitätsentwicklung in den achtziger Jahren* (Opladen: Leske + Budrich, 1991), 135–50.

Friedrich, J.A. 'Die Leipziger Bands', in R. Galenza and H. Havemeister (eds), *Wir wollen immer artig sein: Punk, New Wave, HipHop, Independent-Szene in der DDR, 1980–1990* (Berlin: Schwarzkopf & Schwarzkopf, 2005).

Friedrich, W. and W. Schubarth. 'Ausländerfeindliche und rechtsextreme orientierungen bei ostdeutschen Jugendlichen'. *Deutschland Archiv* 24(10) (1991).

Furian, G. and N. Becker. *'Auch im Osten trägt man Westen': Punks in der DDR – und was aus ihnen geworden ist*. Berlin: Bugrim, 2008.

Galenza, R. and H. Havemeister (eds). *Wir wollen immer artig sein: Punk, New Wave, HipHop, Independent-Szene in der DDR 1980–1990*. Berlin: Schwarzkopf & Schwarzkopf, 2005.

Grünbaum, R. *Wolf Biermann 1976: Die Ausbürgerung und ihre Folgen*. Erfurt: Landeszentrale für politische Bildung Thüringen, 2006.

Günther, C. *Modespezifische Verhaltensweisen von Jugendlichen in der DDR: erste Auswertungsergebnisse zur Studie Jugend und Mode 1985*. Leipzig: Zentralinstitut für Jugendforschung, 1986.

Hahn, A. *Pogo im Bratwurstland: Punk in Thüringen*. Erfurt: Landeszentrale für Politische Bildung Thüringen, 2009.

Hansen, S. and H.-J. Veen. 'Auf Der Suche Nach Dem Privaten Glück'. *Die Zeit*, 5 September 1980.

Hayton, J. 'Culture from the Slums: Punk Rock, Authenticity and Alternative Culture in East and West Germany'. Dissertation, University of Illinois at Urbana-Campaign, 2013.

――――. '"Härte Gegen Punk": Youth Subculture, Western Media, and State Responses in the German Democratic Republic'. *German History* 31(4) (2013), 523–49.

Hebdige, D. *Subculture: The Meaning of Style*. London: Routledge, 1979.

Horschig, M. 'ln der DDR hat es nie Punks gegeben', in R. Galenza and H. Havemeister (eds), *Wir wollen immer artig sein: Punk, New Wave, HipHop, Independent-Szene in der DDR 1980–1990* (Berlin: Schwarzkopf & Schwarzkopf, 2005).

Jugendwerk der Deutschen Shell. *Shell Jugendstudie, 1985: Jugend und Erwachsene '85 – Generationen im Vergleich*. 5 vols. Opladen, 1985.

Lenski, K. *Zwischen Utopie und Resignation – vom Bleiben und Gehen: Jugendkultur in der DDR in den achtziger Jahren am Beispiel der Grossveranstaltung 'Jugend 86' in Rudolstadt*. Jena: Thüringer Archiv für Zeitgeschichte 'Matthias Domaschk', 2003.

Pehlemann, A. and R. Galenza. *Spannung, Leistung, Widerstand: Magnetbanduntergrund DDR, 1979–1990*. Berlin: Verbrecher Verlag, 2006.

Poiger, U.G. *Jazz, Rock, and Rebels: Cold War Politics and American Culture in a Divided Germany*. Berkeley, CA: University of California Press, 2000.

Rauhut, M. and T. Kochan. *Bye Bye Lübben City: Bluesfreaks, Tramps und Hippies in der DDR*. Berlin: Schwarzkopf & Schwarzkopf, 2004.

Reichardt, S. *Authentizität und Gemeinschaft: Linksalternatives Leben in den siebziger und frühen achtziger Jahren*. Berlin: Suhrkamp, 2014.

Reichardt, S. and D. Siegfried. *Das Alternative Milieu: Antibürgerlicher Lebensstil und linke Politik in der Bundesrepublik Deutschland und Europa 1968–1983*. Göttingen: Wallstein Verlag, 2010.

Robert-Havemann-Gesellschaft, e.V., and Bundeszentrale für politische Bildung. Jugendopposition in Der DDR. http://www.jugendopposition.de.

Shahan, C. *Punk Rock and German Crisis: Adaptation and Resistance after 1977*. New York: Palgrave Macmillan, 2013.

Stock, M. and P. Mühlberg. *Die Szene von Innen: Skinheads, Grufties, Heavy Metals, Punks*. Berlin: Links Druck Verlag, 1990.

Teipel, J. *Verschwende deine Jugend: Ein Doku-Roman über den deutschen Punk und New Wave*. Frankfurt am Main: Suhrkamp, 2001.

Wicke, P. 'Music, Dissidence, Revolution, and Commerce: Youth Culture Between Mainstream and Subculture', in A. Schildt and D. Siegfried (eds), *Between Marx and Coca-Cola: Youth Cultures in Changing European Societies, 1960–1980* (New York: Berghahn Books, 2006), 109–26.

Wurschi, P. *Rennsteigbeat: jugendliche Subkulturen im Thüringer Raum 1952–1989*. Cologne: Böhlau, 2007.

Zinnecker, J. *Jugendkultur, 1940–1985*. Opladen: Leske + Budrich, 1987.

Chapter 8

Cultivating the Past

The *Schrebergarten* as a Political Space in Postwar
German Literature

Katrin Schreiter

A llotment gardening has come to be understood in Germany, Hermann
Rudolph finds, 'as deeply and distinctively German'.[1] This is despite
the fact that allotments can be found in many countries around the globe.
Unsurprisingly, the popular pastime of allotment gardening survived
the division of Germany after the Second World War and maintained its
cultural and social importance in both East and West Germany. In the
German Democratic Republic (GDR) alone, 1.2 million people – about 10
per cent of the adult population – were members of the national allotment
association, which was by far the largest non-communist organization in
the country.[2] The widespread appeal of leasing a garden allotment and
creating a personal space seems to have been rooted in the fact that collective property and state-controlled collectivism left private space and
individual liberties rare and precious in the GDR.[3] Certainly, Rudolph
observes 'that it is part of the selfperception of the allotment gardening
movement – and of its public image – that it exists beneath political currents and is merely grazed by social conflict'.[4] Yet this idyllic perception
stands in stark contrast to the socio-cultural and political tensions that
have been inscribed into the *Schrebergarten* in postwar German literature.

To gain more detailed insights into the cultural meaning of the
Schrebergarten in a changing German society, especially in the context of
Germany's division and reunification, this chapter examines the garden
as a topos in modern German literature in its relationship to experienced history. It is interesting to note in this regard that the majority
of German publications on allotment gardens have been published after
reunification. While the German National Library lists fifty-five books,

journals, theatre and music publications before 1990, another 290 have been published since. The pre-reunification absence indicates first and foremost an increasingly specializing publishing sector, which has turned to publishing special interest journals and advice literature for gardening. Nonetheless, projects such as the first historical allotment exhibition, which opened in 2001 at the Film Museum Potsdam with the title *Laube, Liebe, Hoffnung*, and publications such as Wladimir Kaminer's successful humorous novel *Mein Leben im Schrebergarten* (2007), testify to the recent popularity of the allotment garden topos as both a lens through which to view the past and an amusing metaphor for stereotypical German quirks and values.[5] Of course, literary texts are representations of reality, and they are meaningful in the ways in which they are expressions of their time. In the following, four novels whose plot evolve around gardens, Paul Gurk's *Laubenkolonie* (1949), Ulrich Plenzdorf's *Die Leiden des jungen W.* (1972), Jost Baum's *Schrebergarten Blues* (1991), Michael Kleeberg's *Ein Garten im Norden* (1998), are historicized within the political and social context of their time. This interdisciplinary analysis is designed to further our understanding of the different functions the spatiality of the Schrebergarten serves in Germans' (re)imagination of the past, and the role of literature in creating a place of experience.

A Short History of the Schrebergarten

A mass phenomenon emerging with German industrialization, the urban garden movement originated with physician and university teacher Daniel Gottlob Moritz Schreber's pedagogic theories addressing the negative effects of urbanization on children's health. He proposed that such effects could be counteracted with strict discipline including corporal punishment, cleanliness, posture correction and, most importantly, outdoor activities to release excess energy.[6] To honour his legacy, a Leipzig association for parents and teachers named itself after Schreber in 1864 when it first leased land for a children's playground. Small garden lots along the perimeter of the playground were planted to teach city children, from the working class as well as the lower middle class, about nature and gardening. When they lost interest in this activity, the parents took over, displacing the association's original focus on education onto the production of small garden spaces in the midst of urban landscapes.

The movement was emblematic of its time, when the popular illustrated family newspaper *Die Gartenlaube* (1852–1944) linked ideas of education, leisure time comfort and Germanness to the garden: 'We want to entertain you and educate you entertainingly. Over all of this shall hover a whiff of poetry like the scent of a blossoming flower; and you shall feel at home in our *Gartenlaube*, where you will find good German cosiness that touches the heart'.[7] For the middle classes, allotment gardens became a real and imagined space that catered to bourgeois ideals of order and individuality, which were seen to coexist harmoniously in the gardens to create places of calm and reflection in turbulent times.[8] Allotment gardening also became a popular working-class pastime, offering an escape from the dull routines at work as well as at home which industrialization and urbanization introduced into everyday life. The establishment of garden colonies, organized in associations called *Kleingartenvereine* (KGVs), created islands of green in the urban sea of grey concrete. In parts of town where apartment blocks lacked gardens, allotments along the urban perimeter became the only way to interact with nature in a productive and aesthetically expressive way, as opposed to urban parks where one is for the most part limited to looking at nature. Moreover, during times of war and crisis, such as the two world wars and resulting economic collapse, small allotments provided shelter and food for survival.

In the GDR, the 1950s and 1960s saw an integration of the allotment tenants into national food provision. They were sought after as apiarists, as rabbit, poultry and goat breeders, and as producers of precious furs. The honey, meat, eggs, dairy, furs, as well as the vegetables they produced were sold in the state-run local *Handelsorganisation* (HO, national retail organization) shops. After many years of fighting resistance among the allotment associations, the SED eventually won control over the representation structures of allotment gardeners, settlers and small animal breeders in 1959.[9] What followed was an increasing alignment of associational and Party structures, while the allotment tenants themselves continued to resist production quotas to safeguard the joy of self-expression that the garden space offered. Nevertheless, the incomplete integration into the Plan rendered the East German garden colonies an opportunity to diversify the diet of one's family in the later, more stable postwar decades, and to make a little bit of money on the side.[10] In the West Germany of the 1970s and 1980s, the gardens remained first and foremost sites of individual expression. Organized in associations, KGVs reveal allotment gardeners' much denigrated 'petit-bourgeois' values, visible in the strict regulations they imposed on leisure activities and gardening.[11] Records from the West German allotment reconciliation courts (*Kleingartenschiedsgericht*) underline the literal interpretation of associational rules and regulations. Both in the GDR and the FRG, the KGVs thus provided similar settings to negotiate the relationship between individual space and society's norms, expectations and changing political structures. Immediately after unification in 1990, when West Germans claimed former possessions expropriated by the Soviet occupiers and later the GDR government, a network of East German gardening associations lobbied against the re-appropriation of land, and organized conferences and informational workshops that provided legal support for allotment tenants. Such contestations belie the belief that the Schrebergarten is an apolitical space. Rather, it is part and parcel of German political history and imbued with considerable cultural significance for German remembrance.

Memory and Space

The process of collective remembering has found extensive treatment in historiography. Defining the relationship between history and memory has become an important issue for the discipline, not least as a means of defining its social role. Geoffrey Cubitt states that there is only 'a perceived analogy between the mental lives of individuals and of societies: the point is not that history relies on memory, ... but that it does for the society what memory (in the sense of individual memory) supposedly does for the individual'.[12] However, there is an important difference in that history, unlike individual memory, has the status of accumulated trans-generational remembering that performs certain tasks, such as nation building. Cubitt argues that the discipline of history became equated with social, i.e. collective, memory by perfecting itself through the development of a critical scientific method: 'The application of this method strengthened rather than weakened the connection which national communities (and perhaps humanity more generally) had to their remembered pasts'.[13]

Cubitt's critical perspective on historical method not only points to the socially constructed nature of collective memory, it also lays bare the relation between imaginative production, and what have been termed in the historical literature memory places, or (via Pierre Nora) *lieux de mémoire*.[14] The allotment garden, moreover, has been identified in histories of modern Germany as precisely one such memory place. A short essay on the German Schrebergarten figures alongside 120 other 'memory places', including the Volkswagen Beetle or the Loreley rock, in the multivolume oeuvre *Deutsche Erinnerungsorte* (2001).[15] That such an ordinary everyday place should have collective memory value may seem debatable; but, as this chapter seeks to show, there are indications in the post-1945 memorializing of the allotment garden in contemporary literature that it may perform precisely that function.

To pursue this line of thinking further, Henri Lefèbvre's work is a helpful starting point. Lefèbvre's concepts of social spatial production are specifically relevant to the focus below on the garden topos and its literary politicization, both as spatial practices (behaviours triggered and defined by space) and representational space (meanings assigned to space). The interdependency of the two emerges in Lefèbvre's examination of monuments as an example of representational space, which he sees as a place that 'comprehends the entire existence of the group concerned' and gives the individual member of this society 'an image of that membership, ... a collective mirror more faithful than any personal one'.[16] This collective function has been examined in a growing body of literature on places and monuments that are representative of historical events and political developments recognized as important for national or local collective memory.[17] But what about the memory value of everyday places that have not been inscribed with collective meaning? Just like a childhood home or a street scene, gardens are usually insignificant for society, yet, they generate individual remembering. Dylan Trigg differentiates between these two forms of remembering as '*memory of place* as a particular mode of remembering' based on lived experience in which materiality shapes memory, and *place of memory* as the 'formation of memory within a social context, afforded by the power of place and manifest in such entities as monuments and sites of trauma'.[18] His analysis of the connections between remembering and experience of space links back to the questions of power explored by Lefebvre, whose concept indicates that all urban space is politically inscribed: 'What we call "ideology" only achieves consistency by intervening in social space and in its production, and thus by taking on body therein'.[19] Urban space is political, urban studies scholar Grégory Busquet points out in his analysis of Lefebvre, in that it is the subject of public policies, and 'echoes the vision of a specific and desirable evolution of society ... [and] is tied to the question of power held onto or conquered (power over the space but also over the social groups)'.[20] Ideology is inscribed in urban space through spatial projects under the guise of an utopian spirit of social improvement, for example the twentieth-century workers' housing projects that, along with the promise of modern amenities, rationalized and standardized living. For Lefebvre, it is the reproduction of the social hierarchies in the present order of urban architecture that inhibits social change and produces alienation. Uncovering the ways in which spatial production influences practices and behaviours is an important part of Lefebvre's project to expand his critique of the everyday.[21] The Marxist philosopher posits in his seminal work, 'Man must be everyday, or he will not be at all'.[22] He argues that knowledge of the everyday is not encapsulated in meticulous 'realistic' descriptions of 'a peasant at work, or of a worker's oil-stained blue overalls', but rather in 'the totality of labour [which] has modified and transformed the face of the world ... the result of these gestures, their totality, is what contains greatness'.[23] The everyday becomes thus a simultaneous site of alienation and its over-throw, the effective transformation of things as they are.

These theoretical considerations allow us to see the politicization of the everyday space of the Schrebergarten, a space that is often understood as providing refuge from political forces, and to understand this retreat as an expression of individual insurgency that aspires to overcome the experi-ence of individual alienation. Scholarly literature on urban garden allot-ments in Germany, as well as their inhabitable sheds, is surprisingly sparse in comparison to the cultural iconography that surrounds its Russian counterpart, the *dacha*.[24] Perhaps due to the ambiguity of its meaning, scholarly treatments of the German Schrebergarten come from diverse disciplines. Egon Johannes provides a geography of the Schrebergarten in northern urban spaces. Gabriele Hofmann and Dorli Cosmutia's study of leisure time practices in German garden allotments and permanent camp-ing sites as well as Rita Pohle-Schöttler's dissertation on the gardeners' aes-thetic practices approach the topic from anthropological and ethnological angles. Hartwig Stein, whose work follows the development of allotments until the end of the Second World War, offers a cultural history with a focus on Hamburg.[25] The only East German history of the Schrebergarten by Isolde Dietrich is rather a digest of archival sources than a socio-political analysis of the place that allotments held in GDR everyday life.[26] Fascination with the ordinary has also brought forward a small body of popular (hi)stories about the 'Paradise with Garden Shed', such as the work of Christoph Mulitze and Stefan Leppert.[27] Finally, recent academic debates have focused on the role of garden allotments in an increasingly globalized world as sites of alternative subsistence farming and social integration of migrants to Germany, for which Kaminer's *Mein Leben im Schrebergarten* serves as literary anecdotal evidence.[28] Yet the allotment's cultural function as spatial representation of collective memory and as literary space of feelings of belonging and alienation within the German-German context of the postwar era has not gained widespread attention. It is to these issues therefore that attention turns below.

The Garden in German Literature

Nature and landscapes have a long tradition in German literature.[29] In particular, the garden can be found as a topos in German literature across the early modern period, through nineteenth-century realism and on into modern, contemporary and popular literature. Examples include prose fiction, for instance Goethe's *Werther* and Theodor Fontane's *Effi Briest*, or poetry ranging from Friedrich Hölderlin to Sarah Kirsch. Literary scholarship has looked at the garden accordingly as a space of seclu-sion,[30] a space that represents death[31] and connects the personal and the literary[32] in the oeuvre of individual authors.

Part of what might make the garden such a popular image with authors and scholars alike could be the flexibility of the garden topos. From the sacral paradisiacal garden of Adam and Eve to the worldly garden, it has been ascribed manifold literary meanings that go beyond an aesthetic experience for the senses and connect to the mind and inner being: '[The garden] inspires contemplation of world affairs and the meaning of life. Accordingly, it reflects on one hand the notion of transcience (*Vergänglichkeit*) and on the other the notion of immortality'.[33] The meaning of garden topoi has been described as ranging from 'an absolute vision of happiness (*Glücksvorstellung*) in the locus amoenus to a terror scenario in the locus terribilis'.[34] The garden is thus a trope with a long history that gets picked up at different points in literature. The following discussion explores a specific function of the garden topos: the spatial politicization of the garden, and the different meanings and feelings associated with it, explored through an examination of German literary texts across a period from 1949 until 1998.

The concept of urban garden colonies as an emotional counterweight to the fast-moving age of industrialization, with its rapid modernization, urbanization and the rationalizing grip that modern societies gained over the individual, finds application in Paul Gurk' *Laubenkolonie Schwanensee* (1949).[35] This is a late work of an author who was also a major, if less known, contributor to the Berlin Novel genre under the pseudonym Franz Grau. From the age of five, with the exception of the last three years of the Second World War, Gurk lived in Berlin, where he died in 1953.[36] In the autobiographically influenced *Laubenkolonie*, the book's impoverished protagonist Graumann tries to escape the social alienation of the big city in an allotment colony along the northern perimeter of Berlin, which is endangered by the construction of a street: 'The big city has a strange border, absurd, slightly ridiculous, touching and beautiful at the same time, like everything without an immediately calculable and profit-oriented goal: the garden shed! … The area around the allotment gardens, which this story will be about, is odd: an abrupt clash of where the city ends and nature begins'.[37] Gurk juxtaposes the natural wild-ness of the allotment with the calculating profit of the growing city. The motley group of allotment colony inhabitants fit stereotypical images of Schrebergarten oddities: they are engaged in small animal rearing, active at allotment assemblies, and self-absorbed in their cultural activi-ties, reading the colony's newspaper instead of the national or local news. Some of the garden settlers still work, but Graumann has retired from his profession as teacher to follow his artistic passion, and thus considers himself the 'most difficult, the most comical case' in the colony.[38] In this 'tragicomic idyll in which poverty and self-isolation are ironically fractured',[39] the allotment becomes a refuge, a manageable space that allows the protagonist to let his residual creativity and self-expression as a composer unfold. As this refuge comes under threat from the expanding city however, Graumann commits suicide, abruptly ending the utopia of an alternative life in modern times.

Similarly, it is the impetus for self-expression that brings the protagonist of East German author Ulrich Plenzdorf's 1972 short novel *Die Leiden des jungen W.* to a garden allotment.[40] Plenzdorf tells the story of a young man rebelling against the expectations of an increasingly rationalizing and standardizing GDR society. The novel is set in a garden allotment marked for demolition, and from the beginning the space is loaded with connotations that go beyond the materiality of the place. Starting the narrative with newspaper announcements of the protagonist's death, Plenzdorf uses montage techniques such as flashbacks to develop Edgar Wibeau's story. His father, who left when Wibeau was five years old, attempts to discover why his son died, by interviewing the people who were in contact with his son during the last months of his life. These interviews, interrupted by commentary from the dead son, allow the reader to piece together a coherent narrative. It follows the protagonist from his provincial hometown of Mittenberg to East Berlin in the aftermath of an incident at his traineeship. In a gesture that defies authority, Wibeau moves to the capital together with his friend Willi, who eventually decides to return to family and job.

Wibeau stays behind at his friend's family Berlin allotment. It is a typical East German Schrebergarten, with an inhabitable shed and a few scattered bushes, in the midst of a deteriorating garden colony. Wibeau refers to it as his 'Kolchose',[41] a Russian term for an agricultural production collective. The politicized language moves the garden topos from its traditional bourgeois setting to the contemporary socialist one. Yet Plenzdorf instils the term with irony, because the primary function of this garden space for Wibeau is a place to 'drop off the grid' in the highly organized GDR society in order to exempt himself from the scrutiny of the political productivity discourse. The seclusion of the Schrebergarten facilitates his attempt to break free from everyday routine and to explore his 'talent' and creativity as a painter.[42]

The plot parallels to *Laubenkolonie* are striking, as are the autobiographical resemblances of the two protagonists with their authors. However, it cannot be asserted that Plenzdorf knew Gurk's work. The explicit reference in Plenzdorf is instead to Goethe. In the Schrebergarten outhouse,

Wibeau finds Johann Wolfgang von Goethe's famous eighteenth-century novel *Die Leiden des jungen Werther* (1774). The discovery is a laconic commentary on GDR cultural and educational policy, as this text was commonly taught in GDR schools as part of an effort to claim German bourgeois cultural heritage for East Germany. Wibeau begins to cite passages from Goethe's *Werther* to draw parallels between his experiences and those of Werther. The contrast between the eighteenth-century prose of Goethe and the colloquialisms that pepper Plenzdorf's writing could not be any starker:

> I also didn't have especially dazzling visual organs in my old Huguenot bonce. Proper pig's slits versus Charlie's headlights. But brown. Brown rocks, seriously… In short, William, I have made an acquaintance which has warmed my heart… An angel… And yet I'm not able to tell you how perfect she is, why she is perfect. Enough, she has captivated all of my senses. The end.[43]

Mirroring the plot in Goethe's work, a love triangle evolves around Wibeau's chance encounter with the kindergarten teacher Charlie in the garden colony. After falling in love with her, he discovers that Charlie is engaged to be married to another man. The discovery disabuses him of the romance of his off-the-grid adventure in the garden colony. Wibeau decides to find a construction job as a painter, which, eventually, he loses due to his poor attitude. Yet he does briefly develop ambition on the job: he sets out to invent a motorized spray-painting device. It is this machine, patched together with scrap parts found in the garden colony, that causes Wibeau's eventual tragic death, though it remains open whether Wibeau planned his death by electrocution, or whether it was an accident.

The ending has provoked diverging interpretations by critics and literary scholars. Wibeau's drive to build his machine has been called both a submission to and a protest against social norms of productivity and performance in the GDR. Hans-Dietrich Sander attests that, in the end, Edgar wants to be a useful contributor to socialist society and that he is a communist at heart.[44] A more nuanced evaluation by Karena Niehoff sees Edgar's earlier rebellious tendencies confirmed by the ending. She interprets his ambition to invent a sophisticated technical machine on his own as individualized defiance, 'haughtiness against the social collective … conquering for fun, not capitulating because of a sense of order', a game in outsmarting a performance-oriented society.[45]

Unremarked by previous critics, however, is the way in which the traumatic event of Wibeau's death transforms the garden into a place of collective remembering. The montage of Goethe quotes, Wibeau's posthumous narration and his father's conversations connect the spatiality of the garden to the collective memory of the characters. The fact that he lived like a loafer on an allotment is what turns his character into an anti-hero, a counter-example to good socialist citizenship and the heroic archetype in socialist-realist literature. At the same time, it allows Plenzdorf to caricature ideological values and emphasize the country's shortcomings, such as its lack of technological progress. In these ways, Wibeau's story advances to a subtle critique of the GDR's historical development, at least for those among the GDR readership accustomed to reading between the lines.

In contrast to the GDR, allotment gardening in West Germany had to compete culturally with single-family home gardens. Against this back-drop, allotment leasers were viewed as part of the property-less class, 'verhinderte Eigenheimbesitzer' (thwarted homeowners), with a negative connotation in Western materialist society.[46] This limited considerably the cultural function of this space. Accordingly, the Schrebergarten topos does not seem to play an important role in West German literary fiction; yet it has found ample application as a setting for crime novels and tele-vision shows.[47] Jost Baum's *Schrebergarten Blues* (1991) is a wonderful example of this genre. After working for many years in adult education, Baum has used the years spent living in Wuppertal to inspire a series of Ruhrpott crime novels. Published the year after Germany's reunification, *Schrebergarten Blues* carries many West German subtexts relating to allotment gardening. Garden gnomes and petit-bourgeois decorations are ubiquitous, leaving the protagonist, journalist Eddie Jablonski, feeling haunted and ridiculed: 'He sensed how they snickered and chuckled behind his back, and made fun of him while he asthmatically struggled uphill like an old dodderer'.[48] The environment alienates Jablonski; it quickly becomes clear that he has no personal connection to or investment in the Schrebergarten space. This garden colony, located in the Ruhr town of Bochum, is threatened by the city council's urban development plans for a golf course. Jablonski comes to the Schrebergarten on the invitation of one of the protesting allotment gardeners, metalwork retiree Rudi Vollmer, who has reached out to the press to gain publicity for his struggle against the allotment colony's impending demise. The following day, Vollmer is found dead, with a bullet in his head, on his boat on the lake bordering the garden colony. Again, the motifs of impending demolition, death and decay threaten the idyll of the Schrebergarten.

When Jablonski investigates the murder, it becomes clear that this working-class milieu is connected to the power politics of Bochum. The juxtaposition of milieus emerges in the description of the allotment:

> He arrived at a crossroads whose branches each led downhill again. Jablonski chose Rose Lane, as had been explained to him on the telephone, and trudged

down the ash-paved path, lined right and left with high hedges, until he arrived at a garden gate a few meters after a sharp bend. The gate was welded from steel rods that were exactly parallel to each other and in whose centre a small spade was crossed with a metal rake. The whole thing seemed to Eddie like a celebratory monstrance of a long-lost proletarian culture. Rake and spade instead of hammer and sickle, interchangeable and toppled like the Marx and Lenin statues in the ex-GDR. A paltry indication of the faded greatness of a workers' movement that had meanwhile become harmless, degenerated insignia of a formerly powerful force.[49]

The materiality of the garden invokes the history of working-class culture in the industrial Ruhr region and, through simile ('like a ...'), connects the garden to regional political developments. Additional references to the insignia of the then recently collapsed GDR contribute to Baum's 'end of history' representation of working-class idealism. The working-class aesthetic is further underlined by Vollmer's colloquialisms and local dialect:

> 'Pah, Malorka, let me be!' Rudi grumbled. 'Ya'think I'm going into one a'them pensioner silos? A concrete block like that wiv a cat's toilet? Every evenin' a knees-up in the yard, revelry with hanky-panky an' so on? Nope, ya'know, I didn't work miself to the bone all mih life so that they can ship me off to Spain!'[50]

This barrage of idiomatic colloquialisms, administered without measure, not only marks the book as popular fiction, but also firmly places it in a working-class context.

In this and other popular crime novels, the allotment, then, seems to undergo redefinition. The garden ceases to be a place for escape from work and societal norms, and instead transforms into a place of encounter with the sobering realities of power and politics. This is where the West German crime novel intersects with literary fiction in both East and West. Although both Gurk's and Plenzdorf's protagonists pursue a peaceful, self-determined life away from social control and the reach of politics, eventually they likewise face existential challenges in the garden. Their longing for an undisturbed and unconstrained space in which to develop their creativity is not fulfilled. Nothing remains of that longing at the end of the two novels other than an uneasy sensation of nostalgia for a place that is no longer. The same can be seen in Baum's crime novel, where a crime disrupts the tranquillity of the Schrebergarten as the site of working-class retirement, and thus profoundly alters the meaning of the space.

The Garden after 1990

Considering the scant attention that the allotment received in West German literature prior to 1990, it is unexpected that in unified Germany the garden topos has been eagerly picked up. Michael Kleeberg's novel *Ein Garten im Norden*, first published in 1998, takes the topos further than the three texts discussed above and uses it both as a critique of contemporary politics and Germany's history.[51] Among the four texts, Kleeberg uses the aesthetics of nostalgia and the longing for a paradisiacal place most explicitly. His novel not only carries this nostalgia, but also employs it to harness the readers' imagination.

Hailed as 'Der Roman der Berliner Republik' by the newspaper *Die Welt*,[52] Kleeberg's novel imagines an alternative history of Germany, which nevertheless ends with National Socialism and war. The story of narrator Albert Klein, a writer who returns to Germany after twelve years of living in the Netherlands and France, bears resemblances to Kleeberg's own biography.[53] The narrative charts Klein's cultural alienation as he travels through the unified country, until a plot of wasteland in the middle of Berlin, where once the German-German border was, inspires him:

> He pointed at the trees that, in the evening twilight, appeared to be surrounded by rising mist, and I stopped listening. It was almost a small forest or a grove. And there were fir trees, firs and spruces, and even a couple of beeches. A little piece of landscape from my childhood, Black Forest, Schönbuch or Alp, and a hint of nostalgia touched me.

> These forests, this hilly, southern German landscape at a time when nothing had yet been defined, when everything was still possible. The décor of an age in which I didn't have to decide for or against anything, or choose any particular fork in the road. All mistakes could be reversed, no guilt weighted heavily, there was no history, no progress, only a boundless presence.[54]

The garden is presented as an apolitical space, in tune with the cultural coding as a place of respite suggested in François and Schulze's *Erinnerungsorte*. Yet it also provokes contrary emotions, in particular those of *Heimatverbundenheit* (belonging) and *Fernweh* (longing for distant places). Evoking in the phrase 'a little piece of landscape from my childhood' the cognitive absence of politics and history during childhood, an age of innocence, feeds a utopia of undefined possibilities and unwritten (hi)stories. Kleeberg inscribes the garden with longing for a blameless past. Moved by the materiality of the space, the novel's narrator Klein begins to imagine the history of a garden that he imagines may have existed in Berlin, created by his alter ego of the same name, a successful banker in the Weimar Republic and a cosmopolitan philanthropist. What now begins is a novel-within-a-novel, through which Kleeberg evokes a nostalgia that is heightened by the cultivated beauty that the imagined Berlin garden displays. It takes on a Neverland-ish aura:

> Yes indeed, one left this place different from when one had entered it. Elated, more confident as well, just like when getting out of a bath. At the same time also full of a strange yearning and melancholy. And fulfilled by memories ... This much was clear: under the rose tendrils, among the rustling of the bamboo one became peaceful. And curious, he thought, yes, even keen to travel. Who wouldn't be prompted by the lemon-scented blossoms of the summer magnolia or the camellia to think of the Rivera, or of the northern Italian lakes? Who wouldn't long for the orient at the sight of the ebony door, the pagoda and the gentle creaking and rocking of the copper lamp? Seeing the blue cedar, who wouldn't feel the pure air of the Atlas summits high above the Atlantic? And the roses and pear trees, that was home, and the Black Forest – suffused with light and shade, with its firs and spruces and sun-saturated mossy rocks – that might be called *Heimat* and nostalgia for the owner.

> Exterritorial! That was it! The garden was exterritorial. There were no flags flying here, no Prussian military marching through the streets, there was no Tricolour, no Union Jack, no Stars and Stripes, neither Black-Red-Gold nor Black-White-Red, also no double-headed eagle, only the pink of the magnolia blossoms ... A detached idyll? This conclusion seemed somewhat premature.[55]

While Gurk and Plenzdorf describe the garden as a place of refuge where one can preserve, and rediscover, individuality and creativity, the garden in the north – and by implication post-reunification Germany – itself is the main project in Kleeberg's novel. Philanthropist Klein's goal is to create beauty and maintain peace, as he turns the garden into a place where 'good' German artists, scientists and politicians meet with like-minded contemporaries: 'It is a utopia of enlightened civilization, based on dialogue and tolerance'.[56] It houses an archive for audio-visual sources of human culture, collected by stipendiaries Klein sends out into the world. His only requirement for them is to 'keep your eyes open, that is all I ask of you', turning the garden space into a vessel of fictional collective memory with a global reach.[57]

Nevertheless, the fictional garden is not beyond the reach of history; it is eventually destroyed by the Nazis. In the novel-within-a-novel, Kleeberg thus continues the West German usage of the garden topos as the spatiality of failed utopia, while heightening the element of nostalgia by employing the narrative possibilities of an alternative past. Meanwhile, the first Albert Klein, the novel's narrator, realizes that he has written his own prehistory. He learns that the philanthropist Klein was his grandfather, and upon inheriting the plot of land in Berlin, commits himself to rebuilding the beautiful garden. Just like the nation is written through its history in a teleological self-prophecy, so has Klein's story become his reality. Stephen Brockmann has pointed out that in this novel-within-a-novel the writing and the writer cannot be separated: 'it is a process of creation by means of which the writer inserts himself into reality while at the same time subjecting himself to the same process of change'.[58] Klein realizes that the past cannot be altered, that the Nazis and the Holocaust will remain part of Germany's negative past. Yet reunification created the plot of wasteland in Berlin, opening up a hopeful space for a future Germany 'that is no longer defined by the norms of its problematic past'.[59] Even though the reunited Germany that Klein finds upon his return does not seem to have confronted the past in an effort to create a better future, the literary imagination maintains this possibility. The garden in the north, then, guides the gaze backward and forward at the same time; it is both a locus terribilis and a locus aemonus, and leaves the reader with an ironically nostalgic longing for an improved Germany, which remains a dream.

Conclusion

The Schrebergarten as a trope in modern German literature ties traumatic events to a place that is commonly understood as a sociocultural niche of tranquillity and order. The literary works explored in this chapter employ the garden topos quite differently, however. Gurk's protagonist kills himself as his attempts to escape urban modernization and societal demands fail. Plenzdorf's protagonist Edgar Wibeau dies during an attempt to hide from the authoritarian system's expectations, and Baum presents the garden as a material palimpsest of a failed class struggle. Kleeberg's use of the garden as an archive of an alternative past clings to the utopia of a 'good' Germany, which falls into the abyss of twentieth-century events all the same. The dream of having overcome the past, the cultural ideology of the Kohl chancellorship,[60] is shattered by the realization that the German past is always there and cannot be evaded.

Across the four novels, each application of garden topoi is written against major socio-political processes in a changing Germany, and exhibits traces of the specific political systems in which the authors were socialized. The four novels echo Lefebvre's critical view of social spatial production, employing the garden space as a refuge for individuals alienated in modern society. In the process, the meaning of the Schrebergarten opens up, as the garden becomes a space of the 'effective transformation of things as they are' in the literary imagination. The knowledge of every-day life that goes into the writing of these four works circumscribes 'a result to be obtained', extending reality and history.[61] Yet the imagination of the authors, the individual 'memory of place' falters in the face of the collective 'place of memory' that becomes representative of Germany in all its changing forms. The common element in the way in which German authors from East, West and re-united Germany use the topos also recalls Alois Riegl's concept of 'unintended monument': 'a remnant whose pre-vious function has become redundant, but where no new function or use has been established: this allows for the establishment of memory value'.[62] Decay and ruin, caused by political developments, are tropes that transform the Schrebergarten from an everyday space of individual-ized 'memory of place' to a collective 'place of memory'. Accordingly, the Schrebergarten in modern German literature represents the opposite of the stable connotations that popular perception has ascribed to it, and is an example of how the meaning of cultural spaces is renegotiated and politicized through literary practices.

In East and West, the garden is a void that offers the opportunity to write against the currents of history. It is a space that leaves room for imagination, a corrective to the existing reality of quickly industrializing cities, the dystopian outcomes of collectivism, the demise of alternative societal organization to profit-seeking capitalism and the belligerence of Germany's past. It is interesting to see that authors in East, West and reunified Germany use the garden topos to convey autobiographically inspired stories. What they all have in common is not so much that they write an alternative history of Germany, but that they critically voice a desire for such an alternative history. 'And [this desire] is at the same time a – dialogic – narration, a reflection of contemporary historical imagi-nation, the relations between private and political history, and finally of literary fiction and real history'.[63]

Secondly, in the application of the garden topos in literature there emerges a nostalgic sentiment that can provide insights into how every-day places gain meaning, renegotiating their relationship to the past. In the aesthetics of decay, we can find a nostalgic longing for a place that is no more. Following Nietzsche's thoughts on lost paradise in *Untimely Mediations*, Dylan Trigg confirms the memory function of nostalgia in that it relates to the past only insofar as it replicates and forgets it, a coping mechanism for humankind. The ruin is the material manifestation of this process: 'Memories no longer stand as beacons of defined points. They are present, but simultaneously dissolving'.[64] Parallels to contem-porary German memory politics appear, but this is not the place to delve into an extensive critique of institutionalized remembering of Germany's complex and complicated past.

What historians can take away from a literary treatment of the garden is the concurrence of opposing forces. In one way, through decay, the Schrebergarten's stable cultural coding as a sociocultural niche is interrupted. At the same time, tranquillity persists to a certain extent through nostalgic emotions, which the space, even in ruins, conjures up: 'The drive is not toward disorder or disaster. In the ruin, spatially and ontologically, all that will cease to exist is the drive toward permanency, rational progress and static remembrance'.[65] The garden's decay creates new discursive and aesthetic meaning, invoking the milestones of twentieth-century German history, but packaged in nostalgia that allows the readership to acknowledge, and then forget, a place that was and is no more.

Katrin Schreiter is Lecturer in German and European Studies at King's College London. Her research focuses on the interplay of economics and culture of the Cold War era, and how these areas are connected to the politics of German diplomacy and ideas about nationhood. Her monograph *Designing One Nation: The Politics of Economic Culture and Trade in Divided Germany, 1949–1990* is forthcoming with Oxford University Press. She has published on related topics in *Business History Review* and *Europeanisation in the 20th Century: The Historical Lens* (Peter Lang, 2012). Her work on the gendered experience of Second World War trauma was published in *Central European History.*

Notes

1. Rudolph, 'Schrebergarten', vol. 3, 366. All translations from German scholarly and literary texts are by the author.
2. Dietrich, *Hammer, Zirkel, Gartenzaun*, 11.
3. Ibid., 24.
4. Rudolph, 'Schrebergarten', 376.
5. Kaminer, *Mein Leben im Schrebergarten.*
6. Daniel Gottlob Moritz Schreber was born in Leipzig in 1808 and died there in 1861. He published popular works on child rearing and the merits of physical fitness, among them *Die Eigenthümlichkeiten des kindlichen Organismus im gesunden und kranken Zustande* (1839) and *Der Hausfreund als Erzieher und Führer zu Familienglück und Menschenveredelung* (1861). His son, judge Daniel Paul Schreber, is well known in modern psychoanalysis through Sigmund Freud's case study on the younger Schreber's autobiographical account *Denkwürdigkeiten eines Nervenkranken* (1903).

7. Keil, 'Vorwort'.

8. Rudolph, 'Schrebergarten', 366.

9. Dietrich, *Hammer, Zirkel, Gartenzaun*, 130–41.

10. BArch-SAPMO, DY 30 / 2951 (SED: Büro Hager), 169–174. DDR – 'Private Nische Kleingartenkolonie', 10 September 1986. 'Stable' refers here to the end of rationing in GDR, where this economic instrument carried on well into the 1950s, and the rise of détente in the international Cold War.

11. For a discussion of the associational culture in KGVs, see Verk, *Laubenleben*.

12. Cubitt, *History and Memory*, 39–40.

13. Ibid., 42. See also Anderson, *Imagined Communities*.

14. Nora, *Les Lieux de Mémoire*.

15. With this work, the editors strive to document physical and conceptual representations of Germany's complex history. François and Schulze, *Deutsche Erinnerungsorte*. Taking issue with the determinism of the *Erinnerungsorte* collection, Friederike Eigler criticizes the fact that 'despite its thematic diversity and methodological pluralism', Schulze and François's work 'cement[s] a homogenous and backward understanding of German culture and cultural memory' that is no longer in tune with Germany's increasingly ethnically heterogeneous society. Eigler, *Gedächtnis und Geschichte*, 50.

16. Lefebvre, *The Production of Space*, 220.

17. For example, see Carrier, *Holocaust Monuments and National Memory*; Confino, *The Nation as a Local Metaphor*.

18. Trigg, *The Memory of Place*, xvii; emphasis in the original.

19. Lefebvre, *The Production of Space*.

20. Busquet, 'L'espace politique chez Henri Lefebvre', 3.

21. Sheringham, *Everyday Life*, 134–74.

22. Lefebvre, *Critique of Everyday Life*, 127.

23. Ibid., 133–34.

24. The dacha is a common theme in Russian literature, film as well as theatre, and its cultural significance has been explored by scholars over the past decade. See, for example, Lovell, *Summerfolk*; Rumjanzewa, *Auf der Datscha*.

25. Johannes, *Entwicklung, Funktionswandel und Bedeutung städtischer Kleingärten*; Hofmann and Cosmutia, *Über den Zaun geguckt*; Pohle-Schöttler, 'Der Schrebergarten als Ort ästhetischen Handelns'; Stein, *Inseln im Häusermeer*; Mulitze and Papsch, *Übern Zaun geguckt*.

26. Dietrich, *Hammer, Zirkel, Gartenzaun*.

27. Leppert, *Paradies mit Laube*.

28. Meyer-Renschhausen and Holl, *Die Wiederkehr der Gärten*; Dünzelmann, *Von der Yayla zum Kleingarten*; Müller, *Wurzeln schlagen in der Fremde*.

29. See Goodbody, *Nature, Technology and Cultural Change*.

30. Steinlechner, 'Zwischen Heterotopie und hortus conclusus'.

31. Böschenstein, 'Garten und Tod in Gedichten Georges, Rilkes and Trakls'; Roßbach, 'Schläfrige, fremde, tote Gärten'.

32. For example, see Wolting, *Der Garten als Topos*; Toegel, 'The Garden as Literature/ Literary Gardens'.

33. Rossenback, 'Die Welt als Garten', 2.

34. Wolting, *Der Garten als Topos*.

35. Gurk, *Laubenkolonie Schwanensee*, hereafter referred to as *Laubenkolonie*. When Gurk wrote this book is a contentious topic, as the first edition from 1949 dated it to the postwar period. However, the later edition from 1987 claims that the book was written in 1936.

36. Heukenkamp, *Deutsche Erinnerung*, 384.

37. *Laubenkolonie*, 7.

38. Ibid., 24.
39. Heukenkamp, *Deutsche Erinnerung*, 219.
40. Plenzdorf, *Die neuen Leiden des jungen W.*, hereafter referred to as *Die neuen Leiden*.
41. Ibid., 51.
42. Ibid., 49.
43. Ibid., 51. The Goethe passage is taken from Werther's letter of 16 June 1771.
44. Sander, 'Die forsche Welle', 961.
45. Niehoff, 'Gab ihm zu sagen, was er leidet?'.
46. For a discussion of the Western stereotypes about allotment tenants, see Verk, *Laubenleben*, 1–10.
47. See, for example, the TV series *Detektivbüro Roth*, 'Skandal im Schrebergarten', Season 1, Episode 20 (1986) and Kristijan Markoc, *Blackout im Schrebergarten* (Ravensburg 1988). This trend continues in unified Germany, see, for example, Lotte Minck, *Radieschen von unten* (Düsseldorf 2013); Luci Flebbe, *Das 5. Foto* (Dortmund 2013); Günter von Lonski, *Teufelskralle – Hubert Wesemanns 4. Fall* (Hameln 2013); Auerbach&Keller, *Unter allen Beeten ist ruh* (Berlin 2011).
48. Baum, *Schrebergarten Blues*, 22.
49. Ibid.
50. Ibid., 25.
51. Kleeberg, *Ein Garten im Norden*, hereafter referred to as *Garten*.
52. Quoted on the back cover of the novel.
53. Brockmann, 'Michael Kleeberg's *Ein Garten im Norden*', 123–26.
54. *Garten*, 82–83.
55. Ibid., 108–9.
56. Böhn, 'Memory, Musealization and Alternative History', 249.
57. *Garten*, 279.
58. Brockmann, 'Michael Kleeberg's *Ein Garten im Norden*', 126.
59. Ibid., 135.
60. See Herf, *Divided Memory*; Eder, *Holocaust Angst*.
61. Lefebvre, *Critique of Everyday Life*, 134 and 136.
62. See Riegl, 'Der moderne Denkmalkultus'; Ward, 'Material, Image, Sign', 285.
63. Schütz, 'Der kontaminierte Tagtraum', 63.
64. Trigg, *The Aesthetics of Decay*, 249.
65. Ibid.

Bibliography

Anderson, B. *Imagined Communities*. London: Verso, 1991.
Baum, J. *Schrebergarten Blues*. Cologne: Klein & Blechinger, 1992.
Böhn, A. 'Memory, Musealization and Alternative History in Michael Kleeberg's Novel *Ein Garten im Norden* and Wolfgang Becker's Film *Good Bye, Lenin!*', in S. Arnold-de Simine (ed.), *Memory Traces 1989 and the Question of German Cultural Identity* (Oxford: P. Lang, 2005), 245–65.
Böschenstein, B. 'Garten und Tod in Gedichten Georges, Rilkes and Trakls: Eine Skizze'. *Compar(a)ison: An International Journal of Comparative Literature* 1 (2007), 29–36.
Brockmann, S. 'Michael Kleeberg's *Ein Garten im Norden* (*A Garden in the North*)', in S. Taberner, *The Novel in German since 1990* (Cambridge: Cambridge University Press, 2011), 123–35.

Busquet, G. 'L'espace politique chez Henri Lefebvre: l'idéologie et l'utopie' ['Political Space in the Work of Henri Lefebvre: Ideology and Utopia', translated by Sharon Moren]. *justice spatiale/spatial justice* 5 (2012–2013), 1–12.

Carrier, P. *Holocaust Monuments and National Memory: France and Germany since 1989*. New York: Berghahn, 2005.

Confino, A. *The Nation as a Local Metaphor: Württemberg, Imperial Germany and National Memory, 1871–1918*. Chapel Hill: University of North Carolina Press, 1997.

Cubitt, G. *History and Memory*. Manchester: Manchester University Press, 2007.

Dietrich, I. *Hammer, Zirkel, Gartenzaun: Die Politik der SED gegenüber den Kleingärtnern*. Berlin: Books on Demand, 2003.

Dünzelmann, A.E. *Von der Yayla zum Kleingarten: Kleingärten – Räume der Integration und Akkulturation für Zugewanderte?* Frankfurt am Main and London: IKO, 2007.

Eder, J. *Holocaust Angst: The Federal Republic of Germany and American Holocaust Memory*. New York: Oxford University Press, 2016.

Eigler, F. *Gedächtnis und Geschichte in Generationenromanen seit der Wende*. Berlin: Erich Schmidt, 2005.

François, E. and H. Schulze (eds). *Deutsche Erinnerungsorte*. Munich: C.H. Beck, 2001/2002/2003.

Goodbody, A.H. *Nature, Technology and Cultural Change in Twentieth-Century German Literature: The Challenge of Ecocriticism*. London: Palgrave Macmillan, 2007.

Gurk, P. *Laubenkolonie Schwanensee*. Berlin: Peter Selinka, 1987.

Herf, J. *Divided Memory: The Nazi Past in the Two Germanys*. Cambridge: Harvard University Press, 1997.

Heukenkamp, U. (ed.). *Deutsche Erinnerung: Berliner Beiträge zur Prosa der Nachkriegsjahre (1945–1960)*. Berlin: Erich Schmidt, 2000.

Hofmann, G. and D. Cosmutia. *Über den Zaun geguckt: Freizeit auf dem Dauercampingplatz und in der Kleingartenanlage*. Frankfurt am Main: Institut für Kulturanthropologie und Europäische Ethnologie, 1994.

Johannes, E. *Entwicklung, Funktionswandel und Bedeutung städtischer Kleingärten: Dargestellt am Beispiel der Städte Kiel, Hamburg und Bremen*. Kiel: Schmidt&Klaunig, 1955.

Kaminer, W. *Mein Leben im Schrebergarten*. Munich: Manhattan, 2007.

Keil, E. 'Vorwort'. *Die Gartenlaube*, December 1852.

Kleeberg, M. *Ein Garten im Norden: Roman*. Munich: dtv, 2001.

Lefebvre, H. *Critique of Everyday Life*. London: Verso, 1991.

———. *The Production of Space*, trans. Donald Nicholson Smith. Oxford: Blackwell, 1991.

Leppert, S. *Paradies mit Laube: Das Buch über Deutschlands Schrebergärten*. Munich: Deutsche Verlags-Anstalt, 2009.

Lovell, S. *Summerfolk: A History of the Dacha, 1710–2000*. Ithaca: Cornell University Press, 2003.

Meyer-Renschhausen, E. and A. Holl. *Die Wiederkehr der Gärten – Kleinlandwirtschaft im Zeitalter der Globalisierung*. Innsbruck: Studien Verlag, 2000.

Mulitze, C. and C. Papsch. *Übern Zaun geguckt: Geschichten aus Schrebergärten*. Essen: Klartext, 2006.

Müller, C. *Wurzeln schlagen in der Fremde: Die Internationalen Gärten und ihre Bedeutung für Integrationsprozesse.* Munich: Ökom, 2002.

Niehoff, K. 'Gab ihm zu sagen, was er leidet?' *Süddeutsche Zeitung,* 15 May 1973.

Nora, P. (ed.). *Les Lieux de Mémoire.* Paris: Gallimard, 1984/1986.

Plenzdorf, U. *Die neuen Leiden des jungen W.* Frankfurt am Main: Suhrkamp, 1976.

Pohle-Schöttler, R. 'Der Schrebergarten als Ort ästhetischen Handelns'. Dissertation, Free University Berlin, 1993.

Riegl, A. 'Der moderne Denkmalkultus: Sein Wesen und seine Entstehung', in A. Riegl, *Gesammelte Aufsätze* (Vienna, 1996 [1903]), 139–84.

Roßbach, N. 'Schläfrige, fremde, tote Gärten: Ein lyrischer Topos nach 1945'. *Deutschunterricht: Beiträge zu seiner Praxis und wissenschaftlichen Grundlegung* 53(5) (2001), 51–61.

Rossenback, B. 'Die Welt als Garten: Zur Tradition der hortologischen Dichtung im polnischen Barock'. Dissertation, Rheinische Friedrich-Wilhelms-Universität Bonn, 2008.

Rudolph, H. 'Schrebergarten', in E. François and H. Schulze (eds), *Deutsche Erinnerungsorte.* (Munich: C.H. Beck, 2002), vol. 3.

Rumjanzewa, M. *Auf der Datscha: Eine kleine Kulturgeschichte und ein Lesebuch.* German translation. Zurich: Dörlemann, 2009.

Sander, H.-D. 'Die forsche Welle'. *Deutschland-Archiv* 9 (1972), 958–62.

Schütz, E. 'Der kontaminierte Tagtraum: Alternativgeschichte und Geschichtsalternative', in E. Schütz and W. Hardtwig (eds), *Keiner kommt davon: Zeitgeschichte in der Literatur nach 1945* (Göttingen: Vandenhoeck & Ruprecht, 2008), 47–73.

Sheringham, M. *Everyday Life: Theories and Practices from Surrealism to the Present.* Oxford: Oxford University Press, 2013 [2006].

Stein, H. *Inseln im Häusermeer: Eine Kulturgeschichte des deutschen Kleingartenwesens bis zum Ende des Zweiten Weltkriegs, reichsweite Tendenzen und Groß-Hamburger Entwicklung.* Frankfurt am Main: P. Lang, 2000.

Steinlechner, G. 'Zwischen Heterotopie und hortus conclusus: Zur Ikonologie literarischer Garten-Räume', in K. Fliedl, B. Oberreither and K. Serles (eds), *Gemälderedereien: Zur literarischen Diskursivierung von Bildern* (Berlin: Schmidt, 2013), 287–300.

Toegel, E. 'The Garden as Literature/Literary Gardens: Notes on Barbara Frischmuth's Garden Diaries'. *German Studies Review* 32(2) (2009), 267–78.

Trigg, D. *The Aesthetics of Decay: Nothingness, Nostalgia, and the Absence of Reason.* New York: P. Lang, 2009 [2006].

——. *The Memory of Place: A Phenomenology of the Uncanny.* Athens: Ohio University Press, 2013.

Verk, S. *Laubenleben: Eine Untersuchung zum Gestaltungs-, Gemeinschafts- und Umweltverhalten von Kleingärtnern.* Münster and New York: Waxmann, 1994.

Ward, S. 'Material, Image, Sign', in S. Arnold-de Simine (ed.), *Memory Traces: 1989 and the Question of German Cultural Identity* (Oxford: P. Lang, 2005), 281–308.

Wolting, M. *Der Garten als Topos im Werk von Marie Luise Kaschnitz, Undine Gruenter und Sarah Kirsch.* Warsaw: Wydawnictwo Uniwersytetu Wroclawskiego, 2009.

Chapter 9

Painting in East Germany
An Elite Art for the Everyday (and Everyone)

April A. Eisman

In his 2011 article, 'Divided, Yet Reunited – The Challenge of Integrating German Post-War Histories', Konrad Jarausch argued against a history of Germany that 'treats both FRG and GDR separately', what he termed the 'history of one nation in two states', and argued instead for a history that 'draws attention to the demarcation from and entanglement with each other'.[1] Dorothee Wierling made a similar argument in her 2016 article, 'Die Bundesrepublik als das andere Deutschland', showing how knowledge of East German history can help to generate new questions for future studies of the FRG.[2] Such a comparative approach would indeed be a welcome addition to scholarship on the FRG, which often overlooks or marginalizes the East. For scholars of the GDR, however, such a cross-cultural approach has dominated our work to date, often to the detriment of the East.

In the discipline of art history, for example, the assumption has been that the West, and in particular modernism as defined by the West, is the touchstone for 'good' art. Such an approach ignores the very different contexts in which – and to which – artists were responding on each side of the Iron Curtain; it also presumes that only the East was affected by ideology. But modern artists in the West after 1945 were not working in an ideology-free zone. Rather, they were responding to the capitalist system in which they lived and worked – from Pop Art's engagement with advertising and products to performance artists' rejection of creating objects that could be bought and sold on the art market. Once this fact is recognized, it raises the question of why Western modernism should be the touchstone for modern art created in the East? Why should artists working in a socialist society be expected to engage with capitalist art? And if they do, why should it be expected to have the same meaning?

To reject Western modernism, and in particular the American-led post-war doctrine of art for art's sake, is not to reject modern art.[3] As Jacques Rancière pointed out in *The Politics of Aesthetics*, there were two strands of art created in modernity. The 'first variant would have modernity identified simply with the autonomy of art, an "anti-mimetic" revolution... identical with the conquest of the pure form of art finally laid bare': in other words, Western formalism, which as Rancière points out, later went through crisis with postmodernism. The second variant, which he terms *modernatism*, or utopian modernism, was what the East ultimately embraced, often under the term socialist realism.[4]

While the West remains an interesting and important comparative lens for scholarship on the East, the significant differences necessitate that it be just one of many lenses. To do otherwise would simply reassert the West as centre. Rather than a comparative approach with the West, which has already been done in numerous studies, GDR scholars now need to leave the West behind: East Germany needs to be understood on its own terms and in relation to the rest of the world, the so-called Second, Third and Fourth Worlds.[5] Such an approach builds upon work done by postcolonial and post-socialist scholars, from Dipesh Chakrabarty in *Provincializing Europe* (2000) to the many articles and books by the late art historian Piotr Piotrowski. Piotrowski calls for a 'horizontal art history', one that 'is polyphonic, multi-dimensional and free from geographical hierarchies', one that recognizes that the West is just one of numerous narratives in a global world and thus acknowledges the importance of developing these other narratives.[6]

In this chapter I will take a closer look at what art was in East Germany: rather than arguing that East Germans created art that can be valued in the West – which they did and I have shown elsewhere – I want to argue here that East German art was operating on a different set of values, or to cite Raymond Williams, 'a new structure of feeling', one that is related to the development of a new kind of society, a socialist Germany.[7] Rather than creating art for the self or for an intellectual and economic elite as tended to be the case in the West, art in East Germany, and in particular painting, was created for the general public.[8] In the early years, this emphasis often resulted in didactic work based on a simple realism intended to help mould the people into good socialists. Later, however, as East Germany became more established and many of its people more knowledgeable about art – through classes at school, mandatory exhibition visits, coverage in newspapers and journals and artist circles that encouraged them to try their own hand at art – artists began to create more complex paintings intended to engage the public in discussions about important issues of the day. Indeed, in the early 1970s, large numbers of people began visiting art museums in East Germany – more than three times the number visiting them in the West – finding in them an alternative public sphere in which to discuss issues often left unaddressed in other media.[9] A look at the development of art in the East thus reveals the very different premises upon which art in the West is based as well as a significantly smaller audience for that art.[10]

Defining a German Socialist Art

The question of what art should be in East Germany was a topic of much discussion as well as fluctuating policies throughout the first two decades of the Cold War, although the emphasis on a relationship to the audience was a common thread, one that stood in contrast to the West's emphasis on art's autonomy. Such differing approaches to art in the two Germanys, however, were not immediately evident in the early postwar years. In fact, early on, there was openness to modern art within the art establishment in all four occupation zones. The first major art exhibition, *Allgemeine deutsche Kunstausstellung*, for example, opened in 1946 with work by approximately 250 artists, including modern artists – and especially expressionists, whose work had been demonized by the Nazis – such as Ernst Ludwig Kirchner, Oskar Kokoschka, George Grosz, Max Beckmann, Käthe Kollwitz and Ernst Barlach. The exhibition was visited by more than 70,000 people in its two-month run. But after twelve years of Nazi cultural propaganda, which reinforced conservative aesthetic preferences, the general public had little interest in modern art. A poll of exhibition attendees revealed that 66 per cent of them rejected the art shown at the *Allgemeine deutsche Kunstausstellung* as being too modern.[11]

In West(ern) Germany, the people's dislike of modern art did not play a role in art's development, especially after 1950. In the wake of German division, the Korean War and, perhaps most importantly, the implementation of the Marshall Plan, there was a significant shift away from the representational art toward abstraction in the West German art world.[12] In his 1984 article, 'Modernism Restored: West German Painting in the 1950s', Jost Hermand questioned how 'such an elitist, unintelligible, hermetic painting, which by its own admission could only be appreciated by a small "minority"', became successful enough to become the dominant art form in West Germany in the space of just a few years.[13] He argued it was the result of massive organizational support from the government, industry and the art world together with the emergence of a new class of collectors who valued the newness of such works.[14] Abstract art, preferred and promoted by the United States, helped West Germany to escape its Nazi past by embedding it into an international, rather than national framework, a framework dominated by the United States, where abstract expressionism was the reigning art style.[15]

In East(ern) Germany, by contrast, the people's dislike of modern art helped to justify changes in art policy, especially once Cold War tensions began to escalate. In 1948, two articles appeared in *bildende kunst*, the main art journal in the Soviet Occupation Zone; they mark the beginning of the Formalism debates that would define cultural policy in East Germany until the mid-1950s.[16] Titled 'Art and Politics' and 'Politics and Art', these articles, published in the October 1948 issue, were written by the joint editors of the magazine, Karl Hofer and Oskar Nerlinger, who took opposite stances on the role that art should play in society.[17] In 'Art and Politics', Hofer argued in favour of artistic freedom, stating that it is up to the artist to decide on the style and content of his work, including whether or not that work is political. In 'Politics and Art', on the other hand, Nerlinger argued that no art could be free from politics, even that which claimed to be. He therefore concluded that all art, as a public medium, should be accessible to the people.[18]

The Soviet Union agreed with Nerlinger's view. In November 1948, Alexander Dymschitz, the cultural officer of the Soviet Military Administration (SMAD), published an article in the Soviet newspaper in Germany, the *Tägliche Rundschau*, titled, 'About the Formalist Direction in German Art'. In it, he criticized Hofer's view of art for art's sake and argued instead that art should be used to help re-educate the German people who had been compromised by twelve years of Nazi ideology. Art should, in other words, be realistic and didactic.

A second phase in the Formalism debates began in January 1951, when N. Orlow published an article in the *Tägliche Rundschau* titled, 'Directions and Misdirections of Modern Art'.[19] Whereas the first phase ultimately made realism a requirement for art – in order to better reach the people – this second phase argued that art also needed to be optimistic. In his article, Orlow condemned all art created after the nineteenth century, even that by socially committed artists like Käthe Kollwitz, whose realism he found too pessimistic. Although her art was understandable for the time period in which it was created, he deemed it unsuitable for the GDR, which was the embodiment of Socialist victory. What would people think about East Germany if its art displayed such pessimism? A few months later, in November 1951, Walter Ulbricht, head of the East German state, confirmed the East German government's stance on modern art by stating, 'We do not want to see any more abstract pictures in our art schools...

Gray-on-gray painting is an expression of capitalist failure and stands in the sharpest contradiction to the new life found in the GDR'.[20]

The view that art should be both realistic and optimistic and that it should also reject modernist influences reached its height at the Third German Art Exhibition, which opened in Dresden in March 1953. It contained approximately 600 works by 400 artists. One of the most highly praised works in this exhibition was Harald Hellmich and Klaus Weber's *The Youngest Fliers* (1953, fig. 1). This large painting depicts a group of well-dressed boys and girls on top of a hill playing with model airplanes and laughing together in the summer sun. The largest boy, standing just to the right of centre, looks off into the distance as he is about to release the plane in his hand; several of the others watch him expectantly. The meaning of this work is clear and easy to understand: in the GDR, life is good, children are happy and healthy and in them resides much promise. These children can also be read metaphorically as the young GDR itself. Not only easy to understand, this work is also realistic, optimistic and focuses on people, all essential elements of a Soviet-inspired socialist realism.

Despite the East German people's interest in such works – more than 200,000 visited the exhibition in its three-month run – their dominance

Figure 9.1. Harald Hellmich and Klaus Weber, *The Youngest Fliers* (Die jüngsten Flieger), 1953. Oil, 240 × 350. © 2018 Artists Rights Society (ARS), New York / VG Bild-Kunst, Bonn, Photo: SLUB / Deutsche Fotothek.

did not last in East Germany, just as the dominance of abstract paintings in the West did not last.[21] In terms of the latter, already in the mid-1950s, artists like Robert Rauschenberg and Jasper Johns in the United States challenged the exclusion of subject matter in art by incorporating found objects and pop imagery into their canvases. Their art, however, was aimed at a small audience of fellow artists and art critics rather than the larger public.

In East Germany, a shift away from a Soviet-style socialist realism happened in the wake of Stalin's death in March 1953 and the Workers' uprising that June, at which point the East German government loosened its grip on the arts in what was termed the New Course. In part, this change in policy – which had actually begun a few days before the uprising took place – became an attempt to win back intellectuals, including artists, after the violence of the summer when Soviet tanks were brought in to quell the protest. For a few years in the mid-1950s, artists were publicly able – while not exactly encouraged – to experiment with modern art. Picasso, in particular, was thought to be a good role model for the merging of communist ideology with a modern artistic style and was the subject of a series of articles in *Bildende Kunst* in 1955 and 1956.[22]

But the shift to a more open policy was short-lived. In the wake of the Hungarian Revolution in 1956, cultural policy became more restrictive. The editor of *Bildende Kunst* was replaced by one with more conservative tastes, and artists were once again encouraged to create realistic works and to look to the Soviet Union for inspiration. In April 1959, a major cultural conference took place in Bitterfeld that helped to establish a view on art that would dominate official cultural discussions for years to come. Known as the Bitterfeld Way, it called for artists – as well as writers – to work in factories to better understand the workers they portrayed, and for workers to try their hand at creating art and serving on selection committees for exhibitions.

While the Bitterfeld Way has been denigrated in the West, where criticism has focused on the many works of low quality that it produced and the narrowness of cultural policies that resulted, its basic principles were embraced by many East German intellectuals.[23] Indeed, many of the ideas behind the Bitterfeld Way originally came from artists.[24] This is not to say they liked the Bitterfeld Way, but rather that the problem was more with its implementation than its core ideas. Nonetheless, the immediate results – as exemplified by the paintings on display at the Fourth German Art Exhibition in 1959 – were a disappointment to all, including Ulbricht. The question of what art in East Germany should look like was still open for debate. Two years later, official policy loosened in another cultural 'thaw', this time in response to the building of the Berlin Wall. In its wake, a number of artists began to challenge the Soviet model of socialist realism, arguing instead for an art that was unafraid of modern forms.

The question of what German Socialist art should look like was heatedly debated at the Fifth Congress of the Association of Visual Artists (VBKD) in March 1964. The speeches by Hermann Raum, Fritz Cremer and Bernhard Heisig, although controversial at the time, offer insight into the shift that took place – from a government-encouraged didactic realism to an artist-led dialogical one – in the early 1970s.

Hermann Raum (1924–2010), an art historian from Rostock, gave one of the first talks at the conference. Calling for stylistic freedom in the visual arts, he argued that it is the meaning of a work, not its style, that should determine whether or not it is good.[25] In particular, he argued against the Cold War division of the arts into 'two drawers, realistic and modern', noting that there are no enduring connections between style and ideology; the relationships between the two can change. Both the Nazis and the Soviets, for example, had looked to nineteenth-century realism as a model despite their widely divergent ideologies. To adopt a style was not to adopt the ideology behind it, he argued, and thus East German artists should be able to engage with modern art.

Raum also argued that the West's emphasis on 'art for art's sake' would be their downfall as they would eventually have no audience and thus no reason for their work. In the East, in comparison, the emphasis was on creating an 'art for us'. But rather than dumbing art down, it was the artist's duty to educate the people to understand modern art. Lastly, he argued against the idea that socialist realism was a style, stating that it is the intent – the humanism of the work, not its form – that makes something socialist realist.

Fritz Cremer (1906–1993), an internationally prominent sculptor in his late fifties, made many of the same points in his fifteen-minute critique of the artistic situation in East Germany. He began by calling for an 'open discussion about art' and, in particular, for a 're-examination of the consequences of the era of the cult of personality on the visual arts'.[26] In his opinion, the Stalinist era's focus on illusionism and optimism to the exclusion – and denigration – of everything else was unrealistic. He argued instead for a critical realism for socialism, something that could 'serve the further development of our socialist society'. He also called for the elimination of condemnatory labels like abstraction, formalism and decadence.

'We need to understand that our art is for civilized people, for the literate, not the illiterate', he stated. In this, he was drawing a distinction between Germany and the Soviet Union. 'We need an art that provokes the civilized and literate people of our century to ask the question, "capitalism or socialism?" and that gives [them] the right and the responsibility to decide for [themselves] between these two societal systems... We need an art that gets people to think, not an art that takes the thinking from them'.

Later he returned to the subject of art's audience and stated, 'we do not need an art for "ordinary people" *(volkstümlich)*. The people are not "ordinary"' – moreover such an art was what the Thousand Year Reich had propagated. 'We need an art that gives every single artist the freedom to decide the substance and form of his art. We need the search for truth in art, and we need the unconditional personal responsibility of the artist'. What was needed, he argued in the final analysis, was an end to dogmatism. 'We do not need art... to be a poster for Socialism. We need an art that radiates [Socialism's] new feeling for life' in whatever outward form that takes. It was an impassioned speech that clearly resonated with the audience, who interrupted him numerous times with applause and calls of 'very true!'

Like Cremer and Raum before him, Bernhard Heisig (1925–2011), who later became one of East Germany's best known and most successful painters in the West, argued against dogmatic extremes, the ossification of artistic policy, and treating artists and the public like 'children'.[27] Within this framework he made two main points. First, he stated that artists, not theorists, journalists or commissions, should determine what art is. And second, he argued that there should be no more taboos in art: neither modern artistic styles, nor the negative side of life, should be excluded from artistic production.

Heisig's speech began by recognizing that the current emphasis on realism in East Germany 'had developed out of an attempt to protect artists from the extremes of artistic autonomy threatening the West'. The focus on tradition and the human figure, he explained, had been intended to help artists to find inspiration for the new, socialist present, but had resulted, inadvertently, in another kind of isolation: artists had been cut off from a large part of contemporary art because that created in Western Europe had been dismissed as 'rotting fruit on the tree of imperialism'.

Heisig pointed out, however, that the rejection of Western styles was not universal across the arts: skyscrapers in Moscow, for example, were hardly to be distinguished from those built in New York. He then expressed the desire for a similar opening up to take place in the realms of painting and sculpture. Cultural policies such as the Bitterfeld Way, in contrast, had increasingly become ossified rules that led to artistic stagnation. 'In the effort to protect him from dangerous influences, the artist is being treated like a child not allowed onto the street [of modern art] for fear of getting run over'. Such fear and limitation, Heisig pointed out, was leading to provinciality and an uncritical overvaluation of Western art as the forbidden fruit. Heisig then argued that engagement with modern art was the only way to overcome the current artistic impasse. As he stated it, 'Modern art is not poison, it is the art of the 20th century'. Furthermore, it was up to the artist alone – not a commission – to decide what from this tradition is valuable. That was part of the artist's responsibility to society.

Heisig then pointed out that art should not be limited to only portraying the positive side of life. Nothing should be repressed. Fear, imperfection and pain were all valid topics to explore in art. That such explorations were not allowed, however, Heisig saw as stemming from a narrow interpretation of the term realism. It was the result, he stated, of trying to create a new art based on rules rather than stemming from a natural unfolding of the artistic process. Rather than thinking about these questions, he observed, art theoreticians and critics 'reach for the cure-all stamp' of socialist realism.

Heisig argued instead for an art that 'thrills and delights or annoys and provokes, one that is in any case interesting'. Moreover, he argued that people should be allowed to interact with the works on their own rather than always having someone tell them what to think. He then returned to the role of the artist in East German society, stating that 'the artist is also the critic of his time' and thus it was artists who needed to address these issues if they were to be justified in claiming leadership of them. He continued by saying that artists must have better arguments. And he called for room to experiment with ideas rather than be condemned for such experiments. He ended by pointing out that the discussion about art in East Germany needed to be left open to a wide range of possibilities; only in that way could a true discussion take place.

What is striking about these three talks is their shared interest in creating an art for East Germany, one that engages with complex subject matter and modern artistic styles while at the same time being created for the people. Rather than seeing the East German public as something to be feared or talked down to, each of these speakers emphasized the public's competence and his desire for art to engage in a dialogue with them. They wanted art for an educated nation. They wanted a German socialist realism, or more concisely, a socialist modernism.

Creating an Audience

Although the views expressed in 1964 were criticized heavily by the Communist Party of East Germany, and two of the speakers were forced to give official self-criticisms, it was these views of art – with their emphasis on educating the people to understand 'good' art and engaging in a conversation with them – that became the norm once Erich Honecker came to power in 1971. In sharp contrast to the tendency toward a conservative cultural politics under his predecessor, Honecker stated in December of that year that for those artists who truly believe in Socialism, there could be no more taboos on their work, neither in content nor in style.[28] While this lack of taboos did not extend to new media such as performance and installation art – which did not enter the official art scene until the late 1980s – it did signal a much greater openness in the traditional visual arts such as painting.

Indeed, the new era of breadth and variety (*Weite und Vielfalt*) led to an explosion of artistic styles and topics in painting, including non-heroic images of the everyday, *Problembilder*, and mythological images. It was in these years that Heidrun Hegewald (b. 1936), among others, emerged as a people's favourite, with paintings that inspired significant discussion both in the press and in person. In 1977, Hegewald's *Child and Parents* (fig. 9.2), for example, stimulated much discussion about family life in East Germany and, in particular, the difficulties some families

Figure 9.2. Heidrun Hegewald, *Child and Parents* (Kind und Eltern), 1976. Oil on hard fibre, 110 × 190 cm. © 2018 Artists Rights Society (ARS), New York / VG Bild-Kunst, Bonn. Photo: SLUB / Deutsche Fotothek / Reinecke and Walter.

experienced in the face of changing expectations and possibilities for women.

Exhibited in Berlin in 1976 and at the Eighth Art Exhibition of the GDR in Dresden in 1977, *Child and Parents* focuses on three figures arranged around a large, round table that dominates the composition. The young child stands in an open doorway at the centre top of the composition and is bathed in light from the room beyond. At the bottom left of the image, seated at the table with his back to the viewer, is the child's father. At the bottom right, is the mother, her body angled towards us but with her face turned away. Both parents have their right elbows on the table and appear to be consciously ignoring each other, perhaps having been caught in the midst of a troubling conversation. A triangle of lines connects the three figures in an otherwise unadorned and darkened room. It is an image that captures the feelings of isolation existent within a crumbling family structure, with the child caught between parents who can no longer communicate with each other.

Child and Parents sparked a lively discussion amongst the general public that was captured in and encouraged by the widely read illustrated weekly *Für Dich*, which published a series of four articles based on audience responses to the work. The first, titled 'The Door is Still Open' in reference to the door behind the child, opened the discussion with a two-page colour illustration of the work, texts by a couple of art historians engaging with it, one of whom discussed it in terms of divorce, and the statement that 'it is no longer unusual that we confront you with artworks that cause you to think, that find your approval or that shock you and provoke opposition'.[29] This first issue also included a number of quotations from visitors who had seen the work at an exhibition, comments that ranged from a focus on the 'lost and helpless' nature of the child, to a question from one woman who 'searches for beauty in art' about 'why … the artist bother[s] with such themes?' Another visitor questioned whether the painting necessarily showed an impending divorce, seeing this as an overdramatic interpretation.

The next two issues of *Für Dich* that addressed the painting focused solely on responses from readers. Focusing on the content of the work, one wondered if the child was the reason the parents were staying together, while another believed that 'the line between the child and the open door shows the parents the right way [out]'.[30] Another stated that 'the image in issue 15 is hideous! Can someone hang something like this in their living room?'[31] Others called the work 'shocking'.

The final article in the series about *Child and Parents* offered a quick overview of the discussion: 'Approval and rejection, a large spectrum of human perception and insights were reflected in the readers' letters'.[32]

It also included a few more quotations before thanking the readers for their participation and turning to an interview with the artist based on some of the questions raised. The interview included a black-and-white photograph of Hegewald in a painter's smock. In response to the question of how she felt about the differing opinions about her work – did she feel understood? – Hegewald stated, 'a painting takes on a life of its own when one lets it go. It experiences, through engagement with the public, a subsequent realisation'.

What is clear in these articles – and in many others like them about other works of art – is the encouragement that general interest newspapers and magazines in East Germany gave to readers to engage with art.[33] As in this case, they often included texts by experts, who could offer insight into how to understand a work, and encouraged responses from readers. The result was an audience that grew increasingly familiar with looking at and engaging with contemporary art.

Contributing to Hegewald's success with *Child and Parents* was her ability to touch on a topic of interest to the general public, in this case, the impact that policies promoting women's equality in the workforce had had on the traditional family structure. Her ability to choose a topic that resonated with the people was also the result of the increased contact existing between artists and the working class in East Germany. Such contact was encouraged by the East German government through various policies, including who was admitted to study at the art schools. Records at the Dresden Academy, for example, show that the administration kept track of the social background for each student who was accepted to study.[34] Those from working-class backgrounds had a lower bar to meet than those from an academic family as the latter presumably had greater advantages while growing up.

There were also policies that emphasized interaction across different social backgrounds. Male students, for example, had to complete their mandatory military service before beginning their studies, a process that encouraged interaction across different classes. Once at the academies, students of both genders had to spend a week each autumn helping with the harvest, usually picking potatoes, and were also encouraged to visit farms and factories to gain first-hand experience of working life. Angela Hampel (b. 1956), for example, spoke of visiting a farm and a mine during her years at the Dresden Academy (1977–1982).[35] After graduation, the best students often had a three-year contract with a factory, earning money as they made the transition from being students to being professional artists. Although they did not usually have specific commissions to fulfil during this time, the young artists had access to workers if they desired it.

Doris Ziegler is an example of an artist who took advantage of her connection with factories. Indeed, she first became known at the national level in East Germany for her paintings of working women. Her earliest work on the topic was done while a student at the Leipzig Academy. As she explains, she had sought out the opportunity to visit a factory because she wanted to see if the newspaper accounts of women's experiences in factories were accurate. The result was a painting that she submitted as part of her graduation requirements. Then upon graduating in 1974, she was given a three-year contract at the State-owned 'Joliot Curie' automotive plant in Leipzig, which provided her with studio space, money and access to workers.

At the Joliot Curie factory, Ziegler created a series of five paintings focusing on working women. Four of the paintings are small portraits, each showing a woman seated with arms crossed and a sober expression on her face. The fifth, *The Rosa Luxemburg Brigade – Eva* (1974/75, fig. 3), was significantly larger and more complex. It focuses on the dark-haired Eva as she stands outside her place of work, presumably taking a momentary break. She looks at the viewer without smiling. Behind her and through the window, a co-worker stands at a machine, pulling on a lever. Both wear short-sleeved dark shirts and meet the viewer's gaze with a sober expression. When this large painting is hung with the smaller portraits to create a polyptych, their gaze is all the more striking as only one of the four seated women looks out at the viewer.

All five of the women Ziegler painted were part of the Rosa Luxemburg brigade. According to Ziegler, the women in this brigade were mill cutters who worked with big machinery, which included carrying around heavy parts. Eva's sturdy shoes and industrial apron suggests the physicality of the work. The various springs lying scattered on the ground around her feet and the row of machines visible in the window behind her suggest the industrial nature of it.

Exhibited at the Eighth Art Exhibition of the GDR in 1977/78, *The Rosa Luxemburg Brigade* was discussed in a number of articles in the East German press.[36] In each, great attention was paid to the young artist's use of an approach similar to that found in *Neue Sachlichkeit*, or New Objectivity, a style prominent in Germany in the 1920s and evident in her work in the clarity of forms and economy of colours as well as the honesty of the portrayal.[37] In one, the author praised the way that Ziegler was able to 'grapple with societal problems in concrete people'.[38]

Although art critics praised the two paintings of the Rosa Luxemburg brigade that were shown in the exhibition, the women in the brigade were apparently not happy with them, at least, not at first. According to Ziegler, when she travelled to Dresden with members of the brigade to see the exhibition, they expressed resentment, based on pictures they had seen in the press, all the way there.[39] Rather than showing the women as heroic, beautiful figures as was typical for worker portraits since East Germany was founded, Ziegler had shown their exhaustion after working such difficult jobs. Although initially unhappy with Ziegler's paintings, the women ultimately changed their minds, Ziegler noted with satisfaction, once they got to the exhibition and saw the paintings in person: 'they understood the meaning', they understood that people's discussions about the work also led to discussions of their own problems in life, such as the 'double burden' of having to balance a full-time job with taking care of the home and family.[40]

In addition to encouraging artists to engage with topics of interest to the people and getting people to engage with works created by professional artists, the growing interest in art by the general public was further developed by encouraging workers to take art classes. Such classes were part of the East German government's desire to create well-rounded

Figure 9.3. Doris Ziegler, *The Rosa Luxemburg Brigade – Eva*, 1974/75. Oil on hard fibre, 125 × 80 cm. © 2018 Artists Rights Society (ARS), New York / VG Bild-Kunst, Bonn. Photo: SLUB / Deutsche Fotothek / Würker.

socialist personalities. There were many opportunities for workers to develop themselves. Every factory, for example, had a series of clubs, or circles (*Zirkel*), in which workers could participate for free. These included drawing, painting, printmaking and photography and were often led by professional artists who had graduated from one of the four main art academies.[41] These circles were not just in major cities, but even in small towns. And for some, such studies led to becoming a professional artist. Hampel, for example, worked in forestry before she began her studies at the Dresden Academy. Interested in art, she attended the 'evening school' of the Dresden Academy, located in the small town of Bautzen, every Saturday for three years before applying to become a full-time student. Such schools were a way of 'finding talent' among the people, although not everyone who took classes was interested in developing their skills as anything more than a hobby.

In addition to artist circles, there were also cultural centres throughout East Germany that organized concerts, performances and art exhibitions. These included exhibitions of hobby artists, like those who were part of the factory circles. In 1967, hobby artists were even included in the national exhibition of East German art in Dresden. The local cultural centres were also able to get high-quality entertainment regardless of how remote they were. With this kind of encouragement, workers were able to learn how to create art and were thus better able to understand and appreciate it, enabling professional artists to work at a higher level of sophistication.

The Result

The combination of artists aware of and interested in reaching a larger public through works that engaged with important issues of the day, together with years of educating the public about the visual arts through articles, exhibitions and training, led to a significant increase in the numbers of East Germans attending art museums in the 1970s.[42] The Seventh Art Exhibition of the GDR, which opened in Dresden on 5 October 1972, for example, had 655,000 visitors in its six-month run. This is nearly three times the number of people who attended the Sixth four years earlier. It is also three times the number of visitors at the Documenta exhibition in Kassel, West Germany, at roughly the same time.[43] And whereas the numbers attending Documenta remained under 500,000 throughout the Cold War period, in East Germany, the numbers rose to over a million already in 1977 and remained there throughout the 1980s.

A number of representative polls taken during the Honecker era enable us to gain a better understanding of who attended these exhibitions, why they did so and what they thought of the works shown. According to a poll in 1973 asking why people had come to the Seventh Art Exhibition of the GDR, for example, the most frequent response was that they wanted to get an overview of art being created today and to see it in the original.[44] Workers listed both of these reasons, but also had a third: curiosity about how artists see them. In fact, this curiosity was their primary reason for going, and was clearly a reference to the many portraits of workers that had been commissioned over the years.[45]

Another important factor in the increased attendance was, according to Bernd Lindner, the fact that art museums, like books, had become an ersatz public realm for the discussion of topics that were ignored in the mass media.[46] The dialogical quality of art offered viewers an opportunity to discuss issues, and the majority went to the exhibitions with other people, seeing art museums as a collective experience rather than a solitary one.

A breakdown of those in attendance at the Eighth and Ninth Art Exhibitions in the 1980s reveals that a little over half (54–55 per cent) were part of the intelligentsia; students at the primary and collegiate levels were the next largest group (24–28 per cent); and workers, including apprentices, made up the smallest percentage (18–21 per cent).[47] When compared to West Germany, however, where workers made up only 2 per cent of those who visited art museums, these numbers are significant. Of those who attended the Ninth and Tenth Art Exhibitions in the 1980s, 50 per cent knew how to draw and 41 to 50 per cent owned an original work of art. The latter was made possible by the development of an expansive gallery and cultural system in the early 1970s that brought original works of art to even the smallest villages. Indeed, 9 per cent of visitors to the national exhibitions came from small towns and rural communities.[48]

What these numbers show is that art in East Germany was not as elitist an affair as in the West, but rather something in which the larger public took part. In a population of approximately 16 million, over one million (6 per cent) attended the final Art Exhibition of the GDR in 1987–1988. The Documenta exhibition in West Germany in that year, by comparison, had only 474,000 visitors – out of a possible 63 million West Germans (0.8 per cent).[49] When one looks at these numbers, it appears that East Germany did manage, as Heisig stated it in 1959, to avoid the 'artistic suicide' taking place in the West by giving East German artists the socially directed mission of reaching the people with their art – at least, it did until 1989–1990.[50]

Conclusion

After the fall of the Berlin Wall, attendance at art museums in Eastern Germany dropped significantly, from almost 9 million in 1989 to 4 million in 1990.[51] The reasons are multiple. Early on, many preferred to spend their time exploring the West rather than visiting art museums in the East; 25 per cent, however, said that they used their new travel options to expand their knowledge of art. Newspapers and television programmes, now able to discuss virtually any topic, eliminated art's role as an instigator of public discussion. Many people in the new Germany also lacked the leisure time they had had in East Germany; they were either searching for a new job or working longer hours. After a few years, museums also started charging admission at increasingly higher rates, and most had removed East German artworks from their walls, replacing them with Western works. Yet the impact of East Germany's emphasis on the visual arts could still be observed years after the GDR had ceased to exist. In a poll from 1996, Eastern Germans were much more likely to visit an art museum while on vacation (75 per cent vs. 58 per cent of Western Germans).

These lingering differences reflect the very different art world that developed in East Germany, where art was intended initially to offer new role models for a people compromised by twelve years of Nazi ideology and, later, to engage with them on an intellectual level, 'provoking' them to think and, as Cremer stated it in 1964, 'to ask the question, "capitalism or socialism?"' This latter approach was championed by artists themselves, many of whom were concerned not only with the message their works conveyed but also with aesthetics, and they were aware of and responding to modern art as well as the art being created on the other side of the Wall. It was this more complex art that dominated the East German canon of the 1970s and 1980s and that was shown to praise in major exhibitions in the West, including at the Venice Biennale in 1984 and 1988.

That art had a societal purpose – and value – in East Germany has often led Western art historians, especially after the Berlin Wall fell, to dismiss it as ideological kitsch. In 2009, for example, the prominent art historian Benjamin Buchloh called some of East Germany's most important painters 'opportunists' and 'provincial party hacks' whose 'provincial ignorance became the wellspring of artistic abominations'.[52] Yet when one looks at the artwork so labelled, works that are often just as 'modern' as those created in the West, one realizes that these words reflect more about the art historian than the work he was criticizing.

Indeed, Western art and art history are just as ideologically driven as they were in the East, but rather than focusing on the people, art in the West is a form of intellectual and economic capital that tends to be aimed at the elite.[53] Buchloh's words defended this cultural status quo and also fit well within the long-since discredited totalitarian approach common for scholarship on East Germany more generally in the 1990s.

This article, in comparison, addresses key aspects of what Mary Fulbrook articulated as a then-emerging new paradigm in her 2006 article, 'Putting the People Back In'.[54] It shows that art policy in East Germany was not simply top-down, but rather went through a repeated process of negotiation, one in which artists knew 'the rules' but also worked to change those rules over time; in the process their own views on art changed. It shows how artists – and their audience – were formed by and participated in the East German system, and how East German art was not isolated, but rather engaged with broader cultural currents, including from the West.

Art in East Germany mattered, and it mattered to a large number of people. Indeed, it was the focus of so much discussion – and, in the early years, restriction – because it could, and did, change how people thought. Just as Jan Palmowski argues for television elsewhere in this volume, art was a means to make meaning, to connect individuals to larger narratives.[55] But whereas with television this process was largely a passive one, with viewers sitting in front of their television sets and absorbing the contents presented, art was active, albeit reaching a much smaller audience. It usually required viewers to go to a museum or gallery and once there, to enter into a discussion – with the artists (via the paintings on display) or with others in the space. These discussions could also take place outside of the museum, on the ride home for example, or in response to newspaper articles and invitations for reader comments about particular paintings and the issues they raised. Although not everyone who saw art engaged with it, those who did entered into a public sphere where they could discuss issues important to East Germans, issues often different from those faced by their Western counterparts. The study of East German art on its own terms thus offers us an insight into the alternative 'structures of feeling' experienced by East Germans as part of their everyday life.

April A. Eisman is Associate Professor of Art History at Iowa State University. Her research focuses on contemporary art and theory with an emphasis on East German art and its reception. Her first book, *Bernhard Heisig and the Fight for Modern Art in East Germany*, was published by

Camden House in 2018. She has an NEH fellowship for 2018–2019 to complete her second book manuscript, which focuses on the paintings, installations and performances of the (East) German artist Angela Hampel. Co-founder of the Transatlantic Institute for East German Art, Eisman also co-organizes the 'GDR and Socialisms Network' for the German Studies Association.

Notes

Parts of this chapter have been previously published in Eisman, 'From Double Burden to Double Vision'. I would like to thank Grant Arndt, Erica Carter, Jan Palmowski and Katrin Schreiter for their comments on earlier drafts of this manuscript.

1. Jarausch, 'Divided, Yet Reunited'.
2. Wierling, 'Die Bundesrepublik als das andere Deutschland'.
3. I use the term 'Western modernism' here to acknowledge the fact that modernism was redefined in the West after the Second World War by art critics like Clement Greenberg, who removed the artists' political intentions to emphasize the formalist nature of their work instead. In this way, work by Communist artists like Pablo Picasso could be appreciated without having to engage with their political beliefs.
4. *Modernatism*: 'the identification of forms from the aesthetic regime of the arts with forms that accomplish a task or fulfill a destiny specific to modernity … The starting point, Schiller's notion of the *aesthetic education of man*, constitutes an unsurpassable reference point'. Rancière, *The Politics of Aesthetics*, 26–27.
5. Although the global South has come to replace the four-world model, it elides the significant differences between capitalist and former socialist countries, differences that continue to have an impact on the world today. Similarly, it groups indigenous cultures together with those that came later. For these reasons, I prefer the four-world model despite the hierarchy it implies.
6. Piotrowski, 'Towards Horizontal Art History'. The focus on East Germany for East Germany's sake in Anglophone scholarship nonetheless has an inherent contradiction that needs to be acknowledged: most of the people writing about the East in English – and many of the people for whom we are writing – are from the West. The West therefore remains an important, if implicit interest. Studies of other cultures are valuable to us not only for their own merits, but also because they help us to understand our own culture, shedding new light on the West 'according to the principle that one can see much more from the margins than from the centre'. By inverting the typical paradigm and shifting our attention away from the West, GDR scholars can use the East as a platform from which to understand the West and therewith possible alternatives to the neoliberal system in which we currently find ourselves.
7. Eisman, 'The Permeability of the Wall', 134.
8. The idea of creating art for future generations – that one's art is too advanced to be understood in the present – is a common modernist trope, as is the dismissal of popular taste. Although pop artists later challenged the latter by engaging with topics that are appealing to a general public, the costs of such works – and those of their neo pop

successors – are such that, at least since the 1980s, only the rich can afford to own them. For recent engagements with the politics of Western art, see Davis, *9.5 Theses on Art and Class* and Stallabrass, *Contemporary Art*.

9. Art in East Germany was an alternative public sphere, one limited to a smaller, more educated audience, but one that was actively engaged in the East German project and that broadened its reach over time. For more on the public sphere, see Habermas, *The Structural Transformation of the Public Sphere* and Fraser, 'Rethinking the Public Sphere'. For a study of East German literature as an alternative public sphere, see Bathrick, *The Powers of Speech*.

10. Although one could argue that pop and neo pop art have a following amongst the general public, these are exceptions. There are many more important postwar Western art movements – from abstract expressionism, neo dada and minimalism to conceptual and performance art – that are generally not appreciated outside of culturally educated circles; this was even more the case when they were new.

11. Lindner, 'Kunstrezeption der DDR', 63. For a more detailed look at the reception of this exhibition, see Lindner, *Verstellter, offener Blick*, 70–81.

12. Hermand, 'Modernism Restored'.

13. Ibid., 35.

14. Ibid., 36–37.

15. Abstract expressionism was the first internationally important art style to emerge out of the United States. It was exported as part of American cultural hegemony in the 1950s. An exhibition, 'Non-Representational Painting in America', travelled to cities in West Germany in 1958. Hermand, 'Modernism Restored', 25. See also Guilbaut, *How New York Stole the Idea of Modern Art* and Saunders, *The Cultural Cold War*.

16. *bildende kunst* (all lowercase) was the main art journal of the Soviet Zone of Occupation. It ceased production in late 1949. Three years later, in January 1953, *Bildende Kunst* (with capital letters) was founded and became the GDR's main art journal.

17. This debate, which took place in both East and West Germany, can also be seen as a resumption of the Expressionism debate of the 1930s between Georg Lukács, Ernst Bloch and Bertolt Brecht on what art's relationship to society should be. It also finds an echo in the Dr Faustus debate of 1952–1953, which focused on the negative – and thus inappropriate for some – portrayal of the protagonist in Hans Eisler's libretto *Dr Faustus* (1952). In West Germany, this discussion about the visual arts was called the Darmstädter Gespräche.

18. Nerlinger, 'Politik und Kunst', in *Bildende Kunst* 10 (1948).

19. Orlow, 'Wege und Irrwege der modernen Kunst'.

20. Ulbricht, 'Aufgaben der Kunst'.

21. Socialist realism was the term used for art in the GDR until 1989, but it shifted over the course of the 1960s from a style – as is often understood in the West – to a stance or position *(Haltung)*. Indeed, this change is part of the issue at stake at the Fifth Congress in 1964, discussed later in this chapter.

22. Under Herbert Sandberg's guidance, *Bildende Kunst* ran a series of articles debating Picasso's value for East German artists in 1955 and 1956. The first was Lüdecke, 'Phänomen und Problem Picasso'.

23. Mittenzwei, *Die Intellektuellen*. According to Martin Damus, the Bitterfeld Way had three main tasks: 1) to raise the artistic-aesthetic level of the workers; 2) to integrate art into the workers' lives by listening to their opinions; and 3) to integrate art criticism with this new art. Damus, *Malerei der DDR*, 176.

24. 'The Ferry' (Die Fähre) in Halle, for example, was an artists' group that combined artistic experimentation with the motto 'artists in factories! [sic]'. Feist and Gillen, *Kunstkombinat*, 12.

25. Hermann Raum's speech at the Fifth Congress of the VBKD, as reproduced in Goeschen, *Vom sozialistischen Realismus zur Kunst im Sozialismus*, 410–18.
26. Fritz Cremer's speech at the V. Kongreß der VBKD, 24 March 1964. AdK Archiv.
27. Bernhard Heisig's speech at the V. Kongreß der VBKD, 24 March 1964. AdK Archiv.
28. Erich Honecker at the Fourth Conference of the ZK der SED as reported in the Party's main newspaper, *Neues Deutschland* (18 December 1971) and cited in Feist and Gillen, *Kunstkombinat*, 77.
29. 'Noch ist die Tür offen' and 'Im Gespräch mit den Besuchern', *Für Dich* 15 (1977). Divorce rates in East Germany were considerably higher than in West Germany, the result of women's greater emancipation in the East. Rueschemeyer and Schissler, 'Women in the Two Germanys'.
30. 'Noch ist die Tür offen', *Für Dich* 23 (1977).
31. Ibid.
32. 'Aspekte zum Familienbild', *Für Dich* 29 (1977).
33. For additional examples, see Eisman, 'In the Crucible', and Eisman, '"En shock y listos para actuar"'.
34. Archive of the Dresden Academy of Fine Arts, File 03-1421.
35. Angela Hampel, interview by the author, Dresden, 4 March 2013.
36. This was East Germany's most important exhibition of contemporary art and took place every four to five years in Dresden. The painting was mentioned in a number of articles and was the focus of at least two others: Nahser, 'Zu unseren Kunstdruckbelagen', and Neumann, 'Malerei der DDR'.
37. Nahser, 'Zu unseren Kunstdruckbelagen'.
38. Neumann, 'Malerei der DDR'.
39. Großmann, 'Auf Suche nach einem knallblauen Himmel'.
40. Ibid.
41. Circles were not limited to the visual arts. There were hobby circles for activities ranging from writing and art making to stamp collecting. For a great documentary on hobby circles and culture houses, see *An der Saale hellem Strande – ein Kulturhaus erzählt* (Germany, 2010, dir. Helga Storck and Peter Goedel).
42. Between 1965 and 1975 visits to art museums in East Germany nearly doubled from 5.8 million visits per year to 10 million. This doubling was also visible in visits to museums as a whole, which rose from 15.6 million to 30.3 million. Lindner, *Verstellter, offener Blick*, 158.
43. Documenta 5 had 220,000 visitors.
44. It should be noted that for many East Germans, art was synonymous with painting, which was the GDR's most prestigious medium and had long been the focus of governmental policies.
45. In East Germany, worker portraits were an important genre, one that was encouraged by exhibitions and commissions at the state and local level across the entire Cold War period.
46. Lindner, *Verstellter, offener Blick*, 157. This is an idea that David Bathrick also discusses with regard to literature in *The Powers of Speech*.
47. Table 18 in ibid., 161.
48. Ibid., 162.
49. The percentages are rough estimates as the numbers do not reveal the nationality of the visitors nor distinguish between those who attended one time and those who visited multiple times. The percentage of West Germans at Documenta is presumably significantly lower than 0.8 per cent since it is, in contrast to the DKA, an exhibition that emphasizes international art.

50. Bernhard Heisig, Speech at the Fourth Congress, in *Vierter Kongress des Verbandes Bildender Künstler Deutschlands* (Berlin: Zentralvorstand des VBKDs, 1959), 91–99.
51. These and other numbers cited in this section come from Lindner, *Verstellter, offener Blick.*
52. Buchloh, 'How German Was It?', 296.
53. For more on the ideological nature of Western art after 1945, see Guilbaut, *How New York Stole the Idea of Modern Art* and Saunders, *The Cultural Cold War.* For more about art as cultural capital for the elite, see Bourdieu, *Distinction* and Stallabrass, *Contemporary Art.*
54. Fulbrook, 'Putting the People back in'.
55. See Jan Palmowski's contribution in this volume (chapter 1).

Bibliography

'Aspekte zum Familienbild'. *Für Dich* 29 (1977).
Bathrick, D. *The Powers of Speech: The Politics of Culture in the GDR.* Lincoln and London: University of Nebraska Press, 1995.
Bourdieu, P. *Distinction: A Social Critique of the Judgement of Taste.* Cambridge, MA: Harvard University Press, 1984.
Buchloh, B. 'How German Was It? Benjamin H. D. Buchloh on *Art of Two Germanys'. Artforum* (Summer 2009), 294–99.
Cremer, F. Speech at the V. Kongreß der VBKD. 24 March 1964. Akademie der Künste (AdK) Archiv.
Damus, M. *Malerei der DDR, Funktionen der Bildenden Kunst im Realen Sozialismus.* Reinbeck bei Hamburg: Rowohlt Taschenbuch Verlag GmbH, 1991.
Davis, B. *9.5 Theses on Art and Class.* Chicago: Haymarket Books, 2013.
Eisman, A. '"En shock y listos para actuar": Los artistas de la RDA y el golpe de Estado en Chile en 1973', in B. Gutiérrez Galindo (ed), *El arte en la República Democrática Alemana: 1949–1989* (Mexico City: Instituto de Investigaciones Estéticas de la Universiad Nacional Autónoma de México, 2018), 185–204.
——. 'From Double Burden to Double Vision: The *Doppelgänger* in Doris Ziegler's Paintings of Women in East Germany', in D. Ascher Barnstone (ed.), *The Doppelgänger* (Oxford and New York: Peter Lang AG, 2016), 49–54.
——. 'In the Crucible: Bernhard Heisig and the Hotel Deutschland Murals', in E. Kelly and A. Wlodarski (eds), *Art Outside the Lines: New Perspectives on GDR Art Culture* (Amsterdam: Rodopi, 2011), 21–39.
——. 'The Permeability of the Wall'. *German Studies Review* 38(3) (October 2015), 597–616.
Feist, G. and E. Gillen (eds). *Kunstkombinat DDR, Daten und Zitate zur Kunst und Kulturpolitik der DDR 1945–1990.* Berlin: Museumspädagogischen Dienst Berlin, 1990.
Fraser, N. 'Rethinking the Public Sphere: A Contribution to the Critique of Actually Existing Democracy'. *Social Text* 25/26 (1990), 56–80.
Fulbrook, M. 'Putting the People back in: The Contentious State of GDR History'. *German History* 24(4) (2006), 608–20.

Goeschen, U. *Vom sozialistischen Realismus zur Kunst im Sozialismus: Die Rezeption der Moderne in Kunst und Kunstwissenschaft der DDR*. Berlin: Duncker & Humblot, 2001.

Großmann, K. 'Auf Suche nach einem knallblauen Himmel: Gespräch mit dem Leipziger Malerin Doris Ziegler'. *Sächsische Zeitung*, 23 July 1982.

Guilbaut, S. *How New York Stole the Idea of Modern Art*. Chicago: University of Chicago Press, 1985.

Habermas, J. *The Structural Transformation of the Public Sphere: An Inquiry into a Category of Bourgeois Society*. Translated by Thomas Burger. Cambridge, MA: MIT Press, 1991.

Hampel, A. Interview by the author. Dresden. 4 March 2013.

Heisig, B. Speech at the V. Kongreß der VBKD. 24 March 1964. Akademie der Künste (AdK) Archiv.

Heisig, B. 'Untitled', in J. Uhlitzsch, J. (ed.), *Vierter Kongress des Verbandes Bildender Künstler Deutschlands* (Berlin: VBKD, 1959), 91–99.

Hermand, J. 'Modernism Restored: West German Painting in the 1950s'. *New German Critique* 32 (Spring-Summer 1984), 23–41.

'Im Gespräch mit den Besuchern', *Für Dich* 15 (1977).

Jarausch, K. 'Divided, Yet Reunited – The Challenge of Integrating German Post-War Histories'. *H-German* (2011).

Lindner, B. 'Kunstrezeption der DDR', in G. Feist and E. Gillen (eds), *Kunstkombinat DDR, Daten und Zitate zur Kunst und Kulturpolitik der DDR 1945–1990* (Berlin: Museumspädagogischen Dienst Berlin, 1990), 62–93.

———. *Verstellter, offener Blick, Eine Rezeptionsgeschichte Bildender Kunst im Osten Deutschlands, 1945–1995*. Cologne, Weimar and Vienna: Böhlau Verlag, 1998.

Lüdecke, H. 'Phänomen und Problem Picasso'. *Bildende Kunst* 5 (1955).

Mittenzwei, W. *Die Intellektuellen: Literatur und Politik in Ostdeutschland 1945 bis 2000*. Berlin: Aufbau Verlag, 2003.

Nahser, S. 'Zu unseren Kunstdruckbelagen: *Brigade Rosa Luxemburg*, Gemälde von Doris Ziegler'. *Kulturelles Leben* (8) (1978), 26.

Nerlinger, O. 'Politik und Kunst'. *Bildende Kunst* 10 (1948).

Neumann, A. 'Malerei der DDR'. *FF Dabei* 12 (1980).

'Noch ist die Tür offen'. *Für Dich* 15 (1977).

Orlow, N. 'Wege und Irrwege der modernen Kunst' *Tägliche Rundschau*, 20 January 1951, 4.

Piotrowski, P. 'Towards Horizontal Art History', in J. Anderson (ed), *Crossing Cultures: Conflict, Migration, Convergence* (Melbourne: Melbourne University Publishing: 2009), 82–85.

Rancière, J. *The Politics of Aesthetics*. Translated by Gabriel Rockhill. London: Bloomsbury Academic, 2013.

Rueschemeyer, M. and H. Schissler. 'Women in the Two Germanys'. *German Studies Review* 13, DAAD Special Issue (1990), 71–85.

Saunders, F.S. *The Cultural Cold War: The CIA and the World of Arts and Letters*. New York: The New Press, 2001.

Stallabrass, J. *Contemporary Art: A Very Short Introduction*. Oxford: Oxford University Press, 2006.

Ulbricht, W. 'Aufgaben der Kunst'. *Neues Deutschland*, 1 November 1951, 5.

Wierling, D. 'Die Bundesrepublik als das andere Deutschland', in F. Bajohr, A. Doering-Manteuffel, C. Kemper and D. Siegfried (eds), *Mehr als eine Erzählung: Zeitgeschichtliche Perspektiven auf die Bundesrepublik* (Göttingen: Wallstein Verlag, 2016), 391–401.

Williams, R. *Marxism and Literature*. Oxford: Oxford University Press, 1977.

Chapter 10

The Perceptual Fabric and Everyday Practices of Jazz and Pop in East and West Germany

Michael J. Schmidt

Scholarly work on popular music in Germany during the last three decades has shown that jazz has been crucial to Germans' debates on the cultural and social fabric of twentieth-century modernity. A signifier of extraordinary breadth, it has been a conduit to attack, affirm, formulate or transgress normative definitions of race, gender, sexuality and class for roughly a century.[1] The jazz question was most intense and acrimonious in Germany during the music's first forty years, from its arrival in the late 1910s until the mid-to-late 1950s. Scholars have characterized the last decade of this period as one marked by both continuity and rupture. Uta Poiger, Jennifer Fay and Andrew Hurley have demonstrated that while jazz continued to be a social and political lightning rod in the postwar period, the 1950s were ultimately a turning point in the acceptance of jazz in both East and West Germany. Considered a 'degenerate' music for decades, jazz became a legitimate cultural practice by 1960 through Cold War strategizing and the personal proselytizing of Joachim Ernst Berendt, West Germany's most influential jazz critic.[2]

Scholars of jazz in Germany have treated jazz as a stable and coherent musical genre that moved in a pendulum swing between rejection and acceptance, ignorance and knowledge. During the late 1940s and 1950s, a host of critics and activists successfully re-defined it. Scott DeVeaux contends that the jazz tradition – what we understand to be the history and nature of jazz – is 'a construction of relatively recent vintage, an overarching narrative that has crowded out other possible interpretations of the complicated and variegated cultural phenomena that we cluster under the umbrella jazz'.[3] More recently, John Gennari has traced the process of this construction in detail, outlining how our current definition of the music evolved through debates and disagreement over what exactly constituted the music and made it unique.[4] Jazz, their work shows, does not have essential characteristics, but is contingent and historical. What characterizes the music, and which sounds and recordings fall under its label, changed dramatically over the course of the twentieth century.

Seen from this perspective, the late 1940s and 1950s were a key moment in the re-articulation of jazz in Germany. Germans did not simply begin to correctly understand or accept jazz for the first time – the definition of jazz changed significantly in the post-Second World War period. Before the mid-1950s, jazz was highly ambiguous and loosely defined for most Germans. During the 1950s, 'hot' music connoisseurs spearheaded a re-articulation of jazz and pop within the media spheres of both East and West Germany. In this transformation, jazz and popular music fragmented into different genres of music with separate artists, sounds, forms of perception and audiences.

With the re-construction of jazz in the 1950s in East and West Germany, two broad perceptual-medial zones formed for music identified as being outside the Western concert tradition. Jazz became a music that emphasized a type of close listening that was deeply informed by reading. Jazz perception utilized the cooperation and combination of textual reading and the aural focus of the ears. Other forms of popular music – often addressed generically as *Schlager* by Germans in the 1950s – included and accentuated things that jazz fans purposefully minimized: visuality, film, the moving body and the emotions.

The wider re-formation of jazz and popular music in East and West Germany indicated a postwar shift in what Raymond Williams called 'structures of feeling'. Structures of feeling are forms of present-oriented thinking and sensing that do not fit into established institutions or received cultural tendencies and movements. They are 'meanings and values as they are actively lived and felt'.[5] The fragmentation of jazz and pop brought together new combinations of multi-sensory perception, emotions, concepts and media, offering Germans everyday practices and lived experiences through which they could forge alternate forms of sociopolitical belonging after the end of the Third Reich. These experiential compounds of pop music exemplify how aspects of the everyday – the way that one listened to the radio, attended a concert, or read a favourite fan magazine – could bring together communities within and across East and West German societies.

The Re-Definition of Jazz

As a genre and form of music-making, jazz was a conceptual big tent for most Germans until the second half of the 1950s. Although jazz was always associated with twentieth-century entertainment music and the United States, the correlation between the term 'jazz' and its specific sound(s) remained loosely defined between its appearance in Germany during the late 1910s and the end of the Third Reich.[6] There was in fact a significant degree of sonic continuity between the pop music of the Third Reich and the immediate postwar period. All areas of post-war Germany inherited the sound of Nazi entertainment and dance music, which itself stemmed from a host of international pop styles associated with jazz and swing during the 1920s and 1930s.[7] Entertainment and dance orchestras, like the East German RBT-Orchester or the West German orchestra of Kurt Widmann, played these sounds well into the 1950s while absorbing elements of new American styles like Bebop and early Rhythm and Blues (often called 'boogie woogie' in Germany).[8]

Unlike in the Third Reich, however, the label and idea of 'jazz' could be applied positively and publicly to pop sounds and musicians. Like the pre-Nazi era, for most Germans, the genre was associated with a wide range of sounds and styles in the first decade after the war. Looking back on the period in 1966, the German jazz historian Horst Lange argued that there was a 'severe conceptual confusion around jazz in Germany' between 1945 and 1949. 'In general', he remembered, 'every American music that was offered by the diverse AFN (American Forces Network) stations counted as jazz'.[9] The label 'jazz' was applied to many pop music genres that we now consider quite different, including hillbilly music (Country music), Hawaiian music and crooner music.[10] The postwar German dance bands replicated this stylistic breadth and 'absorbed what one heard [on the American and British Forces Networks]: bebop, swing, bar music, boogie woogie and everything else'.[11]

Over the course of the 1950s, however, jazz became a much more specific genre in the two Germanys. 'Jazz' stopped being a description associated with most modern entertainment music (including Schlager) and transformed into a unique, progressively developing musical form. The definition of jazz that became ascendant during this period – and still defines the music today – originated in an international body of pop music connoisseurs dating back to the 1930s. This group, first organizing themselves into 'hot' clubs in Paris, the American Northeast and Berlin during the interwar period, believed that jazz was an elevated form of modern music. As such, it needed to be distinguished from other forms of what they saw as derivative, diluted styles of commercial music.

After the fall of the Third Reich, 'hot clubs' popped up across the damaged landscape in all four zones of occupied Germany. Numbering only a handful in 1945, by 1950 there were at least twenty clubs in West Germany alone.[12] Hot clubs existed not just in Western cities like Düsseldorf and Frankfurt am Main, but also in the East in Dresden, Leipzig, Halle and the divided city of Berlin.

The main mission of these postwar hot groups was educational: they wished to spread their conception of jazz to the broader German public, East and West, and transform the popular music landscape. Fervent in their belief, they were particularly incensed by the diversity of sounds that counted as 'jazz' for postwar Germans. In 1947, the head of the Hot Club Berlin, Hans Blüthner, insisted that although most Germans believed that jazz was ubiquitous, the 'jazz' played on the radio and covered in the press needed to be rejected by 'true jazz fans'. Those who understand correctly what jazz is 'do not support composers, nor do they want to know the development of a Schlager and Schlager texts', he argued.[13] Hot clubs believed that jazz needed to be recognized as fundamentally different from Schlager and other forms of mainstream pop music. In this respect, they contended that Germans' main limitation was aural: the vast majority of audiences could not hear the difference between real jazz and Schlager. Although dance and boogie woogie bands often utilized similar harmonic and melodic material (and ensembles), jazz, they contended, could be identified through the presence of swing rhythm and improvised solos.

In West Germany, the hot club movement successfully created what Paul Lopes has termed a 'jazz art world' during the 1950s. The jazz art world, which Lopes argues was responsible for establishing jazz as a distinct musical tradition and a high art form, consisted of an expansive community of 'record producers, concert producers, club owners, music critics, magazine publishers and diverse audiences'.[14] In the mid- to late 1940s, the German hot clubs had been small private gatherings, which featured local musicians, lectures and record listening sessions. Their publications were largely homemade, distributed by hand amongst their coterie and short-lived. By the late 1950s, there was a large public network: there were clubs in practically every medium to large city, jazz labels like Mod and Old Records in Cologne, record stores which carried both American and European new releases, large concerts with touring American musicians, the yearly *Deutsches Jazzfestival* in Frankfurt am Main, professional jazz magazines like *Jazz Podium* and reams of German-language jazz literature. These institutions identified the proper canon of jazz recordings and artists – from New Orleans music from the 1920s through the contemporary bebop and cool jazz of Charlie Parker,

Fats Navarro, Lennie Tristano and Gerry Mulligan – and the right places to hear live music.

The presence of this network drew more and more West Germans into the hot clubs' orbit of ideas and practices. Although attendance at concerts put on by the hot clubs clearly began to grow before 1955, the second half of the 1950s was a peak period for the jazz movement. The 'huge upswing' between 1955 and 1960 was tied to the new cultural formation of youth culture: it became 'the popular music of choice' for 'a large portion of highly-educated high school and university students'.[15] The growth of the hot clubs into a wider jazz movement could not have occurred without this new, distinct young audience.

The formation of the jazz network brought the hot clubs' musical definitions out of small private circles and into the wider West German public, effectively re-defining what 'jazz' meant. Even if most West Germans did not care about or understand the deep debates amongst ardent fans, they began to recognize jazz as a unique sphere of music making and allowed the institutions set up by the hot club movement to claim ownership over it. By the late 1950s, the mainstream press had largely adopted the language and definitions of the jazz aficionados. Reinhard Fark's survey of West German newspapers and illustrated magazines shows that by the end of 1955, their conception of jazz largely corresponded to the discourse of the jazz specialist magazines.[16]

In 1957, Joachim Ernst Berendt, the most well-known jazz writer and advocate in Germany, declared that jazz had 'arrived'. Berendt had been deeply involved in jazz advocacy through writing, radio broadcasting and concert promotion since the late 1940s. When he wrote his piece in 1957, he had been a prime witness (and indeed leader) of the shifting perspective on jazz in West Germany. An embattled subject at the beginning of the decade, the art world vision of jazz was now widely accepted across the West German cultural landscape, Berendt believed. It had found favour in the churches, one of jazz's strongest opponent just five years before.[17] Moreover, he observed, their vision of jazz had been integrated into established cultural institutions: a jazz film had been sent by Germany to the Venice Biennale (*Jazz und Alte Musik*, 1957) and conservatories, adult education centres (*Volkshochschule*) and literary circles now included lectures on what was previously considered a crass brand of music.[18]

During the late 1940s and 1950s, East German hot club adherents also confronted what they saw as a deep misperception of jazz. Their ability to organize and create a local network was deeply inhibited by their back-and-forth, up-and-down relationship with state officials and institutions, however. In the first few years after the end of the Second World War, the Soviet occupation government had been relatively tolerant of the use of the term 'jazz' and the wide range of US-based sounds with which it was associated. During this period, hot clubs met in Dresden, Halle and Leipzig and maintained relationships with groups in West Germany.[19]

After the creation of two separate states in 1949, East Germany began to assert an opposing identity and culture from the West. Shortly thereafter, state authorities and music institutions began to stridently denounce American popular music, Schlager and jazz, which they saw as integrally, if imprecisely, intertwined. In his 1951 address at the founding of the Union of German Composers and Musicologists, Hanns Ernst Meyer vehemently denounced jazz, boogie woogie, 'entertainment kitsch', and Schlager, which he grouped together. He argued that they '[appeal] to the lower instincts in man' and were 'a canal through which the poison of Americanism invades and threatens to stupefy the brains of workers'.[20]

It was easier to attack the ideas of jazz, boogie woogie and Schlager than to identify what exactly constituted their sound. In a 1952 report on the state of dance music to the music section of the East German Academy of Arts, Max Butting observed that 'the concepts of dance music, jazz and entertainment music are for many people one and the same'.[21] Although it cracked down on repertoire, band names, hot clubs and American recordings, East Germans continued to produce dance music that was clearly associated with or related to what the population considered jazz and Schlager.[22]

Much of the popular music played in the GDR, in fact, stemmed directly from West Germany. In the early 1950s, East German music publishers produced only a tiny number of printed scores and, consequently, East German bands were dependent on West German publishers (who often sent charts for free) for their repertoire.[23] Much of the repression was based in language, not in sound – i.e. East Germans banned American songs and English titled bands, not all the sounds associated with jazz at the time. Recognizing this sonic similarity, GDR music institutions attempted to form their own popular music, socialist *Tanzmusik*, during the early 1950s. After a series of contests and promotions, however, music officials recognized that their efforts had failed to create a recognizably new music culture or garner the enthusiasm of East Germans.[24]

Unable to foster their own network independently, East German hot club adherents embraced this state socialist pop music project as a way to build their own jazz art world and re-define the music. The most prominent and active GDR jazz advocate, Reginald Rudorf, entered the socialist dance music discussion in 1952 and attempted to establish a state sponsored 'Marxist' definition of jazz in East Germany that was rooted in the international hot club movements. Separating jazz from Schlager, he promoted jazz as an authentic form of proletarian folk music, which was fundamentally opposed to the exploitation and racism of monopoly capitalism.[25]

While in a contentious dialogue with state institutions, Rudorf and his collaborator, Heinz Lukasz, began to create a jazz network: in the mid-1950s, he broadcast a series of jazz radio broadcasts on East German stations, he helped to establish the *Jazz-Interessengemeinschaft* (Jazz-Interest Group) in the Leipzig *Freie deutsche Jugend* (Free German Youth), and he gave forty-six lectures in more than seven cities to more than 10,000 people.[26] By the beginning of 1956, the number of jazz groups in East Germany had increased dramatically: there were semi-official jazz clubs in Berlin, Halle, Jena, Frankfurt an der Oder, Dresden, Rostock, Gera, Jütorborg, Böhlen and Plauen.[27] Following Rudolf's example, these jazz organizations had meetings and lectures, produced club journals and held concerts.

Between 1955 and 1957, Rudorf and state authorities continually clashed over his views and his independence. Rudorf's insistence on jazz's unique promise as a foundation for socialist music and his advocacy of jazz-oriented listening practices contradicted many of the Western concert music ideals of party officials.[28] In 1957, Rudorf was arrested after publicly positioning himself and jazz in opposition to DDR authorities. In the months before his arrest, he openly criticized Walter Ulbricht, the head of the SED, in a speech to the medicine faculty at the University of Leipzig and, at a guest lecture in Munich, he characterized jazz as an adversary to ideological dogmatism in East Germany and a source of democratic reform.[29]

Although Rudorf disappeared from East German public life, GDR institutions increasingly promoted a version of the East German hot clubs' definition of jazz. About a month before he was arrested, the Ministry for Culture held a meeting and decided that the state needed to propagate a 'jazz-action', a full audio-textual conception of jazz promoted through radio, records and books. Jazz should be supported, they concluded, and 'real' jazz should be separated from modern dance music.[30] In February 1958, the state magazine for popular music, *Melodie und Rhythmus*, published an article on jazz, 'Metamorphose der Jazzinterpretation' (Metamorphosis of Jazz Interpretation), which clearly defined jazz in the terms set out by the hot clubs: it was a historically developing form with specific characteristics that separated it from other forms of dance and entertainment music.[31] That November, Walter Ulbrich argued in a youth forum on 'American Lifestyle' that jazz is the folk music of African Americans and should not be considered the same as other forms of pop music like rock and roll.[32] Shortly after, in January 1959, the leadership of the FDJ and the local automobile union founded the *Arbeitsgemeinschaft Jazz Eisenach*, the first permanent jazz club in East Germany.[33] A few months later, the group began to produce a house journal, *Die Posaune*, which imitated the information sheets put out by West German clubs earlier in the decade.[34]

The Medial Zones of Jazz and Pop

Music is multi-sensory. It is articulated as an aggregate of different perceptual components and media: historical actors encounter music not just sonically, but in text, images, graphic material and physical media. Music exists in the intersections between LP records, the radio, performance environments, newspaper articles, posters, photographs, books and film. It involves the fusion of the unique practices and content of these source components. In addition to putting fences around sounds, constructing genres also requires different balances and equilibriums between music's different perceptual and media parts.[35]

The redefinition of jazz within the two Germanys over the course of the 1950s also formed two broadly different medial zones. These medial zones had their own separate modes of consumption that comprised different equilibriums of the senses, media, meaning and pleasure. Although there was variation within each sphere, the split between jazz and other forms of pop music created the main experiential axes of popular music during the 'economic miracle', the huge upswing in income and consumption of Germans, during the 1950s and 1960s.[36]

Largely separated by the end of the 1950s, both zones of popular music were intermedial – they both had elements of text, film, image and sound. These two zones placed different stress, however, on different media and, consequently, formed distinct ways to sense and experience music. Jazz emphasized a form of textual-listening. Other forms of pop music – like Schlager, *Heimat* music and rock and roll – stressed visuality, emotion and a form of body-listening. In the latter field, the use of these different components was not uniform, however. Schlager, Heimat music and rock and roll each utilized different degrees and combinations of these elements. For example, Heimat music engaged the feeling body the least (and placed more weight on emotions), while rock and roll appealed to it the most.

The jazz audience that emerged in the 1950s from the hot clubs accentuated the importance of meaningful sound and close listening. Although there was always some diversity in theory and opinion, the cantankerous debates in the international hot club community between fans of traditional and modern jazz in the 1940s had settled out into a consensus by the early to mid-1950s.[37] In Germany, the most influential piece of jazz writing in the 1950s was Joachim Ernst Berendt's 1953 *Das Jazzbuch*. Berendt, often called the 'Jazz Pope', intended *Das Jazzbuch* to be a manual or, as one anonymous German reader inscribed in their copy, 'a guide-book' to becoming a jazz listener.[38]

Berendt hoped that his book would conclusively define the field of 'jazz' for Germans, clearing up all misuses of the term while illumi-nating the music's canon, model practitioners and correct practices. Writing before the hot club understanding of jazz became widespread in Germany, he emphasized that jazz required listening. Those who did not employ listening – i.e. not simple hearing but attuned acoustic recep-tion – could not perceive jazz: 'for the untrained ear', he explained, 'the similarity between jazz and the Schlager of the day is so great that they are both always confused with one another'.[39]

For Berendt, two very important characteristics were at the centre of a proper understanding of jazz and a meaningful listening practice: biographical expressionism and stylistic evolution. Biographical expres-sionism was linked to what he termed *Tonbildung* (literally, the formation of sound). In contrast to the uniform standard of classical music aesthet-ics, Tonbildung was the expression of an individual musician's unique subjectivity and life history. Tonbildung exemplified the primacy of the acoustic within jazz. The sounds of a musician offered up the wealth of their personal experiences: it shared the wisdom of his or her life's trag-edies and the ecstasy of their passions and pleasures.

This form of communication and knowledge was also racialized for Berendt. Positioning sound as a means to understand the 'other', he asserted that 'in every note of real jazz is something living of the long slavery and oppression of a race'. Tonbildung, he claimed, was the 'blackest element of jazz'.[40]

Berendt's interest in biography took another, more macro- perspec-tive. He wanted listeners to hear not just the personal suffering and experiences of individuals, but to hear the larger life story of the music as a whole as well. The second major category Berendt emphasized was stylistic evolution. Jazz was a progressive music: it grew organically over time, from style to style and from decade to decade. Stylistic evolution gave jazz listening a crucial historical component and it became a basic element in making sense of jazz performances and recordings.

In the jazz network of the 1950s, training one's ear also required a con-siderable amount of reading. Horst Lange, the German jazz scene's early chronicler, recognized Berendt's book as 'the foundation of [young fans'] jazz knowledge'.[41] To learn what to listen for meant reading *Das Jazzbuch* or articles in *Jazz Podium*. To know about a musician's life and context or recognize a historical style meant reading a biography, an interview, or a stylistic history. The biographical expressionism of Berendt's theory of Tonbildung necessitated the constant production of textual information to feed and enable such auditory techniques. This was itself clear to Berendt. In his short introduction to the biographical section of *Das Jazzbuch*, he justified the section by arguing that since '[jazz musicians'] lives are constantly transformed into music … it is very important to speak of the lives of the "jazz men"'.[42] In sum, the intelligibility of jazz as a listener's practice was dependent on the presence of text.

To satisfy this demand for text-informed listening, there was an explosion of writing on jazz in West Germany during the 1950s. Between 1951 and 1960, there were at least fifty books published by jazz specialists in German.[43] There were at least eight jazz magazines, including *Jazz Podium* and *Jazz-Echo*.[44] Concerts were also increasingly accompanied by text, as performances began to offer programmes with short essays on the music and musicians. Finally, LP records, which replaced seven inch 78-rpm discs during the 1950s, featured liner notes, which framed the sounds emitted from the turntable. The LP, in fact, was the embodiment of the jazz movement's focus on semantic listening through a combination of sound recordings and text.[45]

As the jazz community built a network of practices and perception around their canon of music, another set of practices coalesced around other forms of pop music: Schlager, Heimat music and rock and roll. One of the main differences between Schlager and jazz's medial zones was the place of film and TV as a musical medium. Jazz was shown and depicted in German film during the early 1950s, but it generally did not correspond to the scriptures and sonic practices enshrined within the hot club movement.[46] They did not, however, totally ignore the moving image: Joachim Berendt did make two jazz films during the 1950s and, beginning in 1955, produced the TV show *Jazz gehört und gesehen*. Despite these forays into jazz film and television broadcasts, these endeavours remained largely peripheral.[47]

Unlike jazz, film (and, in the 1960s, TV) was at the centre of Schlager, rock and roll and Heimat music. This was especially true for Schlager. The most important and popular Schlager singers of the 1950s were also musical film stars: Caterina Valente, Peter Alexander, Fred Bertelmann, Freddy Quinn, Germaine Damar, Peter Kraus and Conny Froboess. Being a major pop music singer in West Germany also meant being an actor or an actress and the movie theatre was a pivotal place for Schlager consumption and reception.

And, in West Germany, there were a lot of filmed Schlager. The 1950s were replete with *Schlagerfilme*, the heir of the *Musikfilm* genre that had begun with sound film in the late 1920s and early 1930s. Beginning with the 1950 film *Die Dritte von rechts*, the Schlager film experienced a 'renewed rise' in postwar West Germany.[48] Schlagerfilme were a central part of Schlager singers' careers: Peter Alexander appeared in at least twenty Schlager films during the 1950s (four in 1958 alone). They were also an enormous part of the domestic film industry. By 1960, Schlagerfilm comprised about a quarter of West German production.[49]

West Germans first encountered rock and roll through the 1955 film *Blackboard Jungle*, which includes Bill Halley's iconic 'Rock around the Clock' as its title song. Haley's tune provided the title and theme for Germany's next major exposure to rock and roll: *Rock Around the Clock*, which was released in Germany with the revealing title *Ausser Rand und Band* (Out of Control). Rock and roll films and music were often associated with Schlager and Schlager films. The 1956 American film *The Girl Can't Help it* – which included scenes with Little Richard, Fats Domino, Gene Vincent, the Platters and Eddie Cochran – was renamed *Schlager-Piraten (Schlager-Pirates)* when it was released in Germany. In 1958, Haley and the Comets appeared with Caterina Valente in the West German film *Hier bin ich – Hier bleib ich*.

Similarly, Heimat music was deeply connected to the soundtracks of Heimat films, one of the dominant film genres of the 1950s. Heimat films situated their narratives in lush, rural German landscapes, 'circl[ing] obsessively around the questions of home and away, tradition and change, belonging and difference'.[50] Many Heimat films 'attempted to sell not only the idea of a Heimat that transcended regional and cultural boundaries but also the accompanying music, the *Schlager*, which functioned very much as a musical representation of Heimat'.[51] There was never a strict separation between these film genres, since Heimat film narrative structures were closely related to and borrowed from Schlager film.[52]

Schlager, Heimat music and rock and roll in the 1950s continued the type of audio-visual performance of music established by the music films of the 1930s. The importance of film to Schlager made the visual important in Schlager in West Germany. When one watched Schlagerfilme, one heard and saw Schlager simultaneously in what Michel Chion has called 'synchresis': the spontaneous melding of sound and image in film.[53] The experience of a song was, amongst many things, tied to the look and demeanour of the performer, the action of a scene and the unfolding plot of the film. The song was not just the sound of the voice and band, but the clothes, facial expressions and movements of the performer within the context of a narrative.

For example, in one early scene in the 1957 film *Und Abends in die Scala*, Caterina Valente, one of the main Schlager stars of the decade, sings a mash-up on a stage in a café. In synchrony with two male dancers, she sings while smiling, flipping a cane and performing a dance routine. Around the small stage, a crowd reacts in enjoyment – they stand up, yell and throw their hands in the air. The scene highlights not just the visual element of Schlager and rock and roll, but also how it appealed to the body and physicality. Schlager and rock and roll were for dancing, excited motion, fun and sensuality (whether it be restrained or not). Although clearly exaggerated and deeply informed by fears of racial and gender transgression, contemporary accounts of swing dancing and early rock and roll audiences give some sense of the use and embrace of the kinetic, energetic body that young fans connected with these forms of pop music.[54] The explosive violence and destruction that erupted in the Bill Haley concerts in West Germany between 1956 and 1958, where the audience smashed chairs and had altercations with the police, were just the extreme end of this spectrum of pop physicality.[55]

The physicality of pop resembles what Roland Barthes calls *musica practica*. There are two musics, Barthes argues: 'the music one listens to and the music one plays'. *Musica practica*, the music one plays, is

> an activity that is very little auditory, being above all manual (and thus in a way much more sensual) ... a muscular music in which the part taken by the sense of hearing is one only of ratification, as though the body were hearing ... a music which is not played 'by heart': seated at the keyboard or the music stand, the body controls, conducts, co-ordinates, having itself to transcribe what it reads, making sound and meaning, the body as inscriber and not just transmitter, simple receiver.[56]

Barthes has in mind amateur playing, but his description characterizes the musical reception of dance as well: one hears and involves oneself in the music through the body. The body feels through the rhythm, reacts and coordinates through the beat. It is a physical reception and participation, not a contemplative one.

In addition to being a music for dancing and physicality, pop music was also a place for experiencing heightened emotion. The critic Carl Wilson has argued that pop is a place to feel sentimentality or, in his words, 'schmaltz'. Countering the intellectual tradition of Theodor Adorno and Milan Kundera which sees sentimentality as kitsch and kitsch as manipulation, Wilson argues that 'sentimentality's promise' is 'feeling emotions fully, bodily, as they are'.[57] Consuming mainstream music, in effect, is an activity that allows one to feel feelings without inhibition; it is a place for emoting at a level that has no other place in normal social life.

In addition to the countless songs of joy, sadness, love and heartbreak by Valente, Alexander and Kraus, the music of the Heimat films also exemplified this appeal by offering a site to connect to difficult emotions like loss, trauma and belonging. Heimat songs, which often spoke of mountains, green valleys and the purity of rural life, played a role in these films' post-war emotional work and nation-building. Although placed in a seemingly unrealistic world of tranquillity and natural splendour, these films and their music also engaged and confronted the processes of modernization. The films exhibit a 'manifest concern with issues of trans-port, motorization, migration and mobility as central aspects of moder-nity'. Not atavistic but modern to the core, 'the *Heimatfilm* responds to the pressing historical question of how to make oneself at home in a world where modernization means, among other things, a fundamental transformation of space and of our sense of place'.[58] In fact, they often thematized the loss of such a home for the millions of expellees who had been displaced from the older German territories in the East as part of the peace settlement. Or, as Sabine Hake has formulated it, 'the genre provided a fictional framework for coming to terms with the loss of nation and for turning the Federal Republic into a new homeland'.[59] Jan Palmowski has demonstrated that in East Germany, Heimat allowed the SED to 'lay claim to a distinctive nationhood for the GDR'. It 'became cen-tral to the public transcript of socialism', a way that citizens confirmed their compliance to the state while privately carving out their own space and meaning.[60]

Jazz listeners and critics consummately rejected many of the percep-tual characteristics embraced by the producers and audiences of Schlager and pop music. In 1948, a member of the Düsseldorf club attacked the so-called *Swing-Heinis*, a subcultural group fascinated by swing dancing and fashion. These Swing-Heinis, he asserted, 'are unfortunately every-where to be found in Germany and they treat jazz not as music, but as fashion and a backdrop for excess'.[61] For the early hot club movement, this 'sensationalist jitterbug public' represented an alternate, incorrect form of reception – one that emphasized the dancing body. Engaged in a fight for the ears and contemplative listening, they 'wanted to work against the emerging dance reception of jazz'.[62]

Members of the hot club movement fretted that visuality was also too important to young fans. Hot club members emphasized the visually ostentatious clothing of Swing-Heinis.[63] Some worried that newspapers repeated this emphasis, reporting only on the 'short hair, bright socks and cord trousers' of the audience and not the sound of a concert.[64]

For one *Jazz Podium* writer, one 1953 concert edged perilously close to being consumed by image. For these young people, the author observed, jazz performances were 'often more a spectacle than a concert'.[65] The largest contingent of those attending jazz concerts, the article maintained, were dancers. For them, rhythm was the be all and the end all: 'the excited figural movement of the music is more important than everything else ... which shows itself in the release from a partner into independent dancing movement'. Such an interest in dancing made them poor listeners – 'this type of jazz fan does not differentiate between purely functional or effect music and stronger musical forms of expression'. Despite their quantitative dominance, these fans of the music were not real jazz fans, the author asserted. The music and its rhythmic effects that they were interested in, according to the author, 'is no longer jazz in an actual sense'. They are 'in every case ... to be described as Schlager'.[66]

In the typology of Barthes, the hot club movement advocated music to which one listened. These practices make 'passive, receptive music, sound music', where one focuses on aural qualities, their decoding and their appreciation.[67] This emphasis on listening was not exclusive within the hot club movement at the beginning. In the first five to ten years after the war, jazz clubs and the jazz audience were mixed: some danced, some contemplated. This heterogeneous audience corresponded to the early looseness of jazz's definition. By the end of the 1950s, however, as the close listeners prevailed within the clubs and 'jazz' became a specific genre, the mode of reception tied to dancing was largely pushed out of jazz and into Schlager.

These perceptual and media characteristics were also largely true for hot club members in East Germany. Adherents to the new jazz in the GDR like Reginald Rudorf and Heinz Lukasz based their jazz perception on the same international literature that Berendt and the West German hot clubs did, even if they emphasized its more socialist-leaning Cultural Front elements.[68] Access to the international network of performances and literature – and the ability to construct one – was considerably more restricted within East Germany before the late 1950s, however. The ability to buy jazz magazines, books or specific records before the construction of the wall was largely limited to entering West Berlin or smuggling them in from the West. The music and mini-lectures available on jazz radio programmes were always available in the East, though, for West German stations, American stations based in West Germany and the short wave broadcasts of *Voice of America* were always a part of the GDR soundscape.[69]

This new perceptual-medial framework for jazz clashed with the goals of the GDR music establishment during the early to mid-1950s, however.

The contrast between their frameworks was especially apparent in a May 1956 meeting between Rudorf and top music authorities, which included the composer and theorist Hanns Eisler. During the discussion, which had been called to clarify the definition of jazz, the group fought over the correct standard for judging music. Eisler insisted that the Western concert tradition was the ultimate foundation for evaluating music's quality, while Rudorf maintained that jazz had its own unique system of musical principles and hierarchies. For Rudorf, jazz needed to be addressed with reference to biographical, historical and stylistic details to be understood; Eisler, on the other hand, forcefully advocated that such minutiae was irrelevant and that only pure, abstract sound should be considered.[70]

Eisler's assumptions about the primacy of Western concert aesthetics corresponded with the SED's blueprint for the national soundscape. In a truly socialist Germany, they believed, all members of society would appreciate and listen to the German classical tradition and *Volksmusik*, erasing the division between elite and entertainment forms and audiences.[71] More than just an end goal, music was essential to the construction of socialism and the socialist personality, for East German 'cultural officials accorded music an exceptional power to shape its audience'.[72] Consequently, they feared that the modes of reception that departed from close listening and the strict contemplation of sound – and the music that went with these modes – could derail the historical progression into socialism.

Although it failed to successfully create an alternative form of pop music (socialist *Tanzmusik*), East German administrators had a general, if ambiguous, vision of what the perceptual and physical practices of this music should be like. For them, the sonic characteristics of music were intimately tied to national sensibility, subjectivity and perception. Sound paralleled reception; consequently, music needed to propagate what they believed to be proper behaviour and an enriched sensorium. In his 1951 report on dance music, the GDR composer Max Butting contended that the 'German dance sensibility' was tied to melody and not rhythm. A product of the social and cultural disarray of modern capitalism, American music was the opposite: rhythm dominated melody. This overwhelmingly 'motorized' American dance rhythm threatened the senses and sensibility of the German *Volk*, Butting warned. Rhythmic variety 'will always support expression and feeling and through it lead to perceptions that are full of life'. Rhythmic monotony, as in America, 'must stupefy and level [humans] out'.[73]

Uta Poiger has demonstrated that East German public figures, like their early Western counterparts, vociferously attacked the physicality and energy of American popular music consumption as 'degenerate' and corrupting. These objections were certainly tied to fears of racial and gender transgression, as Poiger argues, but they were also part of a broader re-definition of, and contest over, the perceptual attributes of jazz, Schlager and GDR music. The engagement with entertainment music through spirited dancing, sensual or acrobatic movement and strong emotion starkly contradicted the perceptual mode that SED music authorities hoped to foster, which was based in the aesthetic practices of Western classical music. Ultimately, the SED was unable to limit the perceptual and emotional field of popular music in the way they wished and, although they continued to reject and repress extremes of pop music receptivity (especially dancing and visuality), they gradually accepted and promoted it over the course of the 1950s and 1960s.

One of the main differences between the musical modes produced by East and West Germany in the 1950s lay in film. Although DEFA made their own Schlager film and imported some from West Germany and Austria, the number of music films made by East Germany was relatively small compared to West Germany (in the 1950s, DEFA only made eight).[74] Furthermore, many of the DEFA productions were operetta adaptations of eighteenth- and nineteenth-century composers and German music films from the 1930s and 1940s 'outnumbered all other releases in this genre of film entertainment' during most years. Until the construction of the Berlin Wall in 1961, East Germans, however, could enter West Berlin to see West German and American Schlager and rock and roll films.[75] Besides seeing West Berlin films, the main source of Schlager and rock and roll was the radio before the pop music TV shows of the mid- to late 1960s. For the East German music industry, 'radio broadcasting networks were the most significant producers of popular music'.[76] Furthermore, like jazz, East Germans could listen to pop music and rock and roll from American and West European stations on their radios at home. And despite DEFA's limited music film production, pop music visuality manifested itself in other ways in East Germany, most notably in the clothes, haircuts and dancing associated with rock and roll and, later, Beat music.[77]

Jazz and Pop as Politics and Structures of Feeling

The two perceptual-medial zones constructed around jazz and other forms of pop music during the 1950s provided broad fields through which Germans could experience and encounter music. Musical genres are not *a priori* distinct forms. They are not clear, fully-formed packages of melody, harmony and rhythm that are simply played authentically or not and accepted or rejected. Genres are (often messy) historical cultural and social formations that involve not just distinctions of sound, but specific sets of affective and perceptual practices and material medias. In the period between the end of the Second World War and 1960, an activist group of Germans re-defined jazz as a genre and, in the process, congealed two distinct ways to engage, receive and practice popular music.

The separation of jazz and Schlager involved the formation of what Raymond Williams calls 'structures of feelings'. In contradistinction to culture as already formed objects, Williams asserted that a structure of feeling is characterized by lived experience and perception.[78] Thinking of it in these terms, jazz was not a finished product that eventually became accepted in Germany during the 1950s. In this period, it became a unifying phenomenon for a type of musical experience that comprised biograph-ical-historical close listening practices that integrated reading and text deeply into itself. It eschewed a focus on the visual, the tactile and sensual bodily listening or dancing and the feeling of sentimental emotions in favour of a more conceptual and abstract kind of reading-listening recep-tivity. When a German put a record from the jazz canon on their turntable or attended a jazz festival, this was the broad fabric of experience and perception that they attempted to utilize in their encounter. On the other hand, Schlager and other types of mainstream pop became phenomena where one felt intense emotions, enjoyed the movement of one's own and another's body and watched the visual elements of a singer on a screen. They offered frames and instruments to engage these broad structures of feeling and experience.[79]

The structures of feeling of popular music offered gathering points for the kinds of political communities and subjectivities that Jacques Rancière has argued form around everyday cultural practices and in contrast to traditional borders and state boundaries.[80] Germans on both sides of the border developed many of the same perceptual experiences around jazz and identified each other as part of the same aesthetic and political commu-nity. The Leipzig *Interessengemeinschaft* and the Halle *Arbeitsgemeinschaft*, for example, maintained a correspondence with the West German Hot Club in Düsseldorf in the mid-1950s.[81] For Rudorf, jazz fostered a transna-tional link between East Germans and Western Europeans and, in a letter to one GDR official, he pointed to the 'countless' letters he had received from West Germany, Italy, France and England about his radio broadcasts. These jazz fans, he argued, were part of an international peace movement and the West German Jazz Federation constituted an 'important reserve for our struggle for peace and the unity of our country'.[82] Seeking to actu-alize this potential, the Leipzig *IG* drafted a letter to the Düsseldorf club calling for a common front against the Paris Agreements, the treaty which had solidified the division of Germany in September 1954.[83]

Politics, according to Ranciére, organizes how people experience and sense their worlds and acts as a form of power by excluding the aesthetic and perceptual practices of certain groups. In opposition to the dominance of Western art music, jazz and Schlager became one of the main ways that postwar German youth asserted their own sensory and affective lives in public and, at the same time, distinguished themselves from one another socially. According to Kaspar Maase, international youth culture and pop music – especially the so-called *Halbstarke* and rock and roll – broke the long, traditional stranglehold of the *Bildungsbürgertum* on the cultural content of the public sphere by asserting their taste in small but visible and auditory ways.[84] At the same time, the everyday practices of music listening also created forms of class/status-related distinctions within and across nations: in West Germany, modern jazz was listened to by middle-class high school and university students, swing and dixieland by middle-class adolescents and rock and roll by working-class teenagers. Children of the educated elite rejected American music altogether.[85] In East Germany, jazz and rock and roll were aesthetic spheres that challenged the dominance of the SED's sensory politics and exclusionary control of cultural institutions.[86]

Finally, these aesthetic practices and structures of feeling pointed postwar Germans, East and West, away from themselves as a racial community and towards their European neighbours and the United States. According to Peter Fritzsche, the media world under the Nazis was characterized by a sense of 'unter uns': representations of daily life, news and cultural consumption were oriented towards the life and history of the German *Volksgemeinschaft*.[87] Jazz and pop music – always connected to the United States and other European countries – re-oriented daily practices and experiences away from racial insularity and towards a sense of community and subjectivity beyond the nation.

Michael J. Schmidt is the Graduate Program Administrator for the Department of Sociology at the University of Texas at Austin. He received his doctorate in History from the University of Texas at Austin in 2014 for his dissertation, 'The Multi-Sensory Object: Jazz, the Modern Media, and the History of the Senses in Germany'. His research focuses on jazz, media history and the history of perception. His work on the Weimar period has been published in *German History* and the *Journal of Social History* recently published his article, 'The Louis Armstrong Story, Reissues, and the LP Record: Anchors of Significance'. He is currently working on a new digital humanities project on the history of music in Austin, Texas.

Notes

1. Rippey, 'Rationalisation'; Petrescu, 'Domesticating the Vamp'; Wipplinger, 'The Jazz Republic'; Kater, *Different Drummers*; Poiger, *Jazz, Rock and Rebels*; Hurley, *The Return of Jazz*; Fay, '"That's Jazz Made in Germany"'.
2. Poiger, *Jazz, Rock and Rebels*; Hurley, *The Return of Jazz*; Bratfisch, *Freie Töne*.
3. DeVeaux, 'Constructing the Jazz Tradition', 532.
4. Gennari, *Blowing Hot and Cool*.
5. Williams, *Marxism and Literature*, 132.
6. For a discussion of jazz's sonic indeterminateness during the 1920s and 1930s, see Schmidt, 'The Multi-Sensory Object', Chapters 2 and 3.
7. In his history of the German jazz scene, Horst Lange observed that the post-Second World War orchestras 'fell back to the swing and dance music from the years 1936 to 1938'. Lange, *Jazz in Deutschland*, 146–47.
8. This sonic continuity between the Nazi and postwar 'liberated' bands is not too surprising, since many of the musicians playing in and leading these postwar bands had been part of the Nazi system. The first leader of the RBT orchestra, Michael Jary, had composed music for UFA films under Goebbels. Horst Kudrizki, who took the baton from Jary in 1946, had arranged music for the Nazi's model pop orchestra, *der deutsche Tanz- und Unterhaltungsorchester*. Berendt argues that the *DTU* was a model for both the Soviet and American radio orchestras in Berlin: the *RBT* and RIAS orchestras. Berendt, *Ein Fenster aus Jazz*, 167.
9. Lange, *Jazz in Deutschland*, 145.
10. Ibid.
11. Jost, *That's Jazz*, 368.
12. Hoffmann, 'Zur westdeutschen Hot-Club-Bewegung der Nachkriegzeit', 67.
13. Blüthner, 'Die Berliner Hotfreunde'.
14. Lopes, *The Rise of the Jazz Art World*, 2.
15. Schwab, *Der Frankfurt Sound*, 83. Many scholars have argued that a global youth culture was born in the unique boom of consumer societies in Europe and the United States during the 1950s. West Germany was no exception and the West Germany economy expanded at an unprecedented rate after 1950. By the end of the 1950s, the young adults used their spending power – and their taste in fashion and entertainment – to form the new social, cultural and generational category of the 'teenager'. Judt, *Postwar*, 347–50.
16. Fark, *Die Missachtete Botschaft*, 227. Fark shows that other illustrated magazines used elements of the hot club language earlier. *Quick*, for example, already used specialist terms like 'bebop' and 'jam session' in 1952.
17. Fark, *Die Missachtete Botschaft*, 236.
18. Berendt, 'Der Arrivierter Jazz', 40.
19. Lange, *Jazz in Deutschland*, 119–33. Bratfisch, 'So viel Anfang war nie', 19–28.
20. Meyer, 'Realismus', 41–42. Meyer defined Schlager as jazz under capitalism and described boogie woogie as 'American *Schlager*-kitsch'.
21. BArch, DR 1-240; Butting, *Tanzmusik Abschlussbericht 1952*, 2.
22. U. Poiger discusses the crack down on band names and repertoire in Poiger, *Jazz, Rock and Rebels*, 59. For the similarities between pop music in the East and West, see von Saldern, 'Der Schlager is grundsächlich ein Politikum', 107.
23. Thacker, *Music after Hitler*, 180–1, 189–90.
24. State music eschewed the term *Schlager* and pop music as a way of semantically distancing itself from West Germany. Larkey, 'Popular Music on East German Television', 178. For an in-depth discussion of the GDR's failed attempt to create a socialist dance music, see Thacker, 'The Fifth Column'.
25. Rudorf, 'Für eine frohe, ausdrucksvolle Tanzmusik'.

26. BArch, DY 24/0392, Copy of the *Jazz-Journal* of the Arbeitsgemeinschaft für Jazz, Halle, December 1955.
27. BArch, DY 24/0392, Copy of the *Jazz-Journal* of the Arbeitsgemeinschaft für Jazz, Halle, January and February 1956.; Rudorf, *Jazz in der Zone*, 74.
28. BArch, DR 1-243, Letter from Rolf Meinig and Horst Wilde to Becher, 7 January 1956; Akademie der Künste, Archiv Hanns Eisler 2854, 'Diskussion über Jazz mit Prof. Hans Eisler in der deutschen Akademie der Künste am 14.5.1956'.
29. Rudorf, *Jazz in der Zone*, 90–95.
30. BArch, DR 1/23, 'Protokoll zur Diskussion über *Jazzmusik* am 8. Februar 1957'. In September, *Ministerium für Kultur* members met with the state record company and recommended that jazz recordings be continued, that work with East German jazz bands be increased and that the radio and music conservatory in Berlin put together a new ensemble. BArch, DR 1/243, 'Aktennotiz über die am Freitag, den 13.9.57 durchgeführte Besprechung mit dem Thema Jazzproduktion des VEB Deutsche Schallplatten'.
31. Elsner, 'Metamorphoses der Jazzinterpretation', 14.
32. 'Fragen und Antworten im Non-Stop-Tempo', *Berliner Zeitung*, 5 November 1958, 4.
33. Lippmann+Rau-Musikarchiv Eisenach, Folder AG Jazz Archiv I, Arbeitsgemeinschaft Jazz Eisenach Sammlung. Blume, 'Die Geschichte des Eisenacher Jazz', 6.
34. See the collection of the *Arbeitsgemeinschaft Jazz Eisenach* in the Lippmann+Rau-Musikarchiv Eisenach.
35. For an extended discussion of the multi-sensory and multi-media aspects of music, see Schmidt, 'The Multi-Sensory Object'.
36. For a detailed discussion of the culture and economy of the economic miracle, see Schildt, *Moderne Zeiten*; Schissler, *The Miracle Years*.
37. Gennari, *Blowin' Hot and Cool*. Germans were also affected by these debates during the late 1940s. For evidence of this, see the short-lived traditionalist magazine *Jazz Home*.
38. Copy of J. Berendt, *Das Jazzbuch* in the author's collection. The best-selling jazz book in German history, *Das Jazzbuch* sold 75,000 copies within a few months and by 1959 had sold 250,000 copies. Poiger, *Jazz, Rock and Rebels*, 45; Hurley, *The Return of Jazz*, 2, note 3.
39. Berendt, *Das Jazzbuch*, 9–10.
40. Ibid., 97.
41. Lange, *Jazz in Deutschland*, 195.
42. Berendt, *Das Jazzbuch*, 24.
43. See the extensive bibliography of Lange's *Jazz in Deutschland*.
44. The other magazines were the *Jazz Revue* (1950–1953), *Der Drummer* (1953–1959), *Berlin Jazz* (1955–1958), *Route 56/57/58* (1956–1958), *Schlagzeug* (1956–1960) and *Fongi* (1958–1959).
45. Michel Chion defines semantic listening as 'that which refers to a code or a language to interpret a message'. Chion, 'The Three Listening Modes', 49.
46. Hoffmann, 'Liebe, Jazz, und Übermut'.
47. Between 1955 and 1960, there were only thirteen shows of *Jazz gehört und gesehen*. Jazzinstitut Darmstadt, Joachim Ernst Berendt Sammlung, 'Fernsehsendungen der Jazzreaktionen'. Furthermore, TV audiences were small during the 1950s in West Germany.
48. Hobsch, 'Die Drei von der Tankstelle', 38.
49. Hobsch, 'Die Drei von der Tankstelle', 39.
50. Von Moltke, *No Place Like Home*, 3.
51. Ludewig, *Screening Nostalgia*, 180.
52. Seeßlen, 'Durch die Heimat und so weiter', 142.
53. Chion, *Audio-Vision*, 63.
54. Poiger, *Jazz, Rock and Rebels*, 56–61, 175–85; Fenemore, *Sex, Thugs and Rock 'N' Roll*, 134–36, 170. The enjoyment of excessive movement in pop music and especially rock

and roll was also linked to a long racialized discourse in Germany (and elsewhere) connecting American pop music to the primitivity, natural rhythm and irrationality of African Americans.

55. 'Haley Krawalle: Saat der Gewalt', *Der Spiegel*, 5 November 1958, 78–79; 'Konzertante Schlägerei: Rock n' Roll Tumulte in der Hamburger Ernst-Merck-Halle – Das Rezept des Paraclesus', *Die Zeit*, 30 October 1958.
56. Barthes, 'Musica Practica', 149.
57. Wilson, *Let's Talk About Love*, 130.
58. Von Moltke, *No Place Like Home*, 17.
59. Hake, *German National Cinema*, 110.
60. Palmowski, *Inventing a Socialist Nation*, 7, 13. For a discussion of GDR Heimat films in the 1950s, see Von Moltke, *No Place Like Home*; Lindenberger, 'Home, Sweet Home'. In the 1960s, TV became central to the construction of Heimat in the GDR. See Jan Palmowski's chapter in this volume (chapter 1).
61. 'Programmblatt 39 des Hot Club Düsseldorf vom 4. 3. 1949'. As quoted in Hoffmann, 'Zur westdeutschen Hot Club-Bewegung der Nachkriegszeit', footnote 43. See also 'Swing vs. the rest', *Anglo-German Rhythm Club* 1 (1949), reproduced in Ansin et al., *Anglo-German Swing Club*.
62. Hoffmann, 'Zur westdeutschen Hot-Club Bewegung der Nachkriegzeit', 71.
63. Hudtwalcker, 'Widersehen mit der Swing Jugend'. Here, Hudtwalcker describes the swing kids' hatbands with stars and stripes, 'short jitterbug pants', 'sombrero-type' hats, red and gold socks and ties. In contrast to many other hot club commentators, Hudtwalcker had a less antagonistic view of these youth at this point and believed their rowdiness could be utilized for a war against conservative taste.
64. Powley, 'A Flying Start'. As reproduced in Ansin, *Anglo-German Swing Club*. Powley was the British head of the joint German-British club in Hamburg.
65. Lucki, 'Die Jazz-Szene vor der Bühne', 11.
66. Ibid.
67. Ibid.
68. In the discussion on jazz in the Academy of Arts described below, Rudorf recommended the American author Sidney Finkelstein's *Jazz: A People's Music* and Joachim Ernst Berendt's *Jazzbuch* to Eisler and the other GDR officials.
69. For a description of radio's role in the history of jazz in postwar Eastern Europe, see Ritter, 'The Radio'.
70. Akademie der Künste, Archiv Hanns Eisler 2854. 'Diskussion über Jazz mit Prof. Hans Eisler in der deutschen Akademie der Künste am 14.5.1956'. The transcript mistakenly spells Rudorf's name as 'Rudolph'.
71. Hermand, 'Attempts to Establish a Socialist Music Culture', 7–11.
72. Tomkins, 'Musik zur Schaffung des neuen sozialistischen Menschen'; Tomkins, 'Sound and Socialist Identity', 112.
73. Butting, *Tanzmusik*, 7–9.
74. Soldovieri, 'Not Only Entertainment', 133–35.
75. Ibid., 134.
76. Larkey, 'Popular Music on East German Television', 178.
77. Visual styles associated with clothing and hair (like jeans, leather jackets, ponytails and 'Elvis curls') were a major preoccupation and worry of the SED. Poiger, *Jazz, Rock and Rebels*, 175–85.
78. Williams, *Marxism and Literature*, 132.
79. This should not be interpreted as an argument that the two different formations necessarily excluded the affects and lived meanings of the other.
80. See the introduction of this volume for a pertinent discussion of Jacques Rancière.

81. BArch, DR 1/243, letter from Hot-Club Düsseldorf to Siegfried Schmidt, 18 January 1956.
82. BArch, DR 1/243, letter from Rudorf to Uszkoreit, 16 February 1955.
83. BArch, DY 24/0392, copy of the meeting plan of the Leipzig Jazz-Interessengemeinschaft, 26 January 1956.
84. Maase, 'Establishing Cultural Democracy'.
85. Maase, *Bravo Amerika*, 18.
86. See Alissa Bellotti's contribution to this volume (chapter 7).
87. Fritzsche, *Life and Death in the Third Reich*, 73.

Bibliography

Ansin, H. et al. (ed.). *Anglo-German Swing Club: Als der Swing zurück nach Hamburg kam Dokumente 1945 bis 1952*. Hamburg: Dölling und Galitz Verlag, 2003.
Barthes, R. 'Musica Practica'. *Image Music Text*. Trans. Stephen Heath. New York: Hill and Wang, 1977.
Berendt, J.E. 'Der Arrivierter Jazz'. *Jazz Echo*, December 1957.
———. *Ein Fenster aus Jazz: Essays, Portraits, Reflexionen*. Frankfurt am Main: Fischer Taschenbuch Verlag, 1978.
———. *Das Jazzbuch: Entwicklung und Bedeutung der Jazzmusik*. Frankfurt am Main: Fischer Bücherei, 1953.
Blume, M. 'Die Geschichte des Eisenacher Jazz – oder die Eisenacher Jazzstory'. Folder AG Jazz Archiv I, Arbeitsgemeinschaft Jazz Eisenach Sammlung, Lippmann+Rau-Musikarchiv Eisenach.
Blüthner, H. 'Die Berliner Hotfreunde'. *Die Jazz-Club News* 17/18 (1947), 26.
Bratfisch, R. (ed.). *Freie Töne: Die Jazzszene in der DDR*. Berlin: Ch. Links Verlag, 2005.
———. 'So viel Anfang war nie: Eine Spurensuche nach 1945', in R. Bratfisch (ed.), *Freie Töne: Die Jazzszene in der DDR* (Berlin: Ch. Links Verlag, 2005), 17–30.
Butting, M. *Tanzmusik Abschlussbericht 1952*. 2 DR 1-240, Bundesarchiv Berlin.
Chion, M. *Audio-Vision: Sound on Screen*. New York: Columbia University Press, 1994.
———. 'The Three Listening Modes', in J. Sterne (ed), *Sound Studies Reader* (New York: Routledge, 2012), 48–53.
DeVeaux, S. 'Constructing the Jazz Tradition: Jazz Historiography'. *Black American Literature Forum* 25(3) (1991), 525–60.
Elsner, J. 'Metamorphoses der Jazzinterpretation: Wandlung der Vortragsweise als Symptom einer inneren Wandlung des Jazz'. *Melodie und Rhythmus* 2(4) (February 1958).
Fark, R. *Die Missachtete Botschaft: Publizistische Aspekte des Jazz im soziokulturellen Wandel*. Berlin: Spiess, 1971.
Fay, J. '"That's Jazz Made in Germany:" "Hallo, Fräulein!" and the Limits of Democratic Pedagogy'. *Cinema Journal* 44(1) (2004), 3–24.
Fenemore, M. *Sex, Thugs and Rock 'N' Roll: Teenage Rebels in Cold-War East Germany*. New York: Berghahn Books, 2009.

'Fragen und Antworten im Non-Stop-Tempo'. *Berliner Zeitung,* 5 November 1958, 4.

Fritzsche, P. *Life and Death in the Third Reich.* Cambridge, MA: Belknap Press of Harvard University Press, 2008.

Gennari, J. *Blowing Hot and Cool: Jazz and its Critics.* Chicago: University of Chicago Press, 2006.

Hake, S. *German National Cinema.* London: Routledge, 2002.

'Haley Krawalle: Saat der Gewalt'. *Der Spiegel,* 5 November 1958, 78–79.

Hermand, J. 'Attempts to Establish a Socialist Music Culture in the Soviet Occupation Zone and the German Democratic Republic, 1945–1965', in E. Larkey (ed.), *Contested Spaces: GDR Rock between Western Influence and Party Control* (Washington, DC: American Institute for Contemporary German Studies, 2000), 4–19.

Hobsch, M. 'Die Drei von der Tankstelle: Schlagerfilme', in P. Rösgen (ed.), *Melodien für Millionen: Das Jahrhundert des Schlagers* (Bielefeld: Stiftung Haus der Geschichte der Bundesrepublik Deutschland, 2008), 34–41.

Hoffmann, B. 'Liebe, Jazz, und Übermut: Der swingende Heimatfilm der 1950er Jahre', in T. Phleps (ed.), *Heimatlose Klänge? Regional Musiklandschaften heute* (Karben: Coda Verlag, 2002), 259–88.

——. 'Zur westdeutschen Hot Club-Bewegung der Nachkriegszeit', in R. von Zahn (ed.), *Jazz in Nordrhein-Westfalen seit 1946* (Cologne: Musikland NRW Band 1, 1999), 64–98.

Hudtwalcker, O. 'Widersehen mit der Swing Jugend: Kurt Widmann in Hamburg'. *Hot Club News* 23/24 (1947).

Hurley, A.W. *The Return of Jazz: Joachim Ernst Berendt and West German Cultural Change.* New York: Berghahn Books, 2009.

Jost, E. *That's Jazz, der Sound des 20: Jahrhundert: eine Ausstellung der Stadt Darmstadt.* Darmstadt: Institut Mathildenhöhe, 1988.

Judt, T. *Postwar: A History of Europe Since 1945.* New York: Penguin Books, 2005.

Kater, M.H. *Different Drummers: Jazz in the Culture of Nazi Germany.* Oxford: Oxford University Press, 1992.

'Konzertante Schlägerei: Rock n' Roll Tumulte in der Hamburger Ernst-Merck-Halle – Das Rezept des Paraclesus'. *Die Zeit,* 30 October 1958.

Lange, H.H. *Jazz in Deutschland: Die Deutsche Jazz-Chronik bis 1960.* Hildesheim: Olms Presse, 1996.

Larkey, E. 'Popular Music on East German Television: Constructing the Televisual Pop Community in the GDR', in Peter Goddard (ed.), *Popular Television in Authoritarian Europe* (New York: Manchester University Press, 2013), 176–93.

Lindenberger, T. 'Home, Sweet Home: Desperately Seeking Heimat in Early DEFA Films'. *Film History* 18(1) (2006), 46–58.

Lopes, P. *The Rise of the Jazz Art World.* Cambridge: Cambridge University Press, 2002.

Lucki. 'Die Jazz-Szene vor der Bühne: Eine Umschau unter Jazzkonzert-Besuchern'. *Jazz Podium* (September 1953).

Ludewig, A. *Screening Nostalgia: 100 Years of German Heimat Film.* Bielefeld: Transcript Verlag, 2014.

Maase, K. *Bravo Amerika: Erkundungen zur Jugendkultur der Bundesrepublik in den fünfziger Jahren.* Hamburg: Junius Verlag, 1992.

————. 'Establishing Cultural Democracy: Youth, "Americanization," and the Irresistible Rise of Popular Culture', in H. Schissler (ed.), *The Miracle Years: A Cultural History of West Germany, 1949–1968* (Princeton, NJ: Princeton University Press, 2001), 428–50.

Meyer, Ernst H. 'Realismus – die Lebensfrage der deutschen Musik'. *Musik und Gesellschaft* 1(2) (1951), 38–43.

Palmowski, J. *Inventing a Socialist Nation: Heimat and the Politics of Everyday Life in the GDR, 1945–1990.* New York: Cambridge University Press, 2009.

Petrescu, M. 'Domesticating the Vamp: Jazz and the Dance Melodrama in Weimar Cinema'. *Seminar: A Journal of Germanic Studies* 46(3) (2010), 276–92.

Poiger, U. *Jazz, Rock and Rebels: Cold War Politics and American Culture in a Divided Germany.* Berkeley: University of California Press, 2000.

Powley, N.A. 'A Flying Start'. *British Voices Network Anglo-German Swing Club News Sheet* 3 (1949).

'Protokoll zur Diskussion über *Jazzmusik* am 8. Februar 1957', DR 1/243, Bundesarchiv Berlin.

Rippey, T.E. 'Rationalisation, Race and the Weimar Response to Jazz'. *German Life and Letters* 60(1) (2007), 75–97.

Ritter, R. 'The Radio – a Jazz instrument of its Own', in G. Pickham and R. Ritter (eds), *Jazz behind the Iron Curtain: Jazz under State Socialism* (Frankfurt am Main: Peter Lang, 2010), 35–55.

Rudorf, R. 'Für eine frohe, ausdrucksvolle Tanzmusik'. *Musik und Gesellschaft* 2(8) (1952), 247–52.

————. *Jazz in der Zone.* Cologne: Kiepenheuer & Witsch, 1964.

Schildt, A. *Moderne Zeiten: Freizeit, Massenmedien und 'Zeitgeist' in der Bundesrepublik.* Hamburg: Christians, 1995.

Schissler, H. (ed.). *The Miracle Years: A Cultural History of West Germany, 1949–1968.* Princeton, NJ: Princeton University Press, 2001.

Schmidt, M.J. 'The Multi-Sensory Object: Jazz, the Modern Media and the History of the Senses in Germany'. PhD thesis, The University of Texas at Austin, 2014.

Schwab, J. *Der Frankfurt Sound: Eine Stadt und ihre Jazzgeschichte(n).* Frankfurt am Main: Societaets Verlag, 2005.

Seeßlen, G. 'Durch die Heimat und so weiter: Heimatfilme, Schlagerfilme und Ferienfilme der fünfziger Jahre', in H. Hoffman and W. Schobert (eds), *Zwischen Gestern und Morgan: Westdeutscher Nachkriegsfilm 1946–1962* (Frankfurt am Main: Deutsches Filmmuseum, 1989), 136–63.

Soldovieri, S. 'Not Only Entertainment: Sights and Sounds of the DEFA Music Film', in M. Silberman and H. Wrage (eds), *DEFA at the Crossroads of East German and International Film Culture: A Companion* (Boston: De Gruyter, 2014), 133–56.

Thacker, T. 'The Fifth Column: Dance Music in the Early German Democratic Republic', in P. Major and J. Osmond (eds), *The Workers' and Peasants' State: Communism and Society in East Germany under Ulbricht 1945–1971* (New York: Palgrave, 2002), 227–43.

————. *Music after Hitler, 1945–1955.* Aldershot, England: Ashgate, 2007.

Tomkins, D. 'Musik zur Schaffung des neuen sozialistischen Menschen: Offizielle Musikpolitik des Zentralkommitees der SED in der DDR in den 50er Jahren', in T. Bendikowski et al. (eds), *Die Macht der Töne: Musik als Mittel politischer Identitätsfindung im 20 Jahrhundert* (Münster: Westfälisches Dampfboot, 2003), 105–13.

———. 'Sound and Socialist Identity: Negotiating the Musical Soundscape in the Stalinist GDR', in F. Feiereisen and A.M. Hill (eds), *Germany in the Loud Twentieth Century: An Introduction* (New York: Oxford University Press, 2012), 111–24.

Von Moltke, J. *No Place Like Home: Locations of Heimat in German Cinema*. Berkeley: University of California Press, 2005.

Von Saldern, A. 'Der Schlager is grundsächlich ein Politikum: Populäre Musik in der DDR', in P. Rösgen (ed.), *Melodien für die Millionen: Das Jahrhundert des Schlagers* (Bielefeld: Stiftung Haus der Geschichte der Bundesrepublik Deutschland, 2008), 106–11.

Williams, R. *Marxism and Literature*. New York: Oxford University Press, 1977.

Wilson, C. *Let's Talk About Love: A Journey to the End of Taste*. New York: Continuun, 2007.

Wipplinger, J. 'The Jazz Republic: Music, Race and American Culture in Weimar Germany'. PhD thesis, The University of Michigan, 2006.

Chapter 11

Alles Geschmackssache?
Shaping (Gustatory) Tastes in East and West Germany

Alice Weinreb

O n 9 November 1989, the Berlin Wall fell. In the days and weeks that followed, throngs of East Germans rushed over the newly open border. That same month, the Federal Republic's satirical magazine *Titanic* published an issue dedicated to this historic moment. The November 1989 title image depicted a smiling *Zonen-Gabi*, or 'Gabi from the Eastern zone'. Gaby was dressed in an ill-fitting jean jacket at least a decade out of fashion, with curly red hair shorn in an unfashionably boyish cut and a goofy grin shining out of her freckled face. In her left hand she clutched an enormous cucumber, carefully peeled so that strips of green skin fell down the cucumber's flesh like a banana peel. The headline was Gabi's proud exclamation: 'my first banana'. This famous image revolves around long-held West German assumptions about East German taste. Gabi's lack of taste is exposed in her lack of (culinary) knowledge – mistaking a cucumber for a banana – as well as in her body itself, with its out-of-date fashion, unflattering haircut and stocky asexuality, reflecting and revealing her 'tastelessness'. The key to the joke is the particular significance of the banana; while the obvious assumption is that the absence of bananas in the GDR has resulted in a chronically underdeveloped sense of taste amongst East Germans, what the image most clearly reveals is how central bananas were to the West Germans' own sense of self – their identity as modern, civilized and tasteful citizens of the world.

Bananas had long been an obsession for West Germans, who recognized them as one of the most important symbols of postwar prosperity and luxury consumption. In the early 1950s, Konrad Adenauer had successfully negotiated the FRG's right to import bananas tax-free, making them one of West Germany's cheapest fruits. (His commitment to cheap bananas was such that he threatened to boycott the formation of the European Community were his country not granted this unique privilege.)[1] As early as 1953, West German cookbooks had chapters titled 'What do I do with all these bananas?'[2] In contrast, the East German SED had little access to cheap bananas, though even the geeky Gabi was unlikely to have never enjoyed the mystical pleasures of the fruit.[3] The GDR's primary source of tropical fruits, Cuba, was not a banana producer, and supplies from North Africa and Asia were unreliable, dictated by politics rather than demand, and often prohibitively expensive. Even during the peak of the GDR's consumer prosperity, bananas, like most tropical fruits, were available only during holidays and then in limited quantities.[4]

This chapter opens with this post-*Wende* invocation of East and West Germany as two populations that were distinguished from one another by the presence or absence of good taste. Throughout Germany's division, the FRG had generally conceptualized the GDR as a space of poor, outdated or 'lower-class' tastes. During the Cold War, such assumptions were often made about communism writ large. However, I argue that the category of (food) taste became especially central to German-German division because of the divided country's fraught relationship with the food economy.[5] It is this longer, twentieth-century history of conflict around food that contextualizes the prevalence of gustatory stereotypes of former East Germans (the prominence of Spreewald pickles in *Good Bye Lenin*) as well as the phenomenon of *Ostalgie* (which often venerates the food products and recipes of the former GDR). More generally, since the severe food shortages and differential rationing plans of the defeated country's postwar hunger years, German-German stereotypes of one another have consistently relied upon invocations of particular foods, flavours and ways of eating.

As Bourdieu famously noted in his classic study of the relationship between class identity and taste, taste as a method of social ordering and hierarchy is intimately connected with food: the kind and amount of food consumed, as well as how it is eaten.[6] Perhaps nowhere is the relationship between food and social status more visible, and more contested, than in the case of obesity. Being overweight generally is a bodily state that has a complicated relationship to the concept of good taste. Fatness had traditionally been linked to someone who has an abundance of taste – a *Feinschmecker* or at least someone who loves to eat. However, modern aesthetic categories have more frequently cast fatness as unattractive and undesirable, visible proof of the person's excessive or inappropriate appetites. As a result, fatness seems to show that an individual's tastes literally shape his or her body. Relative assessments of a body's size illustrate the taste of the person. Too much fat reveals a preference for particular and inferior foods, while a slim body implies better tastes and a superior diet. The twentieth century, and especially the decades following the Second World War, witnessed the rise of the 'tyranny of slenderness', an aesthetic shift that accompanied an inversion of cultural capital and food value. Within the modern industrial economy, the poor and inadequately nourished were increasingly associated with obesity. More specifically, low-calorie and 'fresh' foods (exotic fruits, salads, sushi) became the purview of society's elites, while high-calorie and heavily processed foods (soda, candy, fast food) have become the staples of the lower segments of society.

Divided Germany offers a unique and productive site to explore such patterns linking bodies, tastes and economic development. This chapter uses the so-called obesity epidemic that struck both East and West Germany in the 1970s to explore the entangled economic and cultural histories of the two German states. It does this by tracing the two German states' respective food systems, which it understands as political economies in the sense described by Foucault in his lectures on the birth of biopolitics: 'the organization, distribution and limitation of powers in a society'.[7] This approach suggests that the ways in which the GDR and the FRG managed food production, consumption and distribution expose links between everyday acts of cooking and eating and biopolitical strategies of modern states. At the same time, the particular case of obesity reveals the profound limitations of such biopolitical ambitions.

Fatness, which was recognized as a major medical and economic problem in both German states, seemed to prove to both socialist and capitalist nutritionists the inadequacy of German popular taste. Comparing the two states' medical explanations for why being overweight was becoming such a problem contextualizes the quite different strategies with which they tried to combat obesity.[8] Despite important differences in attitudes and policies towards overweight, however, East and West Germany ultimately had more in common when it came to the 'battle of the bulge'. Both states agreed that the problem of fatness was a problem in popular taste, though they had different methods of trying to shift German taste buds away from a perceived preference for 'the fatty pork leg, the fatty sauce, the fatty sausage, the sweet and fatty cake'.[9] While they developed varied and often innovative strategies for attempting to change peoples' tastes for foods, ultimately they were forced to admit defeat. Neither the individualistic consumer abundance of the West nor the state-managed egalitarianism of the East proved capable of changing German tastes.

The Postwar Rise of Obesity in Divided Germany

Fatness had a long history in the FRG, where doctors began warning about growing levels of overweight almost as soon as the infamous hunger years came to an end. Indeed, the currency reform of 1948 was often seen as the symbolic beginning of a long-term struggle with fatness, a problem that was literally embodied in the *Fresswelle*, or 'feeding frenzy', that emerged in the first decade of the FRG. After more than a decade of strict rationing and several years of extreme shortages and hunger, it is unsurprising that Germans first focused their growing consumer power on food. Less than a year after the founding of the FRG, nutritionists were warning that 'since the general changes in the diet, in a surprisingly short time observations of obesity are multiplying, wherein doubtless an excess of food ... plays a decisive role'.[10] In other words, unlike other Western countries, West Germany's fat problem was understood as a specifically postwar phenomenon and signified a break with the German past.

The nation's first wave of fatness was unabashedly celebrated, linked to the increased consumption of gourmet and expensive food items. Figures like economic minister Ludwig Erhard embodied in his excessive girth the FRG's prosperity. Indeed, excessive quantities of fat came to define postwar Germany, setting it apart from the starvation of the hunger years, as well as the imagined self-control and restraint of the war and pre-war years: 'since here in the Federal Republic all groceries are available again in abundance, the number of overweight people has been growing on a regrettable scale'.[11] The large-scale consumption of food was celebrated in public eating contests, popular songs and private social gatherings. The newly founded industry publication *The Food Economy* (*Die Ernährungswirtschaft*) happily reported in 1954 that 'the consumption of products of a more elevated life style, specifically including high-end food stuffs, has steadily grown since the overcoming of scarcity, since the end of rationing, and with the currency reform'.[12] That same year, ads began to warn the West German public of the need for moderation:

> we indulged in the pleasures of life without moderation and restraint, and barely gave a thought to the fact that at some point we would have to pay for this mindless undertaking, that one day our organism would cease to cooperate and would confront us with a hefty bill. In the meantime, many things have changed entirely. Life is worth living again, and as a result we again regard health as the supreme good.[13]

This wave of eating rapidly reshaped German bodies. While overweight had reached its lowest point in twentieth-century Germany during the occupation, when there was a reported rate of 2 per cent overweight (with pre-war rates estimated at around 12 per cent), by 1951, rates had already risen to 11 per cent.[14] Importantly, this early postwar fatness was linked with prosperity and hard-working German businessmen – as the pseudo-medical label 'Manager's Disease' made clear. In 1953, the *Spiegel* sensationally reported that West Germany's 'educated elite are being worked to death ... compared with the rates of death of the total population looms the death of 50% more leading business men than the statistical average'.[15] These men's fatness was a result not of their excessive consumption but of their excessive commitment to postwar economic production. They were the heart and soul of the economic miracle – and the price they paid was their excessive bulk.

The 1973 Oil Crisis seemed to signal the end of the country's remarkable economic growth; along with a rise in unemployment, painful cycles of stagflation and a widespread sense of discontent, West German society finally moved away from this association of prosperity and celebratory consumption with fatness. Instead, it was in an atmosphere of increasing class tensions, wherein the working class was pathologized as a threat to social stability rather than a productive resource, that nutritionists first began warning of a looming obesity epidemic. This new medical discourse emphasized individual inadequacies (emotional immaturity, inadequately developed tastes, greed) as causes for overweight, rather than, as had been the case with the fat managers, excessive responsibility and an overdeveloped work ethic. In turn, fatness came to be seen as a problem primarily of the working rather than the middle class, as well as being associated increasingly with women and children. In a dramatic shift from reports made just a decade earlier, in 1972 'overweight is more frequent in lower social classes than in higher ones'.[16] New studies revealed that while previously it had been gourmands who were thought to eat excessively due to their embrace of gustatory pleasure, now it was people of lower educational levels who ate too much because they 'hold especially tightly to their traditional eating habits'.[17] This new form of fatness was thus connected to a weaker, rather than a stronger, economy. While wealthy men's fatness seemed proof of their productivity and the country's booming consumer marketplace, the new rise of fat workers made overweight potentially hamper productivity, suddenly transforming fat bodies into an economic liability. As a result, the new obesity epidemic inspired a wave of governmental interventions, including a wide-reaching curriculum reform, marketing and advertising reforms and numerous national and regional healthy eating and weight-loss programmes.

In the GDR, the gradual emergence of widespread overweight as a medical problem was also intimately intertwined with the shape of the postwar economy; however, its developmental trajectory, and thus its meaning, was quite different there than it was in the FRG. In the East, obesity in any form did not become a major medical issue until the 1970s; certainly, the country's lagging economic growth meant that the *Fresswelle* came to the East later and differently. Rationing lasted for a decade longer in the GDR than the FRG, and chronic shortages as well as longer working weeks and more physical labour prevented rapid and extreme weight gain. However, fatness was not simply less present in the poorer GDR; it also occupied a distinct position in the socialist moral economy, where, despite a postwar consensus on the harms of overweight, it was difficult to conclusively condemn fatness. The head of the national Institute for Health Education, addressing the failures of various efforts to improve popular eating habits, explained that 'our current health problems are the problems of a rich society, from the first we should see this, and for all complaints about the widespread overweight and the growing abuse of natural stimulants we should not forget that after all we wanted this high quality of life and fought hard for it'.[18] One reason for this is that socialism claimed as one of its greatest victories the abolition of hunger – something that was understood as literally impossible in a socialist state. A 1973 speech on 'nutrition in a socialist society' noted with pride that 'in contrast to past times and overcome social orders, every citizen of our republic has enough to eat; everyone is free of the misery of watching his children go hungry while others waste food'.[19] A full belly represented economic success and social equity, while hunger signalled moral failure and economic exploitation. Much as they might bemoan excessive caloric consumption, socialist health experts never forgot their hungry past, as celebrity chef Kurt Drummer pointed out in a best-selling cookbook promoting healthier recipes; 'after all we haven't lived for so long in this excess. Less than two centuries ago cakes and tarts were still a luxury of which the poorer levels of the population generally could only dream'.[20] Overweight was linked with egalitarianism and cheapness, rather than, as in the West, with the over-abundance of luxury foods.

Nonetheless, doctors felt increasingly compelled to speak out against growing levels of fatness. In 1970, a national study of obesity in the GDR, which estimated that a third of the adult population was seriously overweight, claimed that obesity's 'spread in the GDR (as in all developed countries) has taken on epidemic character, and everything points to the fact that it will continue to grow in scope and severity'.[21] As in the West, the health threats of overweight were severe. Doctors were especially alarmed by the stagnation of life expectancy, which they blamed on diet-related health problems; with the exception of steadily declining rates of infant mortality, in the 1980s young people in the GDR could not expect to live longer than their parents.[22] In 1985, an analysis of the development of a healthy diet for the population determined that 'in the GDR the nutritional situation is above all shaped by overeating and thus the overweight of about 30% of the population'.[23] A study from the late 1980s determined that more than three out of four deaths in the GDR were 'caused by sicknesses in which an inadequate diet played an especially important role ... in addition to causing a substantial reduction of quality of life for afflicted citizens, the consequences of improper diet are high economic costs and limitations of productivity'.[24]

Changing Tastes in the East

Despite differences in the meaning of overweight – in the West it was seen as a negative reflection of the harms of modernization, in the East as a phase in an ultimately positive and teleological development away from poverty and hunger into a socialist modernity – both states were united by a belief in the need to reduce levels of overweight in their respective societies. Both East and West Germany had well-developed and well-funded networks of nutritional education, both of which, by the 1970s, agreed that obesity and improper popular diets were their primary foci. For these German nutritionists, the goal of modern nutritional education was to tackle diet-related health problems through retraining popular tastes. Through a combination of propagandistic scare tactics and increased interventions in childhood and workplace diets, both states struggled throughout the 1970s and 1980s to change German tastes. Fatness was due to an excessive intake of calories – and these calories were always linked with the consumption of the same basic foodstuffs. Regardless of age, gender or class of the afflicted individual, whether in Bavaria or Thuringia, Dresden or Cologne, both East and West German nutritionists blamed popular preference for the 'traditional' German diet for health problems. This meant that the only way to combat obesity was to change the foods that people wanted to eat – in other words, to change their tastes.

The GDR conceptualized popular diet as an 'issue of all of society' (*gesamtgesellschaftliches Anliegen*); this meant that the food economy – understood as the myriad processes regulating the production, consumption and distribution of the country's foodstuffs – was a political priority, implicitly requiring state intervention in questions of popular diet as well as individual food tastes. No element of this national food economy more clearly represented the societal components of eating than the country's extensive collective feeding programmes; East German nutritionists and economists perceived collective meals as a method of improving popular tastes and thus dietary health. As heavily regulated and thus potentially optimizable sites of food consumption which reached almost the entirety of the country's population, the GDR's network of childcare and school cafeterias and workplace canteens thus represented the much-celebrated pinnacle of the country's food system.

Indeed, East Germany's highly regulated and well-researched collective meal programmes drew international admiration as a low-budget method for improving popular health. In 1975, the British *Morning Star* reported admiringly on the latest innovations in East German canteens. The system, described as 'staggeringly simple – despite the complexity of its details', was essentially an elaborate card catalogue made up of 1350 regional dishes, with each card listing 'recipe, quantities needed for various groups, from infants to heavy workers, caloric content, minerals, vitamins and cost per head ... so the school, kindergarten, old folks home, clinic or whatever fills in a simple form and the computer prints out every suitable menu for the age, type of consumer, season and so on'. The resultant 'carefully balanced meals' promised to provide a defence 'against the main enemy – fat – while ensuring a more healthy diet in other ways'.[25] Indeed, contrary to West German assumptions that automatically equated collective eating with an unhealthy diet, and especially with overweight, a 1969 proposal for the Ministry of Health noted that 'a generous support of collective feeding programs would be far and away the quickest way to an immediate improvement in popular health and in addition would have substantial pedagogical impact on the eating habits of the entire population'.[26] For example, as part of a nationwide initiative to increase fish consumption, experts claimed that the best way to overcome popular prejudice against fish was to target the populations who ate regularly at canteens: 'only through focused influencing of consumer opinion among children, students and workers can an increase in the number of [fish] dishes be achieved ... out of this context emerges the task of the massive popularization of fish and also the responsibility that kitchens bear in their food production'.[27] In fact, despite prioritizing the nation's canteens for funding, research and food supplies, nutritionists consistently found that the canteens and cafeterias that were supposed to shape tastes succumbed to worker desires rather than modifying them. Time and again healthy options were rejected by canteen visitors; reduced-fat meals and vegetarian options inspired personal insults and formal complaints from angry men and women who perceived these undesirable meals as inadequate compensation for their labour.[28] Resultant high levels of waste and hostile atmospheres overpowered modern nutritional training and good intentions on the part of

canteen chefs; even in socialism, workplace canteens proved conservative and reactive rather than progressive and proactive.

This realization encouraged nutritionists to increasingly focus attention on private rather than public food consumption. From the perspective of health, what distinguished the GDR from capitalist food systems
was its centralized structure – which, ideally, meant that nutritionists
actually determined the foodstuffs that were made available to the public.
The idea was that regulating the supply of food products available to
consumers would give nutritionists the ability to directly influence what
people were eating. East Germans should have an abundance of products available to them, but not the sort of excessive capitalist abundance
famous in the West. What distinguished the GDR from the West 'is not
that we principally do not advertise, rather that we see at our core the
human being as the middle point of these efforts, while the capitalist sees
profit as the target'.[29]

As with canteens, however, top-down oversight did not guarantee control over actual food intake. Supply-related pressures shaped the GDR's
food economy at all levels of consumption, distribution and production –
and rarely in ways that accorded to nutritional guidelines or official
recommendations. In this sense, the difference between socialist propaganda and capitalist advertising was blurred, if not erased. Frequently a
food company would decide to modify a product, or a restaurant would
change a recipe, to use up more or less of a particular foodstuff, often at
the expense of popular health. A nutritional study from 1967, for example,
found that the 'the GDR is currently the last country [in Europe] where a
light rye bread without substantial wheat flour added is still the primary
sort of bread consumed'.[30] (The FRG, for example, had switched to primarily wheat-based breads soon after the end of the Second World War.)
For consumers, the continued dominance of rye bread was generally
seen as an undesirable marker of poverty; the switch to more expensive,
lighter wheat bread, and especially fluffy white rolls, was interpreted as
a marker of prosperity. Nonetheless, despite popular desires to the contrary, the author of the study insisted that 'for health reasons we must do
everything we can to retain the role of rye bread in our diet'. The health
advantages were found not simply in the higher nutritional value of rye,
but in the fact that studies found that consumers used smaller quantities of butters, meat and cheese on rye bread than they did on equivalent slices of wheat bread. (This was due to different levels of moisture,
degree of satiation and different 'mouth feels' for the different grains.)
The higher the rate of rye bread consumption, the greater percentage of
diet was made up by actual grains, and the lower the percentage made up
of cold cuts and bread-spreads. For this reason, the lead author claimed

that continuing these high rates of rye bread consumption offered 'a real chance to work against a further increase in our fat consumption'.[31]

The health benefits of rye bread, however, could not outweigh economic and political considerations. Due to its heavy consumption of pure rye bread, the GDR actually began to run short on its primary indigenous crop; by the early 1960s, economists began to worry that 'not enough rye will be available to tide us over until the new harvest'.[32] As a result, the government approved the production and mass sale of a new variety of bread composed of a much higher ratio of wheat to rye flour (40:60); at that time, the standard 'mixed flour' bread was made with a ratio of 15:85. The introduction of this high-wheat bread, which was to be priced slightly higher than the darker rye loaf, was enabled (and inspired) by the fact that the USSR was eager to export wheat flour, but not rye, to the GDR. As a result, despite the recognized health benefits of rye flour over wheat, the SED began to promote bread made of imported wheat flour, accurately predicting that 'throughout the population generally this bread will be experienced as a high quality product because it is, in contrast to the standard [rye] bread, much lighter. Experiences show that the population prefers to buy lighter breads'.[33] A cultural preference previously condemned as both nutritionally and economically disadvantageous became geopolitically useful. Ultimately, East Germans did gradually make the switch to mixed-flour and white breads (though throughout division continuing to consume more rye than West Germans).

The same study that had argued for a health-conscious preservation of the population's rye consumption noted with frustration that the country's supply of rye bread itself was sorely lacking when it came to quality. Lead author Dr M. Rothe's laboratory analyses found that between 40 and 58 per cent of the bread samples tested were flawed or of inferior quality. Indeed, rye breads were of substantially lower quality than the tested wheat breads, precisely because wheat flour was imported; it was thus far more standardized and regulated than regionally produced rye.[34] Despite frequent calls for voluntary 'bread competitions' to motivate bakers to improve their bread quality, rye and whole grain breads continued to be of an unacceptably poor and variable quality, and imported wheat flour continued to produce more consistent, and thus more desirable, bread.

While unexpected shortages, like that of rye, were especially common, unanticipated surpluses could have similarly unhealthful consequences for the popular diet. By the 1970s East German dairies had begun to accumulate an excess of milk and milk fat, which was extracted from milk to produce the reduced-fat versions most commonly drunk.[35] The need to use up this fat inspired a dairy in Brandenburg to produce a new,

higher-fat milk with 3.2 per cent fat content, which the dairy optimisti-
cally hoped would be 'drunk enthusiastically by those people who up to
now were not milk drinkers'.[36] Local newspapers published announcements for the new product using statements provided by the dairy; they
proclaimed that

> Milk is healthy, for its fat is easily digestible and thus especially good for
> the body, milk refreshes, for it rapidly builds up the strength that has been
> exhausted through hard physical or mental energy, and it keeps you slim.
> Thus, you should use the opportunity to drink fattier milk and more often
> limit your consumption of the difficult-to-digest fats in butter and margarine.[37]

Upon reading such laudatory announcements in the local papers, several nutritionists from the East German Central Institute for Nutrition,
in accordance with an at-the-time unquestioned medical consensus that
reduced fat intake was key for popular health and successful weight loss,
wrote angry letters to the newspaper editors as well as to the ministry of
health, reporting that 'mystical and misleading advertisements are being
produced for the new fattier milk products that are in contradiction to
general nutritional knowledge and are certain to create false ideas in
our population'.[38] In a tense exchange between the Central Institute for
Nutrition and the Institute for Milk Research, the nutritionist Dr Grütte
clarified that 'from a nutritional perspective, an increase in milk consumption would be heartily embraced. This does not however include
also an increase in milk fat. Policies that would lead to the excess available milk fat being redistributed to the population through other products cannot be supported from the perspective of nutritional health'.[39]
Dr Spengler reminded the dairy researchers that they had only received
state permission to begin producing this higher-fat milk because they
had agreed 'that ads not be produced that refer to possible health benefits
for products with higher fat content'.[40] And Dr Haenel, in a passionate
letter to the local *Brandenburgischen Neuesten Nachrichten*, dismantled the
advertisement word for word:

> The only accurate argument for the propagating of this milk can be found in
> the words that it is 'pleasantly *vollmundig*' and thus tastes better … that milk
> keeps you feeling fresh is an assertion that cannot be proven and certainly
> one that cannot be generalized … the question of slimness is a question of
> caloric balance, not a question of individual food products. Who eats too
> much, regardless of whether the calories come from milk, pork, eggs, cake, or
> other foodstuffs and who has a tendency to accumulate fat, will become fat:
> he who eats less, even if he does not drink milk, is or will become slim. In the
> GDR it is well known that fat consumption is very high: on average we eat 40%
> more fat than recommended by scientists. A food that, on the basis of 'pleasant

Vollmundigkeit', increases fat consumption, cannot from a nutritional perspective be recommended.[41]

While the *BNN* published Haenel's rejoinder alongside the new milk advertisements, the product continued to be produced and distributed widely and sales were disappointingly high. Despite an official consensus that the population needed to lose weight, and widely circulated medical advice as to how to achieve this goal, both individual tastes and regional economic priorities – in this case the local need to dispose of excess fats – determined popular food supplies. The growing medical consensus that the East German population needed to lose weight directly countered economic principles that encouraged high levels of food consumption; policies as essential to the socialist state as frozen core food prices were condemned as 'diametrically opposed to the principles of a healthy diet'.[42] The constant pressure on the food industry to increase profit while decreasing cost inspired innovations like higher-fat milk and new varieties of candies and chocolates; shortages in artificial sweeteners and limitations in technological and chemical equipment meant that diet foods clearly implied increased costs, rather than representing, as was the case in the West, an important and growing new market share.

Changing Tastes in the West

While the FRG's first *Fresswelle* had been blamed on excessive and celebratory consumption, the more negatively interpreted obesity of the 1970s was seen as evidence of a deeply disordered society. The population's troublesome levels of overweight were attributed to the collapse of home-cooked meals, a shift in eating habits that symbolized the wider shifts in familial structures and patterns of daily living that accompanied the transition to a modern industrial economy. While equating an industrial economy with the disappearance of the family meal is by no means specific to the FRG, typically rising rates of female employment are the primary target for criticism: women abandon their kitchens as they join the industrial workforce. In West Germany, however, both restrictive legislation and tremendous social pressure effectively discouraged female wage labour. Here, the decline in family meals was attributed to the particular demands of the postwar economy on male workers. Nutritionists explained that steadily shortening lunch breaks and growing distances between living and working places made it increasingly impossible for the country's men to go home for a hot midday meal. This in turn forced men to turn to canteens for their meals, a shift which was seen as not only a threat to German culture, but also German health. Indeed, in the West, collective feeding was seen as inherently detrimental and canteens became a symbol and symptom of the disorders of a modern society.

Unlike in the GDR, canteens did not represent promise to West German nutritionists but a clear threat to public health. Canteens did not suggest the possibility of optimizing worker health and thus increasing productivity, as they did in the East. Instead, West German economists conceptualized canteens' primary function as a way of placating the workforce. Thus, although nutritionists recommended that canteen chefs cook healthy and well-balanced meals, they admitted that 'the first and most important aspect [of canteen meals] is that they meet the tastes and expectations of the workers … for them, a good meal is a large piece of roasted meat, a fatty soup or sauce and preferably white bread'.[43] Even when individual chefs might strive to create meals that met new nutritional requirements, factory leaders continually insisted that popular satisfaction (as well as generally maintaining low costs), rather than health, be canteens' main goals.

In the country's first attempt to counteract this normalization of the high-calorie and low-nutrient canteen meal, in 1977, the *Bundeszentrale für gesundheitliche Aufklärung* organized the first ever West German weight loss programme (*Fit statt fett*) that targeted workplace canteens. The official goals of the programme were 'to intensively pursue bringing healthy nutrition and a reduction in general inactivity into the workplace', and to 'make easily available to those workers partaking of the canteen meals information and practical information about false nutrition and inadequate physical activity'.[44] In addition, the programme hoped to use canteens to 'spread knowledge about modern eating into the family … for eating is not only the taking in of nutrients – eating should be fun'.[45]

Despite massive preparations and financial investment, however, 'interest remained substantially below what was anticipated'.[46] Planners anticipated a minimum of 5000 companies participating; instead, 679 mailed in for the educational materials and of those only 19 per cent requested more than the initial introductory package (a portable infocentre with educational pamphlets of eating tips, and table cloths and bumper stickers with the *Fit statt fett* logo).[47] And, despite the programme, canteen chefs noted that 'the favourite dishes for everyone are still schnitzel and *Eintopf*'.[48] The failure of this attempt to remake working-class male eating habits confirmed a growing trend in the Ministry of Health Education to turn its attention to the family – and especially the mothers who were understood as the focal point and primary manager of these families.[49] As a result, by the late 1970s, the 'war against fatness' in the FRG had come to focus primarily upon the mother-child relationship as a solution not only to the current obesity crisis, but as the only way to stave off the rise of future generations of ever fatter Germans.[50]

As a result, diet was a core component of the national health programme 'Family – each for one another', which was initiated in 1978 as a direct response to the new 'epidemic'. The programme emphasized nutritional education for children and parents, singling out pregnant women 'of the well-educated middle class' as its target audience.[51] The growing interest in this new demographic accompanied an increasingly psychological approach to obesity, which was seen as an 'emotional' problem that required therapy, similar to other mental disorders. In this way, the fat body became a visual sign of an internal, and otherwise invisible, disorder. This new approach, which echoed analogous trends in the United States, encouraged the rise of new forms of weight loss techniques based on Behaviour Modification Therapy, a technique which had met with prior success in the US as a way of treating addiction, especially cigarette smoking.[52]

This shift in approach meant new targets of blame; rather than implying that 'modern society' was the cause of the nation's health problems, nutritionists equated obesity with other forms of harmful behaviour which 'increase risk factors', claiming that such negative habits were 'learned false behaviour. Learned false behaviour can in principle be modified'.[53] Traditional nutritional education, which had focused on teaching West German women to cook or shop differently, seemed inadequate; while prior efforts to steer popular eating had assumed that either unfavourable social conditions (the need to eat in canteens, for example) or general ignorance (housewives' inability to prepare proper meals) were to blame, this 'psychological' approach focused on individual fat people as the problem, transforming fatness into evidence of bad behaviour. Thus, losing weight required people to behave differently. The programme coordinator for the nation-wide weight-loss action plan 'Diet and Movement' invoked the eponymous German etiquette guide when describing the requirements for successful weight loss: 'consistency, patience and skill are necessary to get people to change their habits and adopt an appropriate diet that satisfies them psychically. The help of a so-called "behaviour guide" à *la Knigge* would be useful in achieving this change'.[54]

Alongside such calls to remake individual behaviour, West German doctors argued that a return to imagined-as-traditional social structures was the ultimate solution to the rise in overweight, thus explicitly conceptualizing women's behaviour as the determinant factor in the explosion of obesity. According to these experts, maternal cooking, female unemployment and family meals offered the best strategies for fighting overweight. These socio-economic behaviours were cast as individual choices rather than responses to a general economic situation. In other words, women were encouraged to 'choose' to stay at home and cook for their families to ensure individual and societal health. In this way, obesity was associated with inadequate or flawed mothering amongst the working classes, the population least likely to have the idealized stay-at-home cooking mother of West German nutritionists' fantasies. Not coincidentally, this newly classed and gendered way of understanding obesity emerged at the same time as the rise of the West German feminist movement as well as widely publicized experiments in communal living and alternative family and child-rearing strategies. Alongside such challenges to West German social norms, the economic downturn ushered in by the 1973 Oil Crisis meant that prosperity seemed less guaranteed, and the poor and working class potentially more threatening. Anti-obesity propaganda increasingly demonized the unsophisticated palate and excessive appetites of blue-collar workers at the same time as mothers and wives were held accountable for the country's expanding waistlines. Working men were told to eat and drink less of what they were assumed to want (meat, potatoes, beer) and more of what they were believed not to like (fruit, salad). Women, on the other hand, were encouraged to modify their families' food intake by sneaking in healthier ingredients, reducing portion size, replacing tried-and-true German recipes with more exotic and healthier international ones, and by developing better self-esteem for themselves and their children.

None of these strategies, however, resulted in meaningful changes in popular food intake and levels of obesity remained consistent at about one third of the population. Although West Germans embraced 'diet' versions of some favourite foodstuffs, including soda and sweets, they continued to make the 'wrong' choices both in terms of what they ate and how they ate it. Study after study revealed that taste remained the dominant factor in determining what people ate, and that it resisted all attempts at deliberate modification: 'the difficulties with changing customary eating habits, often held since childhood, cannot be underestimated'.[55] Despite increased federal funding for anti-obesity education, a 1973 study found that more than three quarters of the housewives who defined themselves as health-oriented (*gesundheitsorientiert*) in their shopping and cooking habits made their foods purchases based on *Geschmack* rather than health.[56] The situation was even worse at workplace canteens, where both the eaters and the factory managers exclusively valued taste rather than health in evaluating canteen meals. Indeed, 'canteen eaters are generally a limiting factor in the attempt to improve the health [of canteen meals]'.[57] The situation proved exactly as intractable in the socialist food economy of the GDR. Despite state-regulated prices, stand-ardized and optimized canteen recipes and extensive programmes of die-tary education targeting men, women and children, rates of overweight remained stubbornly resistant to change. In frustration, East Germany's leading anti-fat campaigner nutritionist Helmut Haenel concluded that 'in contrast to generally rational behaviour in daily life, be it in the work-place, in social activities, or in the family, emotional impulses control our diets to the point of irrationality'.[58] Even the sudden dissolution of the GDR and the creation of a new, unified German state proved to have unexpectedly minimal impact on popular eating habits, and especially on rates of overweight.

Conclusion

Ideas about who is fat and what fatness means for a particular society are constantly shifting. Throughout the Cold War and well into the 1990s, East Germans were believed by Westerners to be fatter and less healthy than their Western counterparts. Their assumed higher levels of fatness were a proxy representative of the assumed inadequacies of the socialist country's economic and cultural development. Fatness here served as evidence for poorer quality foods, an inadequately developed consumer culture, and a general lack of sophistication on the part of East German citizens, who were believed to prefer less healthy, and less tasty, foods. Indeed, by the 1970s, East Germans overtook their Western counterparts in both meat and potato consumption. These foodstuffs, which had tra-ditionally been the desirable core of the German diet, had become in the context of the postwar obesity epidemic negatively associated with the harms of an old-fashioned and unhealthy German cuisine.[59] Socialism's flaws, once linked with inadequate foodstuffs and reduced caloric intake, was newly associated with too much of the wrong sorts of foods. Fresh fruits and vegetables, notoriously absent from the shelves in the GDR, became the symbol of West German prosperity, combining ideals of deli-ciousness and good health. In fact, East Germans actually consumed more vegetables per head than West Germans; however, the bulk of these vegetables were pickled or preserved, a style of food preparation that was undesirable and perceived as un-modern. East Germans ate fresh fruit enthusiastically, but consumption was highly seasonal.[60] And of course, in terms of tropical fruits, there was no comparison between consumption rates of the two German states. Famously, when it came to bananas, East Germans consumed small quantities and irregularly, while West Germans were leading global consumers.[61] However, despite these culturally significant differences – differences that were deeply meaningful to East and West Germans – from a nutritional perspective, German diets remained largely equivalent across the iron curtain. Thus, despite the very real differences in tastes on the different sides of the border, when both countries faced similar obesity problems in the 1970s, they blamed this fatness on the same source – popular affection for meat and potatoes, which remained the cornerstone of German diets across regional differences and throughout division. Significant as (longed-for) canned pineapples or (maligned) omnipresent sauerkraut might have been for the identities of East and West Germans, from a medical standpoint East and West German bodies and diets looked remarkably similar.

This chapter has argued that obesity, a recurrent problem of modern industrial economies, is a useful expression of the troubled relationship between state economies and individual bodies wherein popular taste is conceptualized as inherently troublesome and troubling. Divided Germany proves an especially interesting case study for complicating our understanding of taste and its relationship to state power. On the one hand, the two Cold War states were clearly aligned with a Bourdieau-ian model of 'good taste'. The wealthier, more powerful West identified itself with a certain more desirable and sophisticated diet and body-type, one that both implicitly and explicitly contrasted with the cheaper, less tasty, and less attractive fare and bodies of the East. In turn, Easterners were imagined, and often imagined themselves, as desperately pining after the flavours of the West, be they bananas, Coca Cola, or imported chocolate and coffee. On the other hand, internally East and West German medical experts looked at their respective populations and saw equivalently recalcitrant individuals who refused to eat what they should. Taste thus simultaneously served as a method of positive collective identity formation against an inferior, though intimately connected, Other, and became a point of unresolvable conflict between both capitalist and socialist states and their respective populations. Thus, a case study of fatness in divided Germany reveals unexpected commonalities between socialist and capitalist rhetorics and lived experiences, while underscoring a common medical pathologization of popular taste as a site of wilful bodily resistance.

Alice Weinreb is Associate Professor of History at Loyola University Chicago. Her book, *Modern Hungers: Food and Power in Twentieth Century Germany*, came out with Oxford University Press in 2017 and was awarded the 2017 Fraenkel Book Prize for Contemporary European History and the 2017 Waterloo Centre for German Studies Book Prize. A specialist in postwar Germany, the history of hunger, gender and the body, and environmental history, she has published articles in the *Zeitschrift für Körpergeschichte, Central European History*, and *German Studies Review*, as well as in several anthologies, and is currently working on a transnational history of Anorexia Nervosa.

Notes

1. West Germany's untaxed bananas were a source of friction in European trade relations during the 1950s and 1960s. France in particular objected, claiming that the FRG's special dispensation was particularly harmful to banana imports from French colonial holdings. (66. Sitzung am 12. März 1957 Deutsch-französische Verhandlungen über den Bananenzoll im gemeinsamen Außenzolltarif des Gemeinsamen Marktes, Kabinettsprotokolle der Bundesregierung‹ online).
2. Aureden, *Was Männern so gut schmeckt*.
3. The woman who modelled Gaby was not from the former GDR, but a saleswoman named Dagmar from the West German city of Worms. See Zips, 'Zonen-Gaby packt aus'.
4. It is worth noting that by the 1970s, the GDR was importing more bananas than most Eastern bloc countries, as well as more than some Western European countries including Belgium, Finland and the Netherlands. It was less the absolute quantity of bananas consumed that set the GDR apart, than the unfavourable ratio of supply to demand, a high demand that was itself rooted in a constant comparison with the extraordinarily high consumption levels of the FRG.
5. See Weinreb, *Modern Hungers*.
6. See Bourdieu, *Distinction*.
7. Foucault, *The Birth of Biopolitics*, 13.
8. East and West German doctors used similar terminology in their discussions of this problem, referring to both the general problem of Übergewicht or 'overweight', and the growing crisis of *Fettsucht* (fatness) or *Adipositas* (obesity). In both states, during the 1970s and 1980s these terms were often used interchangeably; however, doctors generally agreed that being overweight meant having a body weight that was above a standard established 'normal weight', and being 'obese' meant being between 20 and 30 per cent above that normal weight. Generally, East Germany was less concerned about low levels of overweight than West Germany, often advocating a wider range of 'normal weight' than Western counterparts. However, the basic terminology and medical definitions were essentially identical. In this chapter, I try to stay true to the terminology used in specific sources.
9. Zur Entwicklung der Volksernährung, 27 October 1969, Deutsches Institut für Ernährungsforschung (DIfE), Nr. 228.
10. Voit, 'Leitsymptom: Fettsucht', 1106.
11. Bansi, 'Die Fettsucht, ein Problem der Fehlernährung', 151.
12. Sonnemann, 'Was darf die Ernährungsindustrie vom kommenden Jahr erwarten?', 40–41.
13. Wildt, 'Continuities and Discontinuities of Consumer Mentality', 211.
14. Tropp, *Ernähren Sie sich richtig*, 7.

15. Bundesarchiv (BArch), B142/1550, Ein Hauptproblem in unserer Zeit, 15 July 1953.
16. BArch, B310/704, Übergewicht als Risikofaktor, 1972.
17. BArch B310/37, Konzeptionelle Überlegungen und Lösungsansatz für die Kampagne 'Ernährung und Bewegung', 15 November 1974.
18. Voß, 'Wie erreichen wir den Bürger?', 64.
19. Die Ernährung in der sozialistischen Gesellschaft, 25 September 1973, DIfE Nr. 228.
20. Drummer and Muskewitz, *Kochkunst aus dem Fernsehstudio*, 172.
21. Müller, 'Zur Verbreitung der Fettsucht in der Deutschen Demokratischen Republik', 1001.
22. Ernährungssituation in der DDR, 1987, DIfE Nr. 235.
23. BArch DQ 1/24622, Erfordernisse und Möglichkeiten der Gestaltung einer gesundheitsfördernden Ernährung, August 1985.
24. Rahmenprogramm zur weiteren Durchsetzung einer gesundheitsorientierten Ernährung in der DDR, September 1988, DIfE Nr. 195.
25. *Morning Star* Reports Healthy Card-Index Meals, 7 January 1975, DIfE Nr. 233.
26. BArch, DQ 1/2098, Entwurf: Gesellschaftliche Speisenwirtschaft, 6 March 1969.
27. BArch, DL 102/647, Vergleich der Speisenbeliebtheit warmer Hauptgerichte, September 1972.
28. BArch, B310/712, Erweiterter Konzeptionstest für eine Kampagne Gemeinschaftsverpflegung, November 1976.
29. 190 Hosenbund aber sonst gesund?, 1970, DIfE Nr. 233.
30. Zur Perspektive des Brotverbrauchs in der DDR, 13 March 1967, DIfE Nr. 320.
31. Zur Perspektive des Brotverbrauchs in der DDR, 13 March 1967, DIfE Nr. 320.
32. BArch, DY30/IV2/6.10/17, Betr: Einführung einer neuen Brotsorte, 26 January 1962.
33. BArch DY30/IV2/6.10/17, Betr: Einführung einer neuen Brotsorte, 26 January 1962.
34. Zur Perspektive des Brotverbrauchs in der DDR, 13 March 1967, DIfE Nr. 320.
35. The problem of excess stores of milk fat was actually a European-wide phenomenon during the 1970s. The FRG, for example, had begun expressing concern over the financial and health ramifications of its own *Butterberg* (butter mountain) even earlier. (See 'Butterberg', *Der Spiegel*, 27 June 1966.)
36. Zeichen: gelbbrauner Streifen: Ab 1 Juli wird neue fettreiche Milch im Handel angeboten, 13/14 July 1974, DIfE Nr. 465. The dairy hoped that the new milk line, along with an 'increased use of milk fat in cheese ... and the gradual substitution of plant fat with milk fat in the ice cream industry' would use up the region's stores of excess milk fat.
37. Ab 1 Juli wird neue fettreiche Milch im Handel angeboten, 13/14 July 1974, DIfE Nr. 465.
38. An Thymien, 18 September 1974, DIfE Nr. 465.
39. An Das Institut für Milchforschung, 24 July 1974, DIfE Nr. 465.
40. Betr: Trinkmilch 3.2% Fett, 5 September 1974, DIfE Nr. 465.
41. An Redaktion der BN, 17 July 1974, DIfE Nr. 465.
42. BArch, DC 20 / 23106, Information über die Ernährungssituation in der Deutschen Demokratischen Republik.
43. Cremer, *Gemeinschaftsverpflegung*, 2.
44. BArch, B310/832, Erfolgskontrolle der Fit statt Fett Aktion, 1978.
45. BArch, B310/274, Mit Fit statt Fett mehr Spass am Essen, 30 June 1977.
46. BArch, B310/832, Erfolgskontrolle der Fit statt Fett Aktion, 1978.
47. BArch, B310/832, Erfolgskontrolle der Fit statt Fett Aktion, 1978.
48. Siemens-Archiv, Li 158, Schnitzel und Eintopf als Lieblingsgericht, 16 September 1976.
49. BArch, 189/32133, Betr: gesundheitliche Aufklärung der Bevölkerung, 24 October 1974.
50. BArch, B310/717, Übergewicht im Kindesalter und Erziehungsverhalten der Mutter, 1982.
51. BArch, B310/300, Zum Thema Aufklärung zu gesundheitsgerechtem Ernährungsverhalten, 17 May 1979.

52. BArch, B310/706, Verhaltenstherapie des Übergewichts, 1975.
53. BArch, B310/300, Überlegungen zu Aufklärungsmaßnahmen über die richtige Ernährung, 9 March 1979.
54. BArch, B310/328, Änderungsvorschläge, 1974.
55. Voß, 'Wie erreichen wir den Bürger?', 65.
56. BArch, B310/45, Einstellung und Verhalten der Verbraucher zur gesunden Ernährung, September 1973.
57. BArch, B310/712, Erweiterter Konzeptionstest für eine Kampagne Gemeinschaftsverpflegung, November 1976.
58. Kommt jetzt das süße Leben?, 19 March 1974, DIfE Nr. 233.
59. See 'Epilogue: Yes, We Have No Bananas: Negotiating Past and Future in Reunified Germany', in Weinreb, *Modern Hungers*, 237–249.
60. Mensink and Beitz, 'Food and Nutrient Intake in East and West Germany'; Winkler, Brasche and Heinrich, 'Trends in Food Intake in Adults from the City of Erfurt'.
61. Seeßlen, 'Die Banane'.

Bibliography

Aureden, L. *Was Männern so gut schmeckt: Eine kulinarische Weltreise in 580 Rezepten.* Munich: Deutscher Taschenbuch-Verlag, 1953.

Bansi, H.W. 'Die Fettsucht, ein Problem der Fehlernährung', in Deutsche Gesellschaft für Ernährung (ed.), *Probleme der vollwertigen Ernährung in Haushalts- und Großverpflegung* (Frankfurt am Main: Umschau-Verlag, 1956), 151.

Bourdieu, P. *Distinction: A Social Critique of the Judgement of Taste.* Cambridge, MA: Harvard University Press, 1984.

Cremer, H.-D. *Gemeinschaftsverpflegung.* Darmstadt: D. Steinkopff, 1962.

Drummer, K. and K. Muskewitz. *Kochkunst aus dem Fernsehstudio: Rezepte – praktische Winke – Literarische Anmerkungen.* Leipzig: Fachbuchverlag, 1968.

Foucault, M. *The Birth of Biopolitics: Lectures at the College de France, 1978–79.* New York: Palgrave Macmillan, 2008.

Mensink, G.B.M. and R. Beitz. 'Food and Nutrient Intake in East and West Germany, 8 Years after the Reunification: The German Nutrition Survey 1998'. *European Journal of Clinical Nutrition* 58 (2004): 1000–10.

Müller, F. 'Zur Verbreitung der Fettsucht in der Deutschen Demokratischen Republik'. *Zeitschrift für die gesamte innere Medizin und ihre Grenzgebiete* 22 (15 November 1970), 1001–9.

Seeßlen, G. 'Die Banane: Ein mythopolitischer Bericht', in R. Bohn, K. Hickethier and E. Müller (eds.), *Mauer-Show: Das Ende der DDR, die deutsche Einheit und die Medien* (Berlin: Ed. Sigma, 1992), 55–69.

Sonnemann, T. 'Was darf die Ernährungsindustrie vom kommenden Jahr erwarten?' *Die Ernährungswirtschaft* 2 (1954), 40–41.

Tropp, C. *Ernähren Sie sich richtig, Herr Direktor?* Munich: Verlag Moderne Industrie, 1965.

Voit, K. 'Leitsymptom: Fettsucht'. *Münchener medizinische Wochenschrift* 92 (27–28) (1950), 1106–13.

Voß, P. 'Wie erreichen wir den Bürger? Überlegungen aus der Sicht des Deutschen Hygiene Museums in der DDR', in Arbeitsgruppe Ernährung des Nationales

Komitees für Gesundheitserziehung (ed.), *Ernährung – Gesundheit – Genuss: Praxis u. Wissenschaft* (Karl-Marx-Stadt: Warenverzeichnenverband Diätetische Erzeugnisse, 1986), 64–67.

Weinreb, A. *Modern Hungers: Food and Power in Twentieth-Century Germany*. New York: Oxford University Press, 2017.

Wildt, M. 'Continuities and Discontinuities of Consumer Mentality in West Germany in the 1950s', in R. Bessel (ed.), *Life after Death: Approaches to a Cultural and Social History of Europe during the 1940s and 1950s* (Cambridge: Cambridge University Press, 2003), 211–30.

Winkler, G., S. Brasche and J. Heinrich. 'Trends in Food Intake in Adults from the City of Erfurt before and after the German Reunification'. *Annals of Nutrition and Metabolism* 41(5) (1997), 283–90.

Zips, M. 'Zonen-Gaby packt aus'. *Süddeutsche Zeitung*, 22 October 2009.

Conclusion

Erica Carter, Jan Palmowski and Katrin Schreiter

Twentieth-century Germany emerged with strong regional identities from late unification and dissimultaneous political processes as a 'state' that has always been an uneasy entity, its characteristics difficult to summarize, its features difficult to analyse in generalizable terms. Over the past centuries, the country and the cultural realm with which it is associated has time and again extended and contracted geographically, formalized and revised its criteria of belonging and non-belonging, and negotiated relationships amongst its constituent regions. As students of the German territories, the German language, German cultural and economic production, German values, norms and expectations, we are therefore left with the apprehension that whatever we do is less than enough. This anxiety of interpretation has more often than not resulted from disciplinary boundaries, the accepted canon of sources, methodological constraints and dominant theory. Once these boundaries are reached, the question 'How can we know?' confronts us forcefully.

The chapters in this volume propose that we can push the boundaries of the knowable further without sacrificing scholarly rigour. Each of the volume's authors has embedded her or his enquiry into everyday life in a discussion of the formal conventions, genres and technological forms that were constituent of the time and place in which the German everyday was experienced, practiced or produced. Our contributors, therefore, have historicized their research not solely through forms of historical contextualization that embed aesthetic forms and cultural practices in the specific space and time of postwar Germany, but also through attention to the historicity of aesthetic form and practice itself: the capacity of image, text, sound and touch, then, to act in the world by shaping perception, meaning and sense. Chapters in this volume have suggested that an interdisciplinary consideration of the everyday requires a new openness not only to the different disciplinary perspectives outlined in the volume introduction, but also to modes of historical writing that do justice to the operations of the aesthetic in and on social worlds, as well as to the volatility, multidirectionality, spatial fractures and cultural lag of historical experiences at the level of the lived everyday. Exploring the everyday may involve, our contributors have indicated, abandoning for a while the chronological ordering of historical narratives, allowing interruptions and breaks, time taken out to dwell in the slow time of, say, gallery art (as in April Eisman's account of East German art spectatorship), in the fractured space of postwar migration (McMurtry), in the layered temporalities of image-sound experiment (Schmidt, Nössig, Bellotti), or in the simultaneous time of embodied mirror opposites across the East-West divide (Weinreb).

It is the historian's task, we consequently posit, not just to generate narrative reconstructions of the history of the everyday, but to unpeel the layers and intersections of narrative production. Histories of the everyday have always been open to different forms of text (oral history, film, literature, etc.) to inform their approach to social practices.[1] But they have less often engaged with narrative or aesthetic form as such. We argue by contrast that narrative, image, sound, touch, smell or gustatory taste structure meanings and belonging, providing frameworks for ordering and expressing individual experience, forging new avenues for dissidence as well as conformity, and opening diverse scholarly perspectives on everyday experience and its relation to social practices.

This focus on the formal and aesthetic as well as the epistemological and perceptual dimensions of everyday stories, our volume suggests, expands in several ways the possibilities of everyday history. The first contribution of such an interdisciplinary history is its insight into the place of the everyday in cultural and social histories of the Cold War and German division. Understanding the ways in which the space and time of Cold War division is articulated in individual storytelling modes (life writing, prose narrative, oral history) or in everyday practices from gardening, to music-making, to walking, cooking and eating, shows how deeply German division penetrated into lives, how it informed views of belonging, shaped narratives or re-defined the experience of spatiality and historicity in the German lands (and abroad) after 1945. Most centrally, an everyday history of cultural practice dismantles prevailing ontologies of the historical subject, seeking to capture subjects in processes of self-formation that in turn determine capacities for action in the specific setting of the German postwar.

A second, and related conclusion drawn in this volume concerns the relationship between social subjects, power and cultural production. One guiding figure for our exploration of that relation has been Alf Lüdkte, whose historical-anthropological approach has been to date exceptionally influential in shaping approaches by historians to the experience of the everyday. Many (though not all) chapters in the volume share Alf Lüdke's concern with 'those who have remained largely anonymous in history – the "nameless" multitudes in their workaday trials and tribulations'.[2] But the volume also expands Lüdtke's focus on social practice with a diversified methodological toolkit that uses social and cultural theory as well as cultural studies methodologies to reframe the perspectives on politics, power and agency that are germane to Lüdtke's work. Individual and social meanings come to life differently in this volume in chapters that identify the play of power and refusal in everyday cultural practice, showing how communities were fashioned, how individuals related to them (or how they did not), and how power relations were formed and negotiated in quotidian cultural practice. Marcel Thomas thus writes of the German-German border – apparently the clearest possible embodiment of an impenetrable and unchallengeable authoritarian state order – as an entity perpetually displaced and renegotiated in the lived practice and social imaginary of two sets of postwar villagers in Neukirch (Saxony) and Ebersbach (Baden-Württemberg). Áine McMurtry and Heidi Armbruster explore narratives of migration and exile as cultural productions that similarly disturb the binary spatial divisions of East and West, whether by displacing attention onto the global South as a significant site of white German experience (Armbruster), or highlighting fractures in the homogeneous surface of 'German' experience exposed by narratives of migration and exilic flight (McMurtry). Other writers show how a refusal of East-West spatial constraint may occur in the imagination, even while bodies remain rooted to the spot. Franziska Nössig's chapter explores an avant-garde film practice that imaginatively extends 'situational',[3] everyday boundaries (the walls of the apartment that was also Jürgen Böttcher's studio) into the cultural space of the international film avant-garde; conversely, Jan Palmowski's account of televisual narratives, and April Eisman's of the formation of GDR art publics, show how East German boundaries were drawn and redrawn in a popular imagination that needed perpetually to reimagine the frontiers delimiting the GDR and its internal communities.

There were of course quite concrete differences in the opportunities for political participation afforded to individuals and communities on either side of the German-German border. Though our volume does not seek to minimize these differences, our contributions do suggest ways of examining how power was refracted through the everyday for Germans wherever they lived. Contributors suggest many ways in which social actors negotiated their everyday culturally and experientially across stark imbalances of power. Who had power over whom, and how hegemonies could be defined and evaded, was moreover not simply a question of political participation, nor simply one of economic ownership. A third key insight from this collection is its emphasis on senses of belonging as affective forces that are generated through cultural practice, and that frame individual and collective relationships to established structures of power. Numerous contributions highlight the ways in which aesthetic and cultural practice forges common sense attachments to, or detachment from, political formations including the two postwar German states. Our introduction began to explore that process of building commonality by examining the affordances of distinct forms: the capacity of narrative to organize historical experiences of space, time and the body; or of image, sound, movement, touch and taste to shape shared perceptions across common perceptual 'zones' (Schmidt). The conclusion emerging from this volume's various case studies is however that such neo-formalism may not suffice for an examination of the relationship of aesthetic and cultural form to a lived politics shared between social actors and across communities. Particularly in contributions from Bellotti, Schmidt, McMurtry and Weinreb, narrative or aesthetic form (image, sound, taste or bodily movements including walking and dance) are seen instead as vehicles for what Raymond Williams and Jacques Rancière – as we discovered in our shared readings for this volume – term 'structures of feeling' (Williams), or the 'distribution of the sensible' (Rancière).

For Williams and Rancière, there is a perceptual and affective dimension to aesthetic experience that is not captured by formal analysis alone. Michael Schmidt, Franziska Nössig, Áine McMurtry, Katrin Schreiter, Alice Weinreb and others share, moreover, with these and other social theorists of cultural experience an understanding of shared perception and affect as emerging from embodied cultural practices that in turn have a role in generating both social and political communities, and social relations of power. In Williams' Marxist account, structures of feeling are the product of cultural practices that offer 'solutions' to as-yet-unresolved questions of social belonging.[4] Contributions in this volume that see in case studies from postwar literature and film a form of counter-discourse to everyday regulation (including Nössig, McMurtry and Schreiter) can be seen therefore as working in a cultural studies tradition that identifies in aesthetic practice, if not the signs of political resistance, then certainly the capacity to bring to the fore figures repressed from quotidian vision (McMurtry's migrants, Nössig's dissi-dent artists), as well as narrative or audio-visual traces of friction, attri-tion and 'obstinate' refusal of prevailing norms.

Rancière, by contrast, follows not Marx, but Kant, reformulat-ing Kant's notion of 'common sense' (*sensus communis*) – which Kant views as the product of a shared aesthetic experience of the beauti-ful – to explore that shared perception of 'the existence of something in common' which Rancière sees as generated by social processes of 'distribution' of sensible experience.[5] Michael Schmidt in this volume provides historical examples of this material process of distribution in an account of travelling music cultures that foster senses of generational commonality across both German states. Áine McMurtry similarly iden-tifies transnational belonging as one affective product of exile writings in the two Cold War Germanies. In these and other chapters, there are however also evident 'delimitations' between distinct modes and zones of sensible experience.[6] Thus when for instance Alice Weinreb's eating subjects, or Alissa Bellotti's style-conscious punks draw distinctions of style and taste across and between East and West German communities, they are engaging in what Rancière terms a differential distribution of sensible experience that in turn establishes divisions and hierarchies – in Bellotti's case, hierarchical distinctions of generation and class as well as nation, in Weinreb's, most particularly, though not exclusively, distinc-tions between the two postwar German states.[7]

This volume, then, offers a historical perspective on cultural theo-ries of belonging, emphasizing the place of German-German cultural practice in defining who belonged and who did not, who was marginal and who was not. In focusing on experience and belonging – how these were articulated, claimed and shaped in the everyday – our contributors also agree, explicitly or implicitly, that individual experience and social practice were never only about the two Germanies. The fourth shared conclusion from this volume is that Germans operated in a transnational context that was defined not simply by the Cold War (important though this was), but that also included a postcolonial past, and which was strongly influenced by global cultural processes. That German history cannot be understood without reference to transnational influences is hardly a new claim; but our book shows how important the transna-tional perspective is in understanding more fully how social actors who identified as German imagined themselves, and how this refracted in their everyday actions.

A fifth conclusion relates to questions of historical contingency and change. In any volume on national history, there is a need to avoid the pitfall of ethnocentric visions of 'community'. Our contributors do this by presenting texts, artifacts, utterances and events as traces of the past and its social actors as an 'always moving substance', a spatio-temporal and (in Weinreb's Foucauldian formulation) 'biopolitical' configuration that is 'in an embryonic state before it can become fully articulate and defined exchange'.[8] This emphasis on embryonic and not yet fully realized histories – an emphasis therefore on histories of cultural practice as well as communities *in process* – has seemed especially appropriate to a project that attempts to capture modes of shared German belonging that were not fully actualized until the collapse of the Berlin Wall in 1989. Indeed, our contributions invite us to rethink and broaden our concept of the inner German divide itself, and of 'the other' Germany not merely as a social fact, but as a repeated experience of fracture that shaped the most intimate areas of everyday social experience. Even when it was implicit – as in the attempted formation of community on GDR television (Palmowski), or the support of art in the GDR (Eisman) – the border, our contributors show, became constitutive of everyday experience not just by virtue of material encounters with the Wall as physical barrier, but through the repeated assertion of its sensed presence across a range of cultural sites. The border might shape the directionality of looking and thinking (Thomas), or the materiality of everyday space-time experience (Nössig). Or, as contributions from Armbruster and McMurtry in particular show, the unseen border might have a palpable presence well beyond Germany, shaping exilic or expatriate assumptions, practices and experiences indirectly, remaining unspoken and unaddressed, but somehow also tangibly invisible.

But if Germany's boundaries were significant far beyond towns and villages located geographically on the German border, this does not mean (and this is our sixth and final point) that the 'shared experience' of fracture to which this volume's title points took either homogeneous or simultaneous forms. Christoph Kleßmann has observed asymmetries and cultural lag in the development of the two German states: moments of dissonance that are visible in this volume in accounts for instance of the two Germanies' differential access to and use of advanced media technologies (Nössig, Palmowski); their understanding of modern art practice and its relation to the political (Eisman); or their development as consumer economies (Thomas, Bellotti).[9] The verbal exchange between two prominent East Germans (and loyal SED members) that opens this volume shows similarly how the experience of colour, sound and smell was constitutive of difference and cultural lag: specifically in this case, the experiential lag of the East German everyday vis-à-vis a perceived West German experience of consumer abundance within a progressive time of the consumerist modern.

Our history of everyday life in the two Germanies is thus as often as not asymmetrical and dissimultaneous, highlighting relationships not only of mutual mirroring or entanglement, but also of cultural lag and temporal dissonance. The cultural, aesthetic and sensual realms may have been critical to German everyday lives, but these realms were deeply affected by the material: how art was financed and enabled, what production facilities were available to film and television producers and under what conditions, and even the availability of instruments for music-making. These material constraints contributed to distinctions and hierarchies that this volume locates as one product of a 'distribution of the sensible', but that political or economic history would doubtless also identify as the product of differing modes and moments of state intervention, ideological programmes or economic regimes.

If our history, moreover, is dissimultaneous and asymmetrical, it is also multidirectional, moving in some instances towards similarity or even rapprochement across inner German borders; in others, towards ideas of otherness within distinctive national discourses (Palmowski, Eisman), or to transnational relationships (as in Armbruster's account of Germany's relation to postcolonial Namibia) that are understood as simultaneously specific to national discourses, and located experientially within the local and the everyday. Consistently, then, we have aspired to chart an ambivalent, multifaceted and horizontal history that eschews geographical hierarchies, speaking on the one hand of both rapprochement and division between the two German states, on the other, of transnational contexts that interacted with local sensitivities, spaces, ideologies and cultural material (art, literature, television, film) to produce meanings or structures of feeling in which questions of national belonging played only minor roles.

What binds our volume together is, finally, a focus on the everyday as the arena in which the multiple macro-political forces shaping German-German histories were negotiated and refigured through literary, (audio-)visual and vernacular cultural practice. Schreiter points in her contribution to Henri Lefebvre as one of a number of thinkers to have identified the everyday as 'a simultaneous site of alienation and its overthrow'. For the Marxist Lefebvre, the tension between the split subjectivity that is the product of capitalist alienation, and the utopian community that grounds everyday political resistance, is the product of a specific stage in the development of capitalism. In this volume, our more geographically specific claim is that there are within the everyday history of postwar divided Germany instances of a political and ideological ambivalence which, if it did not lead to capitalism's overthrow (quite the opposite, in fact), nonetheless goes some way towards explaining the simultaneous persistence of ideological, political and social divides before and after 1989, and of cross-border political, civic and cultural communities, historical continuities and social bonds.

Erica Carter is Professor of German and Film Studies at King's College London, and Chair of the UK German Screen Studies Network. She has published extensively on German cinema and cultural history; her publications include *How German Is She? Postwar West German Reconstruction and the Consuming Woman* (University of Michigan Press, 1997), *Dietrich's Ghosts: The Sublime and the Beautiful in Third Reich Film* (British Film Institute, 2004), *The German Cinema Book*, 2nd edition (Bergfelder, Carter & Göktürk, 2019) and *Béla Balázs: Early Film Theory* (Berghahn, 2010). She is currently writing a monograph on cinema and late colonial sensibilities in the European 'white Atlantic' after the Second World War.

Jan Palmowski joined King's College London in 1999, and became a professor in 2009. In 2013, he was appointed Professor of Modern History at the University of Warwick. A specialist on the history of the GDR and of contemporary Germany, his books include *At the Crossroads of Past and Present: Contemporary History and the Historical Discipline* (edited with Kristina Spohr-Readman, special issue of the *Journal of Contemporary History* 3, 2011), *Inventing a Socialist Nation: Heimat and the Politics of Everyday Life in the GDR* (Cambridge University Press, 2009, translated into German in 2016), and *Citizenship and National Identity in Twentieth-Century Germany* (edited with Geoff Eley, Stanford University Press, 2008).

Katrin Schreiter is Lecturer in German and European Studies at King's College London. Her research focuses on the interplay of economics and culture of the Cold War era, and how these areas are connected to the politics of German diplomacy and ideas about nationhood. Her monograph, *Designing One Nation: The Politics of Economic Culture and Trade in Divided Germany, 1949–1990*, is forthcoming with Oxford University Press. She has published on related topics in *Business History Review* and *Europeanization in the 20th Century: The Historical Lens* (Peter Lang, 2012). Her work on the gendered experience of Second World War trauma was published in *Central European History*.

Notes

1. Becker and Lüdtke, *Akten*.
2. Lüdtke, 'Introduction', 4.
3. Lüdtke, 'Introductory Notes', 6.
4. Williams, *Marxism and Literature*, 134.
5. Kant, *Critique of the Power of Judgement*. See also Hermann Kappelhoff's elucidation of Kant in relation to political theories of *Gemeinsinn* (which he terms, following Richard Rorty and Hannah Arendt, a 'sense of commonality'): Kappelhoff, *Genre und Gemeinsinn*, 369–74.
6. Rancière, *The Politics of Aesthetics*, 7.
7. Ibid., 7–8.
8. Williams, *Marxism and Literature*, 129–30.
9. Kleßmann, 'Verflechtung und Abrenzung'.

Bibliography

Becker, P., A. Lüdtke et al. *Akten. Eingaben. Schaufenster. Die DDR und ihre Texte: Erkundungen zwischen Herrschaft und Alltag*. Berlin: Akademie Verlag, 1997.

Kant, I. *Critique of the Power of Judgement*. Cambridge: Cambridge University Press, 2002.

Kappelhoff, H. *Genre und Gemeinsinn: Hollywood zwischen Krieg und Demokratie*. Berlin and Boston: de Gruyter, 2016.

Kleßmann, C. 'Verflechtung und Abgrenzung: Aspekte der geteilten und zusammengehörigen deutschen Nachkriegsgeschichte'. *Aus Politik und Zeitgeschichte* 29–30 (1993), 30–41.

Lüdtke, A. 'Introduction', in A. Lüdtke (ed.), *The History of Everyday Life: Reconstructing Historical Experiences and Ways of Life* (Princeton: Princeton University Press, 1995), 3–40.

———. 'Introductory Notes', in A. Lüdtke (ed.), *Everyday Life in Mass Dictatorship: Collusion and Evasion* (Basingstoke: Palgrave, 2016), 3–12.

Rancière, J. *The Politics of Aesthetics: The Distribution of the Sensible*, translated by G. Rockhill. London: Continuum, 2004.

Williams, R. *Marxism and Literature*. New York: Oxford University Press, 1977.

Index

Elaborative endnotes are indicated by the letter n; the following numeral identifies the precise endnote.

The term ill indicates an illustration.

checkpoint Charlie, 134
checkpoint Friedrichstraße, 118
  See also East Berlin; West Berlin
Berlin Wall, 133–34, 235
  building of, 111, 256, 258
  fall of, 70, 130–31, 147–48, 235, 268,
    294
  graffiti (and not), 14, 137
  living with, 107, 113, 118–23, 142–43,
    294
Betts, Paul, 15, 161, 162
Biermann, Wolf, 157, 166, 183
Bildungsbürgertum (educated
    bourgeoisie), 260
black writing, 57
body politics, 20, 21. *See also* obesity
Böttcher, Jürgen, 14–15, 155–68, 169–70,
    171–75, 175n1, 291
  collaboration with Erika Dobslaff,
    162, 163*ill*
  as a painter, 156, 162, 165–68, 174, 175
  as a performer, 157, 159–62, 164–65,
    165*ill*
  Rangierer (Shunters), 156, 157, 172
  as 'Strawalde,' 158, 162, 167
  Verwandlungen (Transformations),
    14–15, 155–65, 168, 171–75
  *Frau am Klavichord (Woman at the
    Clavichord)*, 155, 159, 162, 163, 164
  at international festivals, 172, 173–74,
    175
  Potter's Stier (Potter's Bull), 155, 158*ill*,
    159, 160–61, 160*ill*, 164
  *Venus nach Giorgione (Venus by
    Giorgione)*, 155, 159, 160–61, 163*ill*
Bourdieu, Pierre, 20, 21, 269, 284
Brakhage, Stan, 15, 155, 163–64, 165
Brandenburg Gate, 119, 120–21, 122
Brecht, Bertolt, 134, 149n24, 239n17
  Berliner Ensemble, 134
  The Resistible Rise of Arturo Ui, 134
Bulgaria, 137
Butting, Max, 248, 257

C
capitalism, 38, 46, 47, 89, 93, 98, 117, 144,
    191, 213

and music, 248–49, 257
in Namibia, 59, 61, 62, 70, 76, 77
and nutrition, 276, 284
and punk, 193
and visual art, 18, 219–20, 222–23,
    226, 235–36
  See also East Germany; West Germany
Carter, Erica, 21–22
  contribution by, 1–21, 289–96
Ceaușescu, Nicolae, 13, 129, 130
celebrity/star culture, 19, 37, 183, 192
Central Institute of Youth Research
    (ZIJ), 47, 191, 192
Chakrabarty, Dipesh: *Provincializing
    Europe*, 18, 220
colonialism/postcolonialism, 56–78,
    91, 293
'colonial revisionism', 73–76
Cremer, Fritz, 225–26, 227, 235
Cubitt, Geoffrey, 202
Czechoslovakia/Czechs, 95, 108, 115,
    117

D
dance, 19, 170–71. *See also* pop: dance
    music
de Certeau, Michel: *The Practice of
    Everyday Life*, 5, 11, 109
Deleuze, Gilles, 133
  Cinéma II: The Time-Image, 136, 139
Deutsche Kunstausstellung, Dresden
    (German Art Exhibition, Dresden),
    239n36
  Achte (Eighth 1977-8), 229, 231, 234
  Allgemeine (General 1946), 221
  Dritte (Third 1953), 223
  Neunte (Ninth 1982-3), 234–35
  Sechste (Sixth 1967-8), 233
  Siebte (Seventh 1972-3), 233, 234
  Vierte (Fourth 1958-9), 224–25
  Zehnte (Tenth 1987-8), 234–35
Documenta exhibition, Kassel, 233, 234,
    239n43, 239n49

E
East Berlin, 95, 115, 169–70, 171, 179,
    193, 206, 249

Z
Ziegler, Doris, 18, 231–33
  The Rosa Luxemburg Brigade – Eva,
    231–33, 232*ill*